GAMBLERS,
FRAUDSTERS,
DREAMERS
& SPIES

"Books to Span the East and West"

Tuttle Publishing was founded in 1832 in the small New England town of Rutland, Vermont [USA]. Our core values remain as strong today as they were then—to publish best-in-class books which bring people together one page at a time. In 1948, we established a publishing outpost in Japan—and Tuttle is now a leader in publishing English-language books about the arts, languages and cultures of Asia. The world has become a much smaller place today and Asia's economic and cultural influence has grown. Yet the need for meaningful dialogue and information about this diverse region has never been greater. Over the past seven decades, Tuttle has published thousands of books on subjects ranging from martial arts and paper crafts to language learning and literature—and our talented authors, illustrators, designers and photographers have won many prestigious awards. We welcome you to explore the wealth of information available on Asia at **www.tuttlepublishing.com**.

Published by Tuttle Publishing, an imprint of Periplus Editions (HK) Ltd.

www.tuttlepublishing.com

Copyright © 2024 Robert Whiting

Arranged with Robert Whiting through Japan UNI Agency, Inc., Tokyo

Library of Congress Catalog-in-Publication Data in progress

ISBN 978-4-8053-1798-3

27 26 25 24   5 4 3 2 1   2401VP
Printed in Malaysia

TUTTLE PUBLISHING® is a registered trademark of Tuttle Publishing, a division of Periplus Editions (HK) Ltd.

Distributed by:

North America, Latin America & Europe
Tuttle Publishing
364 Innovation Drive, North Clarendon
VT 05759 9436, USA
Tel: 1(802) 773 8930
Fax: 1(802) 773 6993
info@tuttlepublishing.com
www.tuttlepublishing.com

Asia Pacific
Berkeley Books Pte Ltd
3 Kallang Sector #04-01
Singapore 349278
Tel: (65) 6741-2178
Fax: (65) 6741-2179
inquiries@periplus.com.sg
www.tuttlepublishing.com

Japan
Tuttle Publishing
Yaekari Building, 3rd Floor
5-4-12 Osaki Shinagawa-ku
Tokyo 141 0032 Japan
Tel: 81 (3) 5437 0171
Fax: 81 (3) 5437 0755
sales@tuttle.co.jp
www.tuttle.co.jp

Robert Whiting

Author of *You Gotta Have Wa* and *Tokyo Junkie*

GAMBLERS, FRAUDSTERS, DREAMERS & SPIES

The Outsiders Who Shaped Modern Japan

TUTTLE Publishing

Tokyo │ Rutland, Vermont │ Singapore

Table of Contents

Introduction

EVER SINCE the American Black Ships sailed into the bay of old Edo in 1853, forcing open the nation's long-locked gates and triggering the collapse of its ancient samurai world, a long stream of Westerners has flowed into Japan to impart wisdom and know-how on building a modern nation based on the models of the US and Europe—and to make a buck at the same time. In their eagerness to Westernize, the Meiji-era Japanese, at once wary of outsiders yet extremely inquisitive, welcomed the first wave—military experts, educators in all fields, economic advisors, architects and general fortune seekers who collectively helped to establish the foundations of a modern society.

Within decades, the neophyte imperial nation catapulted itself onto the center of the world stage with a historic victory in the Russo-Japanese war in 1905. The military victory was helped by a massive loan from US banker Jacob Schiff, at the behest of US president Theodore Roosevelt. The subsequent peace treaty, mediated by Roosevelt, who won the Nobel Peace Prize for his efforts, marked the first victory of an Asian country against a Western power in modern times and gave Japan a seat at the global roundtable. However, subsequent Japanese military expansion into the very pocket of influence in China vacated by Russia, snowballed into Japan's alliance with Nazi Germany and Italy, and led to the bombing of Pearl Harbor, with catastrophic consequences. Even before the atomic bombs were dropped on Hiroshima and Nagasaki, every major city across Japan lay in complete ruins from the B-29 bombers.

Following Hirohito's unconditional surrender in August 1945, a war-ravaged Japan saw its second wave of foreign visionaries. At first, these were primarily American military personnel who were tasked with feeding a starving population, rebuilding Japan into a sound and prosperous democracy and, perhaps more urgently, creating a reliable ally (to fight the growing reach of the Red Menace, as the rise of Mao Tse Tung in China and Soviet Communism in North Korea was referred to). Much is recorded in the annals of the Allied Forces Occupation of the exceptional byproducts it bequeathed to Japan—a new constitution, land reform and women's rights, among other advancements.

However, "influencers" come in many shades, shapes and sizes, especially when a nation has sunk to the depths of unbearable poverty, as was the case with Japan. American black-ops groups forging unsavory partnerships with underworld figures to fight encroaching Communist subversives, followed by CIA agents grooming future prime ministers from the ranks of war criminals were but two early examples. Then there was the arrival of post-Occupation Mafia gamblers to build Las Vegas–style casinos and nightclubs where deals at the highest level were made. Among other things, such interchange enabled the growth of yakuza influence over the reconstruction of the nation, as Japan rose to unprecedented heights to host the thoroughly modern 1964 Olympics. Feckless acts by ne'er-do-well itinerants and roaming adventure seekers added a toxic ingredient to the mix, producing many unexpected and likely unintended consequences.

The Japanese leaders of the new postwar order learned extensively from the school of Western-style business and modern entrepreneurial skills. However, they never fully relinquished the insularity that came with a national identity, which held, and continues to hold, that "we Japanese" are unique in a way which other nations and other peoples are not. Attempts at bringing in foreign CEOs were thus more often than not meaningless window displays, yet did on occasion result in notable exceptions that have entered the history books. You can include baseball managers in this group.

Also inside these pages are stories of a different kind of outsider, émigrés from other parts of Asia who overcame obstacles to make a significant impact on the Japanese social, political and business world.

Gaiatsu or "outside pressure" has been a recurring theme in social change in Japan, ever since those Black Ships first arrived. And it is tales of such gaiatsu, intentional or otherwise, that this book tells—many of which have been heretofore unknown or vastly underreported.

CHAPTER 1

The Canon Agency

WORLD WAR II in the Pacific ended with the surrender of Emperor Hirohito and the empire of Japan in August 1945, after nearly four bloody years of fighting climaxed by atomic bombs dropped on Hiroshima and Nagasaki. Japan was brought to its knees. Half of Tokyo was in ashes from B-29 air raids. Millions of people were homeless, many of them living in crude, jerry-built shelters made of cardboard, rocks and chicken wire. Starvation was rampant.

The country was occupied by the victorious Allies, led by the United States, with nearly half a million soldiers stationed in the country. The Occupation was overseen by American General Douglas MacArthur from his perch in the Dai Ichi Insurance Building facing Tokyo's Imperial Palace. The General Headquarters (GHQ), as it was known, provided emergency food and medical supplies, then introduced sweeping social and economic reforms, including land redistribution and a new constitution that gave equal rights to women while outlawing war as a mean of settling international disputes.

The original aim of the Occupation was to make Japan "the Switzerland of Asia" and many of the military and industrial leaders that had taken Japan on a path to war during the 1930s were purged from public life as a result. However the ascent of Red China and a pro-Russian government in North Korea forced a change in policy known as the Reverse Course that focused on combating the growing Communist threat in Japan. Purged wartime political, military and business leaders were reinstated and the goal of the Occupation became remaking Japan into a "bulwark against Communism."

Many of the reinstated were former officers of the Imperial Japanese Army, who went to work for the G-2 or intelligence wing of the GHQ, directed by General Charles Willoughby. Willoughby had been seriously alarmed by the advances of Mao's armies on the mainland, the belligerence of Pyongyang across the Japan Sea, and an increase in demonstrations by leftist groups in Japan that threatened the country's political stability. Willoughby oversaw the creation of numerous extrajudicial intelligence-gathering organizations or agencies, known as *kikan*, including the Hattori Kikan (Hattori Agency), led by ex-Colonel Takushiro Hattori, a former chief of staff to disgraced General Hideki Tojo, Japan's wartime prime minister. But by far the most memorable of them all was the Canon Agency.

The Canon Agency was a black-operations group involved in kidnapping, drug smuggling, midnight shootouts in deserted city parks and other subterranean activities. It set new standards in postwar covert operations in Japan and was one of the most colorful organizations in the long vivid history of the Occupation, which ended in April 1952. It set the stage for the establishment of a pro-American postwar conservative government, one supported clandestinely by the Central Intelligence Agency (CIA) that would remain in place for decades to come.

Originally known as the Z Unit, it was created in 1946 by one US Army Major Jack Canon, a six-foot-two, 220-pound (1.9 m, 100 kg), rugged, charismatic Texan who once worked for the Texas Border Patrol. He had served in Guadalcanal, Borneo and Manila during World War II as an explosives expert and became one of the first Americans to enter Tokyo after the war, arriving in September 1945 as a member of the 411 Counter Intelligence Corps (CIC). One of his first acts upon landing in the bombed-out capital was to blow open the safe at the German embassy, where he discovered documents that showed the notorious Sorge Soviet spy ring was still in operation. Canon, whose mother was from Germany and who spoke fluent German, immediately took the papers to Willoughby, also of German descent. The two men hit it off and Willoughby assigned Canon to establish his group.

The Canon Agency was special for a variety of reasons, one of which was its diverse makeup. The agency recruited a core of twenty-six Euro-American, Japanese nisei and Korean-American agents and trained them to conduct secret operations against Communist sympathizers in Japan. Its members were authorized to carry arms, make arrests and carry out interrogations. Their colorful activities would also include sabotage and masquerading as underworld gangsters.

A key member of the group was Japanese-American Victor Matsui, a US Army–enlisted man, Los Angeles native, and the very first person Jack Canon recruited in November 1945, traveling all the way to Niigata in western Honshu, where Matsui was based with the CIC, to select him on the spot. Canon was impressed with Matsui's language ability, martial-arts background (he had been a former US national sumo-wrestling champion) and the fact that he had uncomplainingly endured three years in a Japanese internment camp in Arkansas, living in a horse stable, before being allowed to enlist in the Army. Canon dispatched the five-foot-nine, 185-pound (1.7 m, 84 kg) Matsui to parachute training camp in Sendai with the 11th Airborne and then awarded him a field commission. Matsui went on to become Jack Canon's translator and right-hand man, serving him for the next six and a half years.

Initially based in Yokohama, the Canon Agency first went after the remaining agents of the famed Sorge spy ring, which had operated in Tokyo during the wartime years. Richard Sorge was a German journalist and Soviet spy, noted for informing the Russians that Germany was going to attack the Soviet Union in June 1941 and that Japan would not participate. Arrested by the Japanese *kempetai* secret military police in December 1941, he was tortured, forced to confess, then tried and hanged along with Japanese coconspirator Hotsumi Ozaki, a journalist for the *Asahi Shimbun* newspaper. Sorge's Radio Operator Max Clausen and his wife were also arrested and sentenced to prison terms but were inadvertently released by

US Army forces entering Japan. Canon and Matsui gave chase but Clausen and his wife managed to escape to Vladivostok, along with a German Soviet spy named Vukovich who, according to Matsui, had been operating in the Yokohama area.

Another key Canon Agency recruit was Al Shattuck who had fought in the Celebes Sea and had initially arrived in Asahigawa, Hokkaido in September 1945 as First Sergeant of HQ company, part of the Occupation forces. Shattuck was astonished at the docility of the conquered forces he encountered compared to the ferocity he had experienced on the battlefield.

"When we first landed in Asahigawa there was a long runway," he recalled, "and it was lined with Japanese soldiers on either side two to three guys deep, all bearing rifles. We only had sidearms and we were worried about what was going to happen. But then the Colonel, our commander, got out of the plane, and the Japanese officer standing there waiting for him handed him his sword and then the soldiers all turned in their arms. When they were done, thousands of Japanese Army rifles were stacked alongside the runway. I'd never seen anything like it. We had no trouble whatsoever there."

In January 1946, Shattuck was transferred to the 2nd Major Port in Yokohama Harbor—under a Colonel C.K. Harder, who was the Provost Marshal—and put in charge of the military police company there as well as the harbor patrol. He earned recognition by ending a massive theft problem on the Yokohama docks—one entirely organized by the occupying American soldiers.

During the years 1945–46, in fact, the Occupation had been losing an amazing one out of every three truckloads of goods that left the port of Yokohama. These were goods from consignments that had come in by ship from the United States to the Yokohama docks and consisted of clothes, food, arms, medicine, and Army Post Exchange supplies, among other things. A full one-third of truckloads that left the pier wound up on the black market, typically at open-air marts like the Matsuda Market in Shimbashi or the Ozu Market in Shinjuku. Theft was rampant.

As Shattuck explained in a later interview, "It was the one particular unit. The trucks had been going in an out without any record of what was going on. So one of my jobs was to deal with that. I instituted tighter controls, improved security and pulled off the guards at the port, replacing them with soldiers from another unit. I took multiple inventories—one as the ship was unloaded, another as the goods were offloaded onto the trucks, and yet again at point of delivery. We cross-checked the lists. I had the drivers inspected and the checkpoints investigated. We eventually fixed it."

Shattuck also managed the recovery of huge amounts of hidden silver, gold, platinum and industrial diamonds that were supposed to have been turned over to the US Military Government by Japan as legitimate booty of war under the conditions of surrender, but had been hidden at various locations.

Somewhere along the way, Shattuck found an interpreter working at the G-2 section, a native of Honolulu named Saburo Odachi, who proved invaluable. Odachi had a most unusual background. In his mid-twenties, born in Hawaii of Japanese parents, fluent in Japanese, and with dual Japanese and US citizenship, Odachi had been sent to Tokyo's elite Keio University to study in 1940. When the war broke out he was drafted into the Imperial Japanese Army. He was commissioned as an officer and served in Taiwan. When the war ended, he found a job as a translator in the GHQ and, was assigned to the Provost Marshal, where he had met Shattuck. Odachi was a ninth dan in judo and also became Shattuck's judo teacher.

As it happened, Odachi knew where there were silver bars hidden at a Japanese aircraft factory. Provost Marshal Harder ordered Odachi and Shattuck to seize the silver as legitimate spoils of war and take anything else they could find. They also picked up a number of silver bars buried in the ground outside the aircraft factory, the Imperial Seal stamped on them, uncovered a carload of silver wire and following that, discovered 1100 karats of industrial diamonds, used for industrial drills, in the backyard of a former Imperial Japanese Army officer. Finally they located some gold and platinum, which had been used in manufacturing Japanese war materials. They turned it all the GHQ and won plaudits from their superiors. (However, not everyone engaged in the same work was so honest. Shattuck told the tale of an Army colonel who was caught stealing silver, court-martialed and cashiered back to the US.)

It was during this time that Shattuck came to Jack Canon's attention and was subjected to one of the commander's famous recruitment tests. Canon showed up on the Yokohama docks one morning in 1947 wearing civilian clothes and a tag which said "State Department" and demanded entry to a secure area controlled by Shattuck

"Show me some identification first," said Shattuck.

"Here it is on the tag," Canon replied.

"That's not it," Shattuck said. "That's just a tag you got from the office up there at the entrance to the pier. I want to see some real identification."

"Well, I don't have to give you identification," Canon said,

"Well then," replied Shattuck, "you're under arrest for attempting illegal entry to a secure area."

The rules in place at the time stated that in order to place someone under arrest, the arresting party had to touch the arrestee and say "You're under arrest." But when Shattuck went to touch Canon's arm, Canon resisted, grabbing Shattuck by the throat. In a flash, the five-foot-eleven, 210-pound (1.8 m, 95 kg) Shattuck threw the much larger Canon to the ground. *Ippon seio nage*, as they say in judo.

"After that, I took him over to the Provost Marshal's office," Shattuck said. "Colonel Harder was there and the both of them started laughing, because Harder knew him. I didn't know Canon from Adam. I didn't know he was a Colonel. I just threw him down on the ground. And apparently that impressed him because he thought he was a pretty good judo man and he would later ask Harder for me to work with him."

Shattuck thus became the liaison between Canon and the police of Yokohama and a year later the point man between Canon and the port of Yokohama in an unprecedented operation involving North Korea and pure heroin.

RED LION HEROIN

Among the many Canon Agency exploits, one of the most dramatic was its 1948 infiltration of the newly established North Korean government, the Democratic People's Republic of Korea (DPRK), which had begun manufacturing heroin refined from opium fields in Manchuria and was attempting to flood the Tokyo–Yokohama area with it.

"The DPRK regime had two goals," said Victor Matsui. "One was to sell as much of their drugs as possible in Japan and channel the profits to the Japanese Communist Party (JCP). The other was to turn as many American soldiers as possible into heroin addicts so they'd be unfit to fight in the war that was coming on the Korean Peninsula, which broke out two years later in 1950."

Until then, there hadn't been a great deal of heroin in Japan, except that brought in from China by the ultranationalist Yoshio Kodama, whose Kodama Kikan group, comprised of yakuza, had plundered China to fund the war effort back home. Kodama's wartime treasure chest would fund the postwar conservative political movement in Japan. However, the DPRK project was far more ambitious in size as it entailed massive shipments to underworld dealers in Japan.

The Canon people came up with a daring counterplan to stymy the North Korean effort. They commandeered a boat and formed a crew to pose as a yakuza gang based in Yokohama, then traveled to Pyongyang where they struck a deal with the generals to distribute as much heroin as they could supply.

The vessel, a PT (patrol torpedo) boat the Canon Agency had procured and converted to look like a fishing boat, was piloted by a Korean naval officer from Seoul named Young Hou, recruited by Canon. Young had been conscripted into the Japanese Army in 1944 when he was a student at Chuo University but began working with the G-2 during the Occupation. He was the only Korean native in the Canon group. (He would later be awarded three Silver Stars by the US for his work during the Korean War, especially in the landing at Inchon.)

Shortly after the fake yakuza gang returned to Tokyo, a North Korean fishing boat dropped off a shipment of Pyongyang manufactured drugs—a dozen aluminum cans in a flotation device—at the mouth of Tokyo Bay. Each aluminum can weighed one kilogram (two pounds) and bore the printed label, in English, *Red Lion*. Inside were packages of 99.9 percent pure heroin. The agents picked up the cans and took them to an office in Yokohama where they unpackaged the heroin and weighed and measured it.

Alonzo Shattuck, who had a marine captain's license, piloted the boat that picked up the heroin canisters. "The stuff was so powerful," he said, "that just the few puffs of powder that escaped into the air during the measuring process would get everybody stoned."

The agents, of course, did not want to deal the heroin, nor did they want to reveal their operations, so they stored it and sent word to the North Koreans that they had lost the shipment at sea and requested another to be sent. That was a lot of heroin to go missing.

The North Koreans sent another shipment, and another one after that, but grew suspicious when no sales or GI junkies manifested themselves. Consequently, they cut ties with Young Hou's impostors and struck deals with a succession of real yakuza gangs based in the Yokohama area. Soon heroin was being peddled on the streets of that city but cut as much as twenty times with other substances, with some of the profits siphoned off to the JCP.

"By the end of 1948," said Shattuck, "there were drugs all over the place. There was a certain bridge in Yokohama where you could buy heroin in any quantity you wanted. The dope was submerged underwater in waterproof packets attached to a string the dealer pulled up to fill your order. To prove how prevalent it was to a visiting officer one day, I walked down the main drag in Yokohama in civvies and got solicited twice by people wanting to sell heroin."

After the real yakuza gangs took over distribution, the Canon Agency mission became one of intercepting the clandestine drug shipments. Violent shoot-outs between Canon's men and the gangs took place on beaches outside Yokohama, in public parks and sometimes even in deserted shrines and temples in the small hours of the night. In one battle at Yokohama's Nogeyama Koen park, Jack Canon was wounded in the leg with a .38 caliber slug.

From 1948 onward, narcotics that were manufactured in North Korea became a fixture of the drug scene in the Tokyo–Yokohama area. Drug trafficking was said to be worth more than a million dollars a year, which was an enormous amount of money at the time. The situation was also exacerbated by GIs serving in Korea who would develop the addiction there, get their heroin from bar girls, and bring their habits back to Japan. Some of them were even dealing. Said Shattuck: "We got a lot of information from heroin users in Yokohama just by incarcerating them and making them go cold turkey."

It was Matsui's job to sniff out the drug dealers. "I had a .38 snub-nosed that I carried with me," he said. "I worked with the narcotics people in the Tokyo and Yokohama area, on the trail of dealers. The 'narcos' would follow me as I went through a neighborhood, going from one house to another, through one house, into the street, then through another house. It was unpleasant work. But I never fired my gun."

Despite all the heroin flowing into the country, the drug never really caught on among the Japanese. As Matsui explained it, heroin was a lethargy drug and Tokyo was a city on the go, where people worked dawn to dusk as much as seven days a week. Speed would have been the perfect drug for a taxi driver working round the clock, a night laborer, a student cramming for exams or a nightclub hostess, but not heroin.

Once the generals in Pyongyang figured this out, North Korea was perfectly willing to manufacture and supply the right narcotic to them in the form of crystal meth, which became Tokyo's designer drug. There had been something called *hiropon* (Philopon), that was supplied to soldiers, factory workers, pilots and others during the war by the Japanese government, but the drug was of such low quality that it left many takers with adverse side effects such as migraine headaches and blackouts. The meth coming out of North Korea, distributed by yakuza gangs such as the Yamaguchi-gumi, however, proved to be a better product and dominated the underworld market for the next several decades. It is still available in Tokyo today (along with North Korean–manufactured Viagra and other products), although China and Mexico are now the primary suppliers of crystal meth, synthetic cocaine and fentanyl. (An interesting fact about the Occupation is that there were more

drug addicts created during those years than there were converts to
Christianity by the missionaries MacArthur had brought to Japan.)

THE IWASAKI HOUSE: GUNS, MIDNIGHT ASSIGNATIONS
AND THE THIRD DEGREE

The headquarters of the Canon Agency, from December 1946
on, was the Iwasaki Estate, built on a palatial scale beside Shinobazu Pond in Tokyo's spacious Ueno Park. On the sprawling sev-
enteen-thousand-acre premises were three buildings: a two-story
Western-style mansion, a large forty-four-room Japanese-style
house and a billiard house modeled on a Swiss chalet. There was
also a garden with a lawn, stone monuments, stone lanterns, a
hand-washing basin and a tennis court. It looked like something
out of *The Great Gatsby*.

Originally the home of Baron Hisaya Iwasaki, eldest son of the
founder of the Mitsubishi Group and its third president, the Iwasaki Estate had been designed by the British architect Josiah Conder
(1852–1920) and completed in 1896. It was the perfect base of operations for the agency.

The Western-style mansion on the estate had the feel of an old
European hotel. On the first floor was a big dining room with a
fireplace, a big kitchen with a pantry, a library, nine bedrooms and
four assorted smaller rooms. The south side had a veranda with a
colonnade. Jack Canon's office was upstairs overlooking the garden.
According to Victor Matsui, Canon had decorated the garden with
empty coke bottles, tin cans, beer cans and light bulbs, and used
them for daily target practice, often firing at them from his desk
with the gold-plated pistol he always carried with him. Once he
took aim at an intruding crow, overshot his target and the bullet he
fired broke a store window in Ueno's Ameyoko-cho, a busy market
area a quarter of a mile away, causing a minor scandal.

Young later described Jack Canon's love of firearms in his entertaining memoir, *Kyanan kikan kara no sengen* [Testimony from
Canon Agency, published by Bancho Shobo, 1973]. "Canon's fondness for shooting guns was a big topic of conversation. When he

was shooting you could see the enjoyment. He would open a window on the left side facing the garden and fire away at light bulbs and cans hanging from the branches in the garden. Bang! Bang! He would go through a hundred bullets a day. The walls of his room were filled with bullet holes that were quickly repaired. He would fire a shot past a new recruit to see how he would react. The guy would open the door, walk in and bang, Canon would scare the heck out of him. The guy would turn white. 'This is a test of the guy's guts,' Canon would say. There was a guy named Choi who thought he had been grazed in the temple by one of Canon's bullets. He grabbed his head, shouting "I've been shot," and collapsed to the floor. But Canon hadn't shot Choi. He had shot a light bulb over Choi's head and Choi had been injured by one of the broken shards . . . There were eight Japanese maids in the house, but Canon would strip down to his underpants and work out in front of them, out punching sandbags in the second floor corridor."

Canon knew more about firearms than anyone else in Japan, according to Matsui. "He was a real gun nut," he said. "He had the *Shooter's Bible* memorized. You could wake him up at three o'clock in the morning and ask him what the weight, length and velocity of a German Walther PK was and he could tell you, even when he was half asleep."

"Canon was also a night person," Shattuck said. "All the agents were. His routine started after dark when he went out to meet undercover operatives, collaborators and rival agents, and also perform recon on suspected Communist activities. He'd assume a false name and go to bars and nightclubs and receptions where he thought he could get the information he was looking for."

"The ladies liked Canon. He was a big guy, burly, good-looking, with a high forehead, and he had this thatch of brown hair. They all went for it. He was the kind of guy who could easily strike up a conversation with a beautiful woman whenever he wanted. It was a talent he used a lot with the Russian ladies. He would get them to invite him to Soviet receptions, and once there, he'd secretly take photos of people he thought were spies."

A popular spot at the time for Canon's agents was Club Cherry, a hostess club on the second floor of a building in Nishi Ginza. It was run by Mama Cherry, a dancer from Kobe, part Chinese, and an extremely beautiful woman according to those who knew her. Her Korean husband worked at the cash register. There were several hostesses at Club Cherry, all skilled at their jobs, according to Shattuck, who had a girlfriend there, a young lady who later married an American Army colonel. Some of the hostesses would sleep with the customers. Others, who had boyfriends, would not. A regular customer was a character named Maurice Lipton. He was famous for his cigar and hat. He had a permanent indentation in his lip from the cigar. He would come in and say to a girl, "As bad as I need money I will go to bed with you for free." But he always paid, said Mama Cherry, and they made so much money there that she and her husband were able to open up the Copacabana club in the late fifties in Tokyo's Akasaka district, which became the place to go for anybody who was anybody.

Another hangout was the Foreign Correspondents Club of Japan (FCCJ) in Marunouchi, with its eclectic mix of journalists from all around the globe. The Soviet Union occupied a building right across the street and two doors down from the FCCJ. The journalists would have a few drinks and go outside with their cameras, aiming them at the windows of the office of a Soviet Consul, a general, who had the shades down, and fire off their flashes.

One of Jack Canon's assets was a Japanese clerk at the Russian embassy who provided him with secret reports including photos and descriptions of communications equipment the Russians were using in Tokyo. Canon also turned a Japanese field operative working for the Russians to the US side and supplied him with misinformation in the form of documents and tape recordings to dispense to his contacts. Canon encrypted his messages, recording and compressing them, so that they could be sent over the radio in bursts lasting a matter of seconds. The receiving operator would record the message, then play it back at slower speed. Meetings with contacts usually took place in the middle of the night in public parks like Hibiya Koen in Tokyo and Nogeyama Koen in Yokohama.

Shattuck had been assigned to handle two double agents, both

Japanese. One of them was a policeman who worked for the Russian embassy.

"We managed to double them," said Shattuck "and we had them in there working for us. They were useless as far as being any kind of spies or what have you, but the advantage was we would get the latest equipment they were given by the Soviets. We'd get it analyzed and we would attempt to feed misinformation through them. There were also Japanese guys in the employ of North Korea but who were secretly working with us. I would meet one guy in Hibiya Park at three o'clock in the morning. I would give him a tape of misinformation that he was supposed to convey to his North Korean bosses."

"Some of our agents were working simultaneously for the Japanese Government and the Communist Party. Two of our informants had even worked for Sorge and for the Japanese Government at the same time! Can you imagine that?! Our informants were never permitted inside the Iwasaki house we worked out of. They were always met outside by one and sometimes two of our own personnel, Americans, well away from our installation. Of course, they would not have been privy to the name Canon or our own names. Most of the intelligence so gathered was always suspect, naturally, especially from the double agents but they were useful for transmitting false information to the Soviets and on occasion they brought us radios and encrypting devices that had been given them by the Soviets for us to study. I have no way of knowing, but my theory is that one or two Japanese intelligence agents, whom we used as sources and who were doubled by the Soviets during the war but were never caught by the Japanese authorities, gave spurious information to the Japanese Government. This type of person was generally a consummate liar and sold information, good and bad, to any willing buyer."

The Canon Agency also used ethnic Korean yakuza, like Hisayuki Machii, aka Ginza Machii, boss of the Tosei-kai, one of the top Tokyo gangs, to suppress leftist demonstrations in and around the city. He once killed a man with his bare hands during a violent protest in Ikebukuro.

POKER FACE

The brains of the operation, as well as the resident expert on fire-arms, was unquestionably Jack Canon. Agents used to comment on just how intelligent Canon actually was. Said Shattuck: "I saw him one time playing chess with a White Russian guy who was regarded the best chess player in Japan, and Jack was carrying on a conversation and answering the phone all the time and he beat this guy at chess. I remember watching him do it."

Canon, who wore a perpetual poker face, was very good at navigating through the dangerous waters of the G-2. The G-2 and the Government Section (GS) did not see eye to eye on a number of things and the general atmosphere was not very good. It was the GS that wanted Japan to be the Switzerland of Asia. They wanted to break up the zaibatsu, the big financial combines, as well as the Japanese military. It was the G-2 that wanted Japan to be a bulwark against Communism. Naturally, with competing objectives, the two departments did not get along. Willoughby was very Germanic. He spoke with a clear German accent and alienated a lot of people because of it. But he knew the business of intelligence very well and because he and MacArthur had fought the war together he had the latter's full confidence. Charles Kades, the brains at GS was just the opposite of Willoughby. Urbane, Ivy League, and Roosevelt New Dealer. The two men could not have been more different.

Canon did not drink. He did not trust people who drank because he thought they would get drunk and reveal secrets, which is why no one in the Canon group was a heavy drinker. He did not touch drugs—except once when he smoked a cigarette laced with heroin to see what it was like. Canon did not chase women either, which made him unusual. It was an era when important people in the Occupation were invited out to fancy *ryotei* inns and geisha houses every night. A lot of these people took on lovers. Charles Kades, one of the most powerful men in the GHQ, had a mistress, the Viscountess Torio, wife of an aristocrat and member of the imperial family, a circumstance which proved his undoing as we shall see later. But not Canon. Although, as noted earlier, he could smooth talk the ladies when needed, he was incorruptible and remained faithful to his wife, believing that as the father of two children and a leader of men, he had a moral responsibility to behave in a certain way. His men believed he was the only American in postwar Japan who had never slept with a Japanese woman.

There were a lot of parties held at the Iwasaki house, at Thanksgiving and other times. One night, they invited the English-speaking actress Yoshiko (Shirley) Yamaguchi who had appeared in Hollywood movies. Others in the group drank copious amounts and made much noise. But not Jack Canon. He would not even raise a glass to his mouth.

"Why do people find these kinds of events interesting," he would ask. "I don't understand. What's so great about playing around with a girl?"

His one great love, in addition to guns, was poker. He would say "Poker is a great way to read a person's heart and soul."

PLAGUE OUTBREAK

One of the most daring missions carried out by the Canon Agency was the raid on Ganzan, a coastal city in North Korea in February 1950, described by Young in his book. It was prompted, he said, by rumors of an outbreak of bubonic plague at an Army hospital there. The UN Command wanted to know if there was indeed bubonic plague and if it would spread. If so, MacArthur was ready to withdraw all US troops from the Korean peninsula. So Young and a team took a ship up the coast, disembarked in a rubber raft, and made their way into the hospital, disguised in North Korean military uniforms. They extracted a corpse reported to have died of the plague, as well as a live patient believed to have been infected, and brought them back down to the beach. There, an American Army doctor performed an autopsy on the spot and examined the living patient. If it had been the plague, they might all have died. As it turned out, however, it wasn't the plague, or cholera or typhus. It was just a virus of some sort.

According to Shattuck and Matsui, Young went on to become instrumental in the Inchon landing later that year, after the Korean

War had started. He knew the geography and detailed information about the twenty-seven-foot (eight meter) tidal difference at In-chon. It was a very difficult place to maneuver and land, and disembarking at the wrong time would have made the landing force sitting ducks. So when the UN forces put out the word that the landing was planned at Inchon, nobody believed them, because it was so problematic. Then the landing went ahead. It was such a surprise, it became a roaring success.

THE KIDNAPPING OF WATARU KAJI

The existence of the Canon Agency remained unknown to the Japanese public throughout most of the Occupation. It wasn't until the kidnapping of a double agent named Wataru Kaji in November 1951 became public knowledge in the early post-Occupation era, that the veil of secrecy was lifted. Kaji was a famous leftist, writer and Chinese sympathizer who had come out of Shanghai where he had been hiding during the war from the Japanese *kempetai* military police. He had been snatched off the street in broad daylight by a Canon Agency team while on his way to a meeting with a radio operator named Mitsuhashi who worked for Mitsubishi Electric—Mitsuhashi was a Russian agent Canon had doubled. Canon himself had personally grabbed Kaji while the double agent was walking on the sidewalk in Fujisawa, after having planted an attractive girl in Kaji's path to distract his attention. Canon ensconced him in a second floor room in the Iwasaki house, a utilitarian office with a desk and a cot. It was this room that Canon and his people would use to interrogate known or suspected Communist sympathizers they had nabbed.

"Victor and I and this Scandinavian guy did the interrogation," Shattuck recalled. "We three kept him under very tight control. I don't think anyone else ever saw him. He was lucky in a sense because he had tuberculosis—he kept upchucking phlegm. He used up a whole box of Kleenex—and our doctors cured him of it, but only after he had given it to a couple of our agents. People from big cities like me—I was from St Louis, which was smoke-filled and

Victor from LA—had developed immunities. But our big blond Swede, who came from a small town in Minnesota, had not. He became quite sick. Kaji actually bit one of our agents, a tall Texan whose name I forget, and gave him hepatitis."

The Canon Agency held onto Kaji until shortly before the Occupation ended in April 1952 and the occupying forces had to leave. Said Shattuck, "We didn't know what to do with him. So we turned him over to our Japanese counterparts in intelligence, who didn't know what to do with him either. They held on to him for a while and then released him. He went straight to the police and the newspapers picked it up and it became a national scandal. Kaji was called to testify in the National Diet. That's how the Japanese public first learned of the existence of the Canon Agency and that it was a black-ops group. The leftists went nuts. And all these bizarre stories started appearing."

There was a young low-level employee named Kozo Itagaki who became well known after he too testified in the Diet in the wake of the Kaji kidnapping. He told lawmakers he had undergone torture while handcuffed in a basement cell and was subjected to a mock execution in May 1951 in the garden at night, which appeared to be part of a vetting process before becoming part of the group. He revealed that all the agents had nicknames or code names with which to identify everyone. Young was called "Big." There was another called "Middle." And there was another one called "Small." Only a handful of people knew them. Zenjiro Yamada, a cook at the Iwasaki house, also testified about what he saw, including a prisoner who suffered a mental breakdown in custody and was taken away.

However, Shattuck was dismissive of the testimony Itagaki gave to the Diet: "The testimony of Kozo Itagaki has to be taken with several grains of salt. There were no cells in the mansion and mock executions did not happen." Added Matsui, "I don't think this guy knows what he is talking about." Said Shattuck of the cook's testimony, "The cook really had no idea what was going on. He had no access to anything."

They were equally dismissive of later reports that Kaji had been in anyway maltreated, given that the original purpose of the operation was not just to see what Kaji knew but also to get him to collaborate with the Americans. As Young put it, "Kaji was a writer. He was good at making up stories." The American outsiders as villains—it's what sold."

THE SHIMOYAMA INCIDENT

Many Japanese people believed that Jack Canon and his men were responsible for the infamous abduction and murder of railroad chief Sadanori Shimoyama and for major train accidents at Mitaka and Matsukawa, all of which took place within the span of six weeks starting July 5, 1949, and were, supposedly, part of a diabolical GHQ plan to discredit the Communist-backed labor unions.

Shimoyama, president of Japan National Railways (JNR), had been ordered by the GHQ to fire thirty thousand JNR employees in a cost-cutting move. Detroit banker Joseph Dodge, MacArthur's tough-minded adviser, had arrived in Japan to impose tight restrictions in order to clamp down on runaway inflation. As part of this effort, Dodge ordered the massive cut in Japan National Railways employees. Shortly thereafter, on July 5, 1949, Shimoyama disappeared on his way to work. His dismembered body was found the next day on railroad tracks outside Ueno, apparently having been hit by a train. A coroner who had examined the body determined it was suicide. However, another autopsy conducted by a professor of forensic medicine at Tokyo University could not establish whether it was suicide or murder. Shortly thereafter, in the Mitaka incident, a Chuo Line train crashed into Mitaka Station killing six people and injuring twenty. This was followed closely by the Matsukawa episode in which a Tohoku Line passenger train overturned near Matsukawa Station killing three crew members. In the former case, the train's conductor was sentenced to death and died in prison in 1967, but he steadfastly maintained his innocence until the very end. In the latter case, seventeen people were found guilty of sabotage and sentenced to death or life imprisonment. However, twelve years later, a high court overturned the convictions, finding all defendants innocent, a decision that was upheld by the Supreme Court.

Suspicions of Canon Agency involvement were stoked by the Diet testimony from Kaji and Itagaki, and the famed novelist Seicho Matsumoto, who in 1960 wrote the best-selling book *Nihon no kuroi kiri* [Black fog over Japan, published by Bungei Shunju], dedicated to the proposition that American black-ops were at work in the tragedies. Over the years other nonfiction writers added to that oeuvre. However, their work was also noted for its glaring mistakes and inconsistencies. Matsumoto, for example, wrote that the Canon Agency was based solely in Yokohama. He also wrote that the Canon Agency consisted mostly of officers of the Imperial Japanese Army, another assertion that was untrue.

In the 2000s, in the wake of the fiftieth anniversary of the end of the Occupation, there was another spate of books published in Japan that dealt with the infamous Shimoyama *jiken* (incident), as it was commonly referred to in the vernacular press. Foremost among them were *Bosatsu Shimoyama jiken* [Willful murder, published by Shodensha, 2009] by Kimio Yada, and *Shimoyama jiken* [The Shimoyama incident, Shodensha, 2007] by Tetsutaka Shibata, which sought to answer the "biggest mystery of the postwar era." Again both were based on circumstantial evidence, secondhand testimony and dubious assumptions that were ultimately inconclusive.

Said Victor Matsui: "There was lots of speculation in Japanese books about the Canon Agency that came out in the wake of the fiftieth anniversary of the end of the Occupation, that was just plain wrong. Pointing the finger at the Canon Agency in regard to the Shimoyama Incident, saying Canon was involved somehow. It was just off base. I knew Jack Canon very well. I was with him every single day from November 1945 until April 1952. And Shimoyama was just not part of the experience. There is no evidence that he was. There were no witnesses. And it doesn't make sense to me to say that Canon was behind the Shimoyama kidnapping and death. It was ridiculous. You have to ask the question, who would profit by having Shimoyama killed? Well, it was the labor unions. To say that Canon was involved goes against basic inductive, deductive reasoning. I think that I can say categorically, we were not involved. Unfortunately, if people keep saying that we were, it becomes fact."

CLOSING DOWN: THE CIA

The beginning of the end for the Canon Agency came shortly before the Occupation closed down on April 28, 1952. A CIA representative simply walked into the Iwasaki house one day—appropriately clad in a trench coat and fedora—and announced that all military intelligence operations in Japan would thenceforth come under the CIA's control.

Said Shattuck later, "It was a complete fiasco. The people they sent over from Washington couldn't find their ass with both hands, starting with the guy who came to the Iwasaki house to deliver the news, a relatively young guy, somewhere I guess in his late twenties, early thirties, wearing this trench coat with the collar up and smoking a pipe, I'll never forget it, leaning on the fireplace, like he was posing . . . and he announced he was taking over the unit. He said the CIA was taking over all the intelligence services—the CIC, Navy Intelligence, Army Intelligence. Well, there was a lot of bitching about that. This new CIA guy opened an office in the GHQ called the Document Research Section, which was not exactly the most ideal cover. Talk about putting up a sign."

There were many resignations as a result, starting with Jack Canon, who immediately asked for a transfer and was sent to Fort Hood in Texas, where he wound up working for the CIA anyway, and later, along with Willoughby, in the employ of H.L. Hunt, an extreme right-wing Texas oil billionaire who later became a major suspect in the assassination of John F. Kennedy.

Matsui, for his part, took a discharge and joined the State Department, while Shattuck resigned and stayed on in Tokyo to go into the nightclub business, opening up the posh Latin Quarter in Tokyo's Akasaka district in 1952 with the Manila-based gambler Ted Lewin and Canon Agency veteran, Saburo Odachi.

Despite the deprecations of Shattuck, Canon and others, the CIA did prove to be effective in its own way, picking up where the Canon Agency, and other intel services left off. The CIA was deeply concerned about massive leftist demonstrations that took place in the wake of the formal end of the Occupation, starting with the riot known as Bloody May Day in 1952, a violent conflict that erupted in front of the Imperial Palace between a large crowd affiliated with the Japanese Communist Party (JCP) that was protesting the recently concluded US–Japan Security Treaty allowing the stationing of US forces in Japan. Police opened fire. Two people died and thousands more were injured in the fighting. Three American GIs were thrown into the moat and stoned while in the water. Sporadic violence followed in succeeding months. Although the JCP suffered at the polls in succeeding elections as a result of the violence, the CIA was taking no chances. Under the authority of US president Dwight Eisenhower, the CIA began paying the ruling conservative Liberal Democratic Party (LDP) approximately one million dollars a month. This lasted through most of the 1950s and 1960s. As described by Tim Weiner in his book *Legacy of Ashes* (Anchor, 2008), the CIA used trusted American businessmen as go-betweens, including executives from Lockheed, the aircraft company then building the U-2 high-altitude reconnaissance jet and negotiating to sell warplanes to the newly created Japan Self-Defense Forces. The money helped the LDP stay in power and continue its support for the US presence in Japan. The aforementioned ultranationalist fixer (and LDP founder) Yoshio Kodama helped deliver the funds.

The CIA also helped elect Nobusuke Kishi, a former Class A War Crimes suspect and descendant of a samurai family, to the presidency of the LDP and subsequently to the post of prime minister. Kishi (maternal grandfather of Japan's future prime minister, Shinzo Abe) was notorious for his brutal rule of the Japanese puppet state of Manchukuo in northeast China that existed from 1932 to 1945, using yakuza thugs to keep Chinese workers in line, and was also noted for his lavish spending as he pursued his favorite extracurricular activities of much drinking, gambling and womanizing. Kishi, who had been imprisoned after the war, was released from Sugamo Prison in 1949 on the very day wartime prime minister General Hideki Tojo and others were hanged, under an agreement with GHQ whereby Kishi would work with the Americans to pursue conservative interests in exchange for political and financial support.

As prime minister of Japan in 1960, the flop-eared Kishi oversaw

the Diet ratification of the extension of the US–Japan Security
Treaty, despite massive public opposition. Kishi also permitted the
Americans to secretly maintain nuclear weapons on military bases
in Okinawa.

Opposition to the American presence in Japan would reach a
peak at that time, when a million protesters descended upon the
Diet to protest that Security Treaty extension. Japanese police and
yakuza gangsters recruited by the LDP helped repel the protesters
and allow the extension to be ratified by LDP lawmakers, thus keeping US bases in the country.

Following the end of the Occupation, new US intelligence agencies came into operation. One was the National Security Agency, established by US president Harry S. Truman in 1952 and funded and
overseen by the Secretary of Defense. Two others were the Defense
Intelligence Agency, which Defense Secretary Robert McNamara
created in 1962 after the Bay of Pigs fiasco, and the National Reconnaissance Office, set up in 1962 to build spy satellites.

But the CIA, with its monetary pipeline to the highest levels of
government, was the most active US agency in Japan, even though at
the time only a very few were privy to everything that was going on.
Ironically, while some people knew about the connection between
the CIA and the yakuza, hardly anyone knew about the pipeline between the CIA and the ruling LDP (or, one might add, the burgeoning relationship of these entities with the Korean Central Intelligence
Agency and the Korean Unification Church, as we will later see).

And no one really knew about the entirety of the operations
of the Canon Agency, the testimony of Itagaki and Kaji notwithstanding. All records were destroyed and the activities of the group
remained secret for a long, long time until Jack Canon granted an
interview to NHK, the national TV network, decades later in 1977
and Young Hou wrote his memoir about Canon.

Jack Canon shot himself on March 8, 1981, the first victim of his
invention, the Glaser Safety Slug, at his home in Maclean, Texas. A
gun he was building accidentally went off and sent two Glaser Slugs
into his chest. Victor Matsui passed away in 2012, and Alonzo Shattuck died in 2023.

By the time the Canon Agency was closed down the GHQ had significantly contributed to the goal of saving Japan from Communism. At the same time, it also had help from the American Council on Japan, a private semi-secret Wall Street cabal that had been trying to influence the early course of the GHQ toward a more anti-Communist stance from about 1947 in an effort to rescue prewar investments and holdings in Japan. These activities were described in the book *Occupation Without Troops* (Tuttle, 2012) by Glen Davis and John Roberts. Involved were John McCloy, James Forrestal, the Rockefellers and other influential figures, including Harry Kern of *Newsweek*, along with future Secretary of State John Foster Dulles and his brother Allan, who were also involved in something called the Office of Policy Coordination. They all spent an enormous amount of money on this endeavor. Kern used *Newsweek* to attack GHQ plans to make Japan Socialist and warn of the mounting Communist threat in Red China and North Korea. Alan Dulles, who had worked in the Office of Strategic Services (OSS) in World War II, participated in the establishment of the CIA in 1947 and became its director in 1953. Both Dulles men were strident anti-Communists and took a big interest in Japan's future after they came to the opinion that MacArthur was being too soft on the Socialists early on in the Occupation. They succeeded, and because of this, the Rockefellers and the Morgans were able to assume significant business positions in Japan when the Occupation ended. Kern was Prime Minister's Kishi's private English teacher. He later became a consultant on aircraft sales for Nissho Iwai Corporation and Grumman Aircraft Engineering because of this closeness to Kishi and his brother Sato, who also became prime minister several years later. This was one of the few times in Japanese history that a Japanese company hired an American to gain influence in the Japanese Prime Minister's Office.

By the time the Occupation ended, the zaibatsu big financial combines, all but deposed during the early days of the GHQ, were back in power again, seemingly overnight. It was as if someone had waved a magic wand.

AN OCCUPATION LOVE STORY: THE COLONEL AND THE VISCOUNTESS

The G-2 intelligence wing of the GHQ and the Canon Agency did more than spy on Communists during the Occupation. They also spied on fellow Americans. One of their targets was the aforementioned Charles Kades, who was having an affair with the wife of a Japanese aristocrat.

Kades, a Harvard graduate, Wall Street lawyer and Roosevelt New Dealer was deputy chief of the Government Section, and a US Army colonel. He was the moving force behind many of the Occupation's postwar reforms under MacArthur, which were designed to endow Japan with modern democratic institutions and do away with the feudal system that had helped put Japan on a path to war. He had arrived in Tokyo in late August 1945 and had overseen the purging and imprisonment of the Japanese military officers, politicians, government officials and businessmen who had led Japan into the war. He further encouraged labor unions to form and supervised the creation of the GHQ draft of a new constitution, a remarkable document that renounced war, stripped the emperor of authority while leaving him as head of state, established an elected government and guaranteed a range of civil rights, including, for the first time, full equality for women (who had previously been subservient under the law to the male head of the household). The new constitution took effect on May 3, 1947.

The head of G-2 intelligence, General Charles Willoughby, thought Kades was going too far to the left. The Cold War with the Russians had begun and Willoughby, concerned about the rising tide of Communism on the China mainland and in North Korea, feared its impact on Japan, where leftist demonstrations were getting larger and noisier. The leader of the Japanese Communist Party had called for a general nationwide strike for economic and political concessions involving six million railway, school, factory, government and other workers on February 1, 1947. The strike was averted only after a sharp public rebuke by MacArthur and the implied threat of retaliation from American soldiers.

Willoughby thought the Occupation could use the services of

Japan's top military officers in combating the rising Red threat, as well as the help of Japan's top industrialists in running the postwar economy, which was caught in an inflationary spiral. Because there were many left-leaning New Dealers in the Government Section and Economic and Science Division, Willoughby suspected there were Communists or people with Communist leanings in both groups operating under the guise of democratization.

Willoughby was also encouraged by the lobbying efforts of the abovementioned group of influential Wall Street executives affiliated with the Morgans, the Rockefellers and other large multinationals with substantial prewar business interests in Japan, who feared the new policies would harm their investments. They used their contacts in the US media and other less openly visible means to push for G-2 investigations into those suspected of left-wing leanings in Tokyo, checking into their histories, family structure and friends, in coordination with the FBI and the intelligence wing of the US Defense Department. In this regard, Willoughby paid special attention to Kades, as well as to his staff, their families and the circles in which they moved.

THE CHARLES BOYER OF THE GHQ

Willoughby was particularly intrigued by Kades' personal life. It seemed that Kades, a married man whose wife was in New York undergoing treatment for cancer, had a Japanese mistress and a very special one at that, a Viscountess named Tsuruyo Torio. She was married to the Viscount Norimitsu Torio and was the mother of two children. The stunningly attractive Viscountess Torio had been involved with Kades since the early days of the Occupation.

The Viscountess had been born in 1912 and raised in privilege and luxury, but during the war years the family fell on hard times, as did most other Japanese. In the early days of the Occupation Japanese officials found her useful in dealing with the Americans. She could speak English, she was beautiful and she looked great in a kimono, something many Americans found enchanting.

Some believed that the Viscountess was an agent for the imperial household, assigned to seduce Kades in 1946 and make sure that there was nothing in the new constitution Kades was helping to create that would limit the emperor's sovereignty or otherwise weaken the emperor system.

The Viscountess was invited to a dinner party for high-ranking GHQ officials hosted by Chief Cabinet Secretary Wataru Narahashi at the home of prominent leftist journalist Tanzan Ishibashi.

It was at this dinner party that Viscountess Torio first met Kades, a man known for his considerable charm and good looks. In fact, he was so dashing that he was nicknamed the "Charles Boyer of the GHQ" after the suave French actor, and enjoyed the attentions of a number of young women. Beate Sirota Gordon, an aide to Kades, raised in Japan, a young woman who had worked with him on the new constitution, and was instrumental in getting an equal rights clause for women included in it (later authoring a best-selling book on her contributions *The Only Woman in the Room*, University of Chicago Press, 2014), said, "He was wonderful. All the girls in the Occupation were in love with him. Including me." Kades' secretary, Ruth Ellerman was quoted as saying, "There were a lot of upper-class Japanese women who tried to get close to the liberals in the Government Section. In the case of Kades, the attraction wasn't just a political or an intellectual one; it was more than that. But Chuck was not the kind of man to chase after women himself; they chased after him."

Nevertheless, Kades was reportedly quite taken with Torio, and she with him. As she put it in her autobiography, *Watashi no ashi oto ga kikoeru* [You can hear my footsteps, published by Bungei Shunju, 1985], she had had an open marriage. Her husband had a mistress and accordingly she was free to pursue her own interests and amusements. After a few subsequent encounters, she and Kades began enjoying romantic weekend getaways at Japan's mountain resort Karuizawa, where the Torio family had a summer home. Kades also became a frequent visitor to the Torio home in Tokyo, parking his 1946 black and silver Chevrolet in front of the house for all to see and bringing presents from the base exchange for the Torios and their two children, including food items and other items forbidden to the Japanese under Occupation rule. He also helped Torio open up a boutique on the Ginza strip, which catered to the wives and mistresses of GHQ officers and wealthy Japanese businessmen thereby bringing extra income to the Torio family.

In turn, as the Viscountess described in her autobiography, she tutored Kades on understanding the ways of the Japanese people and that included instruction as to their love for Emperor Hirohito and the need to keep the emperor system in place. She also explained why it was not absolutely necessary to purge all of Japan's prewar military and financial business leaders. Such people would be needed to help run the new Japan.

Hearing gossip about Kades and his new Japanese girlfriend, General Willoughby had arranged for a plain clothes detective from the Metropolitan Police Department to monitor the comings and goings at the Torio residence and report back via Jack Canon.

This detective who was watching the house remarked that it did not really take a lot of detective work to uncover what was going on because the relationship between Kades and Viscountess Torio was very open and very, very close.

He reported that not only did the husband know about and condone it, he appeared to be proud of it. He seemed to think of it as a family honor. Whenever Kades drove to the Torio residence to pick up Viscountess Torio, the husband would come out to see them off, waving congenially. However, the detective also noted that as soon as they had gone, Viscount Torio would go to pick up his secretary and bring her back to his home. According to the detective, the neighbors could not quite wrap their heads around the goings on in the Torio household. It was all so strange.

With Torio's relationship with Kades public knowledge, many individuals who had been purged by the GHQ contacted the Viscountess to ask her to use her influence with Kades to try to persuade him to remove their names from the purge list. In time, Willoughby submitted his report on Kades to MacArthur.

"Sir," said Willoughby "In the Occupation Policy Manual, there is nothing that indicates it is all right to occupy the wife of another man. Also, I might add that Kades already has a wife."

MacArthur, who was famous for saying of his men in Tokyo that "they could Madam Butterfly themselves to death for all I care," was not moved to action. So, Willoughby did the next best thing he could think of to ruin Kades' career: he sent the report to Kades' wife in New York who made a hasty trip to Tokyo to confront her husband. She returned to the States and filed for divorce.

THE REVERSE COURSE KICKS IN

On March 1, 1948, a pro-Socialist government led by Prime Minister Hitoshi Ashida, and strongly supported by Kades and the people in the Government Section, assumed power. Although MacArthur's ban on strikes and collective bargaining had weakened the leftist movement somewhat, as had increased arrests of Communist agitators by Willoughby's people, there was still sizable public backing for the new government, a state of affairs Willoughby found intolerable.

Willoughby's war on Kades reached critical mass in the spring of 1948 when Torio's husband, now running a car-repair business and struggling to turn a profit, tried and failed to borrow money from the Reconstruction Finance Bank, an institution set up by the Japanese government under GHQ guidance to help ailing businesses get back on their feet. He had asked his wife to ask Kades if he could find out why his loan application was rejected. Kades did investigate and discovered that the bank had channeled all its funds into Showa Denko, a major chemical company, in exchange for bribes to high-ranking officials. Key members of the Ashida government were implicated as well as personnel in the GHQ. When Willoughby got wind of the bribes he leaked details to the US wire services AP and UPI via the Foreign Correspondents Club of Japan. Although censorship had been imposed by the Occupation's Government Section, reprints of the wire-service articles bounced back from the US and the word spread. In June of 1948, the president of Showa Denko, Kozo Hinodera, was arrested.

Shortly after Hinodera's arrest, a glamorous, heavily coiffed woman clad in a mink coat appeared at Viscountess Torio's Ginza boutique. Torio recognized her as a fellow customer at the beauty salon in the Imperial Hotel arcade, a high-ranking geisha named Hidekoma who was also the mistress of the Showa Denko president. Ushered into a back room, she presented a satchel to Torio that was filled with cash yen and begged Torio to take it.

"There's a million yen in there," she was quoted as saying in Torio's autobiography. "And there's more where that came from. Please give it to Colonel Kades and ask him to get Hinodera-san out of jail."

Torio refused. Kades wasn't that kind of man, she replied. He had too much integrity to accept a bribe. She sent the woman away in tears.

In all, sixty-three more people were arrested, indicted and tried, including Prime Minister Ashida himself along with the minister of finance in November 1948. It was Japan's largest postwar scandal to that point. The Ashida government was forced to resign and Conservative leader Shigeru Yoshida, a close ally of Willoughby, became prime minister, ushering in more than four decades of right-wing rule in Japan. This helped to cement what would come to be known as the "Reverse Course" in Occupation history. Purged industrial and military leaders were reinstated and many of the early reforms repealed.

Shortly after that, reports of the connection between Torio and Kades, and Hinodera and Hidekoma began to appear in the Japanese weekly magazines. Some of them portrayed Kades as a corrupt American bureaucrat who had taken as much as thirty million yen in bribes via his Japanese lover Torio, who was portrayed as little more than a prostitute. It was not hard to guess where those rumors originated.

A FINAL, FINAL MEETING

In December 1948, Kades was reassigned to Washington. Before he left, he visited Torio to say goodbye. Torio had wanted to continue the relationship but Kades dismissed it as an impossibility. "I can't stay here because I am too disliked by the Japanese, after what happened with the Ashida cabinet and everything. I can't take you back to the States because there is too much discrimination against Japanese. People remember Pearl Harbor. I don't want to hear anyone call you a Jap."

The downfall of the Ashida government and revelations about Kades' relationship with Torio destroyed Kades' career in Tokyo. But there is no sound evidence supporting rumors circulating at the time that it had all been preplanned or that Torio had had anything to do with Showa Denko or had secretly worked with Willoughby or had been a paid agent of the emperor. That was all speculation.

Moreover, as we have seen, the Reverse Course had other forces behind it as well. A key figure was a man named James Lee Kaufman who had taught English at Tokyo University before the war and as a lawyer represented the interests of General Electric, Standard Oil and Dillon Read among other high profile American firms. He had come back to Tokyo on an August 1947 trip as a member of an economic fact-finding group that wanted to investigate the postwar economic situation. Kaufman then returned to the States and filed a report in which he described the failure of the GHQ labor policy and agricultural policy, the purge of twenty thousand zaibatsu officials and other shortcomings of MacArthur's Occupation, including the juicy detail that GHQ personnel were eating fancy meals for only 25 cents, and staying in hotel rooms for only 50 cents a night, while the rest of Japan was starving. It was a report that Kades claimed was filled with mistakes, but it caused a stir in US business circles, because it presented a picture of the Occupation ruining Japan as a place to do business for Kaufman's clients and people with similar interests. That, and a similarly themed article in the December 1, 1947 issue of Newsweek entitled "Far to The Left Of Anything Now Tolerated In America," helped turn Washington, as well as Wall Street, against MacArthur. Still, some changes remained, such as the new land reform program which redistributed 4,500,000 acres of land and cut the number of tenant farmers from 48 percent of the agricultural population to only 9 percent. This formed the basis of a contented rural population. Consecutive conservative governments, starting with Ashida's replacement, the pro-Willoughby Shigeru Yoshida, who stayed in power for six years, propped up the price of rice and other agricultural products while keeping out foreign competition, thereby guaranteeing rural support at election time over the years and keeping themselves in power.

Kades officially resigned from the GHQ Government Section in May 1949, on Constitution Day, the anniversary honoring the day of the creation of the document that Kades had done so much to forge.

On June 4, 1949, Viscount Torio died of a cerebral stroke. After her husband's death, the Viscountess took a position as the head of PR for Nihon Kaihatsu Kikai Co., in addition to her job at the clothing store. In 1950, she moved to the Aoyama neighborhood of Tokyo and, irony of ironies, fell in love with one Kiyoshi Mori who lived across the street from her: Mori was the fourth son of the president of Showa Denko at that time and would later became a member of the Lower House of the Diet. In 1953, she opened a bar on the Ginza called Torio Fujin but closed it after slightly less than three years of operation.

In 1964, Torio traveled to New York City in an attempt to rekindle her romance with Kades, whom she had heard was once again single. She went on a severe diet, undertook a fitness course, bought some new outfits and booked a room in the Midtown Hilton. Kades kept her waiting for days, finally making himself available on the last night of her stay. He took her out to dinner at a good restaurant. When he dropped Torio off at the Hilton, his final words were, "Got an early engagement. Nice seeing you."

And that, as they say, was that.

CHAPTER 2

Soldiers of Fortune

THE OCCUPATION of Japan lasted approximately six years and
seven months, during which time the American rulers issued a total
of 2,627 orders. Among them were the instituting of reforms which
included the disbandment of the giant zaibatsu conglomerates, the
abolishment of the feudal agrarian system, the implementation
of a war-renouncing constitution, and the elimination of the old
ie system, in which the male head of the family had tremendous
authority over marriage, divorce and adoption. The elimination of
this system meant that women now had equal legal status to men.

Many of those inside the Tokyo-based Occupation General
Headquarters or GHQ, as it was known, and those who wrote about
it, hailed this effort as a huge success. After all, they reasoned, the
Occupiers had remade what was essentially a feudal society into a
modern democratic one and, in the process, had helped their former enemies recover from a horrific defeat—providing food, clothing, medicine and the means to rebuild a shattered economy. In
fact, many termed their time in Japan with their Japanese friends as
a "golden honeymoon," one which created eternal bonds of friendship, mutual respect and admiration.

They pointed with pride to the way Japanese took to such American institutions as dance halls, golf, Santa Claus and "*demokurashi*"
with its refreshing tone of egalitarianism. See how the prospect
of an American-style middle-class existence was intoxicating the

nation, they said. And look at the high number of marriages between Japanese women and American men. Didn't that say something about what kind of occupation it really was?

However, there were also those who thought just the opposite,
pointing to the high-handed manner often displayed by the American policymakers that perhaps did as much damage as the heretofore mentioned reforms had done good. They cited, for their part,
examples such as the perplexing hypocritical policy of promoting
democracy and freedom of speech while simultaneously practicing
broad press censorship, stifling open political debate, and restricting fraternization between Americans and Japanese—even, for a
time, ordaining separate train coaches for Occupier and Occupied,
and declaring local bars, restaurants and movie houses off limits to
all US personnel. In addition, there was the sudden mid-Occupa-
tion switch from a pro-union, almost Socialist philosophy, to one
of hard line anti-Communism, known as the Reverse Course (see
Chapter 1), a policy which, among other things, enabled the zaibatsu to regroup, and depurged many wartime leaders. The switch,
as we have seen, was prompted not only by the rise of Communist
power in China and on the Korean peninsula which threatened to
engulf Japan, but also by the activities of a pro–Wall Street lobby
primarily interested in recovering prewar investments in Japan and
making the nation an attractive place for American multinationals
to do business. All of that, said the critics, combined with the casual
racism displayed by some Occupationaires, made America more
enemies than it did friends.

American hypocrisy was perhaps most evident in the Tokyo War
Crimes Tribunal. Hailed beforehand by Americans as a hearing on
the guilt or innocence of Japanese generals and political leaders
that would be fair and impartial, its outcome appeared to be a foregone conclusion. Famed *Stars and Stripes* reporter Hal Drake cited
a front page story in his military-run newspaper which showed a
photo of the gallows constructed at Sugamo Prison, where the defendants were incarcerated, with a sidebar indicating where Tojo
and the others would meet their makers. Said Drake, with some dismay, "The story indicated not the slightest doubt that some people

were going to be found guilty and hanged, no matter how balanced some people claimed the trial was going to be. It was not a good lesson in democracy."

One of the Occupation critics was a young lawyer named Thomas Blakemore, who had studied in Tokyo at the old Imperial University before the war and who had worked in the legal department of the GHQ as one of the tiny handful of Americans in Japan truly conversant with the language and the culture.

"This business of a honeymoon was an illusion," he would scoff. "It was clear to me and anyone who understood Japan that the majority of the Japanese hated the Americans. In general they viewed those fellow Japanese who associated with Americans as the sycophant type unless they were forced to cooperate in some official capacity or needed to learn English to communicate with the outside world. They had the lowest regard, for the most part, for those women (who, as a rule, were not from the upper class), who did associate with the GIs or American civilians."

Whatever side one took in that argument there was one area where Americans and Japanese got along just fine and that was the field of illegal commerce, thanks to opportunities afforded by the Occupation authorities and a limitless supply of players on both sides of the Japanese–American divide to take advantage of them.

The black markets were in operation well before the first GI ever set foot on Japanese soil, with yakuza criminal gangs selling stolen Imperial Army supplies in open air markets amidst the bombed-out rubble. But it was the participation of nearly half a million Occupation soldiers, along with GHQ policy, that helped them flourish.

The powers that be under MacArthur saw fit to order the severe rationing of much needed commodities like sugar, rice, soap, gasoline, whiskey, tobacco and lighter flints—measures which made them impossible for law-abiding citizens to obtain and therefore increased their value on the black market. The Americans also instituted an arbitrary currency-exchange control system which dramatically reduced the value of the yen and further invited the practice of black marketeering.

The official conversion rate had initially been set at 50 yen to the dollar. Yet, such was the demand for greenbacks that private traders did business at a rate of up to 425 yen. Nearly every Occupationaire needed yen for some purpose or other, if only to buy the popular *kokeshi* dolls to send back home as souvenirs, yet Japanese items and services purchased through the Army Post Exchanges and converted at the official rate were so abnormally high that black-market buying was inevitable.

Rationing and the quest for yen thus put thousands of fresh-faced American operators into the black-market game. They dealt cigarettes, candy, gum, et cetera, to Japanese who were willing to pay dearly for such luxuries in the burgeoning outdoor markets around the war-ravaged city and quite often used them to barter with prostitutes who could be found almost anywhere the occupying troops were. There were so many heavily painted *pan-pan* girls (as they were called) clogging the downtown streets that pedestrians in the area used to jokingly gauge distances by the number of hookers one had to pass in order to get to one's destination. ("The Dai-ichi Hotel? Go straight, walk about 150 hookers down the street. It's on the right.")

A ten-cent pack of *Lucky Strikes* was so valuable that a girl who received one could sell it for ten times that amount to the gangs at the outdoor markets located around the rubble-strewn city. The result of all this was an enormous transfer of wealth from the pockets of Occupation force soldiers to the Tokyo underworld, which via the girls alone amounted to an astonishing one billion US dollars over the course of GHQ rule, according to Harry Emerson Wildes in his classic work *Typhoon in Tokyo: The Occupation and Its Aftermath* (Octagon, 1978).

Historian Yuki Tanaka, author of the book *Japan's Comfort Women* (Routledge, 2001), has written, "It is no exaggeration to say that it was not the textile, chemical or other industries that were rehabilitating the mediate postwar Japanese economy but the sex industry—and that this came at the expense of the physical and psychological health of tens of thousands of Japanese sex workers (who, it might be added, contracted VD at an alarming rate: two hundred thousand cases recorded alone in 1950)."

If the "golden honeymoon" had existed only in the minds of some individuals, the Occupation's dark side was impossible to miss. The forms of illicit commerce varied in scope from the sale of a simple case of booze to large-scale operations that moved millions of dollars a year in black-market goods and dollar currency. The activities covered the entire spectrum of morality—or immorality, to be precise.

For example, there was a US Army doctor, assigned to the 361st Medical Military Hospital in Tokyo, who, while still in uniform, was selling Benzedrine shots to Japanese customers on the side. His off-duty "office" was the black-draped back room of a dingy Ginza coffee shop. A colleague of the doctor, a member of the US Army military police, was a character who could have come out of *The Third Man*. He stole penicillin from the base dispensary, diluted it two to three times and sold it to unwitting Japanese MDs desperately in need of the vital drug.

One might also mention the American civilian who came into possession of several gold bars, recovered from cache of wartime treasure hidden by the Japanese military, which he secreted inside his suit and tried to smuggle through customs at Tokyo's Haneda Airport. He dropped his passport, bent down to pick it up and keeled over from the weight of the gold. When security guards tried to lift him to his feet and found themselves unable to because of the excess weight, the gold was uncovered and the would-be smuggler was arrested.

A major source of illegal dollar currency turned out to be the "specialty" shops, which had sprung up to serve exclusively foreigners ineligible to use the Army Post Exchange. At least nine hundred of these stores existed in July 1950 and much of their $10 million total yearly business was believed to cloak black-market operations. Two of the more successful among them were Ginza-area outfits Evergreen and Lansco. Ostensibly dry goods shops on the first floor, they conducted illegal sales of black-market dollars and other rationed commodities upstairs.

All in all, there was so much backdoor commerce going on— some experts estimated an additional billion dollars had changed hands during the Occupation (above and beyond, that is, the awe-inspiring take of the streetwalkers)—that the Japanese could be forgiven for suspecting that Americans as a people were not honest. It was a suspicion, not coincidentally, which mirrored one the Americans held of their hosts, many of whom thought the Japanese were simply fundamentally crooked, given the latter's eagerness to accept under-the-table gelt.

New York Times correspondent Russell Brines referred to this in his book, *MacArthur's Japan* (Lippincott, 1948): "The Americans arrived with textbook preconceptions about Japan—the charm of the cherry blossoms, the bright kimonos, the clean and intelligent faces, honest pride, and intense industriousness—and found a dirty, slovenly country with a mud-stained culture. Its restless people had become sly and comparatively dishonest . . . The conquerors had caught Japan with its facade down."

Gang boss Noboru Ando put it another way in his best-selling book *Yakuza to koso* [Yakuza in conflict, published by Tokuma Shoten, 1993]. "It was, simply, an era when a man's educational background or family history made no difference, and physical strength mattered more than anything else. Those people who were well-fed before the war were suddenly not so fat anymore. A different type of person was eating well."

GOLDEN GATE

Attempts by the Occupation authorities and the Japanese police to enforce regulations against illicit commerce proved grossly ineffective. For one thing, confusing new anti–black-marketeering laws instigated by newly arrived spit-and-polish generals midway through the Occupation made no distinction between commercial activity and individual bartering for souvenirs or simple gifts. Thus was the lawyer Thomas L. Blakemore collared for giving a Japanese friend the following gifts, all which were used or partially consumed: old fishing magazines, a used cake of soap, a tube of toothpaste, a box of Kleenex, a pack of playing cards, some water purification tablets and a flashlight.

Under Occupation law, Blakemore was as guilty as a black-market ringleader dealing in penicillin, sulfur, cigarettes and American dollars. After a hearing, Blakemore was let off with a "strict warning," it being his first offense, but the experience only reinforced his belief that the Occupation authorities in Japan were unwilling or unable to understand the dire situation ordinary citizens found themselves in immediately after the war, when their homes had been reduced to ashes by American bombers and they faced years of starvation and disease.

Occupation policy reached the height of absurdity in an infamous Christmas episode involving the *Stars and Stripes* military newspaper, an international relief agency, and *Stripes* reporter Donald Richie. The relief agency had wanted to give some Christmas gifts to Japanese street children and requested that their generosity be publicized in the newspaper. So the entire crew of people involved in this quest took off in jeeps to find a couple of street waifs, who were then duly photographed standing on a pile of rubble holding their gift-wrapped boxes, huge smiles of hope and anticipation on their faces. However, the grins quickly turned to disappointment when, the photo session finished, the children opened their presents to find nothing inside. GHQ regulations, it seemed, had prohibited the agency from actually giving away anything. The exercise had been nothing but a photo-op, one which upset Richie so much that he slipped the children some money from his own pocket, an act of generosity for which he was, naturally, disciplined.

Although many military and civilian personnel were in fact being quietly shipped home on suspicion of black-marketing, investigators spent so much time and effort on such insignificant crimes that larger fish were often able to swim away scot-free. In fact, many of the black-market operators were so successful they stayed on after the Occupation ended, contributing in their own unusual way to the reconstruction and revival of the city.

One of them was a young Army-enlisted man, Johnny Wetzstein, who began his flamboyant career selling huge sides of black-market beef purloined from the US military. Discharged from military service in Japan, Wetzstein won forty thousand dollars in a three-day poker game in the mid-fifties and used it to buy a patch of land in Azabu, a largely residential area in southwestern Tokyo near the Russian embassy. There he opened the Hamburger Inn, a twenty-four-hour diner which became a Tokyo institution, as famous for its greasy back-home American menu as it was for the alphabet soup of sexual services available from off-duty hookers and hostesses who plied their trade in an upstairs room.

Wetzstein was a brawny Popeye lookalike whose most famous act came on the Hamburger Inn's first day of business. With a photographer on hand from *Stars and Stripes* to record the event, Wetzstein opened the front door with a key, and then, flamboyantly, threw the key across the street into an empty lot declaiming, "This door will never be locked again. We will stay open twenty-four hours a day, seven days a week, forever." Claiming to have made the first real off-base US-style hamburger ever in postwar Japan, Wetzstein did a continuous booming business, twice changing locations before settling on a site a short walk from the world-famous Roppongi Crossing.

Another more glamorous character was Wally Gayda. He had originally been a support pilot in the famed wartime Flying Tiger fleet led by Major James Doolittle, which bombed Japan in 1942. He then flew for Civil Air Transport, the CIA's proprietary airline which serviced the Kuomintang opium armies in Burma, conducting airdrops into China in support of Chiang Kai-Shek and the nationalist Chinese Army, and later running sorties in Indochina on behalf of the French. Owner of a Master's degree from the University of Chicago, Gayda was reputed to have an IQ of 165. In 1949, with fifty thousand dollars he had saved up from his flying days, he became the first American to open up a nightclub in occupied Japan, operating it with a Chinese business partner from Shanghai.

Located at the southern end of the Roppongi strip not far from the Russian embassy, it was called the Golden Gate and it quickly became one of the most notorious places in town, a vibrant symbol of the free-spirited lawlessness that marked the early postwar era.

Nude dancers, entertainers from the Philippines and, occasionally, blond American songstresses performed on stage nightly while in a back room various forms of illegal gambling went on for the amusement of the customers—including a high-stakes poker game that went on in perpetuity, many of the players Civil Air Transport pilots flying routes to Taiwan, Hong Kong, Saigon and Tokyo, among other Asian destinations. (A sign on the wall read, "If you like pussy, you'll love CAT.")

A major attraction was an earthy late afternoon strip show climaxed by what was billed as the "Magic Moment," when the female performers completely disrobed and employed the creative use of boiled eggs and long-nosed *tengu* masks in their act, just before the lights went out.

The Golden Gate, surviving a fire on the opening night, drew patrons of every stripe, from both the foreign and Japanese communities in Tokyo. It surpassed in popularity the crude dance halls and gangster-run cabarets like the Queen Bee on the Ginza with its gowned hostesses that, in the first years of the Occupation, represented what little nightlife there was. Its muddy boots, rough-and-tumble aura was more accessible to the general public than the more high-end establishments like the Latin Quarter that were also opening up.

The goings on at the Golden Gate fell into the category of things introduced by Americans that the Japanese quite liked. These included Zippo lighters, Whitman Samplers, jazz, bowling, nylon stockings and the idea of democracy in which everyone supposedly got a fair chance. The cabaret-style strip shows, for example, originally introduced to Japan by GHQ Occupationaires, were a facet of American culture that Japanese men could embrace with a passion they could not muster for other American innovations like, say, equal rights for women. So were the new forms of gambling—the poker game in the back with the unusual looking American-style playing cards (played by cigar-smoking men in brown leather flight jackets), and the craps game in the corner. The Japanese had their own games of chance played mainly with traditional *hanafuda* playing cards, but they had never seen anything like the goings-on at the Golden Gate. It all seemed like something out of the Hollywood movies that were drawing standing-room-only crowds in Japan.

Said Tsuyoshi Fukuda, a wide-eyed young lawyer who represented Gayda, "Gayda-san reminded me of Humphrey Bogart in the movie *Casablanca*. His club was just like that. He even had a Black piano player there—a man named Larry Allen—who sang. It was just like Rick and Sam. The place was always packed with foreigners and on the walls there were photos of famous people who had been there, like movie actresses like Ava Gardner. For Japanese people who were struggling economically, the Golden Gate was like a dream. It was a really interesting place, something they'd never seen before."

Not surprisingly, there was more going on than just strip shows and games of five-card stud. Japanese historians would later write that the Golden Gate was not only the scene of heavy black-market trading in dollars and other commodities, but that Gayda and company were also involved in serious arms smuggling, supplying Japanese nationalists with weapons and ammunition shipped in from Hong Kong, Manila and Taiwan for use in suppressing the Communist movement in Japan. Gayda's operation thrived, in part, because as he once put it to a friend, "I wasn't afraid to pay bribes to folks in the GHQ and the Japanese police." One might add that the folks in the GHQ and the Japanese police were not afraid to take them, either.

This peculiar and unexpected chemistry of Western and Japanese interactions would be a major theme of the postwar era and beyond. It was as if the rules of proper behavior had disappeared in this new setting where conqueror and conquered now found themselves and there were no rules at all. This delusion would have repercussions for both sides who viewed their new circumstances as both liberating and exciting.

Gayda was a rugged, mustachioed, smooth-talking figure who oozed charm. He was a magnet to women and would wed several times. His matrimonial stable over the years would include two American wives and two Filipinas, including a young actress named Rosa Rosal who was the number one movie star in the Philippines in the early fifties when she met Gayda. He became an expert in various methods of getting divorced by mail and happily instructed his married friends in all the intricacies of that particular process.

In Tokyo, he was known as *Geiburu-san* to Japanese women, because of a mustache he then sported that made him look strikingly similar to the movie star Clark Gable. Gayda was once quoted as saying of the wealth of available female companionship in Tokyo, "Being married in Japan is like keeping a cow for a pet in Texas." But he was also famous for a torrid love affair he had conducted with Ava Gardner, the internationally renowned film star, ex-wife of Frank Sinatra and regarded as perhaps the most beautiful Hollywood actress of her time, as well as perhaps the town's most promiscuous. She had embarked on an early 1950s world promotion tour, with a stop in Tokyo, during which she toured the famous fleshpots of the Yoshiwara red-light district with a young writer named Donald Richie who had been assigned as her guide. Later that night, in a moment of wild abandon at a gay bar in Asakusa, she removed her panties and presented them to the proprietor who pinned them to the wall. The Gardner panties remained there on display for forty years, gathering dust, grime and mold, until the bar was torn down.

Ava had first espied Gayda in the cocktail lounge of the Nikkatsu Hotel and, deciding he was the best-looking man around, finagled an introduction. At first, Gayda didn't know who she was. It was only later, when they were in bed together in her hotel room that he realized his good fortune. (As he told friends later, "I was looking down at her and it suddenly dawned on me where I had seen this person before. I said to myself, 'My God, I'm getting a blow job from the world's most beautiful film star.'") The affair continued sporadically for years, mostly in Europe at Gardner's Swiss chalet or house in Spain.

For a time, the debonair Gayda was one of the most celebrated figures in Tokyo. Said a Tokyo-based *Stars and Stripes* reporter named Corky Alexander, a close friend of Gayda's, "We were all proud that Ava Gardner had chosen one of our own to sleep with. It was a real honor." He was not just celebrated, he was also rich. The wall safe in his Golden Gate office was permanently stuffed with cash—yen, dollars, Hong Kong dollars, US military payment certificates, even some Korean won. And he was not reluctant to spread it around. Friends told the story of the time an acquaintance of Gayda's, a man named Dick Sykes, came into the Golden Gate and complained about the bad luck he was having in business. If only he had fifty thousand dollars, he sighed, then he could climb out of the hole he was in.

Gayda sauntered into his office, opened his safe and pulled out fifty thousand dollars in cash, which he then proceeded to hand to a thoroughly startled Sykes. It was an astonishing sum of money for those days, roughly enough to pay the salary of an entire professional baseball team for one year. And then some.

"Pay it back when you can," said Gayda, flashing his charismatic smile.

Sykes was stunned. It took him a while to realize that Gayda was indeed serious. When he was finally persuaded that Gayda wasn't joking, he thanked his benefactor profusely and started to write out an IOU.

"Don't need it," Gayda said. "Put the pen and paper away."

"Why not?"

"You're either going to pay me or you're not. And a piece of paper isn't going to make one damn bit of difference."

Sykes took the money. He went on to become head of a huge American firm in Japan, making himself a multimillionaire in the process. He repaid the money in full, with interest, eventually. Later, when Gayda was down on his luck and involved in a costly legal battle, Sykes returned the favor, paying court costs and attorney fees until the matter was resolved.

The Golden Gate flourished for nearly seven rambunctious years. The end came when the Roppongi police raided the place and arrested Gayda on morals charges. Police alleged the shows were getting a bit too explicit and that more than just brief "magic moments" were going on during lights-out time. In fact, they also suspected that other illicit activities like black marketing, illegal currency trading and gun running were going on, which, was indeed the case, although clear evidence was lacking at the time.

Gayda himself was convinced the raid had taken place for one reason and that was because he had stopped paying his monthly bribes to the local police. His attention had turned to other matters and he was considering selling the club. Another explanation was that by the mid-fifties the Japanese police, their authority having been restored to them by the 1951 San Francisco Peace Treaty, began to feel increasingly embarrassed about such vulgar goings on in their neighborhood. Payoffs or no, they felt compelled to make a statement by shutting down the American's notorious juke joint. At any rate, Gayda's run as a Tokyo nightclub mogul was at an end.

Shortly after being arrested and released on bail in 1954, Gayda packed his bags, picked up some money and flew to Hong Kong. And that was the last anyone in Japan saw of Wally Gayda for a long, long time.

THE GAMBLERS

Casino gambling was introduced to the Japanese in the post-Occupation era by two men from the United States. One was named Ted Lewin, a Mafia-connected gambler from New York and war hero who had survived the Bataan Death March and other World War II horrors. The other was Jason Lee, a Korean-American gambler described in a court hearing in his native Chicago as "the biggest gambling operator on the North Side." Both men lived lives that were the stuff of Hollywood movies.

Lewin had been born in New York City in 1907, as one Theodore Lieweraenowski. He grew up to become a heavyweight boxer, but adept at gambling as well, he became friends with Mafia gambling bigwig Meyer Lansky and the New York mob. He moved to Los Angeles in the 1930s, where he worked in offshore floating casinos. Then, after several run-ins with the authorities, he headed to the Far East. He studied Chinese gambling in Shanghai, before moving to Manila in 1939, where he promoted wrestling matches, opened a cabaret and set up a casino on Manila's glittering Roxas Boulevard. In short order, he became a man about town, developing close relationships with prominent Filipino political leaders.

When the Japanese attacked the Philippines, Lewin enlisted in the US Army and was captured in Bataan by the invading Japanese forces in 1942. He endured the infamous Bataan Death March and was imprisoned at Camp O'Donnell, the POW camp at Cabanatuan, forty miles (64 km) north of Manila, where, amidst wretched conditions, he distinguished himself as a kind of King Rat, running a money-lending operation and also organizing gambling activities like poker, craps and blackjack, all of which made him a considerable profit. Lewin's Japanese captors were so impressed with his skills that they had him set up their own private casino. Lewin was allowed to procure food and medical supplies for sick POWs in return. He would sneak out of the camp at night and go to nearby Manila on forays for provisions, aided by his American wife Lou who at the time was living in the city and struggling with a serious respiratory illness. She sold her jewelry to raise funds for her husband.

Lewin was later transferred to the Omuta POW camp in Kyushu. He had initially been sent there on the death ship Oroykku Maru, where he was forced to stand alongside hundreds of other sick POWs in a tiny hold without food or water. The ship was bombed by American planes and Lewin swam to shore, saving others in the process. The Japanese put him on another packed ship for Omuta. Many died on the two-week voyage but Lewin survived.

The camp at Omuta was a hellish place, where prisoners were starved and beaten. Large numbers died of dysentery. Those too sick to work were used for bayonet target practice. Lewin managed to stay alive, ingratiating himself with his captors as he had at Camp O'Donnell. Surviving POWs, including Lester Tenney, author of *My Hitch In Hell*, (Potomac, 2018) remembers Lewin relaxing on the veranda of the Japanese officers' quarters, sipping iced tea, while other prisoners toiled away in the mines below. When the war ended, Lewin was freed and was later called to testify in the Tokyo War Crimes Tribunal in 1949. Lewin was also awarded the Medal of Freedom by Douglas MacArthur.

While in Tokyo, Lewin relieved many a high-ranking officer of their military pay during the course of high-stakes backroom poker games. His poker-playing partners included Jack Canon, according to Victor Matsui, who saw the two so engaged at the Iwasaki house.

Jason Lee arrived in Japan in the early fifties after serving stints in Chicago as the boss of the powerful Oriental Gambling Syndicate and then as an inmate of the Hawaii state penitentiary system, where he was incarcerated for several years for pistol-whipping a Honolulu police officer. The short, broad-shouldered, raspy-voiced mobster promptly set about extorting as much money as he could from his new Japanese friends. Lee capitalized on his ties with the Chicago mob to insinuate himself into the Tokyo Dockworkers Union. He helped run the organization from a fancy Ginza office in cooperation with some friends from a major Tokyo gang, taking a special interest in the union's pension fund. He was usually accompanied by his personal bodyguard Mas Oyama, a fellow Korean and a flamboyant martial arts master who had founded the famed Kyokushin karate school in Japan. Oyama fought bulls barehanded in public exhibitions.

In June 1952, Lewin opened up the Mandarin Casino, above the Chinese restaurant Mandarin located on the Ginza. It was modeled after Monte Carlo's Casino Royale in Monaco, with the help of Lee who had gambled there often. Lee had casino equipment sent out to Japan by TR King, the US gambling equipment company. To ensure no interference from the authorities (legalized gambling was strictly limited to government-regulated horse racing, motorboat racing, and bicycle and motorcycle racing) Lewin had paid a twenty-five thousand dollar bribe to a Japanese politician for protection. For most Tokyo patrons it was their first time to see a roulette wheel up close. For a time, it was said, several hundred million yen a night changed hands

"It was a strange mix of alcohol, women and gambling," went a report in the *Asahi Shimbun* newspaper: "Most of the customers were foreigners. A lot of big yen notes were passed back and forth. To enter the gambling room one had to go through three heavy doors with peepholes. Two red and black fire alarms were on the corridor walls. Inside the gambling room was a roulette wheel and several gaming tables."

The Ginza was an area of the city full of nightspots frequented by foreigners and known colloquially by the disparaging term *Tokyo sokai*, or "Tokyo Colony," in the Tokyo tabloids. It was walking distance to the Dai Ichi building, site of MacArthur's headquarters, and the Imperial Hotel. During the Occupation, and immediate post-Occupation years, the Occupationaires had even renamed the streets. The walk from Shimbashi to Kyobashi in Ginza 8-chome district was called New Broadway, for example. Other names given to Japanese roads included A Avenue for Dentsu-dori in front of the offices of television broadcaster NHK, and Poker Street for Soto-bori-dori running from Toranomon up to Akasaka Mitsuke.

The Mandarin operation did not last very long. It was raided in July 1952 in the midst of an event euphemistically dubbed "Monte Carlo Charity Night." Thirty-two surprised patrons, including fourteen US military officers, were arrested but neither Lewin nor Lee was among them. The event had masqueraded as a Catholic charity affair for nearby Seibo Hospital, whose officials were surprised when police later informed them what was going on. A group photo of those arrested, posing uncomfortably in front of the gaming tables as ordered by police, appeared in the Japanese newspapers the next morning.

The Mandarin reopened months later in a different spot on the Ginza and after a brief period of prosperity was raided again. However, it did live on in spirit. The roulette wheel wound up in the Officers Club casino at the Grant Heights residential base for military families, and the Mandarin's setup was copied by Japanese underworld figures, used in many underground gambling dens in the city and also serving as a model for gaming houses in yakuza films for decades to come.

Lewin went on to open the Latin Quarter, in December 1952, seven months after the end of the Occupation, a deluxe dinner club that featured big-name entertainers from the States like Perez Prado and Tony Scott. Tokyo had never seen anything like it.

The Latin Quarter was located on Poker Street in the Akasaka area of southwest Tokyo, which bordered on Roppongi. It was run on a daily basis by the former Canon agents Al Shattuck and his Japanese partner Saburo Odachi. Shattuck and Lewin had become friends after Jack Canon had sent Shattuck to investigate Lewin. Lewin had also managed to secure the release from Sugamo Prison of two of the guards he had become friends with while imprisoned at Omuta. He gave one of them a job as a "security officer" at the Latin Quarter, and made another a janitor before buying him a small farm in northern Japan, which was not a bad reward for not shooting or bayoneting someone.

The Latin Quarter was very expensive and exclusively black tie—a rarity in a town that was still largely in ruins. The city remained in such a state of disrepair that one could see the five-storied Diet Building from anywhere in the capital. The streets were full of jeeps and GIs (many of them on leave from the Korean Peninsula where war had broken out) and it was populated by people still wearing tattered clothes and old uniforms. The Latin Quarter attracted the capital's diplomats, its CEOs, its leading politicians and budding postwar entertainers. Intelligence agents (mostly from the CIA and the KGB) spying on each other, and Japanese gang bosses added spice to the mix.

The Latin Quarter, in fact, belonged to a complex of buildings owned by the powerful ultranationalist Yoshio Kodama, who had pillaged China, with the help of Japanese yakuza he had recruited from Tokyo, on behalf of the Tojo government during the Pacific War. The short, stout Kodama, nicknamed Little Napoleon by his detractors, had spent three years in Sugamo Prison before the charges against him were dropped, ostensibly for lack of hard evidence, in 1948. However, some believed that he was released because he had paid a massive bribe with plunder he had seized in Japanese-occupied China, where Kodama had run a ruthless wartime procurement machine. Still others claimed he was set free only because he had volunteered to work with the newly organized CIA which needed Kodama's right-wing wartime connections and yakuza friends to help fight the rising threat of Communism.

As an aside, Kodama's prison mate at Sugamo had been

Nobusuke Kishi (see Chapter 1), who had been a key member of Hideki Tojo's wartime cabinet, responsible for forced labor and sexual slavery policies in China as well as the expansion of the opium trade, before climbing into bed with the Americans in the postwar era. Kishi would become prime minister of Japan in 1958, a position he attained with the help of donations from the CIA, as we have seen, and would oversee the approval of the extension of the US–Japan Security Treaty, keeping American bases in Japan, using yakuza manpower to overcome massive resistance from leftist protesters.

Security for the complex of five buildings was provided by one of Tokyo's most powerful criminal gangs, the Tosei-kai, which was simultaneously employed by American intelligence, helping to put down pesky leftist demonstrators. (Their leader Hisayuki "Ginza" Machii carried in his wallet a thank-you card signed by General Douglas MacArthur, expressing his appreciation for such patriotic endeavors.)

The main building had a room called the Lobo Lounge, with a roulette wheel and blackjack and craps tables. It remained shuttered all day and all night because Lewin had been unable to obtain a gambling permit. However, gambling reportedly went on, nonetheless, despite strenuous denials by Shattuck. In a memoir by music promoter Jiro Uchino, *Yume no warutsu* [Waltz of dreams, published by Kodansha, 1997], Tats Nagashima, a Latin Quarter employee, described a pool table in one of the buildings that opened into a crap table, along with other amusements. In the book *Tokyo andanaito* [Tokyo undernight, published by Kosaido, 2011] by Shintaro Yamamoto, a bodyguard named Mogami in the employ of Yoshio Kodama, spoke of gambling by Americans and Japanese in the Latin Quarter complex and said that he had once been arrested during a police raid on a gambling session

Lewin generated further revenue from his base in Manila via a lucrative arms smuggling venture and other black-market operations, in conjunction with the aforementioned Wally Gayda. Lewin was also said to have a partial interest in the nightclub Tradewinds, in Yokosuka, a city in Tokyo's neighboring Kanagawa Prefecture, where there was a US naval base, in partnership with Jason Lee.

The Tradewinds occupied a building next to a hotel that became notorious amongst the populace for its late night activities, including gambling, overly friendly bar girls, and related vices. Lee brought in jazz acts from the US, nude reviews from the Philippines and other Southeast Asian locales, selling them to other clubs in the Tokyo region after they had performed at the Tradewinds. Lee had started out with a partner in the Tradewinds operation, a man named Jerry Zucker from Honolulu. However, after disagreements over money, Lee summarily evicted his opposite number, along with his belongings, and, under threat of death, barred him from ever returning.

Zucker turned to an old friend, an ex-Honolulu cop who flew to Japan to help out. Dan Sawyer, who had brought his policeman's badge and passport with him, along with a couple of handguns, paid a visit to the mayor of Yokosuka, and over a friendly lunch, as one public servant to another, explained his problem. The mayor graciously responded by introducing Sawyer to the head of the city's rickshaw association. That evening, Lee and his men pulled up in front of the Tradewinds in two limousines to find the club completely surrounded by rickshaws whose drivers were armed with clubs and bamboo sticks. Standing at the main entrance was Sawyer, his two firearms visible under his open coat. The scene was repeated the next night, and the night after that, until Lee finally agreed to buy out Zucker for a hundred and fifty thousand dollars, reportedly with help from Lewin.

Sawyer, a karate master, would remain in Japan and go into the entertainment business, bringing in acts from the US to the Latin Quarter in partnership with Al Shattuck, including Luciano Pavarotti, and the Temptations. He also packaged talent from Japan for Las Vegas nightclubs, and hired retired detectives from the Tokyo Metropolitan Police Department to work in his office and deal with undercover yakuza trying to infiltrate his company. Lee, for his part, would expand into other more lucrative operations like his black-market dollar and whiskey businesses that embraced everyone from high-ranking members of the then Yokosuka-based

Inagawa-kai yakuza gang to the lowest members of the Yokosu-ka-based US Navy. He also established a Cadillac importing business in which he sold the deluxe autos to moneyed Japanese crime lords, at several multiples of domestic purchase prices in the US.

In fact, Lee's criminal influence would be so pervasive that for the next forty years some Japanese authorities would reflexively blame the periodic scandals that erupted within the Kanagawa police on the seeds of corruption that were planted by operations like the Tradewinds. When more than 250 Kanagawa prefectural police officers were fired in the year 2000 for various offenses including burglary, narcotics use, the sale of confidential criminal files, murder, hit and run and assorted cover-ups—a level of impropriety unmatched by any other area of Japan—a former detective with the Tokyo Metropolitan Police explained it by pointing to the long, debilitating influence of Americans in Yokosuka.

"Being raised in such an environment, with so many lawbreaking Americans from Yokosuka running around, what do you expect?" he was quoted as saying in a private conversation.

The tough talking Lee lived in Tokyo with his family—a Korean wife, a daughter and a son—and, in addition to his previously described confrontation with the Yokosuka rickshaw association, was involved in assorted contretemps over the years with yakuza gangs and the authorities. For a time he had a gambling operation in the Masonic Building between Tokyo Tower and Roppongi Crossing. In 1956, Lee journeyed to Monaco where he would be arrested for using loaded dice, manufactured by TR King, at the Monte Carlo Casino. He was found guilty and fined one hundred thousand dollars then released by special order of Prince Ranier in honor of the latter's wedding to Grace Kelly.

Lee was shot several times in Japan, but he always managed to recover. Tokyo physician Eugene Aksenoff, a White Russian from Harbin, China, who operated the International Clinic in Roppongi, recalled Lee coming to see him one morning complaining about severe pain in his leg from a .38 caliber bullet that had been imbedded there the previous night by an unhappy underworld associate. At first, said the doctor, Lee had not wanted the bullet removed.

"I can handle it," he said stoically. "Just give me some medicine." But then the doctor explained the dangers of peritonitis and the shame that would fall upon his clinic if Lee died anytime soon after visiting there. Lee finally assented to an operation, but without an anesthetic, fearing the drug would dull his senses and render him vulnerable to attack by his enemies. The doctor, amazed at Lee's bravado, did as requested and was astonished at Lee's ability to withstand pain. (He viewed the gangster more favorably than he did he-man American actor John Wayne, who visited the clinic during the filming of *The Barbarian and the Geisha* in Japan, to have an infected jaw treated. Wayne, said the doctor, was especially difficult to treat because he was "deathly afraid of needles.")

Lee was in the peak of health when he was deported at the end of the decade. He died broke, of heart disease, in a veterans' hospital in Southern California in 1971. He was survived by three daughters a son—Jason Lee Jr.—and two ex-wives.

While splitting his attention between Japan and the Philippines, Lewin ran the Key Club casino on Manila's Dewey Boulevard. He became a sports promoter (staging the world's bantamweight boxing title bout in 1947) and ran a black-market operation behind the scenes. He owned a PT (patrol torpedo) boat which he used to ferry valuable Japanese treasure, uncovered by US intelligence officers in Tokyo, down to Manila for sale on the black markets there. On his return trip he would bring in handguns and ammunition for sale to Japanese mobsters. There was testimony in the Japanese Diet that he transported cash from Manila to the Tokyo office of the CIA. This cash had been wired from the US to the Manila presidential palace by then CIA chief Allen Dulles.

This unusual circumstance might have come about due to a run-in with authorities over Lewin's black-market operations in MPC, or military payment certificates, used by the American military in the Philippines instead of US dollars. The scrip was supposedly tightly controlled: its use, rather than that of normal American currency, was designed to restrict the quantity of goods any single person could purchase in the Army Post Exchanges at one time, and thereby prevent precisely the kind of black-market deals that Lewin was running. It was the practice of the American military to periodically cancel the scrip in use without warning and replace it with newly designed money. However, Lewin had deftly circumvented this hindrance by carrying on an affair with the wife of a US Army Counter Intelligence Corps major, the officer in charge of MPC, who informed him of any impending changes in the frequently redesigned scrip during their trysts at Lewin's Manila penthouse atop the Bayview Hotel, across the street from the US embassy, on Manila Bay.

Unbeknownst to Lewin, however, Filipino and American intelligence officers had bugged his apartment. As detailed in CIA station chief Joseph B. Smith's memoir, *Portrait Of A Cold Warrior* (G.P. Putnam's Sons, 1976), CIA officials were concerned with the growing Communist insurgency in the country, and knowing that Lewin had a close relationship with the Filipino president and other key politicos, thought that monitoring his movements might provide some hint as to what direction the government was secretly leaning vis-à-vis the rebels. According to one report, they used their knowledge of Lewin's black-market activities to blackmail him into becoming a courier for transporting funds to Tokyo. The cash Lewin delivered was transferred to the coffers of the leading conservative parties in Japan to be used in the fight against the leftist movement.

According to various reports, by the mid-fifties the well-dressed, Brylcreemed Lewin was tied into the highest levels of the New York and Chicago Mafias, a close associate not only of Meyer Lansky, but also Frank Costello, Sam Giancana and Johnny Rosselli. When feared mafioso Albert Anastasia was shot dead in 1954 while sitting in a New York City barbershop, rumor had it that the assassins fled to Manila and spent several months in hiding at Lewin's penthouse.

Lewin's second wife Dorothy Wertheimer (his first wife Lou had died of a respiratory disease in 1956) had been married to Mert Wertheimer who ran the Riverside Hotel in Reno before he died in 1958. She had many contacts in organized crime, thanks to her husband, and introduced them to Lewin.

"He was the real deal," said a business associate named Jack

Howard, a tough red-haired insurance executive from Texas, who made a fortune selling policies to servicemen in Asia. "He was the type you didn't want to get on the wrong side of."

Howard said that individuals caught cheating in Lewin's casino would have their fingers broken with a hammer. He also claimed that Lewin employed a professional assassin on his staff, whose MO consisted of taking his victims to a coffee shop, sitting them down in a quiet corner and shooting them under the table using a silencer, before making a quick exit.

Lewin was known in Manila for his charitable activities. He had donated thousands of dollars to a children's clinic among other things. In 1952, Lewin had also staged an international kidnapping for the benefit of the Filipino vice president Fernando Lopez. The VP's daughter had married an American Army lieutenant. The marriage did not succeed and the officer took their son back to the States, setting up residence in New Mexico. The mother was distraught. The vice president turned to Lewin for help, who in turn enlisted the services of the San Francisco mob. He and others traveled to New Mexico, snatched the boy after school, and led the FBI on a breakneck chase, using several cars and two different airplanes, finally getting the boy on a Northwest flight back to Manila. Lewin was on the FBI's wanted list for kidnapping for quite a while thereafter.

Back in Tokyo, the Latin Quarter operated full bore from 1952 to 1956, during which time its landlord Yoshio Kodama dove into conservative politics, his first love. Kodama had been a prominent right-winger since his youth when he had been imprisoned for interrupting an imperial procession and attempting to thrust a petition calling for increased patriotism into Emperor Hirohito's hands.

Kodama had returned from his years in wartime China with a fortune in plunder, which he himself described as "two truckloads of gold, platinum, diamonds and radium," which he intended to use to restore conservative government and preserve the emperor system in Japan. He buried the treasure in the backyards of associates and mountain caves and when he was arrested by Occupation authorities he used some of the lucre, in particular the radium, to buy his freedom—or so it was believed. He used a full half of his fortune to fund the creation of the conservative Liberal Party in 1949.

He was also reported to have handed off numerous satchels, parcels and folded newspapers filled with cash to his favorite conservative politicians. In 1954, for example, Kodama personally delivered a black bag bulging with yen to political strongman Ichiro Hatoyama (another resurrected GHQ purgee), ensuring Hatoyama's triumph in the upcoming conservative Liberal Party leadership race and enabled him to assume the post of prime minister.

In 1955 Kodama provided a private stash of gems to help the Liberal Party merge with the equally right-wing Democratic Party to form the Liberal Democratic Party (LDP), the conservative pro-business, and very pro-American coalition which went on to govern Japan for nearly all of the rest of the twentieth century. Political hacks converted the gems to cash in Tokyo's Ameyoko-cho streetside money markets. (In all, Kodama is believed to have donated $60 million to the LDP.)

Collectively, it was a remarkable operation when one stopped to think about it—the right wing, the Mafia, the CIA and the yakuza gangs all joining hands for fun, profit, the war on Communism and better government. This unholy alliance symbolized more than anything else just how corrupt relations between the two countries could be. It was somehow fitting that when the Latin Quarter finally met its end, it burned down.

Everyone immediately suspected arson because Tokyo was slated to host the 1964 Olympics and Kodama had decided he wanted to build a luxury hotel on the Latin Quarter property to take advantage of that great event and thereby acquire even greater prominence for himself. To do this, however, meant the club would have to be torn down. Lewin vehemently opposed the idea from his HQ in Manila. In his opinion, they were making far too much money to simply shut down. But Kodama could not be persuaded.

It wasn't just the hotel. There had also been bad blood between Kodama and Lewin's right hand man Al Shattuck. Kodama, it was said, was upset over the independent ways of Shattuck, who, as floor manager, ran the Latin Quarter as he saw fit in Lewin's absence. He hired and fired performers and handed out discounts, among other things, without considering the welfare of peripherally connected Japanese talent agencies under Kodama's wing.

What's more, Kodama was miffed at Shattuck for getting himself involved in a sensational crime that was grabbing headlines in all the papers—a diamond robbery at the Imperial Hotel, in January 1956, in which an American professional wrestler named John MacFarland stole fourteen thousand dollars' worth of gems. Although Shattuck had denied any participation, he was nonetheless arrested and convicted for receiving part of the loot and spent time behind bars in the Tokyo Detention House. In the various newspaper reports of the crime, Shattuck's name and that of the Latin Quarter had been mentioned and Kodama had been embarrassed. He thought that it was incredibly stupid of Shattuck to have let himself become entangled in such a scandal.

Shattuck, for his part, felt that Kodama was an unrepentant war criminal who should have been hanged for the murder and mayhem he and his cohorts had caused in wartime China. He had heard the reports of Kodama's men going into villages and shooting the mayor straight off to ensure everyone's cooperation in his search for valuables and materials that might be of use to the Japanese government in the war effort. Rugged and unyielding, Shattuck did not hide his disdain for the man who was also known as "the godfather of all yakuza." As far as Kodama was concerned, he had determined that it was time to part company. What followed would underscore that determination.

One evening in early September 1956, the sky was suddenly alight with a bright orange-red color. It was the Latin Quarter on fire and by the time the fire brigade arrived to put it out, the building was an unusable ruin. Despite the lack of any direct evidence, some observers believed that Kodama had been responsible for the fire, especially when Shattuck was arrested by the Japanese police the very next day on suspicion of foreign currency violations. The fact that Kodama had insured the Latin Quarter building for a substantial amount of money was also hard to ignore.

Kodama also had his own relationship with the CIA on which to rely. The CIA found the highly connected Kodama especially useful in tracking the growing leftist movement in Japan. In fact, the CIA–Kodama alliance would reach its improbable zenith in 1960 when one million people took to the streets to demonstrate against the extension of the US–Japan Security Treaty that provided for Japan's protection by stationing a hundred and twenty thousand US soldiers on Japanese soil. Kodama used his network of valuable contacts with other ultranationalists in Japan and certain yakuza gang bosses, who were all skilled in the art of bashing Communist and Socialist heads, to form a massive security force to control the protesters and support the Kishi government.

Kodama wanted his Latin Quarter tenants out and a fire was one way to do it without any untoward consequences. It was a very memorable event as well as an impressive demonstration of Kodama's growing power. Shattuck took over Gayda's former property and, by the end of the decade, Shattuck had moved on to New York City while Lewin had headed for Africa.

All things considered, it was quite an era, the Occupation and its aftermath. Greed and duplicity just naturally seemed to breed in a city that had been reduced to rubble and chaos, its inhabitants scrambling to survive in an environment where everyone had to watch their back. The arrests of foreign businessmen like Shattuck and Gayda received sensational treatment in the press, and by the mid-fifties, public conviction had become understandably rooted in the belief that foreign businessmen were unruly, immoral and often drunk. Typical perhaps was a 1953 article in the *Yomiuri Shimbun* newspaper which decided to launch an attack focusing on British merchants, labeling them as "dollar speculators" or as tax evaders, and claimed they diverted huge sums of money into illegal channels—a charge that led the finance minister in 1953 to audit the books of 450 foreign firms and 300 private traders.

What the public at large and the press failed to notice—or perhaps *did* notice but chose to ignore—was the fact that for every such crime perpetrated by a foreigner there were also Japanese partners involved, eager to cooperate, eager to share in the booty, eager to buy those black-market dollars or whatever else it was the gaijin was selling. In fact, as previously demonstrated, the locals were perfectly capable of committing wrongdoing all by themselves without the help of foreigners.

In fact, in the late fifties, the Japanese were committing about 1.5 million crimes annually. It was a decade so crime ridden it would take until the 1980s to match it, and by then the population had grown by 50 percent. There were so many stabbings and muggings that police were advising citizens not to go out alone at night. It was a far cry from later years when Japanese would rightfully brag how safe their streets were at any time of day or night.

Many of these terrible misdeeds were committed by members of organized crime, like those in the previously mentioned Tosei-kai, gangland ranks having swollen tremendously since the end of the war. With one-fifth of the nation's total crime (300,000 crimes a year if you are counting), Tokyo could not exactly be described as a peaceful city. If one added political bribery, a phenomenon so common in the capital that a term "money politics" was coined to describe it, 1950s Tokyo also ranked as one of the most corrupt metropolises on the face of the earth during that period.

In such a dissolute environment, one might argue that the foreigners were just trying to fit in.

CHAPTER 3

The Girard And Quackenbush Killings

AS OCCUPATION ARMIES WENT, the American soldiers on the ground had drawn mixed reviews. On the one hand, the mass murder of civilians, such as committed by Japanese forces in China, had not taken place. At the beginning of the US Occupation of Japan, General Douglas MacArthur had made it quite clear he would tolerate no acts of retribution against the Japanese citizenry—no revenge for perceived injustices during the brutal, close-quarter fighting in the jungles of the South Pacific. He made his point quickly in early September 1945 when three GIs—soldiers from the US Army's 1st Cavalry Division which had seen much of the worst fighting on the Pacific islands—killed a Ginza café proprietor and his sixteen-year-old son after a wild drinking bout. In slightly less than a month, the three young men had been court-martialed, convicted of manslaughter and each sentenced to ten years hard labor. That court martial had set the tone. After that there was little trouble reported. *New York Times* reporter Russell Brines, for one, was so impressed with the behavior of American soldiers that he called the US military in Japan "the most disciplined occupation force in history."

On the other hand, however, there *was* substantial evidence of rape and other crimes committed by US soldiers which came to light only long *after* the Occupation ended and the GHQ's strict censorship of the news had ceased. The book *Japan's Comfort Women* by Yuki Tanaka (Routledge, 2001) documented a wave of sexual violence—rape, gang rape and other crimes—occurring in the first year of the Occupation when there were nearly half a million Allied soldiers in Japan. They included 957 such crimes committed by GIs in Yokohama City alone and 119 rape cases reported by the Japanese police. Twenty-four different Japanese women were raped by soldiers on the single day of September 1 alone, the day after MacArthur first landed in Japan. This included the rape of a mother and her fifteen-year-old daughter, committed by two drunken GIs, as the father, bound to a pillar, watched.

A second wave of sexual violence by GIs came in the spring of 1946, highlighted by the invasion of a hospital in Tokyo by fifty US Marines who raped seventeen nurses on night duty, twenty nursing assistants and more than forty female patients in all. A two-day-old baby was thrown out of its mother's bed onto the floor and killed.

Such incidents decreased as order and military discipline were imposed, the number of Occupation soldiers in the country diminished and fresh troops replaced the Allied veterans responsible for the early crime wave. One might also mention that the inability of Japanese to identify Occupation soldiers by their rank and their difficulty in describing foreign facial features made subsequent investigations into the abovementioned cases almost impossible.

The end of the Occupation was determined in 1951 with the signing of the San Francisco Peace Treaty and the US–Japan Security Treaty, the latter of which called for the permanent stationing of US military forces in Japan to augment Japan's budding Self-Defense Forces. But this did not bring with it a great improvement in the quality of the American soldier dispatched to that country. The Occupation-era soldier had been a depression-era youth who saw the Army, even in war-ravaged Japan, as a refuge from the depressing economic conditions back in the US. He was happy just to get his three military meals every day and a warm cot on which to sleep. The post-Occupation draftee, by contrast, was a different breed altogether, secure in a lifestyle created by America's postwar boom, which might have included his own car and an extensive personal collection of rock and roll records. By and large, he did not particularly want to join the Army and leave the more substantial comforts of home for a less-developed country like Japan.

During the 1950s, there were approximately a hundred and twenty thousand American troops stationed in Japan, their numbers supplemented by an unending stream of GIs on R & R from the Korean Peninsula. ("R & R" was an American military term for vacation that meant "Rest and Recreation," but was also referred to by GIs as "Rape and Revel," in reference to the sort of activities that many soldiers took part in during their brief visit to Japan.) Between them, these two groups managed to compile an impressive record of bad behavior and casual destructiveness. There were frequent newspaper reports of GIs stiffing taxi drivers and trashing bars to blow off steam. Consider the bar Hakala in Tokyo's Shibuya district, a drinking establishment that was a favorite of the troops at nearby Camp Drake. One of the walls of the Hakala was covered entirely with mirrors and all of them would invariably be broken on payday night by the rambunctious GIs. The Hakala also had shoji paper screen doors and some of the soldiers, so drunk they were unable to figure out how to slide them open, simply ripped their way through. The Camp Drake legal officer had to set aside a permanent fund just to pay off the monthly Hakala damage bill.

According to the Japanese police, who had jurisdiction over the off-duty, off-base GIs under the Status of Forces Agreement signed at the San Francisco Peace Convention (as an adjunct to the Security Treaty), American soldiers in Japan committed over fourteen thousand infractions of Japanese law in the five years that followed the end of the Occupation, helping to give rise to what many Japanese called "The Era of Anti-Americanism" and laying the foundation for much of the hostility from the Japanese toward the US military that marked the rest of the century.

Even Japanese mobsters who did criminal transactions with GIs, and who were accustomed to a certain amount of perfidy in their daily business dealings, had their complaints. There was a Shibuya-based Ando-gang foot soldier named Joji Abe, for example, who had bought five guns from an American GI at the not insubstantial price of ten thousand yen (about twenty-eight dollars at the time), only to have the GI pull out a pistol of his own and steal the merchandise back. Later that year. Abe was shot in the chest three times by another American soldier from whom he was trying to collect a debt. Said Abe, with some understatement, "There seemed to be a lot of dishonest Americans around in those days." He would no doubt include the three shotgun-wielding GIs who, in 1952, robbed a bank in Tokyo and made their getaway in broad daylight.

To be sure, Japanese people during the fifties were still enamored of American culture. They had seen American movies like *High Noon* and *Gone With The Wind*. They had eaten American food to some extent and drunk Coca-Cola, and they were fascinated by Marilyn Monroe and Joe DiMaggio (who later honeymooned in Japan).

But the American in the abstract was one thing. The American GIs who were physically present there were quite another. Up close, they came across to the Japanese as big, graceless creatures with no subtlety or self-containment. They had a loud, loose, pushy manner to them and a seemingly endless capacity for loutish behavior when they got drunk, like diving into the moat of the Imperial Palace for a midnight swim or hailing taxis barreling down the opposite side of the street, with no intention of getting in, but just for the fun of seeing the driver come screeching to a halt, make a big U-turn and groan in dismay at discovering he was the victim of a cruel joke. One might mention the GI who, one day, learned the Japanese word *bakayaro* (lit., "You stupid SOB") and went down the street slapping people on the back, trying out his new expression. One might also mention the *Stars and Stripes* reporter possessed of an exceptionally long penis which he liked to display in public. Climbing into the front seat of a taxi, he would slide over next to the driver, unzip his fly, remove his member and press the taxi horn with it. More than one startled Tokyo cab driver nearly had an accident because of such antics.

Of course, what made it all the harder to bear was the fact that these boorish, unrefined Americans and their families lived so much better than the Japanese. They had their special foods, their luxuries, the things they were accustomed to having back home— centrally heated on-base housing and access to big autos—while Japanese struggled with privation, living in flimsy, drafty, unheated homes, wearing shabby clothes, riding impossibly packed commuter trains to and from work everyday and having to survive on an abysmal diet.

Indeed, the Japanese in that era were so malnourished that in coffee shops, customers could be seen pouring spoonful upon spoonful of sugar into their coffee cups, doing it half unconsciously, for the calories. They were so thin that American surgeons visiting Japan marveled how easy it was to operate on them. Said a military thoracic surgeon touring Japan giving lectures and performing demonstration operations, "It's great working here. In America people are fat. You have got to cut, tie off the bleeders so the hole doesn't fill up with blood, cut a little bit more, tie off those bleeders and so forth. Here, you make an incision and right away you're inside the stomach wall. You can go to work immediately. It's beautiful working on these people."

In general, the negative image of Americans which emerged during those years was nurtured by leftist groups with a vested interest in making the capitalist Americans look bad. The film *Akasen kichi* [Red line base] described American military bases in Japan as centers of dope addiction, prostitution and crime, while another film, *Hiroshima*, produced in 1953 by the Japan Teacher's Union, showed GIs buying the bones of bombing victims as souvenirs.

It all helped revive some of the xenophobia which had marred the late 1920s and the early 1930s in Japan (and which would later reappear in the trade disputes of the late 80s and early 90s) prompting vitriolic critics to demand that the Yankees go home before Japan became a US colony (although in fact, some Japanese wanted just that). Polls showed that pro-American feeling had fallen from slightly over 50 percent before the San Francisco Peace Treaty was signed to roughly 30 percent in the years thereafter.

Of course, not all Americans were natural born troublemakers. There were, for example, several charitable organizations and orphanages that were supported by military donations. And not all trouble was caused by Americans, as Japanese individuals accounted well over a million crimes a year all by themselves. Yet, such was the reputation of the 1950s GIs that most Japanese simply wanted them to go home.

THE GIRARD INCIDENT

Anti-American sentiment during the decade of the fifties reached fever pitch in what became known as the Girard Incident, so named because of its protagonist, twenty-one-year-old US Army soldier, William P. Girard, a tall, rawboned native of the small Illinois town of Ottowa. His infamous actions in the month of January 1957 rocked US–Japan Security ties to the core, and necessitated a secret deal between Washington and Tokyo in order to save the alliance. It also caused a major reduction in the number of American soldiers stationed in Japan.

Girard had joined the US Army after finishing high school and was sent to Japan shortly before his date with infamy. He was frequently assigned sentry duty at Camp Wier north of Tokyo, a site where US Army members assembled for regularly required rifle and artillery firing practice sessions as well as military maneuvers that often lasted from dawn until dusk. Firing practice was invariably attended by the members of the local Metal Gathering Association (MGA), an organization of some four hundred impoverished individuals who were allowed to pick up the empty shell casings and sell them as scrap metal to junk dealers. It was an activity originally begun in the days of the prewar Japanese military and was reluctantly tolerated by the US Army authorities, because it provided the metal pickers with a continued livelihood, minimal as it was.

It was the habit of some of the metal scavengers to dash onto the firing range in between rounds of shooting and hurriedly pick up the empty shell cases as the GIs were reloading. In fact, some of the more adventurous members of the Metal Gathering Association, eager for a leg up over their colleagues, would stay inside the impact area hiding in holes they had dug and wait for the shells to drop.

The incident that would make the MGA internationally known took place in the chilly noon of January 30, 1957, on a day already marked by trouble. Earlier that morning, large numbers of metal pickers had interfered with firing exercises in their pursuit of expended cartridges. In one particularly egregious instance, a half dozen civilians had pounced on a machine gun position as soon as the operator had ceased firing, before he had even had a chance to clear his weapon and physically pushed him away in order to retrieve the cartridge cases. When the ranking officer on the site saw what had happened, he suspended shooting practice, ordered the area cleared for an early lunch break and instructed SP3 Girard and a co-sentry to stay behind to guard the equipment. Annoyed at seeing several of the metal pickers remain near the field, intently scanning the range for spent cartridges, despite the off-limits order, Girard's platoon commander made it clear that he wanted them kept away, no matter what. But what happened after that was not quite what he had had in mind.

Left alone with his fellow soldier, Girard noticed metal pickers walking tentatively onto the range. He yelled an order for them to disperse. As they began to turn back, he inserted an empty ammunition cartridge into the grenade launcher he was carrying and let it fly in their direction. The cartridge struck one of the workers—a forty-six-year-old woman named Naka Sakai—in the back. It left a gaping wound that severed her spine and caused her to bleed to death on the spot.

By evening, news of the tragedy had been broadcast all over Japan. Official Army accounts of the death initially described it as an "accident," but they were contradicted by other witnesses in news reports, prompting a public outcry among Japanese citizenry against the American military. After first denying knowing anything about the shooting, Girard admitted that he had, in fact, fired his grenade launcher but had not intended to hit anyone. He said that he had used his weapon only to frighten the metal pickers into leaving and thereby protect the firing range equipment he had been assigned to guard. Girard's story was supported by his co-sentry, a young soldier named Victor Nickel.

However, other metal pickers on the scene had a somewhat different account of what had happened, claiming that Girard had set the whole horrific sequence of events in motion with a diabolical trick. They asserted that as the metal pickers began to leave the field, Girard instructed Nickel to toss out a few empty shell cases in the dirt, pointed to the ground at the empty casings, waved his hand at Mrs. Sakai and called out, "It's OK, Mama-san," motioning for her to go ahead and pick up the brass. It was then, they said, that Girard had fired his weapon.

Hearing these eyewitnesses tell their side of the story, it almost sounded as if Girard had shot the poor woman for sport, much like a deer hunter would flush his quarry out of the forest in order to get a clearer shot.

The Girard affair so infuriated the general public that the Japanese government, for the first time, demanded jurisdiction under the Status of Forces Agreement to deal with this act that had taken place on US-controlled property. The Status of Forces Agreement, the aforementioned adjunct to the Security Treaty, did provide for the trial in a Japanese court of US servicemen who had committed offenses not in the performance of duty, meaning those crimes committed outside a US military installation. But now, the Japanese wanted to go a step further.

Japanese authorities insisted that Girard's acts, albeit committed on property being used by US forces in the midst of a military exercise, could not in any way be construed as being in the line of duty because the metal pickers had posed no danger to the equipment Girard had been guarding during the lunch break or to the overall Army mission at that particular time. On the contrary, they argued, Girard had enticed his victim into his line of fire. Moreover, he had employed an unauthorized weapon—replacing his sentry rifle with a grenade launcher—in violation of military rules. Viewed in this light, they insisted, his behavior could only be interpreted as being outside the performance of official duties. The Public Prosecutors Office of Japan quickly indicted Girard on one count of manslaughter with intent to injure and demanded he be turned over.

The US Army refused to accede, arguing that, definitions of the "line of duty" aside, the US government did not have the right to turn Girard over to the Japanese authorities for trial, because of "higher," more profound issues that concerned the US constitution—issues which needed to be discussed in Washington.

With this, battle lines were drawn. As Girard waited in custody at a nearby Army base, the issue escalated into a major cause célèbre in the US, one that would take months to resolve. At first the matter was taken up jointly by the State Department and the Defense Department who had to weigh the arguments of Girard's more vocal accusers that the soldier was no better than a "common murderer" and that for the US government to provide him sanctuary was legally and morally unjustifiable, against that of the American defense lawyers participating in the case who said that the US constitution, which guaranteed every American citizen the right to a fair trial, should supersede all other aspects of the Status of Forces Agreement. Those lawyers used their own inflammatory language to further argue that if the US government gave into Japan's demands and surrendered Girard, they would be guilty of a "sellout" of the soldier's constitutional rights, adding that allowing a soldier to go to jail in a foreign country just for doing his duty would be disastrous to military unity and "imperil soldier morale."

In June, both the Defense and State Departments reached a joint decision which split US public opinion down the middle. Stating that the overriding importance of the non-authorized, capricious nature of Girard's actions and Girard's "unauthorized use of a grenade launcher" trumped any other considerations, they agreed to turn him over to the Japanese for trial, and secured President Dwight Eisenhower's blessing in the matter.

While liberal circles in America welcomed the decision as the "right, fair thing to do," an immediate outcry arose in the country's conservative camp, especially among Army veterans' groups like the American Legion and the Republican wing of Congress who protested vehemently that no American servicemen should ever, under any circumstances, be turned over to a foreign government for trial. They echoed the words of Girard's defense team that it would be morally wrong and "weird" to place US boys sworn to uphold the US constitution in foreign jails, before foreign firing squads or foreign hangmen, no matter what the crime. The powerful House Foreign Affairs Committee went so far as to publicly call on President Eisenhower to cancel or renegotiate the US Status of Forces Agreement with Japan, while Congressman John Butler of the US House of Representatives went a step further and demanded congressional reevaluation of *all* Status of Forces Agreements the US government had signed.

For his part, Girard's older brother Louis, an auto mechanic back in Ottawa, turned to the federal courts for help. He filed suit in a federal circuit court in Illinois, requesting the judicial branch of the US government to overturn the decision by the executive wing (as represented by the State and Defense Departments).

Louis claimed to a reporter that his brother William should in fact be regarded as a "hero" for defending US property abroad and drew immediate backing from the Senate and House of Representatives, led by an influential Republican Senator named Joseph Brocker, who said that Girard was "being sacrificed" on the altar of US foreign policy and Japanese public opinion, when, in fact, his only crime was trying to protect American property.

It was a suit largely based on emotion and it almost worked. On June 19, 1958, a federal circuit court judge named Joseph C. McGarraghy contravened the State and Defense Department rulings and lent his black-robed endorsement to the "performance of official duty" line. He found that Girard's rights under the US constitution had primacy in the matter and that the soldier was accountable only to US federal jurisdiction.

However, his ruling was immediately appealed against by the other side and set the stage for a final, decisive confrontation in the Supreme Court. The eight learned judges at the court heard arguments from both sides and chose logic (and perhaps discretion) over emotion, ruling 8–0 to uphold the constitutionality of the government's decision to turn over Girard to Japanese authorities *without* making any ruling whatsoever on the merits of Girard's actions or his guilt.

In a brief two-page statement, the court said simply that while the Security Treaty might indeed guarantee the US government the right to exercise jurisdiction over its boys in foreign lands, nothing in the US constitution or nearly two centuries of subsequent legislation prohibited granting the request of the Japanese government to try Girard, thereby neatly sidestepping the issue.

For all intents and purposes, that ended the argument and a trial date was set for August that year, although some of Girard's supporters were not yet finished fighting for their man. Most notable among them was the eccentric mayor of Ottowa, a man named Paul Egan, who leapt into the fray by publicly lambasting the US government and sending a cable to Emperor Hirohito, of all people, protesting Girard's forthcoming trial. His cable read as follows: "Because our State Department has sold us down the river, I wonder if you would act to encourage better feelings between the people of our two countries by releasing Private Girard from Japanese custody." When Hirohito replied obliquely through an aide that he "could not possibly intervene in the matter" because of the Japanese constitution (sounding much like a Supreme Court judge himself), the combative Mayor Egan announced that he would fly to Tokyo and "raise a little hell over the matter."

The Japanese public was spared this particular slice of Americana when, at the last minute, the mayor was forced to cancel in order to answer a local court summons: assault and battery charges had been filed against him for punching one of his own aldermen.

THE TRIAL

Back in Japan, Girard was starting to sweat. According to reports, he was just an ordinary, unsophisticated GI who liked his beer cold, his music country-and-western and enjoyed a good fight on Saturday night. He was also one who, in the assessment of a *Stars and Stripes* reporter familiar with him, was "not particularly bright." Like so many youths who had not yet learned to control their baser impulses, he had done something stupid, only the consequences of his irrevocable act were so far-reaching he would never outlive them. He stood a good chance of spending many long years at hard labor at one of the country's prisons—then not noted for their hygiene, their cooling and heating facilities or their sympathetic treatment, but certainly famous for their ability to instill obeisance to authority in a regimen more severe than any Marine boot camp and certainly harder than most US penal institutions. In many prisons at the time, inmates were not allowed to talk to each other or even make eye contact for most of the day. Visitors were not permitted other than family and even family was allowed in very infrequently. This perhaps explained why Girard decided to get married to his girlfriend of several months before the verdict came in.

The young lady's name was Haruo (Candy) Sueyama and she had worked the cash register in an off-base GI bar Club Cherry ("a misnomer if there ever was one," said a US embassy official who was familiar with the establishment). Yet, by all accounts she was not a *kichi no onna* ("woman of the base") as the Japanese derogatorily put it—a term they used for women of loose morals who slept with American soldiers for money. Born and raised in Taiwan, she was a quiet, serious pleasant young woman, seven years Girard's senior, who neither drank nor smoked.

According to an article in a Japanese women's magazine, she had been observing Girard from the sidelines for some time, noting his penchant for wild behavior after two or three shots of whiskey and his careless tendency to allow other more predatory bar girls to relieve him of his loose cash. Finally, she decided she would "save" him. She took him under her wing and did her best to settle him down, persuading him to take up joint residence with her in a tiny one-room six-tatami-mat cold water flat. Despite the unenviable situation her boyfriend now found himself in, she had made up her mind to stand by him—even if he went to prison. She had immediately said yes when Girard popped the question and told acquaintances she would wait for him for the next ten years, if need be.

"I'm the only one who understands him," she said. And thus were the unlikely couple wed at the Army post chapel in a double-ring ceremony, after which Girard returned to his quarters, still under house arrest, while his new bride went home to their tiny apartment.

Needless to say, her devotion to the "evil American," as the tabloids were describing Girard, did not win her a lot of admirers among the local populace. After the wedding, which was reported in the newspapers along with her post-nuptial visit to the grave of the late Mrs. Sakai to offer prayers, she was bombarded by angry postcards and letters from townspeople.

"Your husband should be torn into pieces and thrown to the dogs," went one of the missives.

"Both you and Girard ought to hang," went another.

Another said, "The people are angry with you over marrying Girard. You must pay two million yen condolence money." The police determined that the author of that particular missive was a gangland extortionist, whom they eventually tracked down and arrested.

Yet, despite such vitriol, any suggestions by Girard's defense counsel, which included Army lawyers working with Japanese attorneys, to change trial venue to a more friendly locale were quickly rebuffed. This was Japan, where judges—not a jury—would decide the outcome and judges, as everyone knew in this status-conscious country, were considered immune to public opinion and beyond the reach of mortal influence.

The trial that followed one was one of the most intensely covered in the history of jurisprudence. It began in a courtroom in the Maebashi District Court and, in the midst of a midsummer downpour, quickly moved to the firing range where Mrs. Sakai was killed, the judges wearing raincoats and rubber boots, ankle deep in mud, with some two hundred umbrella-toting Japanese reporters watching from a nearby hill. Also present were Mrs. Sakai's plump, sad-faced eighteen-year-old daughter, clad in a prim yellow dress, along with a sizable contingent of metal pickers.

The prosecutor, from under a soggy outdoor tent, quickly made culture an issue, playing into the hands of those people who said that Girard could never get a fair trial in Japan. After portraying Girard as a "trigger-happy, fun-loving, irresponsible soldier who gleefully took pot shots at metal pickers," he noted with great disdain that Girard had failed to make condolence visits to Mr. Sakai, as required by Japanese justice and customs, that he had further neglected to take any measures to console the soul of the victim and that, worse yet, he had not even seen fit to apologize for his actions.

Of course, Girard, like most of his American confreres, was oblivious to such mores and was naturally unaware of the Japanese need to make tearful public apologies as a demonstration of the sincerity of one's remorse. For GIs in Japan to actually learn something about the culture into which they had been thrust was, as it would be demonstrated again and again, a rare occurrence, (unless it had something to do with getting laid or making money—then they were an incredibly quick study).

Moreover, Girard, being American, and coming from a highly litigious country where such things as apologies and condolence visits could be construed as an admission of guilt and used as effective weapons by the opposing side in court, was naturally advised from the outset by the American lawyers assigned to his case to keep his mouth shut and his cards close to his vest. To the American sensibility, there was no reason to apologize when you were arguing you had not intentionally done anything wrong. Unfortunately, Girard and his American advisors had also failed to understand that in Japan, an apology was not legal evidence of anything, it was just good manners. The failure to show remorse for what had happened to Mrs. Sakai on Girard's turf as a result of Girard's actions—accidental or otherwise—enabled the prosecutors to charge that they could not find any evidence of his "real repentance," which, in Japan, was a black mark against the defendant's character.

The Japanese defense attorney assigned to the case after the US Supreme Court's decision made a trial in Japan an inevitability, did his best to rehabilitate his client's already publicly battered reputation in court. In his opening remarks, he painted a picture of an honest soldier, who was "bewildered, shocked and stunned," and declared that he would finally have his client uttering the magic words, "I'm sorry"—as indeed Girard would.

However, the evidence that was presented against Girard in the following weeks was damning. Girard's co-sentry, Victor Nickel, faced with a charge of accessory after the fact and the possibility of a long detention for his role in the initial cover-up, testified that

Girard had indeed told him to throw cartridges toward the metal pickers to entice them, and not just toward Mrs. Sakai, but another metal picker as well, a man named Hideoharu Onozeki. Nickel also said that immediately after the shooting, Girard had asked him to lie, telling him "if anyone asks you, we didn't hear any shots and we threw no brass."

Nickel added that Girard had further instructed him to say that he, Girard, had held his weapon at the hip, barrel pointed to the sky, and fired one shot, as if to underscore the lack of intent on the latter's part. Finally, Nickel offered his not-very-helpful opinion that Girard had fired only as a joke.

A succession of metal pickers followed Nickel to the stand with damaging testimony, with Onozeki identifying Girard as the shooter—the one who had fired twice. The final nail in the coffin came when Girard's platoon commander also appeared in court to emphasize that he had given no orders to Girard to fire his weapon to keep the metal pickers away and that there was no authorized procedure in either the Army or Marine Corps under which Girard could have conceivably shot the woman. The conclusion was inescapable that, at the very least, Girard was guilty of gross negligence and conspiring to cover up a crime, although whether or not he had actually intended to harm Mrs. Sakai was unclear.

The verdict came through on November 19, 1957. Girard was found guilty of manslaughter, but received a surprisingly lenient three-year prison sentence suspended for four. The judge found that Girard had committed "excessive mischief" in a "momentary caprice," but noted that since Girard had repented his crime and apologized in court, there was no fear of repetition. In a surprise addendum, he also scolded the metal pickers for their behavior saying that they were in part responsible for what had happened. The US Army promptly demoted Girard, discharged him dishonorably and shipped him back to civilian life in the US. Then the US Government cut a check for ¥629,396 ($1,748) as compensation to the victim's husband.

AFTERMATH

The ruling was headline news all over Japan and the leniency shown toward Girard stunned and confused many Japanese who had expected that he would be given a prison sentence, if only for a symbolic period of time. The prosecutor and Sakai's daughter both publicly expressed their anger at the light sentence, while a leading Diet member belonging to the Socialist Party called for an immediate appeal—a call, it must be noted, that was ignored. Some cynics suspected a deal had been struck, especially the leftists who had demonstrated outside the courthouse during the trial with placards that read "Don't put pressure on the Girard Case, America!" But it wasn't until nearly four decades later that it was revealed what had really happened.

Confidential documents, which were declassified in 1991, revealed that US military officials had concocted a *secret* deal with Japanese authorities, one made *before* the US courts had ever become involved. In it, they agreed to turn over Girard to Japanese procurators for trial on condition that Girard would not be prosecuted for murder, but for a lesser offense of manslaughter, or "wounding resulting in death," as the court documents went. Although that might well have been the charge in any event, the under-the-table US demand for special treatment represented, to ordinary Japanese, direct interference in their legal system. The suspended sentence was certainly not preordained but skeptics could not help wondering what effect such pressures might have had on the judge, although on another level, Japanese were reportedly satisfied that the world had seen their court system in action and that it had functioned reasonably well.

As arrogant and intolerable as it may have been, the deal would prove to be only one in a long line of clandestine, duplicitous acts by US and Japanese leaders that marked the postwar era (involving, among other things, matters such as aircraft sales and the storage of nuclear weapons).

In the end, the Girard Incident ignited an "anti-US base" movement in Japan, marked by growing protests, which, as the declassified documents also revealed, directly resulted in the removal of most of the US garrison forces from Japan, cutting by nearly half the total number of American soldiers stationed there. It was during the heated debate over what to do with Girard, for example, that President Eisenhower had seriously begun to rethink the role and purpose of US troops in Japan. During the height of the argument Eisenhower was caught between congressional pressures from those furious that Girard would be tried in a Japanese court on the one hand and, on the other, the desire to maintain good relations with Japan. He agonized over what do to.

"There is no answer," he concluded, according to the documents, "unless you get out of Japan." That sentiment was also shared by most US soldiers on the ground in Japan, who were deeply upset by the animosity the Japanese media and public in general were showing them because of Girard. As one young Marine, Tom Scully from New York, put it at the time, "If that is their attitude, after all we did for them, helped them out when they were starving, then fuck 'em. Let's get out."

Girard's platoon leader, a longtime Army veteran, was, despite his court testimony which helped convict Girard, more upset at the way the Army had abandoned Girard, than he was at Japan's attitude. "If this is the Army," he said, "then I don't want any part of it." And, indeed, he quit.

(They were sentiments that US soldiers in Japan would find themselves frequently expressing over the next forty years as a series of similar events occurred, inflaming passions on both sides.)

Those declassified files released to the public in the mid-nineties were revealing in more ways than one, for they also showed that American leaders were bitterly disappointed by Japan's lack of interest in becoming a world power. The white-haired and perpetually white-suited intellectual Secretary of State John Foster Dulles grumbled during one national security meeting in the mid-fifties, "We have done everything that we can think of to stir up in Japan a desire to assume a position of international influence once again and results have been markedly unsuccessful."

In remarks that through the lens of history must be viewed with wry irony given the stunning performance of Japan's economy that was to come, Dulles further wrote, "Indeed, the Japanese were utterly lethargic and lacking in any perceptible ambition to recover their prewar prestige. Even under proddings which approached the brutal, they remained inert."

Those same documents further revealed that Dulles had earlier told Mamoru Shigemitsu, Japan's foreign minister, that Japan's trade deficit with the US would be a *permanent fact of life*! "There will always be an imbalance in Japan's trade with the US," he wrote, thereby proving that even the brainiest government officials could be just as erroneous in their judgments as anyone else.

It might be worth mentioning that it was in 1965, not so many years after Dulles made his pointed remarks about Japan's lack of economic prowess, that Japan first began running its trade surplus with the US—a surplus which would continue into the twenty-first century and which, at one point, reached $60 billion a year. One wonders how Dulles would have responded had he lived long enough to see it.

Girard was met with a chilly reception upon his return to the United States. The segment of the public that had once hailed him as a public hero had now cooled toward him considerably as the patriotic passions of the moment had subsided. Only a handful of reporters and photographers awaited him as his ship docked in San Francisco. As one reporter explained to a magazine back home: "This is a man who covered the face of America with mud. This is the man who treated Japanese like fools. How can anyone welcome him back?"

Back home in Ottowa, Illinois with Haruo, his new wife, Girard had trouble finding jobs and once found, had trouble keeping them—due in part to his short fuse, it was reported in Japanese publications. Although Girard tried to put the incident behind him (after an abortive attempt at writing a book about his life), the scandal kept dogging him. According to magazine reports, Girard took to spending his nights at the racetrack; he began drinking heavily and hurling abuse at his wife, whose English was still so limited at the time she had little idea what he was saying, although the general meaning was undoubtedly hard to miss.

According to a 1967 article in a Japanese magazine, Haruo had sought solace in prayer, kneeling each night before a religious icon she had brought with her from Japan. But that only made things worse, as her in-laws, perhaps not the most internationally aware individuals, accused her of "putting a curse" on them.

The couple had settled into an apartment in Ottowa (at forty dollars a month, one of the cheapest in town). But with her husband incapacitated, Haruo was forced to take on menial jobs—washing dishes, babysitting, operating a sewing machine at a nearby under- wear factory—to keep the household going and care for the two young daughters the couple had by then. In time, the family moved west, first to Arizona, then to Southern California, in an effort to start a new life. But repeatedly the past would come back to haunt them, as when a neighbor identified Girard as the "one who mur- dered a woman in Japan" and told Girard's elder daughter.

Through it all, Haruo proved surprisingly resilient—and tough. She was the one who had stood fast when all the world seemed against her husband. She'd stuck by him, because she thought that her love could save him. And, in the end, it appeared that this was exactly what she did.

Girard eventually got a decent job, making $150 a week as an au- tomotive technician, and the family settled down to something re- sembling domestic bliss—which may or may not have been marred by the thought that "domestic bliss" was something that Mrs. Sakai's husband and children would not have anymore, thanks to that fate- ful afternoon at the Camp Weir firing range.

The "Girard Pullout," as one writer has described it, began within a year after the conclusion of the trial, when the first of the roughly sixty thousand combat troops that were stationed in the country made their departure.

It was just about this time that a bored nineteen-year-old US Air Force sentry named Peter E. Longpre from Lakewood, California, standing guard at Johnson Air Force Base outside Tokyo, squeezed off a round from his rifle at a passing train, ending the life of a promising young Japanese musician on his way into the base to play in a band. That, of course, started yet another uproar, which would culminate with the soldier's trial and conviction in a Tokyo court for professional negligence and his subsequent incarceration for ten months. (Notably absent were the political and legal histrionics which had marked the Girard case back in the US. Perhaps this time the Americans were just too embarrassed to open their mouths in protest.)

This incident also set the stage for some of the largest and most violent anti-American demonstrations in the postwar era as the 1960 date for the renewal of the Security Treaty approached. Hundreds of thousands of Zengakuren (All-Student Alliance) protesters snake-danced through the streets in massive, virulent protests against the presence of American troops on Japanese soil. They posed such a danger that Eisenhower was forced to cancel a planned trip to Tokyo.

The treaty was renewed, but it took the help of the right-wing and yakuza elements who were enlisted to quell the leftist demonstrators and to keep them out of the National Diet Building where the ratification was being conducted. Still, the leftists managed noticeable small victories. For example, there was a nightclub in Hibya Park called the Keyhole Club, run by the American businessman and ex-cop Dan Sawyer and British entrepreneur Leo Prescott, aimed at GIs checked into the Imperial Hotel. It had been a very successful business until the Zengakuren demonstrations started and the student protesters began ganging up on the GI patrons, shoving and punching them, knocking more than one unlucky soldier into the lotus pond in front of the hotel.

Eventually, the club had to shut down. The hapless Prescott, who had already had one of his clubs trashed by the professional wrestler Rikidozan, next opened a pachinko shop on the Ginza that was quickly taken over by the powerful Tosei-kai yakuza clan, whose bosses simply marched in one day and announced, "We're taking over this place now. It is ours." After that, Prescott could not even get in the front door.

All in all, in the eyes of some observers, both Girard and Long-pre, were "bargain counter soldiers" and a testament to the inanity of US recruitment policy. As *Stars and Stripes* reporter Hal Drake would later put it, "To draft some uneducated country bumpkin like Girard, with a 90 IQ, and hand him a rifle, was a monumentally stupid act. To give a gun to somebody like Longpre, for example, who claimed that when he fired the rifle he 'hadn't realized' there was a shell in the chamber, was typical of the stupidity of the US military." As a result, the US military paid a big price for its actions in terms of goodwill.

QUACKENBUSH

Japan's insistence on trying all off-base crimes committed by US military and related civilian personnel in Japanese courts resulted in its holding one of the more historic and unusual trials of the post-Occupation era. It was known as the Quackenbush Case and the necessity for adjudicating it had come about in June 1961 when Japanese police arrested a slender, attractive American woman from Louisiana named Beverly Quackenbush and charged her with the murder of her husband Henry Quackenbush, a retired US Army major and civilian worker at Fuchu Air Station on the outskirts of Tokyo. She thus became the first gaijin woman in Japanese history to be incarcerated in a Japanese police detention house under suspicion of such a crime. Also arrested was her son, seventeen-year-old Henry, who was charged with patricide, making him the first foreigner so charged in Japan.

The Quackenbush affair began on the morning of June 13, 1961, when husband Henry's body was discovered lying under a tree in the backyard of his home in the sleepy Tokyo suburb of Fuchu. An investigation showed the American had been had been bludgeoned and strangled, and the body moved from inside the house. At first, the wife had professed complete ignorance at the circumstances of her husband's death. But then the police found the murder weapon—a blood-stained iron pipe hidden inside the house—and, under questioning, the sordid truth began to dribble out. In long rambling accounts she described to detectives the unsavory tale of a seemingly ordinary American family hiding a long history of violence and abuse. She told of a series of incidents over the course of their marriage that showed her husband to be a dangerous man, given to violent bouts of drinking and spousal abuse. She testified that years earlier, when the family was living in a small town in Louisiana, for example, her husband would get drunk and beat her, forcing her and her four children to flee into the nearby woods to hide while he sought them with a gun. Once, in 1956, he had even been arrested for shooting her—and at a time when she was pregnant. Moreover, he had been arrested several other times for assault and battery on local townspeople, as well as for the curious crime of cattle theft. Henry Quackenbush had left many unpaid debts in his wake, which had forced his wife to go to work to support the family.

As Beverly Quackenbush told it, the years of violent abuse had culminated in a fierce quarrel on the evening of June 13, the night before the family was scheduled to depart for Okinawa, where Henry Quackenbush had taken a new assignment. He had come home from the officer's club at Fuchu Air Station, intoxicated, and began quarreling heavily with his wife over money and other personal matters—including his wife's suspected lovers. The argument had lasted three hours, and then he had gone into the kitchen, grabbed a butcher knife and threatened to stab her. A struggle ensued in which the Quackenbush patriarch was clubbed and choked to death by his family.

The mother and the two older children then stripped the body of rings and other valuables and removed all the money from the corpse's wallet in an effort to make the death appear as an accidental part of a robbery *committed by a Japanese*. They cleaned and dressed the body and dragged it to the backyard. Then they scrubbed down the bloodstained home, hid the pipe under a bedroom mattress and called the authorities.

Police investigating the matter detected certain inconsistencies in the story Mrs. Quackenbush and her children had told. Under questioning, in one version, Beverly Quackenbush had said that her son Henry, a stocky five-foot-ten (1.8 m) karate student, had sprung to her defense in the middle of the life-and-death struggle. She said she had held her husband from behind while her son Henry wrestled the knife out of his father's hand and began choking him. Fourteen-year-old Diana then picked up a ten-pound (4.5 kg) three-foot (1 m) long rusty pipe and hit her father over the head with it—a blow which was determined to be the primary cause of her father's demise.

Young Diana backed up this account of events and readily admitted delivering the fatal blow. But the police had their doubts about this version as well. It contradicted a statement made by Henry, who said his sister had struck the senior Quackenbush earlier, when he and Henry were wrestling on the floor, not when he was standing up as the mother had claimed. Moreover, the prosecutors believed that the murder weapon, the rusty pipe, had been stolen from a nearby housing construction site, something which a suspicious mind might interpret as an indication that the act was premeditated.

The Japanese authorities decided to charge Beverly Quackenbush with conspiracy to commit murder. They cited her obvious attempt to cover up the crime as well as the disparities in the story she and her son had told.

Prosecutors were particularly disturbed about son Henry's involvement because in a Confucian society like Japan's a son killing a father, no matter what the extenuating circumstances, was considered an extremely serious offense. They filed a charge of patricide, but excused Henry's younger sister because of her age.

The ensuing trial was remarkable for the fact that both the victim and the two accused were all United States citizens. American defense attorneys, trying to get the patricide charge dropped, were brought forth to testify that since the offense was a crime peculiar to Japan and did not exist in any Anglo-American statute, young Henry was being charged unfairly—an argument that failed to move the judge. Moreover, the bilingual nature of the trial necessitated a record number of interpreters and translators to deal with the mountain of evidence and testimony. It was excruciatingly time-consuming and created more than a little confusion.

A bizarre highlight was the dramatic about-faces of fourteen-year-old Diana. Prior to the trial, she had changed her original testimony about her participation in the killing and signed a statement in the prosecutor's office to the effect that she was asleep when her father died. In court, however, she reversed herself again, swearing that it was indeed she and not her mother, as the prosecution was now charging, who had struck the senior Quackenbush on the head and killed him. When confronted with the previously signed statement which contradicted her testimony, she claimed that the document had been coerced out of her by the Tokyo procurator, Kokujiro Ebihara.

"Yes, I made that statement to you," she said, "but I lied. You kept calling me a liar, then I got scared and started crying and said what you wanted me to say."

Prosecutor Ebihara found himself in the position of having to claim that the language difficulty was responsible for the "liar" charge. But Quackenbush's defense attorney Franklin N. Warren gleefully rubbed salt in the wound by pointing out that Ebihara's interpreters were supposed to be among the best in Japan—was Ebihara questioning the competency of his own hand-picked staff, he asked.

Conflicting testimony by son Henry further muddied the waters. In court, he too would change his story again. He now said that he never actually saw his sister Diana hit their father with the iron pipe, only that the father had indeed been hit by *someone* during their struggle, but by whom he could not tell. It just so happened that Diana was holding the pipe when he regained his feet.

In the end, the judges rejected the mother's pleas of accidental self-defense. On Christmas Day 1961, they found her guilty of all charges and sentenced her to prison for eight years. They also found the son guilty as charged and sentenced him to five to eight years. In a prepared statement, the panel of judges called the acts for which the defendants had been convicted, "cold, brutal and a crime against humanity," while totally rejecting Quackenbush family claims that Diana had struck the fatal blow.

Said the chief judge in his ruling, unconsciously reflecting what appeared to be a cultural bias, "It would be a coldhearted, severe person who says that an innocent girl could commit such a crime."

Said one American onlooker, sarcastically, "That was a statement that could only be made by Japanese judge."

Beverly Quackenbush went down in history as the first US military dependent wife to serve a term in a Japanese prison. The sentences were reduced in appeals court fourteen months later, when a judge ruled that Mrs. Quackenbush and son were guilty only of manslaughter, saying that confusion, fear and blind rage were the motivating factors.

By the spring of 1964, both she and her son had been released and reunited with the rest of the family who had been staying with relatives in America.

The whole affair was a fitting epilogue to what some people viewed as America's worst ever decade in Japan.

In totality, this series of infamous actions by this group of outsiders surely contributed to the environment in which others found Japanese society aligned against them.

CHAPTER 4

Elint Agents

MY MEMOIR *Tokyo Junkie* (Stone Bridge Press, 2021) is an account of my life in Japan, but space and editorial requirements did not allow me to tell my own arrival story so I will share it here.

The PACOM Elint Center, where I reported for work upon arriving in Japan in 1962, as a nineteen-year-old airman, occupied a two-story building near the rear gate of the Fuchu base on the outskirts of Tokyo. The windowless structure had walls three feet (one meter) thick and a solid-steel front door which was manned around the clock by Air Policemen wearing Model 15 six-shot revolvers, who inspected the special ID cards Elint Center personnel carried in order to gain entry.

The Elint Center was an electronic spy operation, a tri-service intelligence gathering and analysis unit that was under the joint direction of the National Security Agency (NSA), a wing of the Department of Defense, and the CIA—answerable to a weathered, bespectacled civilian in his sixties named Jack Hobbs. Hobbs sported a dent and a metal plate in his arm, thanks to an injury sustained during the Korean War. Inside the building were several large computer bays and another solid-steel door that could only be opened by punching a secret code, changed weekly, into a panel of buttons. Behind that door, war plans were made.

One had to have a Top Secret security clearance to get in the building. The FBI had sent agents to the small city of Eureka in rural Northern California to interview my family members, neighbors, friends and staff at Eureka High School to make sure that I was a loyal, red-blooded American without any subversive leanings.

The Elint Center was responsible for two types of intelligence gathering. The first, run by the NSA, sent low-altitude flights along the coast of China, North Korea and Eastern Russia, including Vladivostok which had a major Soviet naval and air force presence, to gather data, with occasional penetrating probes inland. The second, managed by the CIA, flew high-altitude missions deep inside the three countries. These high- and low-altitude sorties both came back with reels of photographs and recorded tapes filled with various types of ground radar and telemetric data related to enemy air defenses, for Elint Center analysts to examine. A high priority was placed on getting photographs of known and suspected nuclear weapons facilities.

It was the height of the Cold War and the purpose of it all was to understand the enemy's capabilities and to plot invasion routes if necessary. America was protecting Japan as well as itself, for Japan's fledgling Self-Defense Forces were woefully adequate for the task at hand.

For the low-altitude flights, the Fifth Air Force operated a fleet of P2V and C-135 four-engine propeller craft that flew out of Atsugi naval air station twenty-eight miles (45 km) southwest of Tokyo, as well as from Taipei. When penetrating the Chinese mainland, the planes flew at altitudes as low as one thousand feet (three hundred meters) or less to escape radar detection. For the high-altitude flights, the CIA deployed Lockheed U-2 aircraft. The U-2 planes had been piloted by American civilians and flown out of Atsugi until 1960 when American U-2 pilot Gary Powers was shot down over Russia and was taken prisoner, an embarrassing outcome for the US government which had heretofore issued repeated denials they were conducting such spy missions. After that, all U-2 flights were flown out of Taipei by Republic of China pilots, and mission data was surreptitiously rushed to the Elint Center for analyses by US Air Force jet courier.

Only a handful of people at the highest levels of the conservative

Japanese government knew exactly what the US was doing. In fact, when a U-2 plane crash-landed in a rice field outside Atsugi in 1959, opposition Socialist Diet members opposed to the American military's presence in Japan inspected the wreckage but eventually swallowed the cover story that it was a weather reconnaissance, no need to worry—until Powers was shot down, that is.

I was an analyst from day one. I sat at a highly sophisticated and extremely expensive console called an SLA Pulse Analyzer which featured a six-inch (15 cm) oscilloscope with assorted knobs, dials and switches, and an array of analytic equipment: quarter-inch tape players for two-track recordings used in low-altitude missions and two-inch sixteen-channel players used in U-2 missions; a brush recorder (which produced high-speed images using black ink on white paper); a visicorder (which printed out high-speed images and signals using light emissions); and a continuous loop player among other tools and instruments I was familiar with from Elint School, which I had attended at Keesler Air Force Base in Biloxi, Mississippi before my Japan assignment. I was given a tape every day when I reported for work and ordered to analyze every sound. I would identify a sound by first determining its Pulse Repetition Frequency on the oscilloscope, then measuring the scan or sweep by timing the intervals between each appearance of the sound. Following that, I would check the plane's location on a map versus when the signal was recorded.

The countries under surveillance used three basic types of radar: Early Warning, Height Finder and Fire Control. Early Warning was a coastal radar designed to locate incoming enemy aircraft. Height Finder determined the altitude of the invading plane. The third, Fire Control, usually located further inland, was characterized by an extremely high-pitched sound, as it honed in on the aircraft identified by the Height Finder. Once the Fire Control succeeded in locking in on an aircraft, it could send a surface-to-air missile to knock it out of the sky. The trick for our pilots flying overhead was to make sure that did not happen.

The output from the signal analysis was collated with the data gleaned from photo analysis and combined with other on-the-ground intelligence to produce air intelligence studies. If war broke out, the pilots of our B-52 bombers would have to know how to enter and maneuver through enemy territory without being detected before they unleashed their bombs. Given knowledge of the enemy radar, we could render it ineffective, for example, by jamming the signal or making the enemy think there were many more planes in the sky than there actually were. These tactics were called Electronic Counter Measures (ECM).

It wasn't exactly Brandenburg Gate at midnight. And while it was sedentary work, it was also exciting in its own way, given its importance to US national security. For a nineteen-year-old acned redneck from Eureka, California, it certainly beat bagging groceries at the 7th & E Supermarket, which was my last job before being granted a Top Secret clearance. That we were violating the sovereign airspace of other countries and then denying, at the highest levels, that we were doing so, was something that nobody I knew lay awake at night worrying about. China, Russia and North Korea were Communist nations. And Communists were the enemy. After all, hadn't Soviet premier Nikita Khrushchev banged his shoe on a podium at the United Nations in a scathing attack on American imperialism and declared to us, "We will bury you"?

There were other peripheral operations going on too. There was something called the Naval Security Group (NSG), which had navy ships patrolling the coast of North Korea and picking up intel on submarines and surface vessels. One was the USS Pueblo, which in 1968 would be boarded and captured by North Korean forces.

There was also the Army Security Agency (ASA), which monitored military chatter in Russia, North Korea and China. Both the ASA and NSG had technical representatives at the Elint Center.

Access to the electronic intelligence collected by these operations, however, or even the existence of this information, was limited by a "need to know" policy. No one ever knew all of the missions or even the parts that the different agencies played in the execution of a given mission and analysis of the results. The secrecy was such that married personnel could not even tell their spouses what they did. And mention of key terms like U-2 or Fire Control Radar outside the Elint Center was a court-martial offense.

The Elint Center was the key cog in an overall US intelligence and espionage effort that included a cadre of undercover CIA agents based out of the US embassy in Tokyo, working in the guise of journalists or traders, that was also endeavoring to counter Communism and funneling under-the-table contributions worth millions of dollars to support politicians in Japan's ruling Liberal Democratic Party. It was matched by a network of Russian KGB spies posing as businessmen and newspaper correspondents whose job it was to find out what the Americans were doing in Tokyo and also sow the seeds of mistrust between Japanese and Americans.

We were as clandestine as you can get. But high command did periodically brief high-ranking officials of the Japan Ministry of Defense on what we were doing, to reassure them we were operating in the country's best interests and with the hope and expectation that the Japan Self-Defense Forces would one day be able to conduct their own state-of-the-art surveillance as a true partner in the US–Japan alliance. Article 9 of the postwar constitution, written by MacArthur and his team, limited the scope of the postwar Japanese military:

> *Aspiring sincerely to an international peace based on justice and order, the Japanese people forever renounce war as a sovereign right of the nation and the threat or use of force as means of settling international disputes.*

But we were nonetheless training the Japan Self-Defense Forces to resist attacks in massive joint training exercises, with US help as per the Security Treaty. In fact, it would eventually develop into a sizable and sophisticated fighting force and Japan would become one of the countries often described as "a screwdriver's turn" away from possessing nuclear weapons.

The ratio of officers to enlisted at the Elint Center was nearly 1:1. The whole was an esoteric mix of soldiers, sailors and marines—with a liberal sprinkling of civilians—and there was not a lot of lost love in their relations with one another. Pejorative terms like "swabby," "grunt," "jarhead" and "flyboy" peppered daily conversation.

The schedule called for a forty-hour week, eight till five, Monday to Friday. After work I would lift weights at the base gym and take aikido lessons twice a week—these exertions followed by further instruction in the art of drinking at the Airman's Club or outside the gate on the Han, as the main drag lined with bars was called. But more often than not, we were called in to work twelve-hour shifts on missions that required urgent data analyses.

My supervisor on the military side was a Navy chief from Casper, Wyoming, named Euvern Vorhies. He was in charge of the M1911 45 semi-automatics issued to us in our periodic drills to repel a simulated enemy raid by the Russians or the ChiComms, as we called the Chinese Communists on the mainland.

On more than one occasion we would have to hunt down fellow analysts to haul them in to work, which often entailed searching the bars on the strip and, on a backstreet, the euphemistically named shakuhachi parlor (which offered a nicely appointed waiting room, free drinks and an ample collection of back issues of *Sports Illustrated* to pass the time until your number was called). We might also have to look into another establishment called Derby, where a hand-painted sign proclaimed "Turkish Bath Room: Well Come." There young ladies would wash a serviceman and massage him and attend to any other needs he might possibly have. Some analysts, I'm not saying who, were seen reporting to a late night duty call with suds in their ears.

After I had been there a while, the work at the Elint Center became monotonous and tiring. For U-2 missions you had to sit there for twelve hours at a stretch, three times a week, and watch the same signals appear and disappear. But there was an underlying tension because of the high-priority nature of the work; and the all-too-frequent reminders of just how dangerous it was for the pilots who flew the missions.

The U-2 had a good claim to the title of flimsiest plane ever

built. It was a specially designed single-engine single-seat Lockheed
aircraft. Nicknamed "Dragon Lady," it flew at an altitude of 70,000
feet (21,000 meters), conducting round-the-clock all-weather missions. It had a wing-span of 103 feet (31 meters) and only two permanent landing-gear units set up in bicycle configuration—one
front and one back. That limitation was necessary to give the plane
more lift. Special detachable "pogo" wheels, like training wheels on
a bike, were fixed to either wingtip to balance the plane on takeoff.
Those were jettisoned the moment the plane was airborne.

When it landed, a jeep on the tarmac kept pace with the incoming plane while it touched down; as it was coming to a halt
crew members raced to grab the wings, wrestle them up or down as
needed and re-affix the pogos to prevent the U-2 from toppling over.

The U-2 weighed 25,000 pounds (11,339 kg) when it was fully
loaded. It flew at a maximum speed of 500 miles (800 km) per hour
with a cruise speed of 430 miles per hour. If you flew it too slow, it
would stall and fall out of the sky. Fly it too fast and it would break
apart. It required pilots of exceptional intelligence, skill, persever-
ance and courage.

U-2 planes were cold and cramped and flew so high pilots could
see the curvature of the earth. They had to wear pressurized suits
and helmets, which rendered them unable even to scratch their
noses and required them to suck food and water through a tube.
They had to sit there for as many as twelve hours, then, fatigued,
and with depth perception skewed from the high altitude, they had
to worry about a safe landing, putting the plane into a virtual stall
ten feet (three meters) from the ground to set up the "pogo" align-
ments. After a mission, the pilot was seriously dehydrated from
breathing oxygen and sometimes suffered decompression sickness
if nitrogen bubbles had formed in the blood.

Many of the U-2 pilots were party animals and could run the
strip outside their military base with the best of them. Pilots were
not supposed to drink alcohol a couple of days before a mission
because those pressurized suits were essentially astronaut suits, and
alcohol in the bloodstream mixed with pure oxygen could have adverse effects on the pilot's ability to think and act clearly. Not only

did they have to depressurize after the flight, they had to pressurize before the flight for an hour or two. The more basic human functions were also quite a challenge. So the last thing they wanted to do was spend three or four hours getting suited up and pressurized only to have to strip and beat feet to the loo for a case of "Mama-san's revenge," to use the vernacular of the time. Occasionally a pilot would abort due to this sickness.

Through it all there was the ever-present danger of being shot down as the plane flew in and out of the target country. The high altitudes at which the U-2s flew was supposed to have put them out of range of enemy fighter planes and missiles, but it did not always work out that way, as Gary Powers discovered. Powers' plane was brought down by a Soviet surface-to-air missile (S-75 Dvina) which exploded just behind the tail section, causing the U-2 to flip over and break its wings. Powers bailed out and parachuted to safety, where he was quickly captured. He had carried with him a modified silver dollar that contained a lethal, shellfish-derived saxitoxin-in-tipped needle, but did not use it.

Flying over China was no less dangerous. The strength and capabilities of the Chinese air defense system had improved so much during the 1950s that it became extremely difficult for reconnaissance planes to overfly the mainland. As a result, gaining intel from behind the Bamboo Curtain, as it was often called then, was not an easy thing. Moreover, the communications security systems of the Chinese were so sophisticated and multilayered that the NSA was unable to break most of their codes and ciphers.

U-2 missions over China began in January 1962. Between September 1962 and September 1967, five U-2 aircraft, all flown by Taiwanese pilots, were shot down over the mainland by Chinese air defense fighter interceptors and surface-to-air missiles

The low-altitude P2V flights were also frequently attacked, sometimes more than once during the course of a mission. Ground searchlights would light up the sky, flak would explode all around and bullets would slam into the fuselage. At other times, a MIG-17 fighter might suddenly appear out of nowhere. Planes would take evasive action, diving underneath the ground radar, below a thousand feet (three hundred meters). But the maneuvers were not always successful. During my time at Elint, three P2V planes went down over the China mainland. One of them had thirteen men aboard. In all, fifty crew members that I knew of lost their lives.

The incident I remember most vividly involved a low-altitude flight that was knocked out of the sky by a Chinese missile. An agent had been sent in afterwards to locate the fallen aircraft, destroy onboard equipment and retrieve the tapes, which were then delivered to my center. I was assigned to analyze the tape. I sat there and listened to the pilot's commentary in halting English, as a navigator called out coordinates, marking radars as he flew toward Shandong and his death:

> Coordinates 37 degrees North, 121 East.
> Coordinate 37 degrees North. 120 East.
> Over land now.
> Coming up on Early Warning.
> Coordinate 36 degrees North, 119 East.

Then I heard the distinct high-pitched Fire Control sound, followed by an awful screech, which signaled lock-on. Next I heard the Taiwanese pilot say, "I'm sorry. Goodbye."

That was the last sound on the tape. No bang. No boom. No sounds of explosion. Just silence.

I felt nauseous. For the first time in my life I understood completely the meaning of the word courage.

Try as it might, the CIA garnered very little human intelligence from within China. It was extremely difficult to recruit and control agents on the Chinese mainland and efforts to infiltrate it with CIA or Taiwanese spies often ended with the agents being captured or killed. In 1962, for example, as I learned much, much later, 873 Chinese Nationalist commandos were sent into Communist China on raiding missions to capture prisoners and collect intelligence, but 172 of them did not make it back. Subsequent missions in 1963 suffered an 85 percent loss rate.

What was left for the CIA to do was to buttonhole refugees from mainland China who had made it into Hong Kong, then a British Crown Colony, but the reliability of the information gathered this way was suspect, to say the least. That left overflights as the primary source of intelligence, which we shared with high-ranking Japanese officials and passed on to Washington.

THIRTEEN DAYS

By far the most stressful time at the Elint Center was a two-week period in October 1962, during what became known as the Cuban Missile Crisis. We fully expected a Soviet nuclear warhead to take out our facility as part of a global conflict.

On October 14 of that year, it had been discovered by American U-2 spy planes flying over Cuba, that the Soviet Union had installed medium-range atomic missiles there, just 90 miles (145 km) from Florida. The weapons were SS-4 missiles, 72 feet (22 meters) long and carrying megaton warheads. Their presence placed large swaths of the US within range of attack. A missile launched from Cuba could reach the White House in just fifteen minutes.

On October 19, the US military was put on "high alert" and ordered to be ready to invade Cuba at a moment's notice. At Fuchu, we were all confined to base, placed on twelve-hour shifts, seven days a week, and remained on standby during off duty hours.

On October 22, US president John F. Kennedy told the nation about the discovery of the missiles. Branding Soviet premier Nikita Khrushchev an "immoral gangster," he demanded the removal of the missiles and set up a naval blockade around Cuba. He also had his generals draw up plans to bomb the Cuban missile sites should that prove to be necessary. In response, Khrushchev wrote a letter to Kennedy in which he called the blockade "an act of aggression propelling humankind into the abyss of a world nuclear-missile war."

An agonizing standoff ensued, the anxiety level moving off the charts, as we monitored Russian and Chinese movements in the Pacific region, increasingly convinced that some sort of attack was imminent. The crisis dominated the news as the world watched and waited. The people on the base, both American and Japanese, were eerily subdued as they went about their business, transistor radios (made in Japan) held to their ears to catch the latest news. The television set in the day room alternated between the English-language military broadcaster FEN TV and the Japanese-language national broadcaster NHK, where grim-faced announcers gave round-the-clock updates on the crisis. Demonstrators outside the base waved banners appealing for peace. But everyone seemed much quieter than usual.

A number of Soviet ships tried to run the blockade. US Navy ships fired warning shots at them. On October 27, after a U-2 was shot down by a Soviet missile crew in Cuba, the Pentagon raised the Strategic Air Command's Defense Condition (DEFCON) to level two, which was the second-to-last step to nuclear war. It meant that armed forces had to be ready to deploy and engage within six hours, and that US nuclear-armed B-52 bombers would be on continuous airborne alert around the world. It was the highest confirmed DEFCON level ever in the history of the United States. Historian Arthur Schlesinger Jr. would later call this showdown "the most dangerous moment in human history."

At the beginning of the standoff, the Elint Center military commander, a Navy admiral, had assembled us and we all held our breath as he explained the situation.

"This is not a drill," he said solemnly. "I cannot overstate the danger we are facing. There is a very real chance that nuclear war could break out and that we might all be blown to kingdom come." He then added, "If you have any letters to write I suggest you write them now. You might not get another chance."

What neither the Soviets nor anybody else knew at the time was that the Americans had also installed ballistic missiles of their own, similar to the ones the Russians had delivered to Cuba, in Okinawa, just south of Kyushu. There were eight Mace missiles in all, trucked in six months earlier and hidden in underground missile sites. Each missile was 43 feet (13 meters) long and weighed eight tons. Packed inside each one was a 1.1 megaton nuclear warhead that had seventy-five times the ferocity of the bomb dropped on Hiroshima. It could obliterate everything within a five-kilometer radius, create a crater twenty stories deep and irradiate the landscape for decades to come. The range was relatively short but Vladivostok was within reach and so was China. Many at the base thought it likely that the Okinawan Maces might be used to annihilate Shanghai and Beijing, prompting a retaliatory attack on the 900,000 residents of Okinawa, and perhaps the millions more living in Osaka and Tokyo. The Elint Center would of course be a priority target.

So we wrote letters home, suspending our doubts about Herodotus's encomium to the postal carriers (which did not include nuclear winter among the snow, sleet, gloom of night and other atmospheric conditions which left them undeterred). Unable to leave the base, we commiserated with each other at the Airmen's Club, scared out of our wits, and got blindingly drunk each night, trying to deal with the reality of it all

It was in that state that I turned twenty years old on October 24—an appropriate way, I thought, to celebrate the fact that under Japanese law, which the US military followed under the Status of Forces Agreement, it was now legal for me to get that way. It was hard to find anything else worth celebrating at the time.

"Whiting," said my friend, Douglas Victoria from Iowa "Happy Birthday. Let's all hope you make it to age twenty-one."

The people in my age group thought we were too young to die, until someone reminded us that the average age a soldier died in World War II was not that much older.

So we sat there scared out of our wits, slowly going blotto.

As chance would have it, unbeknownst to us, secret back-channel negotiations were taking place between Kennedy and Khrushchev, and sanity prevailed. On October 28, the two leaders reached an agreement whereby the Soviets would publicly dismantle their Cuban missiles and return them to the Soviet Union, subject to verification by the United Nations, in exchange for a US public declaration and agreement never to invade Cuba, and a secret dismantling of all US-built Jupiter medium-range ballistic missiles deployed in Turkey and Italy. A further outcome of the Kennedy–Khrushchev talks was the creation of a Washington–Moscow hotline.

With the announcement of the deal, we all started breathing again. A couple of men started going to church.

SPIES AND DRUGS

At Elint, we were constantly reminded that our enemy was Communism—Russian, Chinese, North Korean Communism—and warned that there were Communist spies in our midst. We were instructed to always be on guard.

"Loose lips sink ships," was the pet phrase of the aphoristic Navy chief who was my immediate boss. "If you're asked what you do, just say you're a radar operator. And don't get drunk in the presence of strangers—and that includes the women off-base."

The Japanese Communist Party (JCP) had been active since the first days of the Occupation. It had only fifty thousand members, but it was supported by both China and the Soviet Union, which had helped to subsidize demonstrations against the US presence in Japan.

Tens of thousands of ordinary Japanese, normally apolitical, had opposed the extension of the US–Japan Security Treaty in 1960 and marched in protest in the months of May and June of that year. But the most virulent opposition came from the ideologically committed students of the Zengakuren, the tightly disciplined Communist-led All-Student Alliance, who spearheaded violent clashes with the riot police and who, according to firsthand reports, were financially supported by the JCP. (Student protesters were said to have been paid two or three hundred yen a day plus a free bento lunch.)

On the evening of June 5, 1960, some fourteen thousand members of the Zengakuren had attacked the Diet Building compound in a futile attempt to block the passage of the extension of the revised Security Treaty, throwing stones and wooden spears at a phalanx of four thousand steel-helmeted riot police. In the melee, a twenty-two-year-old Tokyo University student was trampled to death. The protests were so violent that a planned visit by US president Dwight Eisenhower had to be canceled.

"Moscow and Peking have made it abundantly clear that the

neutralization and eventual takeover of Japan is their number one objective," said the previous US Ambassador to Japan, Douglas MacArthur II, nephew of his illustrious namesake.

In the minds of most US military officers, everybody outside the center was suspect—Japanese nationals waving political banners near the entrance, photographers on the other side of the chain-link fence taking photos of the facility through zoom-lens cameras. We were told to be vigilant at all times, to beware of the Japanese drivers who took us on intelligence exchange trips to the Yokosuka and Atsugi naval bases, the Japanese waitresses that served us in the Airman's Club, the manager of the Korean-style *yakuniku* restaurant up the road where we sometimes ate, the proprietor of the Chinese chain restaurant down the street and any patron of the bars on the strip who was not an identifiable American military or civilian worker, such as the old White Russian drunk, a longtime Fuchu resident who hung around the bars on the Han speaking to us in his broken English. They were all potentially spies.

There was also the odd shady character hanging around outside the gate, in the bars and on the strip, looking to buy weapons. It was hard to tell whether they were simply yakuza doing yakuza business or red agents with more sinister motives. Others were there to peddle drugs, some for profit, others, or so we were told, for the purpose of addicting GIs so that they would spill military secrets or, at the very least, be useless as enemy soldiers.

If there was a visible trade in weapons, however, I never saw it, although there were occasional reports of GIs from other US bases in the Tokyo area arrested for selling guns. I knew an Air Policeman who was stupid enough to sell his sidearm for a couple of hundred bucks and then claim it was stolen. He wound up in the brig. (He was almost as dumb as the Air Police guard doing an overnight at the Elint Center who was so bored he started playing with his sidearm and wound up shooting himself in the hand. The desk by the entrance was covered in blood and bits of flesh as we walked in the next morning. They sent him back to the States.)

Drugs were a little more conspicuous. Every now and then you would be approached by someone on the Han who asked if you were interested in *shabu* (meth). I never took the bait but I knew of a couple who did and were caught and cashiered back to the States and out of the military.

There were also heroin dens outside the base in Tachikawa, the drugs supplied by bar girls who got them from Chinese and North Korean agents. There was a large population of Chinese and Koreans residing in Tachikawa City that was said to be sympathetic to the Communist cause, engaging in espionage and sabotage. According to one report in the *Nippon Times*, by the end of the Korean War in July 1953, there were dozens of heroin dens and hundreds of users. GIs serving in South Korea added to the mix. They would develop the habit there, usually getting their heroin from bar girls in South Korea, and when they came to Japan on leave they would bring their drugs with them. Some of them were even dealing, selling it to the yakuza.

The military had cleaned things up some since then, but not completely. I knew a guy named Deckman, an airman in the admin department who lived in the room next to mine in the barracks. He went to one of the dens and wound up hooked. He pointed the den out to me as we walked by one day on our way from Tachikawa train station to the base. It was just a house, a nondescript, Western-style house not far from the base's main gate. He said you went in and sat down in the living room and some mama-san presented you with a menu. "Of course, this being Japan," he said, "you always get a nice hot towel and a cup of steaming green tea to go with it."

The options were the pipe, the cigarette and the needle. You licked the cigarette and dipped it in a bowl of heroin powder, then lit up. Well, he kept going back and soon he had graduated to the needle. Medics responding to an emergency call from the house found him writhing on the floor in agony. They shipped him back to the States as well. The last I heard he was living on the streets of downtown Los Angeles.

We were told to exercise particular caution in the Roppongi and Akasaka areas on our sojourns to Tokyo because, according to the Navy chief I worked for, "it was a hotbed of Communist spies." The Russian embassy was just steps away from popular gaijin haunts the Club 88 and Nicola's—the latter being the first pizza restaurant to open in Tokyo—to both of which Soviet agents were frequent visitors. We received reports of Russian agents attempting to bribe American employees of the *Stars and Stripes*, for example, for information on the activities of the US military inside American bases. One of them, an editor named Tom Scully, whom I later befriended, was wined and dined repeatedly by a Soviet agent, who offered him thousands of dollars in cash and other perks to come over to the other side. Scully enjoyed the wining and the dining, but turned down the money and reported the agent to the Japanese authorities and got him deported.

A locus of activity that aroused interest was the International Clinic across the street from Nicola's, run by White Russian doctor Eugene Aksenoff, whose parents had fled to Harbin, China during the Bolshevik Revolution. From there he had come to Tokyo in 1942 as a medical student, earning money for his tuition fees by playing captured American pilots in Japanese war propaganda films—speaking American English with a thick Russian accent—and stayed on, stateless, a man without a passport. The doctor spoke fluent Russian and the leather chairs in his waiting room were filled with patients from the nearby Russian embassy, reading Russian-language periodicals. With the Cold War at its peak, that alone was enough to attract the attention of Japanese authorities, who suspected that a Communist lurked behind every cherry tree.

The Koan-ka (Public Security Division) placed Aksenoff under constant surveillance. Undercover detectives followed him around Tokyo in taxis and unmarked cars. They dined at the same restaurants and they tapped his phones (so badly, in fact, that Aksenoff told friends that he could hear the cops talking to one another). Eventually they would gather enough evidence to make an arrest.

It was later learned that the authorities had based their suspicions in part on a report prepared by US military intelligence in 1954 that designated Aksenoff as a Communist agent, after a defecting Soviet diplomat had fingered him as such. The diplomat had been an associate of the infamous Soviet secret police chief Lavrenty Beria, who had just been executed in Moscow.

Fearful for his life, the diplomat had decided to cross over to the American side. Lacking anything substantial in the way of information to barter, he'd concocted a story that Aksenoff had been providing treatment for young GIs with venereal diseases—STDs as they are now called—who were afraid to go to the base hospital and thus run the risk of being discovered and punished by their superior officers.

In return for doing this, according to the diplomat, the GIs were giving Aksenoff US military secrets, which Aksenoff then passed on to his friends at the Russian embassy.

There was never any evidence produced that this was remotely true, and logic dictated that Aksenoff, whose family had escaped the Russian Revolution, would not be a likely Communist sympathizer. However, because of the aforementioned reports and the indisputable fact that Aksenoff's clinic was, in fact, only a city block from the Russian embassy in Azabu, Japanese police, not exactly sophisticated internationalists, reasoned constant surveillance was warranted.

As for me, the exposure to the city of Tokyo during my Elint career proved addictive and for reasons that had nothing much to do with espionage. Thus when my military term ended in March 1965, I turned down an offer to work for the NSA in Washington and enrolled in a Tokyo university instead.

CHAPTER 5

Saints

PEOPLE WHO LIVE on the edge of society are always more interesting to read about, in my opinion, than those who operate in the mainstream. We all have a dark side and are fascinated to see it come out in other people because it tells us something about ourselves. The content might be unpleasant, but such stories tell us who we are.

The characters in this book, among the millions of foreigners who have been to Japan, have had a hand in shaping the history of this country and the attitudes of Japanese toward the West, and in particular, the US, given the great presence of Americans in the country since the end of the war in the Pacific.

These characters all remind us that the field of international relations is a lot broader and more diverse than some people realize. It is more than trade conferences, international political summits, diplomatic teas and cultural exhibitions. They teach us that not every foreigner who comes to Japan comes for the purpose of studying the language, learning about the culture and contributing to society in a meaningful way.

That having been said, there are those who will no doubt complain that this book and its predecessor, *Tokyo Underworld* (Vintage, 2010), dwell too much on the negative side of the ledger and that people who led less colorful lives and thus make less interesting stories—even though they made positive contributions to cross-cultural understanding—get overlooked.

Thus, to remedy that: a peace offering. A chapter that focuses on a select group of foreign individuals who have made positive contributions to relations with Japan. In reality, of course, there are many, too many to cover in this space (just as there are too many bad guys for just one book), but, for what it's worth, here is a purely arbitrary sampling of those who have made a difference.

WOLFHOUNDS

Consider first of all the 27th Infantry Regiment, nicknamed the Wolfhounds—an organization one hears little about these days. The Wolfhounds belonged to the US Marine Corps Infantry Division sent to Japan as part of an Occupation force police unit after World War II, but wound up doing something far more important.

It started with one of their members, Hugh O'Reilly, a square-jawed marine who had fought on Guadalcanal and Iwo Jima, and who so hated the Japanese that he asked for assignment in postwar Europe, not Japan. It was a request that, fortunately for a large number of people, was ignored.

In 1949, while based in Osaka, O'Reilly found himself dragooned by Army Special Services into giving a Christmas party for a destitute orphanage run by the Catholic Daughters of Charity in Osaka. He went to a drafty, crumbling wood-frame house that had once been a barracks for the Imperial Japanese Army, and was so moved by what he saw—forty war-orphaned children living there, with only one small hibachi brazier for heating and only rice gruel to eat—that he went back to his unit at the Wolfhound post and took up a collection for them from his fellow soldiers.

Soon, other units in the Wolfhound regiment began chipping in and donations continued even after the Korean War had started and contributing soldiers were dispatched to the Busan perimeter. A *New York Times* reporter picked up the story and soon the Wolfhound-sponsored orphanage became big news in the United States—so big, in fact, that a Hollywood studio turned the tale of O'Reilly and the Wolfhound regiment into a movie called *Three Stripes in the Sun.*

O'Reilly romanced and married a Japanese woman and then fathered six children. He retired from the military in 1962 and settled down to run a language school in Osaka, acting as a consultant to a Japanese firm that shipped engines to the US. The contributions kept rolling in from the Wolfhounds, who had their base of operations moved to Hawaii and, for a time, Vietnam). Over time the cold drafty barracks that housed the orphanage was transmogrified into a sturdy two-story dormitory and clinic complex. At its peak 120 children, including 38 infants, lived in the building.

Moreover, every Christmas without fail, Wolfhound soldiers would show up from headquarters. One would play Santa Claus and pass out presents. In May each year, two children would be chosen to fly to Hawaii to be guests of the regiment.

As Japan's economy grew and the populace accumulated wealth, the Japanese government and Japanese business gradually took over the financial support of the orphanage, but the gifts and contributions from Hawaii still kept rolling in.

There were other such stories of good deeds by US military personnel: the sailors in Sasebo in Kyushu, who, every year, would take children from a nearby orphanage to the base galley for a huge Christmas party; the marine who jumped into a river, risking his life to save a one-year-old child in Okinawa in 2001. But such acts seldom made the Japanese press.

THE DOCTOR

Other philanthropists include Eugene Aksenoff, mentioned in Chapter 4, who compiled a record of human kindness that was unmatched: in his fifty years as a doctor in Tokyo's international community, he never turned down a patient who couldn't pay.

Aksenoff was born in Harbin in Manchuria to Russian aristocrat parents who had been forced to flee there in the wake of the Russian Revolution. He came to Japan, by himself, in 1943. He studied the Japanese language at Waseda International Institute and was the first Caucasian ever to enter the Jikei University School of Medicine in Tokyo, and got his medical license soon after the end of the war.

He earned his tuition fees by playing foreign spies in Japanese films. Invited by the Japanese authorities to join the party greeting General Douglas MacArthur at Atsugi Airbase to begin the Occupation, he joined a hospital that was run by the US Army, and was assigned to treat Japanese war criminals at Sugamo prison, for whom he also served as an interpreter. "During the war, I was never treated badly in Japan," he once told an interviewer. "And since I was so well treated, it was natural to want to help people charged with war crimes. Mind you, this caused some people to distrust me."

Married to a Japanese woman who was a former medical technician, he treated an average of eighty patients a day until his International Clinic closed in 2014 upon his death.

Aksenoff has no nationality.

"I didn't obtain Japanese citizenship," he said, "because I wanted to tell the world about the good things Japan offers and such praise carries more conviction when spoken by a foreigner. And perhaps you'll agree that an international clinic is best run by a doctor who has no nationality . . . I'm prouder of the fact that I've never turned away someone who couldn't pay my fee than I am of anything else."

THE NETSUKE COLLECTOR

Ray Bushell, who prided himself on being the first American lawyer to hang out his shingle in Japan, was one of some seventy foreign lawyers given special permission to practice there by GHQ, with approval from the Japanese bar. Bushell had a lifelong love affair with Japan during which time he made himself one of the world's foremost experts on Japan's treasured art form of netsuke and became one its greatest benefactors.

Bushell's admiration for Japan was born as a result of his early post-Occupation experiences as a lawyer, when he had ample opportunity to observe local courts in action. He came to believe the Japanese legal system was more merciful than the American one. He saw numerous examples of people who had committed crimes and were genuinely sorry about it, given lenient sentences or often mandated to do nothing more than write an apology.

He liked to tell the story of a case he witnessed in 1953, when three young GIs had gotten drunk, run out of money and stolen some cash from a cab driver, roughing him up in the process. In those days, drunkenness could be a mitigating factor in some cases. According to Article 39 of the Criminal Code, an act of a person of unsound mind was not punishable—and drunkenness was considered being of unsound mind. Partly because there were so many instances of drunk driving in those days of limited traffic (it was possible to drag race down Sanno-dori street in central Tokyo at night), the judges used to apply this article in court very liberally.

In this particular case, the GIs pleaded not guilty due to their unfortunate state of inebriation. The judge proceeded to ask the first soldier, "How many beers did you drink?" The youth said, "Five large bottles." The judge asked the second soldier and he replied, "Four bottles," And then he asked the third who answered, "Three." The judge decided to test them in court.

Adjourning for the day, the judge ordered the court officers to bring in a case of Kirin beer. At the next session, each GI would be ordered to drink the amount that he had told the judge he had consumed on the night the assault of the taxi driver occurred. Then they would be questioned. By the time the soldiers had worked their way through the nicely chilled brew put before them, the judge decided they were indeed not responsible for their actions, invoking Article 39 and its application to drunkenness. As a result, he gave them each a suspended sentence of eighteen months and the three GIs walked out of court as free men.

It was shortly after arriving in Japan, very early in the Occupation, that Bushell became an avid fan and collector of netsuke, the ornately carved ivory figurines that date back to the seventeenth century. Transferred to Kobe, where he was given charge of all the docks in the area, Bushell met a long-time local resident named Fred Jones, a half-Japanese, half-British man, who worked with the business firm of Nicholas and Lyon, which had been tasked with the job of unloading the Liberty supply ships docked in Kobe. Jones' father had come to Japan as a tea merchant at the turn of the century, married a Japanese girl and started a family. Jones showed Bushell a book about netsuke along with some figurines he had collected, and from then on Bushell was hooked. Jones helped Bushell buy a few pieces and Bushell was off and running.

Over the span of his forty years in Japan, Bushell put together a collection of the small sculptures that would grow to be one of the most formidable in the world, valued at several million dollars, with some pieces worth over $200,000. (The record for a netsuke at the time of writing is $1,066,000—sold in Paris on June 15, 2023.) Bushell sold many pieces through auction houses and art dealers but he also donated the bulk of his collection of several hundred pieces to one of the best art museums in the world, the Pavilion of Japanese Art in Los Angeles, on the condition that the collection would be kept on permanent display and that the pieces would be no closer than six inches (15 cm) apart from each other.

By the time of his death in 1997, Bushell was recognized as the world's foremost authority around the world on netsuke, about which he wrote eight books. His basic book is *The Netsuke Handbook of Ueda Reikichi* (Tuttle, 1989); others include *The Wonderful World of Netsuke* (Tuttle, 1970); *Collectors' Netsuke* (Weatherhill 1971); *Netsuke Masks* (Weatherhill, 1995); and *Netsuke, Familiar and Unfamiliar* (Weatherhill, 1999). He also coauthored a book called *The Art of Netsuke Carving* (Kodansha International, 1981) by Masatoshi as told to Ray Bushell, which was the only book written by a craftsman, in other words, a man who is not a collector.

Bushell was also noted for being a defender of the Japanese way. During the height of trade friction between the US and Japan in the late eighties and early nineties, he was one of the few Westerners who took the Japanese side in the dispute. He argued that, to his mind, the Japanese were *more* democratic than the Americans, the very people who were supposed to have introduced the concept.

"People say America is a democracy," he was quoted as saying in one interview, "but in reality it's not. In business, if the word from the boss comes down, everyone has to obey. The American boss is an autocrat. He thinks he has to show profit in the next quarter or he's screwed. The Japanese, by contrast, start from the bottom up.

They get a consensus . . . in business, at least. They think in the long term. So in my view, Japanese are more democratic."

"It's we who should learn from them," he said in 1995, shortly before his death, summing up his long, long life in Japan.

FRANCES BAKER

Another leading patron of the Japanese arts, was Frances Baker, a University of Washington graduate in painting, sculpture and design. She came to Japan in 1936 as the wife of an American missionary, and left half a century later, as the wife of a prominent American lawyer, having forged a trail of goodwill activities in between.

Frances's first marriage was over in six months (a huge mistake, she liked to call it—a hot-blooded girl married to a cold blooded man with the only good thing about it being it brought her to Japan). Upon her divorce, she moved into a one-room Tokyo apartment, and, to support herself, taught English (to groups of students from Keio and Waseda Universities). She also painted murals in Ginza coffee shops, bars and nightclubs, where the sight of a young red-haired Caucasian girl was enough to attract a full house at anytime of day or night. Japan was in the middle of a military buildup—its government shouting insults across the Pacific to Americans who had been complaining about Japan's advances into Manchuria—but still the Japanese people were intensely curious about foreigners because there were so few of them in their midst. At the time Frances was one of five hundred English-speaking foreigners in the city. She was such a big attraction that one coffee shop advertised her painting on the walls of the Ginza Line subway stations!

Frances became friends with the family of Dr. Muramatsu, an internationally renowned Harvard-trained psychiatrist and with his daughter Hideko, a well-known actress. She also became friends with the daughter of a politically prominent family, who took her on guided tours of Formosa and Manchuria, chauffeured around in a Buick wearing furs, like some Hollywood film star of the era.

In 1941, when the US placed an embargo on all shipments to Japan, and war became inevitable, Frances left for Hawaii, where, as chance would have it, she would be an eyewitness to one of history's most famous attacks. She was working in her backyard garden on a Sunday morning in December that year when Zero fighter planes flew overhead and she marveled to her Japanese gardener "how realistic the Army Air Force training was."

During the war, she put her artistry and knowledge of Japan to work on behalf of the US government, which, in her opinion, had little understanding of the psychology of the Japanese. For example, nearing the end of the war, the US was urging the populace to surrender in air-dropped leaflets depicting scenes of destruction, fire and brimstone, with messages of surrender or die.

To the Japan-knowledgeable artist Miss Baker, however, employing a different type of psychology, for example, showing a woman holding her kimono-clad daughter with the message, "It's always sad to see young men die because of the many things they have left undone . . . Don't throw away your lives. You can't prevail against our vast equipment and endless supplies and resources."

She believed that the leaflets were more effective if they cited US numerical superiority while paying tribute to Japanese fighting spirit, which, in her opinion, was the "best in the world." Thus, another of her leaflets depicted a Japanese samurai warrior on horseback brandishing a sword against American planes and technology.

Her leaflets also frequently portrayed America and Japanese civilians and soldiers as mutual victims of the same thing—the Japanese military establishment, the Gunbatsu.

"Come over to us," read one of the leaflets, "and then when peace comes, soon you will do all the things which are in your heart. You will be reborn, and with that rebirth will come great happiness and contentment. The world is vast and good. You are too young to die now."

Honorable life over honorable death.

When the war ended, Frances returned to Tokyo to work in the US Occupation for the State Department. She resided at the Dai-ichi Hotel (built in Shimbashi in 1940 for the Tokyo Olympics that was then postponed), one of the few buildings left standing amidst the rubble of the city.

She found her Japanese coworkers so hungry for food that she would steal extra pieces of toast and bacon from the Dai Ichi breakfast buffet, wrap them up and give them to her staff, who, she discovered, sometimes hadn't eaten for days. She would also find ways to get sewing needles, soap and other valued commodities to them.

As Director of Fine Arts in the Occupation and post-Occupation State Department, Frances was called upon to do the decorative paraphernalia for the 1952 San Francisco peace conference, held at the San Francisco Opera House, at the conclusion of which, Emperor Hirohito pulled her aside and thanked her profusely.

Among other things, she did exhibits for the Japanese public on aspects of democracy, including one on women's rights (the idea being such a new concept in Japan that it took a whole exhibit to explain) and a famous exhibition which occupied all of Hibiya Park, extolling the peaceful uses of nuclear energy—which featured exhibits using radioactivity to hatch chickens, among others. It was, improbably, an enormous success, touring nationwide and seen by a third of the Japanese public, among them Emperor Hirohito, rapidly becoming one of Frances Baker's fans. It repaired some of the damage caused by the infamous Lucky Dragon incident of 1954, when captain and crew of a Japanese fishing boat were irradiated by spray from a US nuclear test blast in the Marshall Islands, with several eventually dying from related diseases. (One of the fishermen was especially unfortunate: he'd been living in Nagasaki when the atomic bomb was dropped. He committed suicide a few years later).

The diplomatic fallout from the Lucky Dragon Incident was particularly bad because the US government had, not uncharacteristically, failed to come clean at first about its responsibility, refusing to acknowledge that the crew's health problems had been connected to the Marshall Islands test blast.

Although many Americans, within the government and without, had had mixed feelings about the atomic bomb—most thought Hiroshima had been necessary to end the war, fewer bought the argument that Nagasaki was necessary to scare the Russians from invading Japan from the north—the Lucky Dragon incident was a clear case of US guilt and officials in the State Department had obsessed about repairing the US–Japan breach. As a result, they were extremely grateful to Frances Baker for her exhibit. It is one of the reasons why Japan wound up using nuclear energy.

One day in the early 1950s, weary of life in the tiny rooms of the Dai-ichi Hotel, she decided to buy some land on a hill in Ichigaya and build a house there, land being extremely cheap in Tokyo at the time. She consulted an American lawyer, Thomas Blakemore, who had only recently opened up his own practice in Kyobashi.

"Why do you want to spend your good American dollars on a piece of devastated rubble like that?" he asked, incredulously.

Frances ignored Blakemore, bought the land and built the house. Then she started dating the lawyer and wound up marrying him. The two ultimately moved into Frances' new home. Eventually she and her husband built a luxury apartment complex on the site called Pine Manor, with seven Western-style units furnished throughout with General Electric equipment and a swimming pool, which, of course, grew in value to tens of millions of dollars.

Then, with Frances Bushell, wife of the lawyer Raymond Bushell mentioned earlier, and another American woman, she opened up the Franell Art Gallery in the new wing of the Hotel Okura, which made them the only foreigners to operate a business in the whole posh arcade. She spent much of her time, energy and money promoting young Japanese artists, including potter Shoji Hamada, whom, it is said, Frances did a great deal to make famous.

She also authored many books on Japanese art, including *Who's Who In Modern Japanese Prints* (Tuttle, 1975) and *Japanese Design Through Textile Patterns* (Tuttle, 1978), and put together a collection of Japanese textiles, stencils and costumes that was shown in the Los Angeles County Museum of Arts, the Cleveland Museum and other places.

In 1989, she and her husband were forced to move to the United States for medical reasons. They gave away luxury units in their housing complex to their longtime maid, chauffeurs and cook, before selling the rest to set up a scholarship for American students who wanted to study about Japan.

It was just the last of many in a long list of acts of kindness.

THOMAS BLAKEMORE

However, it was Frances' husband, Thomas, who got the coveted Kinshi Kunsho Order of the Golden Kite award—given for bravery or leadership in battle—from Emperor Hirohito, not Frances or Ray Bushell, both of whom had wished for an imperial decoration. But then that was because Tom Blakemore's contributions were really something special, starting with his work in the GHQ—which he always described as an effort to prevent the Americans from destroying what he viewed as the core of a perfectly good system.

Blakemore was a tall, rangy, soft-spoken graduate of the University of Oklahoma, who had originally came to Japan in 1939 to study law at the Imperial University in Tokyo with a fellowship from the US Institute of Current World Affairs (after a stint in Berlin studying law in Nazi Germany). At Teidai, as the Imperial University was called, he was known for his superhuman effort to soak up everything he could about Japanese language and culture. There wasn't a dish he wouldn't try, a place he wouldn't visit, an experience he didn't want to have. He would walk around with kanji flash cards in his hand, constantly memorizing new kanji characters. (He also became famous in one Ginza department store for the time he walked in attempting to ask for *kenuki* (a pair of tweezers), but mistakenly used the term *hekoki* (fart).

By 1941, as war was about to break out, he had come to know Japan and the Japanese quite well and had concluded that the image in the Western press of the Japanese as mindless, obedient robots who were tools of the military was all wrong. Etched in his memory was one lecture he had attended given by a Teidai law professor, in which the professor implicitly criticized the Japanese government by describing the adoption policy of Frederick the Great as a transparent tool to get more men for his army. Even though it was expressly forbidden to say anything bad about the Japanese government or military, the message was crystal clear, because the militarists who were in control of Japan at the time needed more cannon fodder and were encouraging people to build large families. The class buzzed in astonishment at such defiance.

Blakemore was finally forced to leave Japan in November 1941, returning to the US via Shanghai. He spent most of the war years in Washington, D.C., working for the newly formed Office of Strategic Services (OSS). As one of the few people in the US government who could read Japanese, he spent days and nights at the Library of Congress, poring over the Horei Zensho, the Statutes at Large for Japan, for the radio call letters and other vital statistics of all Japanese military naval and aircraft, to create an order of battle for all Japanese ships that was more complete than the order of battle of any military department. Its thoroughness so impressed the US Congress that it ordered an increase in funding for the fledgling OSS, an organization which went on to become the CIA after the war.

When the war ended Blakemore returned to Japan where he worked for a time with the State Department and then with the Legal Reform Section of the GHQ which was then endeavoring to write a new Japanese constitution. It was there that he came to the conclusion that the Occupation was more or less a waste of time.

It started with the Tokyo War Crimes Tribunal. Hailed beforehand by Americans as a hearing on the guilt of Japanese generals and political leaders that would be fair and impartial, its outcome appeared to be a foregone conclusion.

Although Blakemore's colleagues were sometimes accomplishing some things he agreed with (like granting women's rights), in general, he found the Americans he worked with arrogant, heavy-handed, possessed of an overweening sense of their own moral superiority and with little respect for Japan, the Japanese or the culture.

He liked to tell the story of the time he took three GI acquaintances on a trip to a village outside Tokyo. During the ride, his traveling companions had referred to the Japanese derogatorily as being "just like children."

"They have to be led toward democracy," one of them had said.

When they had arrived at their destination, his friends began playing with the village kids, spinning tops, doing other things, while off to the side, Blakemore, the only one present who could understand Japanese, smiled sardonically as he listened to village elders viewing the scene, talking among themselves about how the Americans were "just like children." To Blakemore, that was symptomatic of the vast gulf that existed between the two sides.

He also liked to tell the story of the internal GHQ survey conducted to judge Japanese attitudes toward Americans in which the main question cited was "What does the date December 7 mean to you?"—a reference to the day in which the attack on Pearl Harbor took place. When the survey showed the respondents replied overwhelmingly that the date meant "nothing at all"—often scratching their heads in the process—the Americans concluded that this represented a major shift away from the old anti-American pro-nationalist wartime thinking among Japanese people. It never occurred to the polltakers that because of the international dateline which divided Japan and the United States that the attack actually occurred on December 8 in Japanese time.

Blakemore, himself, was perhaps the only American on the scene who had read Japan's law books in Japanese and to whom was thus left the task of liaising with Japanese legal scholars on the GHQ's proposed changes to the legal system. He described himself as "a man with one-eyed vision in the land of the blind."

The Civil Code Section of the GHQ, where Blakemore was assigned, was given the task of devising a new civil code which would, among other things, grant equal rights for women and eliminate the *ie* system in which the male head of the family had the power to make all decisions regarding marriage, divorce and adoption. But there was also almost daily commentary among Blakemore's colleagues in the Civil Code Section about other things the United States wanted to change vis-à-vis Japan.

One reason for such discussion was the essential difference between the US and Japanese legal systems. The US approach was based on precedent—or past rulings by judges—while the Japanese modus operandi was codified, meaning it was composed of a pattern of laws designed to cover everything in the legal universe. Many on the US side wanted Japan to become more Americanized in this regard. As Blakemore liked to put it, "They viewed Japan with the apprehension they would view a rattlesnake."

To Blakemore's great amazement, lawyers in his section who could barely handle chopsticks were busy rewriting the Civil Code, employing in its stead laws from backward, rural states like Arkansas and Texas.

"They were just bloodsuckers," said Blakemore. "The country already had the core of a very good system dating back to the 1880s and they were legislating it back to the Stone Age. They were throwing the baby out with the bath water."

Blakemore tried to promote some sort of continuity by pushing for reform within the prevailing legal system. As a conduit between the Occupation and those reforming law on the Japanese side, he met daily with high-ranking prosecutors and a committee of constitutional scholars. They would have dinner and work over different drafts of the criminal code. Blakemore quietly tried to put the brakes on the overzealous reformers and keep the heart of what he believed to be a basically sound system.

He worked with the Japanese in getting their opinions on the new constitution brewing in the corridors of the GHQ. They would propose new legislation and Blakemore would look at it and either filter it to MacArthur, or if he thought it had no chance of getting anywhere, delay and defer it.

"The Japanese realized that there were areas where their law had to change," he said, "and that's what we tried to focus on." For his sympathies and sentiments toward the Japanese (and open criticism of the 8th Army officers who committed unnecessary acts of insensitivity, like arrogantly appropriating Emperor Hirohito's prized white horse and riding it in a military parade), he earned the title "Jap lover"—something which Blakemore accepted cheerfully.

"Sure, I like the Japanese," he would say. "Aside from some of the militarists, they are pretty nice people, in general."

Blakemore was suspicious of Americans who claimed that the Japanese loved MacArthur. When MacArthur announced his intention to run for president, a sign appeared outside the US embassy in Tokyo, where MacArthur resided, with the words "We Play For General MacArthur's Erection"—an embarrassing, even insulting misspelling—which Blakemore believed was no mere confusing of the letters "l" and "r" as Japanese tend to. Then, after thousands of people had lined the street to say goodbye to Macarthur, a group of citizens tried to raise money for a statue of him. But they were never able to gather enough funds to start the project. Perhaps it had something to do with MacArthur's Senate testimony in which he referred to the Japanese as a nation of twelve-year-olds. But it was clear to Blakemore what the message was—in both cases.

Despite the difficulties, Blakemore did make certain significant contributions to the Japanese legal system, which are still in existence today. One was in the area of jail confinement for arrested suspects who had yet to be indicted. In prewar times, the procurator (to use the term in vogue at the time) in Japan was an extremely powerful person who had sole authority to determine periods of pre-indictment confinement for arrested suspects. Such power was thought, by Japanese authorities, to be important since they believed that the best way to get a subject to talk was to confine him alone for extended periods of time, to interrogate him and make him sweat. To Americans, however, unlimited confinement without an indictment was a violation of an individual's basic civil rights.

Now, Blakemore did have the highest respect for the Japanese procurators and he was one of the few Occupationaires who felt that way). He saw them not as scheming fanatics, obsessed with power (as some of his colleagues did), but as devoted, diligent and capable. They were the smartest people in the land, the cream of the crop, people who were exceptionally good at what they did. He was also deeply impressed with their esprit de corps, their discipline and their sense of propriety. Unlike in the US, if a procurator was seen having coffee with a defense lawyer, even if the lawyer was an old classmate, the procurator would be reprimanded.

But he sided with the Americans on the particular issue of unlimited confinement without an indictment. No matter how effective such a system was in getting, say, a pair of criminal suspects to contradict each other's story, Blakemore could also see the potential for excess and he understood the US demand for change in the Japanese way of doing things. So he worked to help introduce modifications in the old system—which he sincerely believed would benefit the Japanese people as well as placate those Americans who wanted the procurator's unbridled authority trimmed.

And as a result, a new MO was implemented that relied not on a procurator, but on a judge as a decisive figure, whereby the procurator would be forced to go to court to get a judge's OK to detain a suspect. Thus, it became the job of the procurator in the postwar era to work up a case and have a judge take a look at it. The procurators did not particularly like this change, nor did they like the new rules which reduced the amount of time a suspect could be kept in jail (to twenty-three days), before an indictment had to be handed down. But the new system stuck and is still in place today.

Another change made primarily at the urging of Blakemore was the formation of a citizens' watchdog group to analyze and pass judgments on the actions of the prosecutors. Initially, some individuals in the GHQ had demanded the establishment of a grand jury to replace the procurator in passing down indictments, thereby copying a Western tradition born in England. However, in Japan, the idea of such a radical reduction in the role of the procurator was too extreme for most Japanese people, given the high level of pride and status long associated with that position.

As a compromise, an Inquest of Prosecution was set up in which there would be a Citizens' Committee: a group of citizens assembled periodically to look at what the procurator did and didn't do. They had the power to question the procurator, to call witnesses and issue findings. The Citizens' Committee could undo what a procurator did although they did not have the power to indict. But, the committee's finding would be publicized, which in Japan, was censure enough and it would serve as a guide for the future.

At first, the procurators fought the idea of an inquest into their work tooth and nail, viewing it as a serious impingement of their authority. But later, in the end, they came to realize it was a good thing because it gave them a forum to argue why they did what they did and to defend their decisions. The code was enacted on July 10, 1948, and was enforced from June 1, 1949.

And everyone primarily had Thomas Blakemore to thank.

Blakemore left the GHQ in 1949. He took the Tokyo Imperial University Law School graduation test, entirely in Japanese, and passed

it, making him the only American—indeed, the only Westerner—
ever to accomplish such a feat (It was an achievement that would
not be matched for nearly another half-century). Then he opened
up a law office in Kyobashi, essentially a desk in a burned-out hutch
in a makeshift building which he shared with a foreign newspaper
correspondent, and hung out his shingle to practice law.

There were two classes of foreign lawyer at the time in Japan,
Class A and Class B. Class A attorneys were just like Japanese lawyers, which meant they could be retained by a Japanese client and
argue in court before a judge. Class B lawyers could be retained by
home-country nationals if the dispute was covered by Japanese law,
but a Class B lawyer was not really licensed to practice in Japan. He
served as a kind of "Rump Bar."

Tom Blakemore was the only foreign lawyer in Japan in the
Class A category. All other foreign lawyers were Class B.

But Blakemore was reluctant to argue in a Japanese court.
"There are too many things an American lawyer can do, unconsciously, to irritate a Japanese judge," he said. "I would never inflict
myself on a client that way."

Instead, he used his talents to help top US foreign businesses
navigate entering the Japanese market in matters involving negotiations, buying and selling, registration, land purchases, tax reports
and personnel problems. He taught American executives about the
importance of gift-giving and creating human bonds with Japanese business contacts, the type of relationships which, back home
Stateside are a very low priority—the quality of a product being
the top priority.

As he put it, "I helped alleviate any anxiety they may have felt
over any legal 'Pearl Harbors' happening to them in Japan."

An early boost to his career came when John D. Rockefeller II
walked into Blakemore's unheated office one day, introduced himself and said, "Young man, I am a philanthropist and I want to make
an endowment to an international goodwill organization in Japan.
Can you help me?"

"Who are you working with in Japan?" asked Blakemore.

"Count Kabayama. Matsumoto Shigeharu," Rockefeller replied,

naming two men that were as distinguished as you could get in Japanese society. The former was a highly respected businessman who had served in the House of Peers and the latter a top journalist and one time head of the Domei Tsushin, the official news agency of the Empire of Japan.

"Mr. Rockefeller," Blakemore replied, "you don't need a lawyer like me if you're working with people like that."

John D. Rockefeller II thanked Blakemore, excused himself and walked out, ending one of the shortest legal consultations in history.

After that the word spread, somehow, that Blakemore was such a good and successful lawyer that he was too busy even to take on someone as wealthy and important as a Rockefeller, which only made the demand for his services grow and eventually ensure that Blakemore would become one of the wealthiest people in Japan.

Throughout his long career, Blakemore was nothing if not civic minded. He was one of the founding members of the International House of Japan (along with John D. Rockefeller II). He was active in the Japan–America Society. He translated the Criminal Code of Japan into English and he reported on Japanese Law and Japanese legal firms for the Oklahoma Bar Association Quarterly.

He was an avid outdoorsman and a member of the Hunters Association of Japan, once killing a bear in southwest Hokkaido that had terrorized villagers in the area and mauled at least one local forester to death. He introduced species of Japanese wildlife to Western museum collectors and was honored in return by the Museum of Natural History in New York with the title "Field Collector." He also introduced a breed of dog to the Japanese: the Vislad—a Hungarian Labrador Retriever. One of his Vislads, a dog he donated to a village in Ibaragi Prefecture, proved to be so dedicated and efficient in tracking down wild boar that the animal was honored by the prefectural government.

His other accomplishments included popularizing fly-fishing in Japan, setting up an outdoor fly-fishing park along the Yozawa River, and establishing an experimental farm in the town of Itsukaiichi outside Tokyo where students from Tokyo University came to work as interns, and where friends of Blakemore, like explorer

Naomi Uemura could be seen heaving rocks, digging holes and otherwise helping out. On Blakemore's departure from Japan (he had to move to Seattle in 1989 to be treated for a serious illness), he turned the farm over to an organization called the Seikatsu Club, a voluntary organization set up by women with the aim of reforming their lives and local communities.

He used proceeds from the sale of property and other assets to set up a scholarship foundation for students of Japan, one of whom was a young lawyer named Mark Brazeal, now a San Francisco based attorney, who did legal work for the Hiroshima Carp in their suit against the baseball agent Don Nomura.

Blakemore, who received awards from the Prime Minister's Office and Emperor Hirohito, perhaps made one of his most important contributions to Japanese society when he did the legal work that enabled Tokyo Disneyland to be built and opened in 1983—and which went on to become a national institution in Japan.

At the peak of the economic bubble when the term "Japan bashing" came into being in North America, and people all over the world were attacking Japan for perceived collusive business practices and closed markets, Blakemore became one of the few Americans to stand up and defend Japan. For example, during the height of the trade friction between the US and Japan, when Japan was running a $50 billion annual trade surplus with the US, he told a reporter, "It's not a question of the Japanese being unfair, at all. The problem is Americans who are just not really hip to what it takes to sell in Japan. Americans, Westerners in general, will always say the Japanese market is closed if they can't make a deal to sell their product. But sometimes their product just doesn't suit the market— like autos with the steering wheel on the wrong side. The reality of business in Japan is simply that Japanese companies and the Japanese government would rather deal with their Japanese friends and acquaintances. It is a fact of life which has nothing to do with the quality of a given product. You can't pass a law and force them to deal with you, even if your product is superior . . . and the construction industry is one good example in that regard." (Note: At the time, the construction industry accounted for a fifth of the GNP in

Japan and had deep ties to the long-ruling Liberal Democratic Party and the Japanese underworld).

When critics accused Japan of taking over the world, Blakemore is quoted as saying that "the Japanese system helped save the world from economic collapse. The Ministry of Finance kept their stock prices high in the late 1980s, providing capital to invest in the US market and buy T-Bonds which are the pillar of US wealth."

Such perorations kept a lot of US–Japan joint ventures together.

Perhaps Blakemore's best contribution to Japan, to be somewhat corny about it, was pure, unadulterated love. A few years before he died, he gave a long series of interviews to a reporter (me) about his affection for his adopted country, the Q&A sessions taking place in his apartment high on a hill in Seattle, overlooking Puget Sound.

Excerpts follow:

"People called me a 'Jap lover' and I was. I listened to the Japanese side and issues—before, during and after the Occupation. It was my character and also my legal background. I was able to accept Japan and see both sides. I was sympathetic . . . Why did I stay in Japan? Infatuation, sympatico feeling toward the language and culture."

"Some people complained about discrimination, but it was never a problem to me. If a cab didn't pick me up, I just shrugged. I didn't curse at it and yell racism . . . I never had that love–hate relationship with the country that some people did . . . If, say, Japanese businessmen took a long time to commit to a decision, say, or the Japanese wanted to change the terms of a contract after it was already signed—two things that usually bothered American businessmen, it didn't bother me, because as a lawyer I was always open to peaceful solutions to a problem. I tried to negotiate. Consensual arrangements are always better than unilateral action . . . Filing a lawsuit as some people back in the States might, was usually the wrong thing to do in Japan."

"I liked the Japanese because I found them generally to be more courteous. If, for example, a man had to be fired or replaced, I liked the way the Japanese did it. They found another spot for him or tried to smooth the way with a generous separation package.

Generally speaking, they didn't embarrass the guy or put his head on the chopping block. They showed sensitivity to the guy's feelings. They didn't just kick him out like Americans usually did."

"They had class even when the long knives were out. Americans were frank, but they were also too loud, too belligerent and too aggressive. The Japanese way was just more pleasant."

"If I had a complaint about them, it would be that they were so polite that it was a little inconvenient at times. It was hard to tell what the other guy was thinking because they never showed their anger. It was hard to get to know them because they always kept their feelings to themselves. A lot of Americans thought Japanese were tricky and devious because of this, but that's just the way the Japanese were. They didn't open up, cry on your shoulder and tell you their life story. They were just more reserved—unless they had a lot to drink, that is."

"At times, depending on place or circumstance, the Japanese gave the appearance of being arrogant or being racist, but that was because they didn't know how to behave politely in front of foreigners in certain situations. In Japan, superiors can behave in an arrogant manner to subordinates. That's a cultural, historical behavior pattern. The Japanese accept it, but foreigners don't like it. They think it's undemocratic. But that's just the way it is here."

"The more that Americans understand that, the fewer problems they are likely to have. Of course, the Americans have to understand that as gaijin, they are always *suketto*, [lit., 'helper'] like the gaijin ballplayers were, no matter how well they spoke the language or understood the customs. In Japan you were always a gaijin and you just had to understand that. Period."

"But then, I was top dog at my own law firm. I wasn't anybody's suketto."

"It takes a lot of living to make a house a home . . . But we . . . America and Japan are getting closer. The US has become more savvy these days about the way things are done in Japan. And Japan is starting to see the cards on the table. The big gulf doesn't quite exist anymore."

Amen.

CHAPTER 6

Con Artists

TO MANY WESTERNERS, Japan, with its justifiable reputation for personal honesty, is a paradise. It is a place where, generally speaking, purses seldom get snatched and late-night pedestrians can walk through any part of town, sober or drunk, unmolested by muggers. Leave an item like a scarf, a wallet or a passport in a cab, chances are that the taxi driver might very well return it in person the very next day (such practices attributed to Japan's lost goods law and moral education traditions in the school system). If not, it would most certainly have been turned into a police-controlled lost and found.

In contrast to some urban areas in the USA, where crime is almost a way of life, big city Japanese are so trusting that at some restaurants, the staff will ask diners what they had eaten as they arrive at the cash register to pay and the diners tell the truth and pay the correct amount. It is an honor system wherein walking out on the bill, as some dishonest Americans might do, is just unthinkable. You can leave your laptop on your table at any Starbucks in Japan to visit the rest room and be assured it will still be there when you return. Some even leave their wallets on the table to hold their seats while they wait in line to buy their coffee.

Japanese journalist, Hiroshi Kubo, author of a book entitled *Sagishi no subete* [All about scam artists], published by Bungei Shunju, 1999) once explained this by saying, "It's a special characteristic of the Japanese to not be suspicious of people. One can say that it is part of Japanese culture, dating all the way back to the fourth century when royal court scholar Shotoku Taishi produced a constitution for the nation which emphasized the importance of harmony and the necessity to resolve all matters through peaceful discussion. If you have *wa* (harmony) as the basis for your society, then trusting others is imperative [. . .] Europeans and Americans are naturally distrustful of each other and this is a fundamental difference between the two cultures, because Japanese are not. [It] is part of Japan's beautiful, traditional culture."

Organized crime figures in Japan have long taken advantage of the trusting nature of their fellow Japanese. Scam artists have tricked the unsuspecting elderly out of their bank accounts, posing as long-lost relatives in need of help or as government officials demanding payment for some imagined offense. Many unscrupulous visitors from abroad have been delighted at discovering this aspect of Japanese life. To them, the trusting soul of the average Japanese, combined with a certain naivete and gullibility some Japanese display in dealing with non-Asian foreigners makes Japan a foreign scam artist's dream.

Of all the things that Americans bequeathed to Japan that fall into the rubric of gullibility, perhaps language schools are among the worst. Such institutions proliferated greatly after the war in response to the Japanese desire to learn English. There, for the longest time, hiding behind cleanly pressed shirts, one could find a motley assortment of drifters, subliterate high school dropouts from English-speaking countries and other impostors occupying teaching positions. The logic behind this sorry state of affairs was simple. At the end of the Occupation, the Japanese realized they increasingly needed English to interact with the rest of the world. The native English speakers they saw were mostly Caucasian. Thus, many Japanese believed that a teacher had to be white to be any good. A Japanese-American with a PHD from Stanford arriving in the country and looking for work as an English language instructor might find it difficult to get one precisely because he would *look* to the Japanese as though he *couldn't* speak English. On the other hand, a blond-haired, white-skinned thickly accented traveler from a non-English speaking land like Germany or Russia, could.

In the 1950s, when Japan was a wilder, less regulated place, fake jewel salesmen and bogus insurance agents were also much in evidence. However, many of them headed off to Saigon when the Vietnam war started. In their wake, a different, more sophisticated type of operator appeared on the scene, attracted by a Japanese economy that was expanding so fast it almost seemed to grow before one's eyes, like bamboo sprouting in the spring.

Among the new sophisticates was an American named Donald Zubriskie, a visiting New Yorker who introduced himself to trusting Japanese as a Harvard professor and set a record for passing bad checks during his stay in Japan. He bought millions of yen worth of goods—cameras, tape recorders, jewelry—using counterfeit travelers checks and a fake passport for identification. In one astonishing stretch of twenty-three days in May 1967, he committed twenty-four separate acts of fraud (including six in one day), beginning in Tokyo and ending up in Kobe, where he was finally nabbed by Japanese police—but only because they had been tipped off by the FBI.

Even more daring was an inventive American businessman named Howard Baron, who managed to get himself appointed to the fairly important post of general manager of the Tokyo American Club, that exclusive preserve of well-to-do American executives, diplomats and their families. Upon assuming his post, he casually eliminated the club's watchdog committee and other committees in what he termed a cost-cutting, restructuring move. Then he quietly and clandestinely set about trying to sell the land upon which the club stood to a Japanese consortium. Baron's plot was discovered and he absconded to Hong Kong where he began working with the US military crime organization known as the Khaki Mafia and where, shortly after his arrival, for reasons unknown, he was shot dead while sitting at his desk.

A special point of entry for foreign schemers was Tachikawa Air Base. Up until the end of the Vietnam war, it was one of the largest US military bases in the world, housing thousands of soldiers and civilian employees with their families, as well as assorted clubs, movie theaters, bowling alleys, BXs and whatnot. It was like a small city, until it was returned to the Japanese in 1977, after the American withdrawal from Saigon. The area around the main gate was alive with American salesmen flown in from the States to ply their wares to vast market of unsuspecting military personnel with spending money in their pockets ("shearing the sheep," as some of them liked to put it). There were peddlers of gold, silver, stocks, mutual funds, plots of land, automobiles, US golf club memberships and a hundred other commodities for which the American soldier or civilian worker might be willing to part with their pay check.

One real estate company made a fortune selling plots of land no sane person would want to buy to unwitting customers—properties bordering a rural alligator-infested Florida lake, or in the middle of a Hawaiian jungle lava bed, or on the side of a mountain in Arizona accessible only by parachute. Tachikawa was sort of a testing ground for the would be con artist. Try the thing out on the Americans, smooth out the wrinkles, test the local waters, then move on to the Japanese population in general where the real money lay.

Among those who found Tachikawa Air Base and its nearby cousin Yokota Air Base fertile ground were representatives of the global mutual fund Investors Overseas Services (IOS), which had amassed $2 billion by the end of the 1960s to became one of the world's most important international financial institutions (making its founder and CEO Bernie Cornfeld a multimillionaire who enjoyed a lavish lifestyle befitting that of a Saudi sheik).

The IOS men opened up a Tokyo headquarters in 1962. Starting with the US military bases, they then fanned out across the country, selling shares in the IOS fund as well as sales staff positions to Japanese and Americans alike. Their bible was a best-selling book authored by Cornfeld, entitled *Do You Sincerely Want To Be Rich?* (Viking Adult, 1971).

However, it turned out to be a massive pyramid scheme in which tens of thousands of investors around the globe were jilted out of their money, proving that where people like Cornfeld were concerned, gullibility knew no borders. Many Tokyo-based IOS investors went broke, unable to redeem or cash in their investments, while a number of IOS employees lost their salaries and commissions. More than one Tokyo-based IOS sales representative would be visited by well-muscled organized crime figures, hired by angry clients who wanted their money back. The finance ministry eventually closed down the operation. By the early 1970s the IOS empire would crumble and Cornfeld would spend a year in a Swiss prison. However he kept enough of his fortune to wind up living a lavish lifestyle in Beverly Hills, hobnobbing with film stars like Liz Taylor, Warren Beatty and Richard Harris.

MR. T.

One of the more audacious operators in the gaijin pantheon of con artists, if little known at the time, was a former US Air Force captain who shall be called "Mr. T." in this narrative, for legal reasons. Mr. T. had been based at the Tachikawa Air Base, when, in the early 1970s, after twenty years of duty, he was given a discharge from the service. Infatuated with Japan, its women and its friendly, gullible citizenry, he decided to hang around and seek his fortune.

A tall, gray-haired man in his early forties whose angular features and distinguished looks reminded people of a fox, Mr. T. had considerable talent for smooth talk and so he quite naturally gravitated towards the sales industry. He teamed up with a partner, a mechanic, in a venture to sell Japanese autos (Toyota, Nissan, Mazda) originally manufactured in Japan for export to the United States but rejected for minor flaws such as a malfunctioning window or a loose steering wheel. The partner fixed the cars as best as possible, Mr. T. sold them to Americans in the US military as brand new, and the two partners made a tidy profit. If a soldier complained about the quality of the car, Mr. T. would brush him off with a wave of the hand.

"This car was made in Japan," Mr. T. would say. "What did you expect? If you want a Lincoln or a Ford, you'll have to wait until you get back to the United States."

Needless to say, it was still an era, albeit one which was nearing an end, when most Americans still thought American-made cars were the best in the world and naive GIs were unaware of the high quality of Japan's rapidly growing auto industry.

The venture went so well that the pair opened a civilian taxi service on Guam, purchasing a fleet of used taxis from the US military base in the island's capital Hagåtña (formerly Agana). The partner stayed behind in Tachikawa, while Mr. T. moved to Guam to run the operation. It proved to be a mistake on the partner's part. Mr. T. used the taxi fleet to borrow money from the Chase Manhattan Bank on Andersen Air Force Base, located on the island. Then he sold the taxis, took all the money from the cab sale and the bank loan and returned to the US, leaving his partner and the bank high and dry.

No one heard from him for several years until one day, long after his ex-partner had departed the scene, Mr. T. suddenly appeared in a Japanese television commercial, wearing a white smock and looking very doctorish. It was an advertisement for a new health clinic which "Dr. T." had opened up near Roppongi Crossing called The Diet and Quit Smoking School.

Visitors to the clinic were greeted by a staff of several very serious-looking Japanese male and female nurses, all "specially trained," according to the clinic brochure, to help patients kick the cigarette habit and lose weight at the same time. There were several partitions, each one containing a scale, measuring equipment and other important-looking paraphernalia, while in the back, accessible only with special permission granted at the receptionist's desk after a thorough interrogation was Dr. T's office. In this windowless enclosure, behind a locked door, sat Mr. T., the room usually filled with a thick, blue haze from cigarette smoke.

Prior to his advance on the Japanese market, the good doctor had attended a special six-month course at an "institute" in Texas. On completion, he was awarded a diploma, prominently displayed on a wall in the lobby of his clinic, which, according to the large print, authorized him as qualified to instruct people on how to diet and quit smoking at the same time. Shortly after graduation from the Texas institute, he had put an advertisement in the *Japan Times* newspaper, and as luck would have it, he was able to find two

Japanese investors (and one Czech) to help finance the establishment of his Roppongi clinic.

On the basis of a few conversations, these investors had paid his airfare (first class) across the Pacific. They set him up in a fashionable and very expensive Western-style apartment in Tokyo. They paid him a handsome salary, giving him a big advance, as well as a loan of three million yen to buy furniture and decorate his new residence. On top of that, they had allowed him to invest in the venture, making him a full partner with access to the company books and bank accounts. They also gave him a full investment credit until he could arrange for his stateside funds to be transferred to Japan.

Their generosity was a tribute to Dr. T's ability to bamboozle total strangers, and simultaneously, a monument to their stupidity. It hadn't taken much to persuade them that this great new breakthrough discovery in the US, combined with the sheer force of his magnetic American personality, would make them rich. Amazingly, in the months they had done business together, Dr. T. had not paid them even one single yen of the money he owed them. He had promised to pay just as soon as he could manage to redeem his money, which, unfortunately, was all tied up in stocks and bonds in the US. It would take a little time, he said, if only they would be just a little more patient.

And then, one day, soon after the business had taken off, Dr. T. vanished with all the company's funds and that was the end of that.

Dr. T's unsuspecting Japanese partners were not unlike many other Japanese businessmen—status-conscious businessmen, one might add—who, for years, during that era, viewed Americans in a special light, giving them the benefit of the doubt, simply because America was such a superpower and Japan, through growing rapidly, still lagged behind, relatively speaking. Government leaders often referred to their country as the "little brother" of the United States.

As for Dr. T., it took more several years, but one day in the early 1990s, he resurfaced again in the unlikeliest of places—a new English school that had just opened in Tokyo's Yoyogi district called the East–West School. The school, which had a good reputation, specialized in teaching English and Japanese to foreigners from various Asian countries—Pakistan, Bangladesh, China and the Philippines. The brochure for the multistoried school boasted it had nearly four thousand students.

The era of the immigrant worker, legal or otherwise, was just beginning, thanks to the expanding economic bubble in Japan and the reluctance of so many young economically well-off Japanese to do manual labor, which they found dirty, demeaning and uncool. There were so many migrants looking for such work, in fact, that a market had sprung up for this kind of school, providing "students" with visas that allowed them to live in Japan.

Ensconced in a top floor office, dressed in a double breasted Giorgio Armani Italian suit and sporting a shiny gold chain around his neck, was Dr. T.

Only now he was "Professor T."

Or more accurately, "Dean T.,"because that was his official position, according to the sign on the door and the desk plaque. Mr. T., now in his sixties, completely gray and hands shaking from Parkinson's, had answered an ad in the *Japan Times* and had somehow talked his way into becoming the head man of one of the new language schools in Japan. The fact that he had barely passed high school English and spoke in a broad Texas accent many Japanese found indecipherable ("Whatamaset?" he would say when asking the time) apparently did not matter.

Secretaries scurried about bowing obsequiously to *Kocho-sensei* (School Principal), as they called him in Japanese, treating him as if he were a Harvard Regent and not a scam artist who belonged in jail—which is where he eventually wound up.

After a span of several months service as headmaster, Dean T. was arrested for bringing Pakistanis into Japan to go to his school, then farming them out, for a substantial fee to factories that needed workers. It was, of course, illegal to work on a student visa and by brokering jobs for his students, Dean T. was therefore breaking the law. So were the factory owners by hiring them, and, of course, so were the students themselves by accepting the jobs.

Dean T. was charged with several crimes, including tax evasion. There was a court trial at the end of which "Dean T." became

"Inmate T." at Fuchu Prison. After serving over a year, Mr. T. was released and deported, thereby putting an end to one of the most colorful careers in the history of US–Japan relations.

CHEAP MEAT

The postwar history of Japan's relationship with the *furyo gaijin* (delinquent foreigners), as some Japanese like to term them, was rife with colorful episodes, but none were quite as strange as that involving an Australian liquor salesman named Eric Drew. Drew specialized in fake ID cards and other activities that eventually landed him in a Tokyo jail and on the front page of the country's leading daily newspaper the *Asahi Shimbun*.

Drew's own particular specialty arose out of the fact that he did not like Japanese food very much. He much preferred beef instead. Since Japanese beef was too expensive for his budget, however, and he had no military privileges to allow him to shop at BX butcher shops, he decided to manufacture a false US military identification or ID card to gain access to such places. He went to a Japanese printer, had the ID design copied and a card made up, identifying himself as a civilian employee of the American government. It worked like a charm, so well, in fact, that he had five hundred more of the cards printed up and distributed them to all his friends. Among them were his Chinese tailor, a West German import-exporter, a Russian salesman, a Greek businessman, an American teacher, fellow salesmen at the Yokota branch of the IOS where Drew also worked temporarily, as well as assorted Japanese acquaintances, including a professor from a university in Tokyo. All of these friends of Drew were living in Tokyo, and all of them began to experience the joys of shopping on Army Post Exchanges where the goods were of fairly high quality and the prices dirt cheap, thanks to military discounts. Since there were already several thousand civilian workers of various nationalities on US government payrolls in Japan, all with their own IDs, no one noticed the addition of five hundred new card holders.

Profits in hand, culinary demands met, Drew shifted his attention to a new kind of business: buying and repairing old military transport and patrol aircraft and parts no longer needed by the US military in Japan and then selling them around the world through his Tokyo contacts. The idea was the brainchild of a certain member of the US Air Force on the Yokota Air Base. He picked Drew as his middle man and Drew would sell the merchandise to wealthy patrons and flying clubs in Japan, Hawaii, Hong Kong, Taipei and Athens, hiring pilots to make personal delivery.

Making such sales was not illegal under either US or Japanese law, but considering the Cold War that was raging at the time between the United States and the Soviet Union and the fact that Japan and Australia were American allies, Drew set new standards for chutzpah when he sold aircraft to his Russian friends and endeavored, unsuccessfully, to persuade the Soviet government to give him a salaried job as a procurer. Some of the planes, according to reports, made it all the way to China, another US Cold-War enemy.

The audacious operation proceeded smoothly for some time. Indeed Drew might have continued forever. But then one of Drew's colleagues, an impoverished German trader named Gottlieb fell ill, and things began to unravel, in a highly improbable, almost slapstick, fashion. Gottlieb, struggling to make ends meet and subsisting primarily on gifts of Army Post Exchange beef from his friends, was suffering gall bladder problems. Gottlieb's neighbor was an American actor whom we will call by the pseudonym Eric Money to protect his identity. Money was appearing in a nightly drama on NHK, Japan's national TV network, introduced Gottlieb to Eugene Aksenoff, the White Russian doctor running the International Clinic in Roppongi, just up the street from the Russian embassy.

Aksenoff was known as a man of integrity and honor, a physician who would never turn away a patient merely because he or she was unable to pay for his services, and an individual who was would even dig into his own pocket with a loan for people down on their luck. Learning how financially strapped Gottlieb was and that he had a wife and family to care for, Aksenoff, as was his wont, invited the man for lunch and slipped him a few ten-thousand-yen bills (ten thousand yen was then about thirty US dollars) to tide him over temporarily until his situation improved.

"Here," he said. "Take this and buy some things for your kids."

And that was when the plot began to thicken.

With the Cold War reaching its full-blown peak, the Koan-ka (Public Security Division), had come to believe that Aksenoff was a spy given his proximity to the Russian embassy. On this particular day, the ever vigilant police witnessed the good doctor handing Gottlieb money and, suspecting some kind of intelligence payoff, immediately began investigating Gottlieb's background.

They discovered that Gottlieb, like Aksenoff, had also been born in Manchuria, in the city of Harbin, where his German father was in the beer and movie theater business. They learned that Gottlieb was fluent in Chinese, Russian, German and English, that during the war he had been a materials procurer (in one instance, he stripped Shanghai houses of their corrugated steel roofs in order to get metal for the Japanese government), and after the war he had worked briefly for US intelligence. Then they found out about the fake IDs and the airplane parts business. They put all these suspicious facts together and determined that they had uncovered a communist spy ring, a ring that was infiltrating US bases with false papers, and that Gottlieb was a double agent.

In October, 1976, the authorities arrested Gottlieb, the American actor Eric Money and a thoroughly surprised Drew, an event that made the front page of Japan's leading daily, the *Asahi Shimbun,* replete with mugshots and headlines announcing a Japan-based spy ring was supplying military secrets from US bases to the Russians. In the body of the article was a cryptic reference to a "fifty-one-year-old White Russian, Mr. A." It was strategically displayed next to the newest revelation about the huge Lockheed sales bribery scandal that had taken Japan by storm—an affair in which the US-based aircraft manufacturer was found to have bribed Japanese government officials and airline executives in order to get sales contracts—and thereby raising, yet again, suspicions in the minds of many readers of that august publication about how untrustworthy the gaijin in their midst were (suspicions that were no doubt increased by subsequent reports that Gottlieb had been traveling around Tokyo on a fake train pass).

The police subjected their prisoners to intensive interrogation, in an effort to get at Aksenoff whom they were certain was their ringleader. They also made their captives look at photos of every member of the Tokyo American club and the Foreign Correspondents Club of Japan, demanding they identify "which ones were communists." A search of Drew's office revealed several hundred US military ID cards.

After reading the newspapers about the Big Bust, Aksenoff paid a visit to the police and told them they were making a huge mistake. He certainly wasn't the ringleader of any spy group. The police were unwilling to admit error, but fortunately, one of Aksenoff's patients just happened to be the ex-prime minister and behind-the-scenes LDP wirepuller Kakuei Tanaka, still running his party despite his indictment for bribes in the Lockheed case. Aksenoff made a call to the powerful politician's residence in Mejiro, Tokyo to plead his case, whereupon Tanaka placed a call to the Chief of Police and suggested that perhaps his investigators were overreacting.

The Koan-ka (Public Security Division) backed off Aksenoff, albeit temporarily, and when, after five days of intense questioning, they proved unable to produce any evidence linking the other members of the Communist spy circle, they were reluctantly forced to release the three arrestees.

In the wake of the great airplane-parts, ID-card, cheap-meat scandal, Gottlieb remained penniless. He retuned to Germany in 1980, again with the help of Dr. Aksenoff, who, sympathetic to Gottlieb's plight, paid his airfare—an act which further convinced the police that Aksenoff had been "running" Gottlieb. Eric Money's career as a thespian took a temporary forced hiatus, but Drew, the man who had started it all with his fictitious military IDs simply because he did not want to eat his vegetables, was not charged with anything either. Despite the fake IDs, there was no Japanese security law Drew had violated, nor were there sufficient records to prove he had *used* the IDs to enter the base illegally or make illicit purchases. Moreover, as an Australian, the US government had no jurisdiction over him, and so the gaijin carnivore blithely continued with his aircraft sales. He made a fortune and left Japan a wealthy man.

The Drew affair prompted yet another of Japan's frequent bouts of moralizing about the evil influence of *gaijin* on the public at large. NHK, ever conscious of its image and the adverse publicity that the scandal might have on its squeaky-clean image as the country's national broadcasting corporation, announced it would never hire the American actor again (albeit quietly hiring him back a year later).

Yet, for all the talk of spies and the considerable newspaper and magazine print expended on the "Drew Gang," as one writer called it, the affair all boiled down in the end to a case of false representation, one of 1,300,000 crimes that were committed in Japan that year and one that drew a disproportionate share of media attention primarily because its participants were *furyo gaijin*. In the end, all it really proved was how desperate the Koan-ka was to uncover a communist spy ring or even a solitary spy.

The Japanese police kept up their campaign against Aksenoff, and arrested him again, in 1980, this time on charges that he had installed a radio transmitter in Kawasaki near a new clinic he had set up for visiting sailors. The authorities had received an unconfirmed report from an unidentified witness that Aksenoff had been seen burying equipment at the site and when they unearthed it, they found that part of the device was marked with what looked like a Russian Cyrillic "4." That was the clincher and the detectives came to Aksenoff's residence, hooked him up with handcuffs, tied a rope around his body, as per police custom, and led him off to jail, where they kept him for several days. He was released only when an embarrassed Toshiba engineer came forth, after reading about the matter in the newspaper, and explained that the transmitter was an experimental device which belonged to his company and the symbol that had so impressed the police as evidence of Russian espionage was in fact a symbol Toshiba used for digital equipment. Whoever identified Aksenoff as being at the scene, Aksenoff later surmised, was probably a business rival unhappy that the new Kawasaki clinic was taking away patients.

Said Aksenoff summing up the whole experience when it was

all over, "In both cases, the police knew there was nothing there. They had to create fear that there were Russians in the country to keep anti-communist feeling high. They needed a Russian spy and I was it."

As chance would have it, in the process of pursuing Aksenoff, the police had totally missed the activities of a Major in the Soviet Union secret police, the KGB, who had been stationed in Tokyo under the guise of a Soviet journalist, until he defected to the United States in 1979. His name was Stanislav Levchenko. He became one of the few known KGB agents ever to defect to the US. Levchenko was instrumental in detailing the KGB's Japanese spy network to the US government, including Congressional testimony he delivered in the early 1980s.

Levchenko told a House of Representatives panel that in addition to acquiring intelligence on Japan, the KGB's mission there was to create distrust between the Japanese and Americans in order to weaken US influence. He testified that he was in charge of ten Japanese agents, four of whom he said he recruited himself. They included journalists, an editor, members of parliament and a high-ranking official of the Japanese Socialist Party.

Levchenko gained information by posing as a writer who was collecting data for a confidential bulletin circulated only among high-ranking Politburo members. His interviewees—mostly influential Japanese—were charmed and flattered to be approached and were usually happy to cooperate. But the bulletin never existed.

CIA deputy director John McMahon said, at the time, the information he provided "was so damaging to the Soviet cause that it would be inconceivable that he might be under Soviet KGB control."

He left a wife and son in Tokyo, who were forbidden to join him. They were forced to return to Moscow where they lived in disgrace. Once in the United States, Levchenko adapted to American fast food and movies and even did a cross-country tour in a Chevy Monte Carlo with fellow defector Viktor Belenko, the MiG pilot who flew from Vladivostok to Hokkaido in his bid for freedom.

Levchenko accomplished his defection by going to the US-run

Sanno Hotel in Akasaka in central Tokyo, one evening where he corralled a US Navy captain and asked him for help in obtaining political asylum in the US. A few hours later it was granted.

In 1981 a Soviet court sentenced him to death in absentia.

With the fall of the Berlin Wall in 1989, the Soviet Union ceased to exist and along with it Soviet (if not Russian) espionage.

THE FINANCIER, THE COUNTESS AND THE LOBBYIST

Japan's economy moved like a high-speed bullet train through the 1970s and 1980s, the yen zooming in value from 360 to the US dollar in 1973 to 120 by 1987. New buildings and businesses opened up every day. The amounts of money being thrown around by Japanese business and government officials in an effort to win overseas markets was amazing. So were the types of people from abroad who showed up to try to get their hands on that lucre at the source.

Donald Louis Mages, who claimed to hail from "high US financial circles," was one of the many interesting characters. Mages was a tall, stocky, balding man in his fifties who spoke very good Japanese, which he had learned, he said, during his days working in intelligence in postwar Japan. Mages returned in the mid-1980s attracted to Japan's bubble era wealth and "looking for investments." He told people that he was the trustee of an American consortium of financial investors who controlled a whopping $150 million worth of funds. Funds, he said, he had full authority to invest anywhere he deemed fit.

Mages used his trust as a prop to make leveraged buyouts of businesses sorely in need of money and to perpetrate other scams. For example, Mages persuaded the executives of a real estate company in Hokkaido, to part with ¥60 million, in an investment scheme involving a 21,500 square foot (2,000 square meter) gold mine in Nevada and a French bank in Los Angeles. The Hokkaido firm would invest US$2 million worth of shares in the Nevada gold mine to serve as a guarantee for a huge loan from the French bank for the mine's development. The gold would be excavated and everyone would share in the profits.

Another of Mages' scams involved a very expensive, Persian restaurant in the Roppongi–Akasaka area, which was also debt laden. He proposed contributing ¥30 million in exchange for which he would receive 25 percent ownership in the company, with the owner, an Iranian businessman, signing a document saying that if he didn't repay the loan, then Mages group would have the right to take over the whole restaurant. The owner, desperate for fresh capital, said yes. The papers were drawn up and signed but after two weeks the money had not arrived.

Growing suspicious, the owner checked the Texas address of the company on Mages' name card; it was located in a small city in that huge state. He called a state governmental bureau in the city of Austin and was told there were no records certifying the company in question. Next, they called Dun and Bradstreet, who replied, "There is no record of Mr. Mages name or his company."

The owner went to Mages office to confront him.

"We checked," he said. "You have no credibility. You're trying some kind of fraud."

"We still have a contract," Mages replied.

"It's worthless," the owner replied.

"Get the hell out of here," Mages replied, getting up out of his office chair. "I'll be instituting legal action and I'll see you in court about this."

No one was quite sure what scam it was that Mages was trying to pull. Perhaps it was a plot to sell his shares in the restaurant to other investors, without actually paying for them? That was a scam that was not unknown in New York business circles and a quick way to make a cool buck illegally.

In the end, for whatever reason, Mages was unable to obtain control of the restaurant. Perhaps it was because the restaurant's owner's next move was to go to the yakuza loan sharks to get his money—not one, but *two* different loan sharks who lent him cash.

It was an incredibly stupid thing to do because it set in motion a battle between yakuza gangs for control of the restaurant that culminated in a bloody brawl involving guns, knives and samurai swords, one beginning in front of the main entrance and causing great property destruction and the eventual bankruptcy of the place.

It was shortly after that, in March 1986, that Mages was arrested for fraud. Tokyoites picked up their copies of the morning edition of the *Asahi Shimbun* to read that Mages had been charged with perpetrating a massive swindle: the aforementioned imaginative, if fraudulent, investment scheme involving a gold mine in Nevada.

THE JOURNALIST

Another entertaining individual was Genevieve de Vilmorin Giscard d'Estaing, a bubbly, petite, self-described "journalist" in her early fifties, who arrived in Tokyo in 1983. She introduced herself around town as a writer working on a book, a sister-in-law to former French president Valery Giscard d'Estaing and a "confidante" of aristocracy around the globe. With such credentials, she soon became a fixture at embassy parties around town.

Genevieve had checked into the posh Hotel Okura, at the time regarded as the best hotel in the city. One night, shortly after her arrival, she filed a robbery report, claiming that nearly ¥9 million in cash had been stolen from her room, along with ¥850,000 in travelers checks and the manuscript of the book that she had been working on for two years. She also reported that there was some "jewelry" missing.

The Okura management, worrying about the hotel's reputation, obligingly reimbursed her for her stolen checks and let her stay free from the date of the robbery onward, which was June 6. But then the Tokyo Metropolitan Police began an investigation of the crime. Through Interpol, they discovered that she had an extensive file of unresolved charges, including unpaid hotel bills, unpaid loans and bad checks. They also obtained a statement from ex-president Giscard d'Estaing that she was not related to him. (As it turned out, she had been married to the ex-president's cousin in 1964 for two months, but in the opinion of the d'Estaing family was using the name fraudulently.)

On July 1, Genevieve was deported although she doubtless left in somewhat better financial shape than when she had arrived, thanks to the Okura's naive generosity. Her exploits were described in great detail some years later in a lengthy article in *Tokyo Journal* magazine.

THE LOBBYIST

Perhaps the most ambitious and certainly the most famous of the gaijin operators was a Washington lobbyist named Craig Spence, a man who demonstrated an uncanny ability to worm his way into lofty government levels in both Japan and the United States on little more than hot air and audaciousness, even as he ultimately went down in flames in a male prostitution scandal that damaged political careers on both sides of the Pacific.

A pale, slender, fast-talking Bostonian with a degree from Boston University in broadcasting, Spence had been fired from a promising career as an ABC correspondent in Vietnam because of his off-duty activities in Saigon's black market. (He had been caught cashing his paycheck at an illegal Saigon sidewalk currency stall.) He eventually made his way to Tokyo, that great haven for foreign opportunists, in 1973, where he worked as an ABC radio news stringer and taught English until he wangled a better-paying job at a government organization called JETRO—Japan External Trade Research Organization—conducting seminars for Japanese salarymen headed for the US in which he lectured them on American customs and business practices. Soon after that, he began writing reports and "diplomatic assessments," based on open sources, for JETRO's Overseas Research Division, anointing himself with the imaginative title of "research journalist," for which he was paid handsomely.

Spence was a shameless self-promoter ("I've always been a first class person in a second class world," was a favorite expression). He used his contacts with former ABC colleagues like journalist Ted Koppel to impress Japanese clients whom he often invited to parties at his house in the Kudanshita area of Tokyo. He also began describing himself, very self-importantly, to Japanese authorities as a "major intellectual force" in the American intelligence community, dropping hints of special ties to the CIA and often referring to associates as "operatives" and "friends."

Openly gay, with a taste for Edwardian suits, red-lined capes and silver-tipped canes, Spence cut a striking figure at the Foreign Correspondents Club of Japan where he also managed to make himself a major annoyance by lecturing members in the Club Bar in his haughty Back Bay accent on everything from the importance of color coordinating socks and ties to what questions to ask at press conferences.

The gregarious Spence made many friends in a lot of different places. One of them was Motoo Shiina, LDP Diet member, son of a one-time deputy-prime minister of Japan and president of something called the Political Study Group (PSG), a Tokyo-based non-profit organization, funded by politicians, whose goal was to bring Japanese businessmen together with influential Americans and promote commerce.

Japanese were not (and still are not), very good at networking. In Japan, what mattered was where one went to school. Outwardly shy and reserved around strangers, especially foreigners, they lacked the easy manners and unabashed spontaneity of Americans in social situations.

At the same time, however, many Japanese needed, if not in substance then at least the appearance of, having American connections. Japan was a status conscious society. The US was a world leader in many areas, which was why it was not unusual to hear people in positions of importance boasting of their friends in high places—in Washington, D.C., in New York, in Hollywood—be they real or imagined. It was one of the ways Japanese had to impress each other.

Spence persuaded the PSG that if they really wanted the attention and respect of American business and political leaders, then they needed representation in the United States. He further persuaded them that the best way to do that was to hire him as their US-based representative. Thus, it was, in 1979, that Spence moved to Washington, D.C., to become the PSG's man in the capital. There he began holding seminars and receptions inviting well-known Washingtonians like Senator John Glenn, Senator Richard Stove, Richard Holbrooke (then Assistant Secretary of State for

Asia Affairs), and renowned political commentator Eric Sevareid to come and speak (for a fee) and to hang around afterwards to meet the Japanese dignitaries Spence always had present.

Registered as a foreign agent, Spence was paid a not-insubstantial monthly retainer of over ten thousand dollars by Shiina's group. He also persuaded Shiina to buy a deluxe Washington house for use by the PSG, explaining the need for a place where the group's activities could be conducted in a sophisticated fashion and in a manner that would reflect an appearance of success and well-being. Spence, of course, said it would be necessary for him to live there, as well.

Once ensconced in the United States, Spence took the same approach he had taken in Japan, only in reverse, using his contacts with the Japanese as a way to impress Americans. Since Japan was in the process of becoming a superpower, Americans who had connections there had become a hot and valued commodity. He convinced his Washington friends that his influence in Japan spread far and wide and deep that it was actually he, Craig Spence, who had been responsible, among other things, for the decision made by the Japanese government to allow the Palestine Liberation Organization to open an office in Tokyo. (He also boasted of a friendship with Prime Minister Yasuhiro Nakasone and would later claim that he was the one who had personally talked Nakasone into giving US President Ronald Reagan the gift of a saddle in lieu of the more traditional gift of a set of golf clubs.) It was a remarkable feat of political ju-jitsu and it ensured a steady flow of important people to the dinner parties Spence held at his expensive new residence.

Spence's efforts earned him a laudatory profile in the *New York Times* in 1982 (in which he listed as his friends such luminaries as ex-president Richard Nixon, ex-Attorney General John Mitchell, and the actor Peter Ustinov). *New York Times* reporter Paul Gailey compared Spence, improbably, to Jay Gatsby: "What most impresses, if not benefits his clients, is his ability to master the social and political chemistry of this city, to make and use important connections and to bring together policy makers, power brokers and opinion shapers at parties and seminars." It was all the more extraordinary given that no one knew anything about Spence's background—not where he was born, not who his parents were, where he grew up. Not even Spence's closest friends could tell you that information. It was one of the best-kept secrets in the world.

However, it was Motoo Shiina who suddenly found himself unable to share the *Times'* enthusiasm. In 1983, he wrote to Spence that the PSG had become a "personal burden" and he had found that "in Japan, having a representative in a foreign capital is not considered as commendable, but rather as dubious behavior." Then he filed a lawsuit against Spence in a D.C. federal court in an effort to force the sale of the house Spence had bought using Shiina's money.

What he was really worried about, no doubt, were the risqué private parties Spence was widely known to give. That became evident in a subsequent *Washington Post* interview with Shiina's Tokyo attorney Chikahiko Soda, who said that Shiina had taken the court action in part because he had concluded that Spence was carrying out "his own individual business," from the house.

As Shiina said later in court papers, "I was advised that staying at the house while Spence was there could be damaging to my reputation and I therefore did not use the house again." There was no further elaboration, but the true meaning was not hard to miss.

Although homosexuality is tolerated in Japan, and certainly not subjected to the condemnation by religious groups that has been seen in other countries, it is not the most popular after-dinner topic of conversation. Politicians who are suspected of supporting a gay lifestyle are not looked upon kindly by the electorate.

Spence responded by countersuing Shiina and an out-of-court settlement was reached. According to a *Washington Times* report, Spence told friends that he had "won the suit" by "blackmailing" Shiina through a threat to expose supposed irregularities in Shiina's transfer of Japanese cash to Spence to buy the D.C. house, which Spence thought potentially embarrassing to Shiina because of Japanese currency restrictions in place at the time. (Shiina denied through his attorney that he had been blackmailed and that there was any problem in connection with the cash payment—which, in any event, was already on public court files.)

Spence also fell into disfavor with a number of Washington

journalists whom he had hired to write reports on American officials. When they found out their work was not for "a Japanese publication" as Spence had promised, but for Spence's Japanese clients
instead, they broke off their relationship with Spence.

Although such activities prompted one acquaintance to say "I
seldom knew of a man who had more enemies," the irrepressible
Spence was able to maintain contact with some of the Japanese officials whose friendship he had cultivated. He did some work for
JETRO's New York office and other Japan-related industries. He
also did research for Becton-Dickinson & Co., a New Jersey–based
health-care company with a plant in Japan. He continued to brag
to anyone who would listen about his close relationship with Nakasone, while simultaneously trying to cultivate new ties with the
Chinese government.

He boasted to friends in private that he was a CIA agent who,
acting on behalf of the agency, regularly bugged government and
foreign officials appearing at his house. The friends remained skeptical, even as he surrounded himself with a phalanx of bodyguards
and lackeys who had code names like "Hawk" and "Thunderbolt,"
while dropping hints that they were all CIA related somehow, too.

It was during the 1980s that Spence embarked on a bold new
effort to increase his influence by engaging the services of male
prostitutes and escorts for certain Reagan and Bush administration
insiders as well as Japanese business interests he represented.

By the time the decade was out, rumors were circulating that
there was a list of two hundred prominent Washingtonians who
had used Spence's callboy service, including a White House officer
in charge of filling all the top civil service positions in the federal
prosecutor's offices and the chief of staff for Secretary of Labor Elizabeth Dole. So wired had Spence become to the movers and shakers
in Washington that he had even conducted late night tours of the
White House for his Japanese friends and their gigolo companions
while President Reagan slept upstairs. It all gave new meaning to
the term "Japanese-American relations."

In July 1989, D.C. police raided the male prostitution service
Spence was using and found thousands of dollars' worth of credit

card receipts with Spence's signature on them. (In one month, it was discovered, Spence had spent more than twenty thousand dollars on the service.) Soon, the wire services were humming with stories about the DC callboy rings with *underage* youths, late-night White House frolics and the acrimonious influence of Japanese and their lobbyists like Craig Spence who had infiltrated the nation's capital.

Given the trade tensions that had been rising between the US and Japan at the time and fears that Japan was "buying up" America, after high-profile purchases of Rockefeller Center and Columbia Pictures, Spence was suddenly a pariah. Moreover, headlines like "Homosexual Prostitution Probe Ensnares officials of Bush, Reagan," in the *Washington Times* of June 28, 1989 and the *Mainichi Daily News* headline, "Washington Lobbyist Used Callboys To Help Japan," in July 1989, did not help the future of certain aspiring politicians in Washington and Tokyo, especially those connected to the PSG (and no doubt Shiina, who ultimately proved unable to follow in the footsteps of his father). Spence's name even popped up in the 1989 elections in Japan with one conservative candidate circulating a pamphlet that attacked a rival candidate for having associated with the notorious American.

Since evidence of hidden microphones, two-way mirrors and video cameras were discovered in the Virginia mansion that Spence had acquired, successive reports speculated that Spence's callboys were part of a CIA sexual blackmail operation.

The *Washington Times* reported that when asked who had given him the "keys to the White House," Mr. Spence had hinted the tours were arranged by "top level persons," including a former National Security Advisor to Vice-President Bush and later US Ambassador to South Korea, named Donald Gregg—charges that Mr. Gregg heatedly denied.

Later reports indicated that Spence had merely bribed a White House guard for access and that the supposed bugging equipment had nothing to do with US intelligence activities. Most people believed that Spence had simply invented the CIA connection to make himself look important.

Some people, like Murray Sayle, the respected Japan-based

Australian reporter who had known Spence since his Saigon days, and admired him for his intelligence, thought he had a death wish, or at least a strong self-destructive urge, given the lack of elementary prudence he displayed that was astonishing for a grown man in the news business. Exhibit A was that fact Spence had lost his very good job in Saigon by foolishly cashing an easily traceable ABC payroll check with his name and address on it in a Saigon black market shop. Most people playing the black market in Vietnam during that era limited their transactions to cash and other non-traceable exchanges. He also had held bawdy parties at his Virginia house when surely he must have known he was being watched by his Tokyo sponsor and moreover he had used his credit card to pay for a male prostitution service when more cautious people might have used cash. "It seemed he had unconsciously created the conditions for his downfall," said Sayle. "For after his arrest, he had nowhere to go but down."

After his police bust, Spence disappeared for several weeks. He did not surface until early November, when he was arrested again, this time in New York City, for carrying a loaded weapon and crack cocaine. He was in the company of a twenty-two-year-old male prostitute whom Spence had picked up on 42nd Street. Facing a federal investigation for the callboy scandal, as well as the drugs and weapons offense in Manhattan, and said to have contracted AIDS to boot, Spence opted to commit suicide. On November 12, 1992, he was found dead in a room in Boston's exclusive Ritz-Carlton, an empty bottle of sleeping pills on the bedstand. He died in predictable Spence fashion, wearing a black tuxedo, a white bow tie and suspenders, while listening to Mozart on headphones. Scrawled on the mirror was the following notice:

Chief, consider this my resignation, effective immediately. As you always said: you can't ask others to make a sacrifice if you are not ready to do the same.

It was a last final attempt to keep with the persona Craig Spence had tried to craft for himself, and to continue conning the rest of the world, even in death. In the end, there never was any evidence uncovered that he was a CIA agent.

Sayle wrote Spence's obituary in the Foreign Correspondents Club of Japan newspaper, the *No. 1 Shimbun*. In the opening paragraph he recalled the terms that had been applied to Spence during his lifetime, sometimes by the man himself—Braggart. Faggot. Fantasizer. Bully. Dandy. Bon vivant. Influence-peddler. Name-dropper. Secret agent. Snob—and ended it on the following perceptive note:

> *Craig had quite a few friends, perhaps no less than the rest of us, but he certainly had many determined enemies. It was in my opinion, the most vindictive, the most implacable, the most tireless of the latter, who eventually raised the fatal tablets to his lips.*

In Japan, he was one outsider the Shiina family and their associates wished had never come.

CHAPTER 7

Danny's Inn

IN THE DECADES following the end of World War II, Western businesses coveted access to the Japanese domestic market. Few honest brokers, however, were actually able to succeed in carving out a decent market share. There were simply too many protective barriers to contend with and that was, unfortunately for the Western businessmen, a state of affairs that did not seem to bother the US government, its priority being the creation and maintenance of a strong anti-Communist ally in Japan and not necessarily a trading partner for US goods. If the Japanese wanted to keep their doors closed to imports in order to cultivate their own economy, that was just fine with the American mandarins. In addition, if they wanted open access to US markets, where they could sell their newly manufactured products, like Sony transistor radios, then that was fine too. US thinking amounted to: let them have their way, because fighting the great global red menace is the most important thing. The result of this was a comparatively limited American presence in the legitimate business community. There were a handful of big, multinational companies that the Japanese government had allowed in, as well as a handful of small, independent businesses. And that was basically it until the late 1960s when capital liberalization occurred.

One of the more memorable of the independent businessmen was American Jack Dinken, an East Side New Yorker who had initially traveled to China at the end of World War II to buy a hair-net factory and wound up relocating to Tokyo in the fall of 1947 as a "commercial entrant," opening up Dinken Sangyo K.K., an import-export company, at a small office based in Yurakucho.

Dinken got his first big break in the midst of the Occupation, when Communist demonstrations had become so much of a problem that the authorities decided to arm the Japanese police with modern new weapons. Dinken, then representing two American ammunition makers, was given the contract to supply the necessary weapons to them. He provided Japanese law enforcement with the Colt 45 firearm. Since the six-inch (15 cm) barrel was nearly half the length of the Japanese arm, he also sold them Grip-Rite devices to steady the weapon as they aimed and fired.

So far, so good. Then the chief of police asked Dinken for some tear gas grenades and Dinken procured something called NSG (Nauseous Gas Grenades) from the Lake Erie Chemical Co., a device which when fired caused instant vomiting or diarrhea. He arranged for a demonstration on an island in eastern Tokyo's Sumida River, an exercise which proved disastrous. With five hundred policemen from all over Japan assembled to watch, Dinken tied dogs to stakes at a spot in the middle of the island where the gas bombs were to be set off. It was his idea of an experiment designed to demonstrate graphically the harmful effects of NSGs. However, when the grenades were detonated, the wind suddenly changed direction, blowing the deadly gas toward the onlooking crowd. A consequence of this was that many of the visitors developed sudden gastrointestinal problems. This left the island in a terrible odiferous mess and Dinken with a lot of apologizing to do, as well as some very confused and shell-shocked dogs!

Legal businesses, like the one Dinkens ran, faced myriad barriers and restrictions. However, illicit commerce involving Japan and the West intensified, in fact, with the advent of two events. One was the holding of the 1964 Tokyo Olympics, which showcased, via the global media, the city's sparkling new architecture designed specifically for the games, as well as modern office buildings and high-rise hotels, demonstrating to the world that the ravages of war were a thing of the past. It gave the Japanese economy a tremendous shot in the arm by attracting tourists, curiosity seekers and fortune hunters from all over. The second great event was the Vietnam War which brought hundreds of thousands of American military men, civilian personnel and their dependents flowing to the city on R & R, medical leave, temporary duty or simply in transit, their existence presenting all types of new opportunities—and opportunists to go along with them.

DANNY STEIN

One of these visitors was a man named Daniel Stein who decided to stay and who would ultimately make his mark on the Tokyo nightscape in a most indecorous way. Danny, as he was known to his friends, was an ex-New York policeman, an officer in Brooklyn's 82nd precinct, who had left the force in the late 1950s, having had "problems" he preferred not to discuss with anybody. Stein had gone onto stints as a security guard at Florida's Hialeah racetrack, then as a salesman for a Florida real-estate company, and next to Saigon, where he worked for a major US construction company, supplementing his income in the evenings by running a bar and trading in the city's hyperactive wartime black market. While in Vietnam, however, Stein developed rheumatism and was advised by doctors to leave the country. Thus, it was that in 1966, at the age of fifty, he set his sights on Tokyo.

At first, Stein worked as a croupier in the Grant Heights military club in the Nerima suburb of Tokyo where, as historical accident would have it, he operated the very same roulette wheel initially brought to Japan by the mobster Ted Lewin, who was living in comfortable retirement in the Canary Islands by this time.

However, seeing the hordes of Vietnam-related US government and military personnel swarming around the Roppongi–Akasaka axis in central Tokyo, Stein sensed he had found the right place to start his own nightspot. With the exception of the high-ranking officers who stayed at the US-military-owned Sanno Hotel in the heart of Akasaka, very few people in this teeming swarm of temporary Tokyo residents could afford to go to the glitzy new restaurants and pricey clubs that dominated the area—especially the grand-sized, big band hostess clubs with names like the Getsusekai, the New Latin Quarter, the Copacabana, the Benibasha and the Hanabasha. Such establishments were the preserve of the politicians, the celebrities, the captains of industry, the gang bosses and other rich, influential people.

To give a little detail on the lay of the land at the time from just one of these storied establishments, Copacabana hostesses earned more money a month than most corporate executives. A story circulating at the time had it that touring crooner Frank Sinatra once gave a Copa hostess five thousand dollars to spend the night with him and even that was not enough to win her lasting devotion, as Sinatra discovered on his next visit to the Copa, when the hostess, a Liz Taylor lookalike, bedecked in Givenchy and Mikimoto, rejected his demand for a free rematch.

"Yesterday was yesterday," she reportedly said to the famously hot-tempered American singer. "Today is today, and who do you think you are anyway?" Copa hostesses, after all, had a certain standard to live up to.

Sinatra became very indignant and began behaving obnoxiously. So the girl arose from the booth where she had been sitting with the Hollywood legend, went over to the owner of the Copa, Mama Cherry and borrowed five thousand dollars in cash on the spot. She then took it back to the table, and threw it in Sinatra's face. It was one of the great tales of the Copa, even if no one knew if it was true or not.

Still another episode, this one verifiable, involved Wally Gayda (see Chapter 2) and Ava Gardner, who showed up at the Copa together to find Ava's ex-husband Sinatra at one of the tables. Ava said hello, but Sinatra, in an apparent jealous huff, refused to talk to the actress. Ava then wrote out a note and when the singer went into the men's room, she asked Gayda to deliver it. A reluctant Gayda did as he was told. He stood uncomfortably at a urinal next to Sinatra, introduced himself and tried to hand over the letter. Sinatra refused to take it.

"Screw that whore!" he said as he zipped up his pants and left.

If the Copa and its ilk were too expensive, still others—the cheaper cabarets and bars—were usually "Japanese Only," vast segments of the new postwar generation preferring to do without the company of foreigners during their after hours. Even once gaijin-friendly places like the Albion on the Ginza and the New Yorker in Shimbashi with their pounding music, pulsating lights and dancing miniskirted waitresses were not quite as receptive in the new post-Olympic era. Since most military and government personnel in transit—even when dressed in civilian clothes—were easily identifiable by the inevitable short-cropped hair and white socks, a bar hostess would simply write "Nam" on top of the bill in the Japanese katakana script (ナム) which would cause the total amount charged to automatically double. The assumption was that all such customers were loaded with leave and travel pay.

Danny Stein was convinced he could do better. So in 1968, he opened a restaurant on the main drag, Sanno-dori street, across the from the US-military-owned Sanno Hotel (where Imperial Japanese Army officers had famously plotted a failed coup in 1936). Replete with a long brass bar and outsized tables with red-checkered tablecloths, Danny's Inn served reasonably priced cold draft beer, American-style hamburgers and provided a different type of female to keep the young, inexperienced and budget-conscious foreign male clientele company. Stein had spread the word that all aspiring, amateur ladies of the night looking for a little money on the side would be welcome at Danny's Inn—be they college girls, secretaries or bored housewives. They could eat for free at his place, he said, and conduct negotiations there for services to be rendered elsewhere later.

He instituted two basic rules: one, there would be no hardened pros allowed in his place competing with his neophyte girls. Two, equally important, there would be no yakuza. The thirty thousand members of organized crime syndicates located in the Tokyo area were free to extort other places for tribute, as far as he was concerned, but they would not be tolerated at Danny's Inn. Anyone with a scar, a nasty swagger, a missing fingertip (the chopping off of which was a ritual punishment in the yakuza world) was not going to get in through the door. As an ex-New York cop, medium-sized, but sturdy and muscular and still in reasonably good shape despite the rheumatism, he felt confident in his ability to keep such people at arm's length. Moreover, Stein still had his NYPD badge and a gun which he knew how to use to good effect—despite the fact that one was no good in Japan and the other was illegal.

Stein hired a dozen Japanese "Papillon" ("butterflies," as they were called in Akasaka), touts who patrolled the streets, snagged passing GIs and guided them to his place. He also enlisted the services of the Akasaka flower girls—elderly ladies selling cellophane packs of flowers—to spread the word about Danny's Inn on their own nightly sales routes through the area's watering holes.

The smorgasbord of food, drink and fresh-faced girls, at affordable prices, turned Danny's into an overnight hit. On any given evening, one could walk in and see the entire bar lined with conservatively dressed, well-mannered, presentable young Japanese females engaged in conversation with customers. All of the back tables were filled as well. Moreover, the clientele was comprised not just of R & R military personnel, as Danny had first expected, but also included a wide cross-section of young foreign men from other walks of life—bankers, traders, insurance executives, multinational corporate employees and other businessmen—who found the beer and cheeseburgers to their liking and the all-night services provided by the friendly young budding "professionals" eminently reasonable at a flat rate of ten thousand yen (roughly twenty-eight dollars at 1968 exchange rates).

It was an international lovefest of a highly unusual sort and it stood in marked contrast to the other nightspots in the city. It also provided an interesting counterpoint to the student-led demonstrations against the Vietnam war which were taking place regularly on the main thoroughfare outside Danny's front door. The protesters, who frequently stopped in for a cold drink and a look around, were also demanding the United States revert to Japanese control the southern island of Okinawa, which had been under US administration since the end of the war and whose bases the US government was using to prosecute the war in Southeast Asia. (The island was indeed handed back in 1971.)

As an ex-policeman, Stein felt an obligation to keep up appearances. He enjoyed a certain status with Japanese law enforcement and did not want them thinking he was a common pimp, despite the sexual trading that was going on at his establishment. Thus, he took pains to make it clear that what money the girls made at Danny's Inn was their own business as long as the customers ate and drank a lot before leaving with them for the night. Stein would make all his money from food and beverage sales. (And what he would make was a lot.)

Prostitution had a long, rich and legal history in Japan. Before World War II, thousands of young girls had been sold into prostitution each year by their parents. There was not exactly the stigma attached to the business that existed in some other parts of the world. In fact, many people had once considered the profession a kind of art form, the girls wearing colorful tattoos on their bodies and, at times, the names of their favorite clients emblazoned on their inner thighs and buttocks. The colorful brothels of Yoshiwara, for example, which dated back to the Edo era, gained worldwide fame as grist for the works of some of Japan's top writers and artists.

It was only when the American Occupiers came along that, prompted by pressure from religious groups back home, legislation outlawing the sex trade was passed, banning sex in public establishments. The anti-prostitution law went into effect in 1956 causing the formal closure of Tokyo's brothels. Fortunately for those irrevocably wed to the sex industry, the law was mercifully full of loopholes. It prohibited buying and selling sex, but did not set forth any penalties for those acts. It made roadside solicitation and pimping punishable offenses, along with forced prostitution, but did not interpret oral, anal and other sexual services as "sex." Thus, a myriad of substitute enterprises popped up in place of the brothels, such as massage parlors, telephone clubs, "pink salons" and bathhouses that served essentially the same purposes, promoted by thousands of explicitly sexual ads appearing in some of the seedier weekly magazines and evening tabloids, or in the leaflets that were dropped in neighborhood mailboxes by yakuza delivery boys. A convenient clause in the Prostitution Prevention Law which stated that prostitution was something between two *strangers*, allowed many establishments, such as the so-called "soaplands," to charge a large service fee then claim that anything else that went on in its private rooms was based on mutual consent between two adults who knew each other, having become friends during the thirty minutes it took to disrobe and bathe.

The police correctly reasoned that the world's oldest profession was not going to go away and, as befitting the general laissez-faire attitude of Tokyo's finest, left such places alone. That included Danny's Inn, as long as everyone remained relatively discreet. According to some reports, the police sincerely believed that places like Danny's would somehow keep the crazies and the sex maniacs off the streets and under control, which was why they seldom tried to make any arrests.

In fact, a major source of Stein's profit came from sales of hard liquor drinks—top-of-the line whiskey, brandy and other products which he had obtained through his contacts at the Sanno Hotel across the street. Sanno customers, and, by extension, those at Danny's, paid a fraction of what Japanese were forced to pay on the open market where imported whiskey was subject to extremely high protectionist duties. Maintaining this arrangement on a constant basis, however, required a certain amount of skullduggery. Under Japanese law, each legally imported whiskey bottle had to have an "import approved" stamp on it. Bottles without this import stamp were deemed illegal contraband if they were found being used or sold outside American bases or other US government-owned property like embassy or consular compounds. Stein circumvented this restriction by filling up used, empty, import-stamped bottles with contents from new bottles purchased at the Army Post Exchange. Japanese authorities would come around to check the whiskey and remark how strange it was that Stein-san never had any new whiskey bottles on his shelf. Stein would always reply simply that his customers were more interested in cheeseburgers and cheap beer than fine whiskey. That was the problem with having foreigners for customers, he would say. They were cheap. No class. Certainly the Japanese could see that.

As the profits poured in, Stein bought himself a huge home on a residential back street of Akasaka, a lavish, four-bedroom Western-style structure which soon became a refuge for any friend or acquaintance of Danny's—male or female—needing a place to stay. Said one middle-aged guest who had enjoyed an extended stay there, "It was like a twenty-four-hour orgy. Booze and women all the time. It made me wish I was twenty-one again."

Stein himself, not blessed with movie-star looks, wasn't much of a ladies' man. He was a serious, sober individual, not given to small talk, or to revealing his innermost thoughts. "He had no lightness about him at all," said one acquaintance.

His passion was gambling—compulsively so. He made frequent trips to Las Vegas to play poker and amuse himself at the craps tables, and he was very good at it. In fact, he won several professional poker tournaments in Las Vegas and held weekly games at his Tokyo residence as well, in which he invariably came out ahead, until a masked man armed with a gun appeared during a game one night and relieved the poker table of tens of thousands of dollars. That marked the end of the poker get-togethers at the Stein home.

Stein also had a strong sense of fatherly responsibility toward the young women in his charge. He was always willing to help out with college tuition and medical bills. If he thought a girl was particularly bright, he would send her to English school to polish her linguistic skills and then arrange for a visa to the States if she wanted to go there. One girl from Danny's Inn went on to graduate from UCLA and become a CPA, eventually marrying an American man and raising two children. Another went to law school. In time, Stein went on to compile a record of such benevolence that friends cracked he could start his own Rotary Club branch.

As the US involvement in the Vietnam war began to wind down in the early seventies, American GIs and government civilians slowly disappeared from the scene, reducing Stein's clientele somewhat, although the Western businessmen still came around in impressive enough numbers to keep Danny's Inn in the black. Then, however, the oil shortage crisis in 1973 plunged the nation into darkness, as energy conservation measures forced the city's multitudinous neon lights to be temporarily switched off for a time, and triggered a recession. Stein was forced to rethink his approach to business.

The Olympics had brought with it an influx of high class Caucasian call girls to Tokyo, who stayed around to prosper in the booming Japanese economy (fueled by auto and TV exports). These girls were expensive, but despite the hard economic times in the early seventies, they had no difficulty in finding Japanese businessmen willing to pay the exorbitant fees they charged. Leggy, large-busted, blond foreign girls, popularized in Japan by the hit movies of Marilyn Monroe, were a rare breed. Indeed when the famed actress honeymooned in Japan in 1954 with her new husband Joe DiMaggio, it was the biggest news story of the year. Japan was a baseball crazy country but the actress's following there even exceeded that of her legendary spouse. The movies in which she starred, such as *Gentlemen Prefer Blonds*, were shown again and again in first-run theaters long after her death in 1960. She represented a vision of booming postwar American culture that had resonated with the male populace of the country. Thus, girls with similarities to Monroe and willing to have sex with Japanese men were in such demand that the girls could literally set their own prices. Moreover, having a young, good-looking Caucasian girl on one's arm was considered such a status symbol that some men would pay dearly just for the escort service.

It was customary for newly arrived girls to start out at a place like Byblos, a wildly popular discotheque in Akasaka, in search of a swinging young entrepreneur or some refined upper-echelon gangster who might be in the market for a mistress. A girl lucky enough to get herself set up in an expensive apartment with a handsome monthly stipend and a steady stream of gifts of jewelry and overseas trips, could live very comfortably and still make money on the side with outside clients.

Failing that, they might set up shop at similar, but lesser, operations at Manos, a bistro owned by a former OSS agent or occupy a bar stool at the Red Baron, an establishment operated by a professional poker player Las Vegas entrepreneur, Ken Judd. However, most of the girls operating out of Manos complained of not-infrequent demands by the proprietor for private excursions to the back room free of charge. The Red Baron was not high on their list of favorites either due to the tendency of a certain foreign bartender there to get violent with them.

MARIA

To avoid such problems, a voluptuous German born blond named Maria, in Japan by way of New York and a temporary Japanese husband, opened up her own place, a Roppongi club called the Balakan. There, she assembled an unparalleled coalition of high-end Portuguese, German, French, Spanish, Canadian, as well as Thai, Korean and other ladies of the night, who practiced their profession uninhibited, as it were. It was believed to be the largest selection of foreign sex workers in the history of the city. The Balakan was but a short walk from the highbrow Rockefeller-funded International House, where scholars and dignitaries from all over the world were invited to discuss the important issues of the day with their Japanese hosts, many of whom, it might be noted, could be found later in the evening practicing a different kind of international intercourse with their lowbrow, but more worldly Roppongi neighbors.

However, the Balakan had problems. Maria suddenly found herself under pressure from her building's landlord and the local police to move. Owners of a new family-oriented restaurant in the building had begun complaining about the activities of their co-tenants and the effect they might be having on the morals of the young adults who frequented their dining establishment with their parents. Thus it was that Maria approached Danny Stein one summer afternoon in 1974.

Stein was sitting at a back table of his restaurant, talking with a friend, an American businessman named Rick Roa (who coincidentally hailed from the same Brooklyn neighborhood as Stein, and doubled as a bartender at Danny's Inn), when Maria abruptly walked in. She introduced herself, said she was being forced to move her business and asked if Stein might want to sell half of Danny's Inn to her and let her move her girls in immediately to share the space.

"I don't know," said Stein, shrugging in surprise. "How much are you offering?"

"How much do you want?" Maria replied.

Stein thought for a moment, and then replied, half jokingly as he later confessed, "$250,000."

It was an extremely high price just to buy one-half of what in Japan was called a "Business Right." But Maria did not even blink.

"Done," she said.

She told Danny to have his lawyer draw up the papers immediately and that she would be back the next day with the money. Stein asked Roa to be a witness and what Roa saw the next afternoon was something he would never forget. At three thirty, Maria walked in with her attorney, carrying a big brown paper bag. The bag contained $250,000 worth of yen, in cash, which she unloaded onto the table in one fell swoop, much to Stein and Roa's amazement.

It took about an hour to count the money, sign the papers and stamp the documents with the assorted requisite seals. That done, one of the strangest joint ventures of the postwar era was officially in business.

"That night at seven," said Roa, who hung around to view the arrival, "it was like a UN convoy. "About forty broads, perfumed and coiffed, dressed to the teeth, came parading in from the street to start work at their new headquarters. It was the damnedest thing I ever saw."

Included in this group he was introduced to was a variety of exotic women: Renée, a petite French girl; Jenny, a tall, big-boned Australian lass; Erin, an Irish-American girl who specialized in two men at the same time; Alice, a studious, bespectacled New Zealander who usually had a book with her; Sophie, a beautiful, if hard-looking French-Canadian; an athletic Israeli-American named Hannah; a Korean homosexual in the process of a sex change named Kim—beautiful, but also pushing forty; and Adrian,

a stunning thirty-year-old blond American intersex (or hermaph-
rodite, as we said in those days), who stood six feet two (1.9 m).
Adrian had made some twenty visits to a plastic surgeon in Cairo
for assorted eye tucks, tummy tucks and hind tucks, as well as breast
augmentation. Her blue-eyed movie-starlet image was flawed only
by a hard, deep baritone voice and a vocabulary befitting a Marine.

The news traveled fast. Soon, a surprising thing happened: Danny's clientele doubled. Over 90 percent of the new customers were
Japanese. Men who had never shown the slightest interest in the
old Danny's Inn were now suddenly crowding through the door,
elbowing their way past the foreign men and their schoolgirl companions to a section in the rear of the restaurant where the ladies
from abroad were seated, powdering their noses.

The system Maria initiated might have been described as "Rapid
Service," to borrow a term used by the Japanese National Railways.
In her way of doing things, which was a departure from that of the
Balakan MO, there was no such thing as an all-nighter: only brief,
thirty-minute flings at a whopping ¥50,000 a shot ($138 at the ex-
change rate in place at the time), all activity taking place at a neigh-
boring "love hotel," minutes away.

A customer would come in, pick a girl, sit down and order drinks:
by design only expensive foreign whiskey was served, at ¥3,000 a
shot. After an appropriate interval, discussing perhaps the weather
or the price of rice, the couple would hop into a cab for a two-min-
ute trip to a gabled and turreted multistory mock-Tudor stucco
structure called Chante, where all the subsequent action occurred.

Everyone involved in the business made a fortune. Danny and
Maria from peddling drinks; Maria and the girls from selling their
wares; the Chante Hotel from renting out rooms at ¥3,000 for half
an hour several hundred times a night. Even the cab companies
made big profits by ferrying everyone back and forth. It was capitalism at its unfettered finest.

However, if the United Nations Division of Danny's Inn was
busy to the point of overload—tables occupied, people waiting in
line, the phone constantly ringing with calls for the girls—the other
half of the operation was not. It was still functioning as before, still

charging the same prices as before (which for all-night services amounted to a fraction of what was being charged on the other side of the room). But it was gradually being squeezed into one corner of the place. This situation made Danny's Inn an interesting study in international trade and the laws of supply and demand—the basic lesson being that a Japanese man would pay more to sleep with a foreign girl than the foreign man would pay to sleep with a Japanese girl.

"Business 101" was the way a patron of Danny's, a Japanese economics professor at a Tokyo University, liked to put it, "The rarer a commodity is, the higher its value."

In time, finding the competition for customers and for space was getting too stiff, as it were, some of the Japanese girls moved on. But others stayed, enabling Danny's to maintain its unique, multi-dimensional character.

The mid-to-late seventies was a time when Japan's rising trade surpluses with the rest of the world were beginning to cause tension. A massive flood of low-priced, high-quality exports, from VCRs to automobiles, had catapulted the Japanese economy to number two in the world and created a trade deficit that with the US alone had climbed to tens of billions of dollars. Government and business leaders on both sides of the Pacific were starting to tentatively voice complaints about each other—the American governmental leaders suddenly "discovered" closed markets and unfair trade practices, while the Japanese, for their part, found themselves pointing to the "poor quality" of products made in the US, like TV sets and cars that broke down too easily. Yet, Danny's remained one area of international commerce where Japanese and foreigners got along just fine. Consumer access and satisfaction were guaranteed.

Danny's fame spread, attracting patrons such as wealthy businessmen, company presidents, baseball players, movie stars, gangsters and politicians—noticeably ruling Liberal Democratic Party politicians, who stopped by for quick relief on their way to the Copacabana. As Danny's bartender put it, "It seemed that there wasn't a big name who hadn't put in an appearance."

But that wasn't all. There were customers who came in from the big island of Hokkaido to the north and Kyushu to the south. Rice farmers from the provinces appeared, still wearing their straw hats. Rich Japanese college students—male *and* female—dropped in. There were also visitors from abroad. Tourists. Airline captains looking for female companionship. Airline stewardesses looking for female companionship. There was even a man and his wife from New York who came in periodically just to sample the young Japanese ladies who worked out of Danny's. Word was getting around. If you were in Japan, go to Danny's Inn. It was the place to be. Everyone was welcome, regardless of race, creed, color, gender or sexual orientation, as long as he or she had money—and management did its best to provide companionship of any race, creed, color, gender or sexual orientation for its clientele. With its convivial, egalitarian atmosphere, it perhaps offered as much, if not more, in the way of international communication and cooperation than that other Tokyo bastion of cross-culturalism, the International House. It certainly provided more in the way of services and entertainment.

The only exception to the equal opportunity rule at Danny's was, of course, the yakuza. And that was a state of affairs that separated this place from other establishments in the area, which increasingly seemed to be at the mercy of the area's mobsters, in particular those of the ethnic Korean gang, the Tosei-kai, and its chief rival, the Sumiyoshi-kai, Tokyo's largest gang with eleven thousand members across the country. At the nearby Manos bistro, the yakuza would come in to punch the cash register and take their "protection" fee, and the owner would pretend not to notice or would disappear into a back room.

Danny Stein, however, absolutely refused to be intimidated by anyone. Occasionally some open-shirted yakuza would come staggering in, drunk, gold necklaces jangling, missing appendages in evidence, growling at customers and staff alike. But Stein would just stand in his way, affix him with a thick-lidded stare and tell him to leave. If necessary, he would flash his New York City cop's badge. The mobsters always left. Perhaps it was because to the mind of the

Japanese yakuza, being a New York cop automatically meant that Stein was cozy with the New York Mafia—because that was the way things worked in Japan; cops and robbers came from the same mold.

The only times the police ever bothered Stein was if the girls started soliciting in the streets, something they were wont to do during slow periods, early in the evening or very late at night, which would cause the neighborhood shopkeepers to complain. The cops would call Stein over to the Akasaka station, an easy five-minute walk from Danny's, for a polite discussion over a cup of green tea amidst bureaucratic gray office furniture and smoke-clouded air.

At such sessions, the police would produce a very thick file from a row of metallic cabinets with updated descriptions of all of Danny's girls and, often, letters of complaint from the drugstore around the corner or the Korean restaurant down the street.

"See?" the cop would say. "Now please go back and tell the girls not to solicit customers in the street. You've got to get things under control. Otherwise we'll have to start making arrests."

It was revealing of the laissez-faire attitude of the Japanese police—and perhaps the fact that Stein was a comrade in arms—that in all the years Danny's Inn was in operation, not one of the girls was ever convicted of prostitution. Not a single one. In fact, there had only been one crackdown. And that had come in 1977 after a Japanese magazine published a feature story on the girls of Danny's Inn and made them all more famous than they really wanted to be. A number of the girls were arrested and the police raided the apartment of one of them and uncovered a tin box with ten million yen in it. However, since no Japanese male wanted to admit to a tryst, the girls were eventually released and the charges dropped. A listless follow-up attempt to infiltrate Danny's with undercover detectives proved equally fruitless, because the police, with their government issue shoes and socks, military-style haircuts and uniform facial expressions, were even easier to spot than GIs on leave.

As one of Danny's girls so aptly put it, "They might as well wear a sign that says, 'I'm a cop.'"

And perhaps that was the way the police wanted it.

Of all the girls, Adrian would prove to be the most in demand. She claimed that her great popularity was caused by her anatomy, which, to be perfectly graphic about it, featured a one-inch (2.5 cm) penis fortuitously positioned above a small vagina. Adrian was followed on the hit charts by Maria, Renée and Kim, while the least popular of the lot was the French-Canadian Sophie, known for a mean temper. (Once, espying a colleague making a move on one of her regular customers, Sophie grabbed the offending woman and flipped her unceremoniously out of her seat on to the floor with a ruthlessly efficient *uwatenage* arm throw that would have impressed a sumo stable boss.)

Still, no matter what her ranking, every girl made money, several thousand dollars a night in fact, in a work day that stretched from seven in the evening until three in the morning, With little upkeep required, aside from new clothes, the occasional abortion and the odd cocaine habit, they squirreled away their nightly income in savings accounts and overseas investments, providing an interesting, if small, counterpoint to the rising current account surplus in Japan.

Erin, who took up reading stock market investment guides, kept millions and millions of yen in a safe deposit box in the Mitsui Bank at Roppongi Crossing. She would periodically withdraw money and change it into US dollars on the black market—to avoid nosy Japanese banking officials, who might report her to the tax authorities, and to circumvent pesky currency exchange restrictions. Up until 1973, when the dollar exchange rate had been fixed at 360 yen, she had been paying an underground dealer from Yokota Air Base a usurious 900 yen per greenback.

Then she would take her dollars to the Hongkong and Shanghai Bank in Hibiya and have a friendly teller transfer them incrementally to her overseas account. Eventually, she used her savings to buy a house in London, putting what was left over into IBM stock. Maria, for her part, shipped her money overseas through the IndoChine Suez bank in Toranomon. She used her funds to buy an office in New York and set her sister up in the real estate business. In those days of restricted foreign currency exchange (the legal limit at the time frozen at three thousand dollars), such sub-rosa transactions had been standard operating procedure for people dealing in black market dollars.

The most money-conscious of the very money-conscious Danny's Inn group was the Australian girl Jenny, who lived in an apartment complex in Akasaka, known as Riki Mansion, home to assorted denizens of the Tokyo underworld. Residents there included gangsters, itinerant foreigners, drug addicts and even a couple of murderers. But Jenny was oblivious to them all and just about anything else that did not concern the advancement of her bank account. She had no hobbies. She did not play the guitar. She did not keep a cat. She could not have cared less for the tea ceremony or other facets of Japanese culture. The only Japanese words that she knew had to do with her profession and they were terms like "*Ikura desu ka*" and "*I-kai go man yen*." ("How much?" and "Fifty thousand yen for one time."). She had but one interest and one interest only: making money. And she worked extremely hard to that end. Unlike the others, Jenny never took a day off. Not even on Sundays. She kept to her 7 p.m. to 3 a.m. shift and worked after hours at a nearby pub. That was her schedule for all the years she worked in Japan (which would be a total of ten in all). She saved everything she possibly could, including all her one-yen coins, the equivalent at the time of one 360th of a dollar. She just put them in a big flower vase and then took them to the bank once a month.

Said her roommate Lea, a young student from New Zealand, "She was the cheapest person I ever met."

It was the dream of all of them to strike it rich in one fell swoop, so they could stop working, but Renée was the only one who actually accomplished that goal. Renée found herself a rich man, a forty-year-old married Japanese plastic surgeon from Osaka, who was unaware of Renée's true profession. She used her charms to persuade the man to divorce his wife and marry her. She moved to Japan's second largest city to set up household with her new husband and less than a year later, she was on her way back to Paris, having relieved her hapless *shujin* (husband) of nearly a million dollars, which would buy her a chateau in Paris. It was a famous story at Danny's and the girls were envious.

In 1975, still bothered by rheumatism, which was aggressively worsening, Stein was advised by his doctor to move to a warm dry climate. Thus did he decide to sell out and relocate to Las Vegas. He put his remaining half-interest in Danny's Inn up for sale and began laying the groundwork for a Vegas-based travel agency aimed at capitalizing on a growing new trend, the large numbers of moneyed Japanese gamblers (some of whom were Danny's Inn customers) who were flying to the States to play in Nevada's casinos—the only legalized forms of gambling in Japan being horse, boat, motorcycle and bicycle racing.

The most interested prospective buyer was Kim—her sex change now complete. But Kim could not afford the forty million yen that Stein wanted for his half of the enterprise. Twenty million was all she and her husband could afford. Stein refused to budge. Negotiations continued: Danny lowered his price to thirty million but this time Kim would not budge. It had to be twenty million. It took a bizarre meeting in Kim's tatami-matted apartment one afternoon to break the impasse. Stein was finally persuaded by a negotiating technique straight out of a Toei Film Studios yakuza movie.

At first, Kim had tried pleading. She said that she had to have Stein's share of Danny's Inn, no matter what. She was over forty and needed security for herself and her husband in later years. The price had to be twenty million and not a yen more because it was all she had. When Stein again refused, she went to her closet, pulled out a long, razor-sharp samurai sword and took a swipe at Stein with it, the blade barely missing him by intention and instead slicing open a *zabuton* floor cushion. That was just a warning, she said, eyeing him malevolently and raising her sword again. Stein agreed to terms.

"I'm getting too old for this," he said to his American friend Roa later that afternoon, blood drained from his face, hands still shaking slightly. "My health is no good. I'm packing it in."

Taking his twenty million yen, Stein moved to Nevada. Danny's Inn continued under its new joint ownership for several years more, until, one by one, the girls moved on as well. The popular Adrian left Japan for Manhattan where she bought an expensive apartment in an exclusive Upper East Side building, pretending to be an investment counselor in order to pass a tenants screening test for propriety. It was, ironically, she wrote back to Tokyo, the same apartment building whose management had rejected former US president Richard Nixon's application on the grounds that his presence would attract media and be "too disruptive."

Maria became a part timer. She kept a little black book with over a thousand names and numbers of clients in it (whom she liked to call her "cute, adorable little boys") that was in itself worth a lot of money. Semi-retired in New York, she would fly back to Japan during the summer and winter gift-giving seasons—a time when Japanese businessmen were flush with cash—and start making calls.

However, Maria went to the well once too often. One chilly evening in 1978, while hanging out in an Akasaka bar, she propositioned a man visiting Tokyo on holiday from Fukuoka. Two hours later she was dead, strangled to death. The man had come out of the bath in the hotel she had taken him to and had caught her rifling through his wallet. That was what had set him off, or so he claimed to police.

Maria's death was reported in great detail in Japan's leading newspaper, the *Asahi Shimbun*, which also saw fit to run an article about the Akasaka gaijin sex trade, bemoaning the specter of foreign "queens of the night" who were corrupting the morals of Japanese men. The Japanese television network TBS later produced a drama about the life and times of Maria and her friends at Danny's Inn. It was telecast nationwide in prime time and was one of the few such television shows in Japanese broadcast history ever to feature gaijin as leading characters.

Danny Stein lived and worked in Las Vegas for several years after leaving Tokyo, running a very successful travel agency. He had set it up so that any Japanese tourist who flew into Vegas and was looking for a hotel reservation at the airport lobby hotel ad billboard would have his call routed to Stein's business office. But, like Maria, his life did not have a happy ending either. On one occasion, returning home from an extremely profitable evening at poker, he was attacked and robbed. Then, on another occasion, he was severely beaten up by an unknown assailant, believed to be a disgruntled gambling opponent.

On top of that, he had marital problems. Stein had married a Japanese girl twenty years younger than he—a girl he had met in Tokyo and whom, friends said, he treated like a queen. But once in Las Vegas, she became involved with another man, also a professional gambler. In the end, Stein died alone, of a heart attack, while on a trip to Florida. Friends maintained he actually died of a broken heart. He left most of his estate to his assistant in the travel business, and that was that. According to an acquaintance, his wife was last seen working as a change girl in a Vegas casino.

Danny's Inn, predictably, deteriorated too, as a former patron discovered one night in 1980. When walking down a street in Akasaka, he passed a relocated, "new and improved," Danny's Inn and curious to see what was going on, popped his head inside. The place was empty of customers, except for one old, obese Australian man sitting in a corner, talking heatedly to one of the staff. It had all the ambience of a tomb—a very brightly lit tomb, thanks perhaps to the authorities who, at the time, may have been making one of their periodic sweeps of bars and restaurants in Tokyo trying to enforce lighting laws. About ten aging women were sitting at the bar, wearing fierce makeup which only looked more ferocious under the hot lights. The former regular did not recognize any of them. The only person left from the old days was the bartender.

Still, Danny's Inn had left a legacy, above and beyond that enshrined in the TBS video archives, dubious though it may be and even if not one Stein had set about to create. That legacy could be seen for years after on Akasaka side streets in the form of very high class, very expensive rapid-service sex clubs, featuring attractive young Western women catering to wealthy Japanese for half an hour at a time. The old big band hostess nightclubs, the Latin Quarter, the Copacabana, the Getsusekai, had grown out of fashion, and in their place, quieter, smaller, more intimate clubs had sprung up. An era of postwar Tokyo nightlife had ended.

CHAPTER 8

The Sadaharu Oh Story

SADAHARU OH, the greatest home run hitter in the history of Japanese baseball, was cut from a different cloth than those we've surveyed so far. Although born in Sumida, Tokyo, Oh was registered as a citizen of the Republic of China (ROC), as mainland China and Taiwan were known from 1912 to 1949. He became an iconic figure among the Japanese populace, a man whose achievements moved an entire generation and gave sport in Japan international credibility, yet he still paid a price for his "otherness."

In the 1960s and 1970s, Oh and his legendary Yomiuri Giants teammate Shigeo Nagashima formed the powerful cleanup duo known as the "O-N Cannon." They were often compared to Babe Ruth and Lou Gehrig of New York Yankees fame. Together, they led the Tokyo-based Giants to fourteen Central League pennants and eleven Japan Series championships, including an unparalleled nine in a row, starting in 1965. The success of the proud Kyojin (the Japanese name for the Giants) in that era cemented baseball's position as the country's national sport, with telecasts of Giants games dominating prime-time television. It also symbolized the new status Japan was acquiring as a world economic superpower, conquering global markets with Japanese-manufactured cars, cameras and TV sets. It was a time known as the "Golden Age of Japanese Baseball."

In Oh's twenty-two-year career with the team, ending in 1980, he won every major title and award there was, many times over, including fifteen home run crowns. He slammed a total of 868 round-trippers, a world record.

He then went on to a successful second life as a manager, winning several pennants and two Japan Series titles. He reached the zenith of his managerial career in 2006 when he led Team Japan to a stunning triumph in the inaugural World Baseball Classic.

Yet, throughout it all, curiously, Oh was less popular than Nagashima, despite far more impressive accomplishments as a player and manager. It was Nagashima who always was known as Mr. Giants or Mr. *Puro-Yakyu* (Mr. Pro-Baseball) in Japan, not Sadaharu Oh. Some said the fact that Nagashima was a pure-blooded Japanese, whereas Oh was not, may have had something to do with it.

Oh, also known as Wang Chen-chih on his ROC travel documents, was the Tokyo-born son of a Japanese mother and a Chinese immigrant father from Taiwan, who had chosen to retain his ROC citizenship. Oh overcame discrimination in his youth to lead Waseda Jitsugyo High School to glory in the 1957 High School Spring Championship Tournament at Koshien Stadium.

Before a nationwide TV audience, Oh pitched four complete games in four days in the final stages of the tourney, despite infected blisters on his pitching hand that covered the baseball in blood, earning glory for himself and his team. However, his Chinese nationality disqualified him from membership in the national high school team, which represented Japan in international competition. Like all foreigners in Japan, the Tokyo-born Oh carried an alien registration card, which he had to renew with periodic visits to the Immigration Office.

Nevertheless, Oh became a national hero when he broke Hank Aaron's career home run mark. His achievement moved prime minister Takeo Fukuda to create and confer on him the country's first People's Honor Award (*Kokumin eiyo sho*). Only a few critics protested that he was not a *kokumin* (lit., "person of the country.")

On the other hand, the Yomiuri Giants made clear where their affections were by constantly demonstrating their preference for Nagashima over Oh. Nagashima was hired as field manager twice, compared to Oh's one time, and it was Nagashima who was made a lifetime honorary chairman of the Giants, not Oh. Oh had to move to Kyushu to the Korean-owned Softbank Hawks baseball organization to find a permanent spot after he retired as a player.

The story of Sadaharu Oh's development as a batter is the stuff of legend. Joining the Yomiuri Giants in 1959 as a pitcher, he was adjudged to have lost the pop on his fastball and converted to first base to take advantage of his natural power at bat. However, Oh experienced a lengthy period of adjustment because of a serious hitch in his swing. He went hitless in his first 26 at-bats as a professional and put up mediocre statistics during his first three seasons.

In 1961, for example, he hit but 13 home runs with a .253 batting average. Said Hiroshi Gondo of the Chunichi Dragons, a 30-game winner that year, "Frankly, it was easy to get him out. He could not hit a fastball. You could just blow it by him."

To overcome Oh's defect, the Giants hired a batting coach named Hiroshi Arakawa, who was also a martial arts sensei. From January 1962, the portly, moon-faced Arakawa began working with Oh every morning at his aikido dojo and devised a most unusual remedy.

"Oh's problem," said Arakawa, "was a tendency to stride too soon and open up his body. I devised a one-legged stance to focus his center of gravity on a smaller area. I got the idea from watching batters like Kaoru Betto of the Hanshin Tigers, who also lifted his foot somewhat before swinging. But I made Oh lift his leg higher, to waist level, and stand there like a flamingo as he waited for the ball.

"At first, Oh found it very difficult to do. We practiced and practiced and he slowly got better, but he was afraid to use it in a game for a long time."

But then came the time he had to try—a rain-soaked game versus the Taiyo Whales at Kawasaki Stadium on July 1, 1962. The Giants had been in a slump. The team had lost six games in a row and fallen back in the standings. Many were blaming it on Oh, who was hitting .250 with nine home runs and had killed many rallies by striking out.

The word "Oh" means "king" in Japanese and the sports dailies had begun to denigrate Oh by labeling him the *Sanshin Oh* or

"Strikeout King." Giants manager Tetsuharu Kawakami despaired Oh would ever step up to the next level. In desperation, Oh decided the moment had come to try his new stance in a game. He stepped into the batter's box against the Whales wiry right-hander Makoto Inagawa for his first at-bat, raised his right knee as high as he could, and stood there, waiting.

Out on the mound Inagawa thought to himself, "What the hell? He'll never hit me with that stance."

Inagawa wound up and fired a fastball, which Oh promptly lined into right field for a single. Arakawa watched from the sidelines like a proud father. In his second at-bat, Oh slammed an Inagawa fastball into the right-field stands. Arakawa leaped to his feet cheering. Oh finished the night with three hits, and a beaming Arakawa told him afterward, "That's it. You've got it. You'll never go back now."

Indeed, from then, Oh was off and running. Using his new stance, Oh hit 10 homers in July, and then 20 more, finishing with 38 to win the Central League home run crown.

Oh intensified his efforts in those morning sessions at the Arakawa dojo. He spent hours shadow swinging with Arakawa kneeling in front of him. Arakawa was not just watching, but also listening. He wanted Oh to produce just the right "whoosh" as the bat cut through the air to signify a perfect swing. Oh also began swinging a samurai long sword, slicing sheets of paper suspended from the ceiling, to strengthen his wrists and arms.

Yomiuri shortstop Tatsuro Hirooka, who witnessed some of those excruciating sessions, marveled at the effort Oh was making. "What he was doing was extremely difficult," said Oh's teammate. "Especially the sword. The displacement of air when you swing it pushes the paper away. To cut it you have to hit it just right and that takes great wrist strength."

"What we were doing," said Oh, "was applying the principles of budo martial arts to batting."

The following season, Oh hit 40 homers to capture his second straight home run crown, and raised his average to .305.

It was becoming increasingly difficult to get Oh out. Pitchers tried often and, increasingly, in vain.

Masaichi Kaneda, the great 400-game winner who had once boasted that nobody could hit his 96-mph (155-kph) fastball and roundhouse 12–6 curveball, was forced to change his tactics with Oh. He employed a stop-and-start delayed delivery to throw Oh's timing off. But that didn't work either.

By this time, Oh had reached the point where he could stand in the batter's box with his right knee lifted up to his waist for a full ten seconds, enough to outlast the most dilatory of pitchers. As Kaneda put it ruefully, "Oh could hit any pitch at any speed. And you simply couldn't break his focus."

In desperation, Dragons right-hander Kentaro Ogawa even tried throwing pitches from behind his back. But he was as unsuccessful as anyone else.

However, Oh was just getting started. In 1964, he hit 55 home runs to set a Japan record and raised his average to .320. It was his third straight home run title in what would be an unprecedented string of thirteen in a row. He also won three batting championships in a row, starting in 1968, hitting .326, .345 and .325, respectively. In 1973 and 1974, he garnered back-to-back Triple Crowns. That '73 campaign was arguably his best single season; he hit .355, with 51 home runs and 114 RBIs (runs batted in).

It caused Hanshin Tigers manager Minoru Murayama to utter at one point, "I get a headache every time he comes to bat. I can't bear to watch him anymore."

Before he was finished, Oh would have thirteen RBI crowns to go with his monopoly on the home run title, five batting titles and nine MVP (most valuable player) awards. On September 3, 1977, Oh reached the pinnacle of his playing career, when he blasted his 756th home run, surpassing American Hank Aaron's lifetime Major League Baseball (MLB) record.

Yet, throughout the O-N era, as it was called, Oh, again, was never the most highly regarded player. That honor always belonged to his teammate, cleanup hitter Nagashima. In favorite player surveys, Oh always finished a distant second to the exalted Nagashima, even though Oh surpassed him in every statistical aspect of the game.

There were a number of reasons for this, other than ethnicity. Nagashima was older than Oh, which counted for something in Japanese society. He had come out of Rikkyo University to win the Rookie of the Year award in 1958 and then went on to capture the batting crown in each of the next three seasons, all while Oh, the high school graduate, was still struggling to find his form. Nagashima was charismatic, ebullient and a crowd pleaser, who looked good even when striking out. He generated so much bat speed that his batting helmet would fly off his head when he swung and missed with one of his famous roundhouse cuts at a ball outside the strike zone. He was also entertaining in the field—a third baseman who could somehow turn ordinary groundballs into fielding gems.

Oh, by contrast, was somewhat dull, his unique foot-in-the-air hitting stance and prolific home run output notwithstanding. He had turned himself into a precision machine that almost never malfunctioned, but he also lacked a certain excitement. He was shy, stoic and a bit too mechanical for some fans.

Moreover, Nagashima had a flair for the dramatic. He had walloped a "sayonara" home run in the only official pro game Emperor Hirohito ever attended, in 1959, a feat that was replayed ad nauseam in highlight reels for the next half-century.

Oh, for his part, had hit a record four home runs in a game in 1964, and homered in seven consecutive games in 1972, another record, but far fewer fans remembered those particular achievements. It wasn't until after Nagashima retired in 1974 and Oh approached the Aaron mark, that Oh began to enjoy the spotlight alone and even earn some attention in America.

Ironically, Oh, by virtue of batting third in the order, made the cleanup-batting Nagashima a better hitter. Oh was so disciplined, that he would never swing at a pitch outside the strike zone. He averaged a walk per game.

With the game on the line in the ninth inning, Oh quite often would draw a base on balls, even with a runner on base, because the pitchers were so afraid to pitch to him. Nagashima would then come up to bat with the opposing pitcher having no choice but to challenge him and Nagashima would often get a hit. It was how he developed his famous, if not entirely deserved reputation for hitting in the clutch. He was just given so many chances, many of them thanks to Oh.

However, the pure-blooded factor could not exactly be ignored. Nagashima was a natural-born Japanese, as they say, while Oh now carried a Taiwanese passport (as the island had broken away from the new People's Republic of China). He remained a member of a minority group that was not always welcomed in Japan. And perhaps that counted for something in certain quarters.

Another upshot of all this was that Nagashima's salary was always higher than Oh's and he made far, far more money in endorsements. It was his uniform, No. 3, that all the schoolkids wanted to wear, not Oh's No. 1.

A generation after both men had ceased playing, Oh held 18 different batting records that were all seemingly unassailable, including his 13 RBI titles, 2,170 career RBIs, 9 MVPs, a .634 lifetime slugging percentage and 5,862 total bases. This was in addition, of course, to his equally unassailable home run marks. Nagashima held less than half that number of titles, including four Japan Series MVPs, six Central League Batting titles, ten Opening Day home runs, and leading the Central League in hits ten years in a row.

Yet, Hall of Fame pitcher Kazuhisa Inao, appearing in a 2004 Japanese television retrospective on the history of Japanese professional baseball would place Nagashima at the top of the Nippon Professional Baseball (NPB) pantheon. "Before Nagashima there was no one," he said. "And after Nagashima there was no one"—not even Sadaharu Oh, apparently—such was the emotional attachment to Japan's Golden Boy.

Oh faced a different kind of challenge in competing for attention on the world stage. He made the cover of *Sports Illustrated* (August 15, 1977) during his assault on Aaron's record and was featured in the *Washington Post* and *Newsweek*, among other major US publications. Thus, many Americans knew his name, while by contrast, almost nobody knew who Nagashima was.

However, MLB fans in America, not overly familiar with the Japanese game, hotly objected to Oh's 868 home runs being called a world record. They charged the level of play was lower, the parks smaller and the players not as physically imposing as those of the US major leagues. Typical, perhaps, were the remarks of an irate reader who had responded to a *New York Times* article about Oh's record by suggesting the "records in his neighborhood whiffle ball league should also be recognized."

Although the level of the Japanese game was indeed regarded by experts to be inferior to that of the MLB, the fact is, Oh did bat against some very tough pitchers, including wickedly effective breaking ball artists and a surprising number of speedball throwers.

It was generally agreed at the time by experts familiar with the Japanese game that there were at least two or three MLB-level pitchers per team in Japan and whenever a team played the Giants in the O-N era, they were used to the maximum. It was a practice the ever-quotable Clyde Wright, a former major league pitching star who played in Japan in the mid-70s, once described as "kamikaze baseball."

Consider Yutaka Enatsu, a chunky left-handed fireballer with the Hanshin Tigers, whose performance against the visiting St. Louis Cardinals in 1968 prompted Cardinals manager Red Schoendienst to say, "He is one of the best left-handed pitchers I have ever seen. He is as good as Steve Carlton."

Enatsu, who combined a 100 mph fastball with a devastating curve, struck out a record 401 batters in that '68 season, a total higher than the MLB mark of 383 set by Nolan Ryan in 1973, who played in a league with 32 more games per season.

In his prime, whenever the Tigers played the Giants in a three-game series, Enatsu often would start the first and third games and often come on in relief in the second contest.

(The starter in the second game of those three-game sets for a number of years was usually Minoru Murayama, a forkball artist rated highly by ex-MLB players who faced him. Murayama's lifetime earned run average [ERA] was a jaw-dropping 2.09.)

Enatsu dominated the Giants, but not Oh, who compiled a lifetime mark of twenty homers off Enatsu and a .287 batting average.

The oft-heard criticism about smaller parks admittedly had

some validity. The old Korakuen Stadium, where Oh played, was listed as 90 meters (295 feet) down the line, shorter by about 10 meters (32 feet) than many MLB parks, and insiders secretly confessed that the real measurement was actually several meters less. But Oh's home runs were usually not of the high flyball variety that landed in the front rows of the outfield stands, but rather hard line drives and majestic shots whose flight was terminated by the presence of the right-field seats, many rows back.

Oh, at five feet eight (1.78 m) and 176 pounds (80 kg), was not a big man. But, as he himself put it, he had "the right muscles" to hit home runs. He had huge calves and tremendous leg power. That, combined with the strong wrists he had developed and his great bat speed, helped turn him into a slugger par excellence.

It is also worth noting that Oh hit all of his 868 circuit blasts in 155 fewer games and 597 fewer at-bats than Barry Bonds, who holds the present MLB record with 762.

There is no shortage of testimonials from former major league stars who saw Oh in action. Davey Johnson, a slugging second baseman who played with both Aaron (in 1973 and 1974 in Atlanta), and Oh (in Tokyo from 1975 to 1976), declared that Oh was as good a hitter as anyone he had ever seen. Clyde Wright said, "Oh hit better on one leg than most guys in the big leagues hit on two."

And then there was this insight from Clete Boyer, the former Yankee great who also played alongside Hank Aaron in Atlanta from 1967 to 1971 and then against Oh in the early seventies when with the Taiyo Whales: "I think he's super. He's one of the best ballplayers I've ever seen. If Oh played in the US, he'd be a superstar. He would probably lead the league in home runs and would hit with the best of them. People say they would brush him back in the States because he crowds the plate, but he would learn fast. He's got great reflexes. He's got a perfect swing and the perfect mental attitude. I would compare him to Hank Aaron. And, in his own way, he's like Ted Williams. His eye is that good!"

Oh played 110 games against MLB teams in postseason, goodwill exhibition games. He hit .260 with 26 home runs, which projects to 38 homers a year and 836 over a 22-year career.

Said Pete Rose, who played against Oh in 1978 when the Cincinnati Reds visited Japan, "I think he would have hit .300 and averaged 35 home runs a year if he had played in the majors."

Of course, we'll never know.

(Just as we'll never know how well Bonds and Aaron might have done playing in Japan. Would they have ever seen a pitch in the strike zone?)

Over the years more than one MLB team tried to recruit Oh. Los Angeles Dodgers owner Walter O'Malley and Chicago White Sox general manager Bill Veeck both tried to sign him. But they were blocked by a long-standing reserve clause that bound a player to one team in Japan, and the quaint notion prevalent at the time that one should be loyal to one's team.

As Oh put it, "I wanted to go, but even if I had found a way, the fans would have never forgiven me. It was a different time."

TOKYO

I watched Sadaharu Oh through much of his career with the Yomiuri Giants, living as I did in Tokyo, first as a student, then as an employee in a Japanese company and after that as a journalist.

During that time it was impossible to miss what was going on with him and his team. You could get in a cab after work and the Giants game would be blasting away on the radio. Walk into any restaurant and bar in the city and there would be a TV set tuned in to the game. Headlines in the sports dailies at the train station kiosks the next morning were all about the mighty Kyojin. And it was like that all over the country. Cynics have compared the wall-to-wall coverage to brainwashing and it was not far from the truth.

I went to Korakuen Stadium whenever possible to see the Giants play in person. It would cost me a couple of hundred yen to sit high up in the jumbo stands on the third-base side. With the nighttime neons of Tokyo as a backdrop, I would quaff Kirin beer and watch Oh do his stuff. I saw him play several times in 1964 when he hit his 55 home runs to set a new single-season record.

I saw many of the homers he hit off Hanshin Tigers southpaw

Yutaka Enatsu. I also saw him hit a home run off Bob Gibson, and another off Tom Seaver in postseason exhibition play and still another off Jon Matlack that went completely out of the park.

Someone once showed me a seat in the right-field stands with a crack in it. "An Oh home run," the man said.

Perhaps the most memorable incident I witnessed involving Oh was the famous televised brawl between the Giants and the Hanshin Tigers in September 1968 at Koshien Stadium, in which Oh, Hiroshi Arakawa (a Yomiuri Giants coach) and a big, swarthy pitcher from Louisiana named Gene Bacque were key participants.

Bacque had risen from the Tigers' farm system after passing a tryout in 1962 to become one of the best pitchers in the game. He had won the Sawamura Award (Japan's equivalent of the Cy Young) for best hurler in 1964, when he won 29 games and led the Tigers to the Central League flag.

In 1965, he had pitched a no-hitter against the Giants, and three years later he was still at his peak. Bacque liked to play the role of Ugly American. He liked to scowl in disdain at Giants batters, make mocking gestures and throw an occasional brushback pitch, especially at Nagashima and Oh, all of which he thought was good psychology, not to mention additional entertainment for the fans.

Brushback pitches may have been part and parcel of baseball in the United States, but they were frowned on in the more genteel Japanese game of that era. Thus, in this environment, Bacque was like a touring foreign professional wrestler, playing the villain to pure-hearted, well-mannered Japanese opponents.

Oh, for his part, usually shrugged off such antics. The Giants had a code that demanded they "always act like gentlemen," and so Oh kept his cool and still got his normal quota of hits. On this particular night, however, the atmosphere was unusually heated. It was September and the Tigers trailed the first-place Giants in the standings by a single game.

In the fourth inning, trailing 1–0 and with two runners on base, Bacque delivered two inside pitches in the direction of Oh's head, both of which sent Oh sprawling to the ground. Oh got up and started toward the mound, bat in hand, but he was beaten there by a furious Arakawa and a horde of angry Giants players. A brawl ensued and fans poured onto the field to participate. Despite being knocked down and taking several blows, Bacque got up and hit Arakawa with a right hook, a punch that permanently embedded an outline of Bacque's knuckle on the famous coach's forehead.

It took nearly an hour for the umpires to restore order. When action resumed, a Tigers relief pitcher named Masatoshi Gondo promptly hit Oh in the head. Oh was carried off the field on a stretcher and was taken to the hospital where he spent the next three days. The Tigers lost the game and eventually the pennant. Many blamed Bacque, who had sustained a broken thumb and missed the rest of the season.

"Bacque and I were friends," Oh explained later. "I often went to dinner at his house, over behind Koshien Stadium. I didn't think he was trying to hit me. But I did think he was overdoing it that night. So I was going out to tell him to knock it off. But Arakawa went by me like a rocket. And then everybody went crazy."

That winter, Bacque was traded to the last-place Kintetsu Buffaloes of the Pacific League. Many people believed that Bacque's banishment to the worst team in Japan was punishment for causing so much trouble. Bacque completely lost his effectiveness and was forced to retire after an 0–7 record in 1969. Some Giants fans believed it was divine retribution.

By virtue of the books I wrote, I was in a position to see Oh up close, in interviews, at the ballpark, at receptions, and I can say that I never encountered a more gracious superstar. He was constantly being approached for autographs—by little kids, adults and even ballplayers from other teams. But he never said no and he always treated everyone he met with courtesy and respect, even lowly freelance journalists.

I first met Oh in 1977, when I visited his house, a modest two-story affair in Tokyo's western suburbs. I was a young, unknown journalist, there with a *Newsweek* crew to chronicle Oh's assault on Hank Aaron's home run record. "Oh-san," I stammered upon being introduced, "it is an honor to meet you." He replied to my surprise, "No, Whiting-san, the honor is mine." Then he ushered me into his living room and sat me down in his favorite chair, a huge leather contraption shaped like a baseball glove.

When the interview was over, we drove with him to the stadium, but not until he had posed for pictures and signed autographs for everyone in the crowd of people that was waiting outside his house.

Arriving at the Korakuen clubhouse, he then sat down and started to tackle the stacks of autograph boards, buckets of balls, T-shirts and other items he had been asked to sign, patiently writing his name and along with it the Japanese letters for the word *do-ryoku*, which means effort. That, we learned, was his routine every single day of the season.

When Oh passed Aaron, on the night of September 3, 1977, all of Japan celebrated. Even the US ambassador joined in the festivities, offering a tribute and congratulations.

Yet Oh humbly refused to compare his record to Aaron's. "I'm just a man who happened to hit a lot of home runs in Japan," he told reporters. "The home run I hit today is just one of many."

During the commemoration ceremony, the lights at Korakuen dimmed and a spotlight shone on Oh standing on the mound in front of a microphone. The first thing he did was to bring his mother and father onto the field beside him to thank them for their support and give them the credit for his achievements.

It was characteristic of Oh that in 1980, at the age of forty, when he hit 30 homers with 84 RBIs, but with a batting average that had sunk to .236, he quit. Some players might have thought those statistics warranted playing another year, but not Oh. He was embarrassed. The Giants had finished out of the running for the third year in a row. Shigeo Nagashima, in his sixth year as manager, was forced to resign. Although Oh and Nagashima were not particularly close, Oh felt responsible and so he announced his retirement at the same time.

If you are guessing that Nagashima got more media coverage that fall than Oh, you would be right.

Upon retirement Oh was appointed to the unusual post of "assistant manager" with the Giants, under 1950s pitching star Motoshi

Fujita (who later led the Giants to a Japan championship in 1983, their first in a decade). This assistant manager post was an apprenticeship designed to ease him into the top spot and avoid the difficulties the club had experienced with Nagashima, who had retired from playing at age thirty-eight in 1974 and had immediately been pushed into the manager's slot to capitalize on his huge popularity.

As manager, Nagashima's movie star good looks and bubbly personality were predictably a big hit with the fans, but his inexperience showed, as did his famous absent-minded streak. (Once, during his playing days, he had brought his young son Kazushige to the park and gone home without him.) As manager he would forget how many outs there were. He would go to the mound twice in the same inning without realizing that what he was doing was a violation of the rules and would be forced to take the pitcher out. He would even forget the names of some of his own players.

In Nagashima's first year at the helm, the Giants suffered the humiliation of finishing in last place for the first time in their proud history. Nagashima had to lead his team in a tearful, on-field apology, accompanied by deep bows, on the last day of the season.

Although Nagashima did go on to win two pennants, he also failed to win a Japan Series in his six years at the helm, a state of affairs which, in the Yomiuri worldview, was unacceptable, and the front office brain trust forced him out the door. The move may have been deemed necessary, but, unsurprisingly, caused angry protests from his legions of adoring fans who thought he could do no wrong and that the managerial post of the club should be his for life.

Oh took over as field pilot in 1984 and managed the Giants for five seasons, winning a pennant in 1987, but losing in the Japan Series. During those years, prejudice still continued to rear its ugly head and the overall experience gave him gray hair.

There was still a strong Nagashima faction on the team and many of the players resented the fact that Oh had taken their leader's place at the helm. They would make disparaging remarks behind Oh's back.

Team captain and infielder Kiyoshi Nakahata was among the worst offenders. Oh's name in Chinese was pronounced "wan," which was also a homonym for the sound of a barking dog in Japan. Nakahata, a dyed-in-the-wool Nagashima man, would insultingly refer to Oh as *wanko*, a term that might loosely be translated as "mongrel" or "mangy cur."

"If Nagashima came around to visit," said Warren Cromartie, a former Montreal Expos star, who played for Oh during that period and wrote a book about the experience, *Slugging It Out In Japan* (Signet, 1992), "everyone, from the guys in the front office, to the coaches, to the media, would kiss his ass. But they treated Oh as if he was a second-class citizen. You could tell just from the body language. I'm a Black son of a bitch and I can spot a racist a mile away. They were just rude to Oh in general. But Oh, in my opinion, is worth ten of Nagashima."

At times, in fact, the deposed Nagashima seemed to act as if he were still in charge. Whenever star third baseman and cleanup hitter Tatsunori Hara fell into a slump, Nagashima would appear at the park during pregame workouts to offer advice. Some observers thought that this confused Hara, because the team already had a batting coach. But nobody ever asked Nagashima to cease and desist, including Oh, who seldom complained about anything.

Cromartie could not understand it. He thought Oh was the best batting teacher anyone could have. Oh had taught Cromartie to shorten his big major league swing, to swing down, and just make contact with the ball to hit Japanese-style pitching. He made Cromartie take batting practice with a book under his right arm, to keep his body from "opening up."

Under Oh's tutelage, Cromartie went from being a .280 hitter in 1984 to a .363 hitter in 1986. Later, Oh would pay Cromartie the ultimate compliment. "Cro-san," he said, "you have truly mastered Japanese baseball."

Cromartie, who won a batting title in 1989, hitting .378, became so close to Oh than he named a son, born in Japan, after him: Cody Oh Cromartie (who is now a Miami record producer).

"He showed me how to overcome the handicap of being an outsider," said Cromartie, "because he did it himself. It was comforting to me to have him as a manager."

Oh was an intelligent man. That much was clear.

Oh worked as hard at being a manager as he had at being a player. He was the first one at the park each day and the last one to leave. At home he immersed himself in game data. He was so committed to his job that when his father died in 1985, aged eighty-four, Oh did not allow himself to miss a single game. He took a flight from Hiroshima, where the team had just finished a three-game series, back to Tokyo to attend the noon wake and then boarded a bullet train to Nagoya where the team was scheduled to play, arriving at the antiquated Dragons park worn out and bleary eyed.

But he was never regarded as a particularly apt manager during his tenure with the Giants.

The rap on him was that he was just too nervous and too insecure. He would issue signs on every single pitch. He would pinch-hit in the early innings. He would make his best hitters bunt and was constantly moving his players around. He would not hesitate to remove a starting pitcher holding a lead with two outs in the fifth inning if he thought said pitcher was starting to weaken. Moreover, he relied on intuition and he was superstitious. He would sprinkle salt and use other talismans to ward off evil spirits.

Nakahata and other members of the Nagashima faction would shake their heads in derision at some of his moves. Even Oh's own handpicked coaches, unwilling to take the blame for his mistakes, would criticize him to the press. Some said they took their lead from Giants head man Tsuneo Watanabe who looked down on Oh because unlike Nagashima, Oh had not gone to college and worst yet, lacked charisma. Thus in Watanabe's view of the world, Oh had never met the criteria for superstardom.

Through it all, Oh suffered from intense stress. He took vitamin shots and medicines such as ginseng herbal tea to calm his nerves. But the pressure mounted with each passing season that the Giants failed to win a national title, as sniping from press intensified.

"Oh Screws Up!" a typical sports daily headline would scream.

And there were painfully critical attacks such as the one written by ex-catching great and TV commentator Katsuya Nomura, another pure-blooded Japanese star, in which he adjudged that Oh was the "worst manager in the history of Kyojin." Also, letters from angry fans poured in, demanding that he quit, or be fired. Reporters joked that the only person in Japan who truly liked Oh was his mother, who attended every game, sitting behind first base in her kimono. Oh's wife, a baseball devotee he had met at the Giants practice ground at Tamagawa, stayed at home.

Failing to win the '87 Japan Series, and finishing second the following year, Oh accepted the club's invitation to resign. He stayed on the sidelines for many years working as a media commentator.

But in 1995, he found a managerial niche that fit him, when he was hired by the Daiei Hawks of Fukuoka. While not a national institution like the Giants, the Hawks had a strong fan base and they would treat Oh as the national treasure that he was. Their managing executive was ethnic Korean, a despised minority in Japan, which made him naturally more sympathetic to Oh's position. The Hawks were a downtrodden team that hadn't seen a top-three finish in seventeen years. But Oh (with the help of a skillful general manager named Rikuo Nemoto) took over and molded a winning team.

He took a group of young players—many of whom were youngsters when he retired but nonetheless idolized him for his great achievements—and turned them into one of Japan's hardest-hitting squads. The team included future major leaguers Kenji Johjima, a big, broad-shouldered brute, who would become the best catcher in Japan; Tadahito Iguchi, who would become, arguably, Japan's top second baseman; first baseman Nobuhiko Matsunaka, who would win a Triple Crown; and perennial All-Star third baseman Hiroki Kokubo. All of them would put in seasons in which they hit thirty or more home runs and drove in over a hundred runs.

In Fukuoka, Oh developed a reputation as one of the most demanding managers in Japan. He was one of the few who still made his players do the exhausting spirit-strengthening "thousand-fungo drill" (which requires players to field ground balls until they catch a thousand or collapse), a staple from his own playing days. He also required intensive bullpen sessions from his pitchers and exceptionally high pitch counts from his starters. But he also developed an unusual rapport with team members. Said well-known Meiji

World War II in the Pacific ended with the surrender of Emperor Hirohito and the empire of Japan in August 1945. The country was occupied by the victorious Allies, led by the United States, with nearly half a million soldiers stationed in the country. The Occupation was overseen by American General Douglas MacArthur from his perch in the Dai Ichi Insurance Building facing Tokyo's Imperial Palace. (Chapter 1)

ABOVE: The headquarters of the Canon Agency was the Iwasaki Estate, built on a palatial scale beside Shinobazu Pond in Ueno Park. (Chapter1)

LEFT: Leftist writer and Chinese sympathizer Wataru Kaji was snatched off the street in broad daylight by a Canon Agency team. (Chapter 1)

ABOVE: Charles Kades, right, deputy chief of the Government Section of the GHQ, with his mistress, Viscountess Tsuruyo Torio (center). (Chapter 1)

LEFT: Jack Canon, creator of the black-ops group the Canon Agency. (Chapter 1)

Another key Canon Agency recruit was Al Shattuck who had fought in the Celebes Sea and had initially arrived in Asahigawa, Hokkaido in September 1945 as First Sergeant of HQ company, part of the Occupation forces. (Chapter 1)

LEFT: US Army–enlisted Japanese-American Victor Matsui was the first person Jack Canon recruited to the Canon Agency, in November 1945. (Chapter 1)

BELOW: Yoshio Kodama (front row, left). His Kodama Kikan group, comprised of yakuza, had plundered China to fund the war effort back home. Kodama's wartime treasure chest would also fund the postwar conservative political movement in Japan. (Chapter 1)

Hideki Tojo, former Japanese war minister, takes the stand at the Tokyo War Crimes Tribunal. Hailed beforehand by Americans as a fair hearing on the guilt or innocence of Japanese generals and political leaders, the tribunal's outcome appeared to be a foregone conclusion. Famed *Stars and Stripes* reporter Hal Drake cited a front page in his military-run newspaper which showed a photo of the gallows at Sugamo Prison, where the defendants were incarcerated, with a caption indicating where Tojo and the others would meet their makers. Said Drake, with some dismay, "The story indicated not the slightest doubt that some people were going to be found guilty and hanged. It was not a good lesson in democracy."

Ted Lewin was involved in the postwar introduction of casino gambling to Japan. (Chapter 2)

Wally Gayda, the first American to open up a nightclub in occupied Japan. (Chapter 2)

Jason Lee arrived in Japan in the early fifties after serving stints in Chicago as the boss of the powerful Oriental Gambling Syndicate. (Chapter 2)

Ted Lewin opened the Latin Quarter, in December 1952, seven months after the end of the Occupation, a deluxe dinner club that featured big-name entertainers from the States like Perez Prado and Tony Scott. Tokyo had never seen anything like it. (Chapter 2)

Shibuya in 1952. The crossing at the center of the picture is today's world-famous scramble crossing, and the landmark statue of Hachiko can be seen in the bottom left-hand corner.

A US soldier stands in front of the Dai Ichi Insurance Building, from where General Douglas MacArthur oversaw the American Occupation of Japan from 1945 to 1952.

A Western customer is served a drink by a geisha in a hostess bar in Tokyo in the 1950s.

Craig Spence demonstrated an uncanny ability to worm his way into lofty government levels in both Japan and the United States on little more than hot air and audaciousness. (Chapter 6)

Frances Baker was a leading patron of the Japanese arts, who first came to Japan in 1936. (Chapter 6)

Tom Blakemore, husband of Frances Baker, made significant contributions to the Japanese legal system that are still in existence today. (Chapter 6)

週刊 ベースボール 12月18日号

〈特集〉ついに長……を追い越す王の実入り
●師走に吹きま……、契約更改の嵐をさぐる●

ベースボール・マガジン社 発行

100円

Sadaharu Oh graces the cover of *Shukan Baseball* magazine.

Oh breaks Hank Aaron's home run record. (Chapter 8)

Before his 2018 arrest in Tokyo on charges of false accounting, Brazilian-born CEO of Nissan was by far the most successful foreign executive in Japanese history. (Chapter 11)

American Bobby Valentine had the stormiest career of all foreign baseball managers in Japan, filled with astonishing highs and mortifying
lows. His dynamic leadership electrified Chiba Lotte Marines fans and
changed the face of Japanese baseball. (Chapter 12)

Frenchman Mark Karpelès, who ran a Tokyo-based Bitcoin exchange named Mt. Gox, was another individual who would make his mark on the Tokyo criminal justice system. (Chapter 13)

Sadao Aoki was a prewar Korean immigrant to Japan who rose from abject poverty to revolutionize the taxi industry with his MK Taxi company. (Chapter 14)

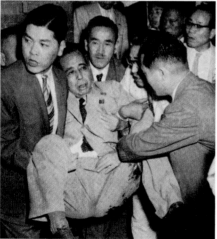

Shinzo Abe's own grandfather, Nobusuke Kishi, a former prime minister of Japan, was the victim of an assassination attempt in 1960. (Chapter 15)

The funeral of former prime minister Shinzo Abe in 2022. Abe's assassin told police he was motivated by his hatred of the Korean Unification Church, an organization long supported by the Abe family. (Chapter 15)

Tokyo in 1964 and 2017.

University communications professor and author Takashi Saito, who had made a study of Oh, "Oh was a superstar when he came to Fukuoka, but he didn't act like one. He didn't behave as if he was above his players. He got down and worked alongside them. He demonstrated his passion and commitment. And they responded to that."

Johjima was one of Oh's biggest supporters. "Oh was cool," he said. "He was the kind of guy who made you feel you had to do something for him."

In 1993, Nagashima was brought back to manage the Giants by new Yomiuri headman Tsuneo Watanabe, a longtime Nagashima fan. Nagashima, now sporting his own crop of gray hair, won a Japan Series in 1994. Oh's Hawks won a Japan Series title in 1999, setting up an historic face-off between the two men in the 2000 Japan Series, described by sports writer Masayuki Tamaki as a "nostalgia fest for old geezers." Nagashima won that encounter, as destiny would have it. But a year later, he retired from baseball. In 2004, he suffered a stroke that left his right arm partially paralyzed.

After the Daiei Hawks were sold to the Softbank Corporation, owned by ethnic Korean billionaire entrepreneur Masayoshi Son, Oh went on to win another Japan Series crown in 2003. He also won regular-season titles in 2004 and 2005, only to be eliminated both years in a new playoff system.

The one big black mark on Sadaharu Oh's reputation was, of course, the unsportsmanlike behavior of the pitchers on his team whenever foreign batsmen threatened his single-season home run record of 55.

The phenomenon had first surfaced in 1985, when American Randy Bass, playing for the Hanshin Tigers, went into the last game of the season—against the Oh-managed Giants at Korakuen Stadium—with 54 home runs.

Bass was walked intentionally four times on four straight pitches and would have been walked a fifth, had he not reached out and poked a pitch far outside the plate into the outfield.

Oh denied ordering his pitchers to walk Bass, but Keith Comstock, an American pitcher for Yomiuri, reported afterward that a certain Giants coach imposed a fine of a thousand dollars for every strike Giants pitchers threw to Bass.

An investigation by the magazine *Takarajima* concluded that the instructions had probably originated in the Giants front office, which wanted the home run record kept in the Giants organization.

Except for an editorial in the *Yomiuri Shimbun's* archrival newspaper, the *Asahi*, demanding to know why Oh did not run out to the mound and order his pitchers to throw strikes, the media remained silent, as did then NPB commissioner Takeso Shimoda, who had often stated his belief that the Japanese game would never be considered first class as long as there were former MLB benchwarmers starring on Japanese teams.

Of course, the reality was more complex. There were many imports who were in fact gifted hitters, but were kept out of big league lineups by other shortcomings in their game or by bad luck—simply being in the wrong place at the wrong time. However, Shimoda and like-minded critics failed to see such shades of gray.

A replay of the Bass episode came during the 2001 season. American Tuffy Rhodes, playing for the Kintetsu Buffaloes, provided the next threat to Oh's record. With several games left in the season, Rhodes hit the 55 mark. But during a late season weekend series in Fukuoka, pitchers on the Hawks refused to throw strikes to Rhodes, and catcher Kenji Johjima could be seen grinning during the walks. Again Oh denied any involvement in their actions and Hawks battery coach Yoshiharu Wakana admitted the pitchers had acted on his orders. "It would be distasteful to see a foreign player break Oh's record," he told reporters.

The NPB commissioner on watch, Hiromori Kawashima, denounced Wakana's behavior as "unsportsmanlike," and there was some outcry from the media.

However, this did not help Rhodes, who went homerless the rest of the way. Rhodes remained convinced that there was a "Code Red" that kicked into action whenever a foreign player did too well.

A replay occurred in 2002, when Venezuelan Alex Cabrera also hit fifty-five home runs, tying Oh (and Rhodes) with five games left to play in the season. Oh commanded his pitchers not to repeat their behavior of the previous year, but, not surprisingly, most of them ignored him. There was more condemnation from the public, but, curiously, not from Oh, who simply shrugged and said, "If you're going to break the record, you should do it by more than one. Do it by a lot." Such behavior led an ESPN sports channel critic to call Oh's record "one of the phoniest in baseball."

In Oh's defense, there was probably nothing he could have done to prevent his pitchers from acting as they did. Feelings about gaijin aside, it was (and still is) common practice for teams to take such action to protect a teammate's record or title.

In all three assaults on Oh's record, the respective front offices had a decided interest in the outcome. Oh's 55 homers was a Yomiuri record, while executives with the Hawks believed Oh's status as a record-holder brought the organization favorable publicity. No pitcher on any of Oh's teams wanted to be the one who gave up the homer that cost Oh that particular spot in the record books.

Finally, there was the question of Oh's own personality. He was a product of his life experiences and his father's life experiences as a member of a minority group in Japan. He surely knew better than to make waves and to embarrass the executive suits that had so much invested in him.

Still, amid all the fuss about protectionism in baseball, it is noteworthy that no one in the Japanese game ever saw fit to mention the discomfiting fact that Oh hit most of his home runs using rock hard, custom-made compressed bats. A batter using a compressed bat, it was said, could propel a ball farther than he can with an ordinary bat. Compressed bats were illegal in the MLB when Oh was playing in Japan, and were outlawed by the NPB in 1982 after Oh retired, but well before Bass, Rhodes and Cabrera had Japan visas stamped into their passports. Curacao native and former major league player Vladimir Balentien hit sixty home runs for the Yakult Swallows in 2013. Critics argued that Balentien hit his sixty in a season when there was a juiced ball—which was true. The scandal caused the resignation of the NPB Commissioner. Nobody said anything about Oh's compressed bat.

Oh's finest hour as a manager was perhaps his performance as manager of Samurai Japan, the national team, in the 2006 inaugural World Baseball Classic (WBC) tourney. He was sixty-five now and his age was starting to show. Moreover, he was not in the best of health, and was months away from a bout with cancer that would spare his life but require a rearrangement of his digestive system.

The tournament was the promotional brainchild of the Major League Baseball Commissioner's Office, but setting it up had been a long and contentious process. At first, the NPB Players Association refused to cooperate. They were upset over the March schedule which they felt would interfere with their spring training. Another thing that bothered the players was that they had been completely left out of the loop in the discussions leading up to the WBC, both by the NPB owners and the American organizers of the event.

The NPB owners, with typical arrogance, had not bothered to inform the players of what had been going on, much less seek their consent or consult with them about the terms of participation in the WBC, until long after the tournament was announced.

More important, the players were skeptical of the event itself. They did not particularly think it was a worthy use of their time.

To break the impasse, senior executives from Yomiuri (which had agreed to sponsor the Asian round) prevailed upon Sadaharu Oh to manage the team, hoping that the presence of one of the most revered names in Japanese baseball history could somehow change the dynamic. Their first choice, Shigeo Nagashima (naturally), was not available due to the aftereffects of his stroke.

Oh had his own (secret) misgivings about the event, but true to his agreeable nature, finally consented to take part. "I'll do it for the welfare of Japanese baseball," Oh had said in a well-publicized remark. "I'll do it for the future. For fifty years from now."

Among others, Ichiro Suzuki, the Japanese batter who starred with the Seattle Mariners, was initially not impressed. "What difference does it make if some old guy is going to manage the team?" he reportedly told acquaintances. "That doesn't make it a real event." But the "old guy" was persistent. He threw himself into the job with typical gusto.

Oh began a courtship of Ichiro and Hideki Matsui—the former Yomiuri slugger who went on to fame with the New York Yankees—and he did it with the grace and diplomacy that was his trademark style. He worked very hard to persuade them individually how important it was that Japan participate, that they participate. Japan's greatest slugger approached them as if they would be doing him a personal favor if they joined the team. In the end, Ichiro agreed to play, although Matsui felt too strong an obligation to the Yankees to leave spring camp.

Oh drove his players hard and the cool, aloof Ichiro somehow magically transformed into a fiery leader, exhorting his team to greater effort in practice and in the actual competition.

Japan went on to win the tourney—despite its three defeats overall—on a succession of steadily improving performances and a managerial strategy which combined caution with aggression. The final, a 10–6 triumph over Cuba played at Petco Park in San Diego, riveted the nation. It was watched by one out of every two Japanese, a total audience of roughly sixty million people, which made it one of the most-watched sporting events in the history of Japan. It ignited an enormous national cheer back home. It was an ironic ending for a team that had not wanted to participate in the first place.

With the WBC victory, Oh was now more popular than ever and it was a fitting cap to his career. Yet in a survey conducted by Sangyo Noritsu University to determine the "Boss of the Decade" the following year, Oh finished well behind Nagashima in the voting, despite having a higher lifetime winning percentage at the time.

The results were not surprising.

Oh had fought against adversity his whole life, it seemed, and his years with the Hawks, successful as they had been, were marred by other difficulties. Among them was the premature death, in 2002, of his wife Kyoko, who succumbed to stomach cancer. That was followed by the inexplicable theft of her ashes from the family graveyard, never to be retrieved.

And then came Oh's own bout with stomach cancer. In the middle of the 2006 season, Oh underwent laparoscopic surgery in which his cancerous stomach was completely removed.

But the thing about Oh was that you never, ever heard him complain—about anything. He just sucked up whatever misfortunes life dealt to him and went on to the next challenge. He always tried to look at the bright side.

When he returned to manage the Hawks in 2007, several pounds lighter and looking, as one reporter put it, "like an underfed jockey," he acted as if coming back to work was the most natural thing in the world to do.

"Yes, I don't have a stomach anymore," he said, the last time I saw him, in the fall of 2007 when he appeared at a Foreign Sportswriters of Japan event to pick up a Lifetime Achievement Award, "but now I can eat as much chocolate as I want."

However, the Hawks fell further out of contention in that '07 season and were eliminated in the playoffs for the fourth straight year. In 2008, the Hawks dropped into last place and Oh announced his resignation and his retirement from field managing. He referenced ill health, but also took responsibility for the team's failure to win another championship. "Managers should not stay that long in one place," he said.

The announcement of his retirement prompted a wave of tributes from the Prime Minister's Office on down, as well as special newspaper editions and TV reports lauding his accomplishments.

People seemed to sense that with Oh's retirement they had lost something more than just a baseball hero, they had lost a connection to an era in Japan where the values of hard work, selflessness and responsibility mattered a lot more than they do now.

Professor Saito summed it up when he honored Oh in an interview with national broadcaster NHK. "We are living in an era of instant gratification," he said. "People these days want everything now and they give in too easily to adversity. But not Oh. He has shown us what the true meaning of *doryoku* is."

Johjima flew back from the States to attend Oh's farewell game on October 7, 2008. "Oh was a great human being," he said when it was all over. "He was special, as a player, as a manager, as a man. He was a father figure to me. It was a huge honor to play for him."

Taiwan president Ma Ying-jeou later honored Sadaharu Oh with the Order of Brilliant Star on February 5, 2009, in Taipei. Oh called receiving the award "the highest honor of my life."

Oh continued to work in the Softbank front office, as general manager, team president and honorary president. He could be seen in the spring of 2022 at the Softbank Hawks training camp working as a batting instructor.

OH AND HANK AARON

Oh was a great friend of Hank Aaron, the man whose career home run record he broke. They spent a lot of time together before Aaron died in 2001 at the age of eighty-six. They had a number of things in common.

Aaron, who came from a poor Black family in Alabama, joined the Milwaukee Braves in 1954—seven years after Jackie Robinson broke the color line in big league baseball—and played for the Braves franchise for the next twenty-one years, the team moving to Atlanta in 1966. He won his first batting title in 1956 with a batting average of .328 and was chosen the National League's Most Valuable Player in 1957, when he led the Braves to a world championship. That year, he also won his first home run crown with 44 homers. He was voted to the All-Star team twenty-one times.

Aaron's life was marked by racism. As a boy, his mother hid him under the bed if the Ku Klux Klan marched down the street. Early in his career, Aaron and his Black teammates were often barred from hotels in the Deep South where his non-Black teammates were staying.

As Aaron neared Babe Ruth's MLB career record of 714 homers and began to receive more national attention, including a million-dollar endorsement deal with TV manufacturer Magnavox, he also started getting racist mail containing death threats from people who did not want a Black man to break Ruth's sacred mark. The letters were so alarming that he needed an FBI detail to protect him and his family. The Braves front office was even compelled to hire two Atlanta police officers to sit in the stands behind Aaron's outfield position to watch for trouble.

Aaron believed he would be assassinated, but finally hit number 715 on April 8, 1974, in Atlanta in a game versus the Los Angeles Dodgers that was broadcast live nationwide. An eleven-minute ovation followed and he was showered with accolades. But the abuse continued. Aaron complained in his memoir, *I Had a Hammer* (Harper Perennial, 2007)—a tribute to his nickname, Hammering Hank Aaron—of being verbally abused and "racially ravaged" in his own park.

"I thought I had earned the right to be treated like a human being . . . it seemed that the only thing that mattered [in Atlanta] about the home run record was that a nigger was about to step out of line and break it."

After retiring as a player, Aaron was given a well-paying job as a vice president in the Braves' front office. But he complained that he was never asked to be the manager. Frank Robinson became the first Black MLB manager in 1975 when he was hired by the Cleveland Indians. Since then there have only been twenty-seven others.

Aaron developed a special relationship with Sadaharu Oh as the Japanese star chased Aaron's home run record. The two men faced off in a home run derby in Tokyo on November 4, 1974, before a Yomiuri Giants–New York Mets exhibition game at Korakuen Stadium during the Mets' goodwill tour. The event was sponsored by CBS News and broadcast to the US. A capacity crowd of fifty thousand in Tokyo watched Aaron win 10–9, with the American shaking Oh's hand warmly afterward. People in Japan still remember that event.

Oh topped Aaron's record on September 3, 1977, at Korakuen, hitting his 756th career home run before a crowd of fifty-five thousand wildly cheering fans. An office building lit up a sign that said "Congratulations, Oh 756" and the US Ambassador sent his regards in a telegram. Japanese television broadcast a videotaped message from Aaron stating: "I would have loved to have been there tonight to put the crown on top of his head because he certainly is quite a gentleman and the people of Japan have a lot to be proud of. I want to wish him the best of luck in the world. I know he is capable of hitting more home runs."

Aaron had respect for the Japanese game and for Oh's accomplishments, unlike many in the US who viewed Japan's version of baseball as somewhat inferior, and one that was played in smaller parks. But a fair analysis would also note that Oh hit his homers in shorter seasons against pitchers who preferred to walk him rather than challenge him. Final career statistics showed that Aaron hit a home run in every 18.46 official at-bats, while Oh's rate was one of 13.67. Moreover, even though the pitchers he faced were generally speaking not as fast as their American counterparts, they threw a sophisticated array of breaking pitches that most batters, including MLB imports, found difficult to hit.

"There are a lot of big-league level players [there]," Aaron said. "Oh could be a big star in America." Aaron seemed to take issue with those who felt Oh's achievement was not a real "world record."

Aaron and Oh formed a long friendship. They reenacted their home run derby ten years later on July 21, 1984—again at Korakuen—and later created the World Children's Baseball Fair to increase awareness of the game among youngsters around the world. The inaugural event took place in August 1990 and was held every year until Covid-19 forced cancellations. Oh and Aaron attended many of the sessions.

In 1992, the two men also initiated the establishment of the World Children's Baseball Foundation to complement the fair. Aaron last appeared in Japan in 2015. That same year, he received the Order of the Rising Sun from the Japanese emperor for his furtherance of US–Japan friendship through baseball.

Aaron passed away in 2021. Sadaharu Oh, who was eighty at the time, expressed his condolences in a statement in which he said: "He had a long career and was a tremendous gentleman. He was great in everything and the epitome of a major league baseball player . . . I thank you for so many things and pray for your soul."

The two great men had much in common.

CHAPTER 9

Hostesses

NIGHTCLUB HOSTESSES have a long tradition in Japan, originating in the world of the geisha house—a richly colorful social institution, centuries old, where graceful kimono-clad women, trained from childhood in the art of music, dance and subtle praise, entertained well-to-do men of high social standing behind closed doors. The modern-day hostess club has evolved as a more egalitarian and Westernized form of nighttime amusement—one that did not demand the hard apprenticeship and unyielding servitude that geisha were subjected to—and one that was also more accessible for the common man.

Hostess bars have flourished in Japan primarily because of the highly demanding Japanese business culture, which, especially in the postwar era, has required salarymen to work brutally long hours and display strict obeisance to authoritarian bosses. Japanese employees need to work off stress before heading home on long crowded commutes to the wife and kids and a tiny cramped apartment. One good way to do it, the reasoning goes, is to spend a couple of hours in the company of a friendly, attractive young lady skilled in the art of flattery. Also, corporate executives need a venue to impress their clients. This is where higher-end clubs with their glamorous hostesses came in.

It is a modus operandi that distinguishes Japan from the US. Whereas in the West, it has largely been the quality of the product and its price that are important in sales and marketing, in Japan it has long been the case that personal relationships are equally vital, if not paramount. Indeed, that is why the majority of bar tabs have been put on company expense accounts and, why the total amount spent annually by Japanese business on "entertainment" has often been more than the entire national defense budget.

Contrary to popular belief, though, Japanese nightclub hostesses do not automatically sleep with their customers. Indeed, in the better clubs in Japan, hostessing at its best is a highly refined Japanese art, requiring patience, a willingness to listen raptly to men complain about their jobs, to laugh at their stupid (often sexist) jokes and, on occasion, to carry on an intelligent conversation on a variety of topics ranging from the state of the economy to sports. Looking one's best is also a must, which means enduring daily trips to the beauty parlor, regularly purchasing new wardrobes at expensive boutiques and making an occasional visit to the plastic surgeon.

"We are far from being common prostitutes," said one Ginza hostess, describing her chosen profession. "Our task is to flatter, to provide attention, to pamper. Our job requires a certain amount of art. Japanese men have a tough corporate life. They have to work hard. There is a lot of stress. We try to provide a kind of nursery service, so they can revert to childhood. We're more like child psychologists than anything else."

Or, as a middle-aged Tokyo geisha once put it to the *New York Times*, referring to the same MO: "It may sound impolite to wives, but men have a world that wives cannot understand. Men release their inner self in a place like this and then go home. Professional women can draw out a man's inner self, but it requires experience. There is a technique to good listening."

THE APALON

One of the most famous, most elegant, most exclusive and most expensive clubs in Japan during the seventies and eighties was the Apalon on the Ginza. It featured rugs made of polar bear hide, deep cushioned sofas covered with tiger skins and a bevy of the most beautiful and gracious women in the city.

The Apalon's exclusively Japanese clientele included some of the most important people in Japan in the latter part of the twentieth century: Liberal Democratic Party kingpin Kakuei Tanaka, multi-billionaire Yoshiaki Tsutsumi, famed actor Shintaro Katsu and others who thought nothing of dropping ten thousand dollars a night on food and drink and female companionship.

The owner was one Akira Shimizu, a short, cognac-drinking, Marlboro-smoking man, who was nicknamed "The General" because he always stood at the bar, drink in hand, every evening, vigilantly watching everything that went on in his club. Subtle eye signs and hand gestures, as sophisticated as those of the third base coach for the Yomiuri Giants, would inform his charges when it was time to order another round, to rotate to another table in order to "create a fresh feeling" for the guests, or to convey some other critical instruction like padding the bill for particularly obnoxious customers to make sure they would never come back.

To Apalon aficionados, places like the supposedly elite Copacabana or the nearby Mikado with its 1,200 numbered hostesses and pagers in bras, were lower class because it was easy to spend the night with the girls. All that was required was a lot of money. The Apalon clientele preferred the psychological game that their club offered, one in which a love affair, not just sex necessarily, was the end goal—this, even though a night at that club would bankrupt normal men. It was the excitement of the chase that appealed to them.

There was an aspect at play here that sociologists and Japanologists had long commented on, a pattern of dependent servitude in family life where mothers devoted themselves so intensely to their male offspring's child's care that when the son grew up he was unable to relate to his own spouse as an equal partner in love—especially after his own children were born. (It was this same psychology that would later drive wealthy Japanese men to patronize certain exclusive clubs which allowed them to don diapers and regress to early childhood, sucking at the breast of a professional mother figure. Seriously.)

Although being a nightclub hostess in Japan offered more immediate material rewards than a job in the corporate world—an overwhelmingly male-dominated preserve where most women were relegated to serving tea, licking stamps and waiting for Mr. Right to come along—it also had its downside.

Said a longtime Ginza "mama"—as the women who manage hostesses and geisha are known—speaking on condition of anonymity, "Nightclub mamas in Tokyo are notoriously neurotic, especially those who've been around for twenty years. Far from learning how to 'really listen,' you become mentally deranged. You get tired of having to cater to people all the time. It's such an emotionally hard, boring job that no one wants to do it forever. After a while you stop remembering your customers names. It's all one big blur."

If being a hostess posed strains for Japanese girls who, one might say, were culturally attuned to such subservient behavior given Japan's reputation as a bastion of male chauvinism, it would go without saying that Western women would be even more taxed, given their independent and opinionated ways and, their comparative lack of interest in nurturing the male ego.

The Apalon's Shimizu, for example, quit hiring foreign hostesses after an experimental trial period because he knew that sooner or later he would have to fire them for one or more violations of his code of conduct, the most common of which were an inability to keep the Japanese customers' names straight or remembering their favorite whiskey. He was once quoted as saying that "Putting a Western girl in a club like mine is like serving cheap wine at an imperial banquet."

There were lesser, if still expensive clubs, in the nighttime entertainment business (or *mizu shobai*, literally "the water trade," as it is called in Japanese) and one could more easily find foreign hostesses there. The clubs wanted them because they believed that Caucasian women would reel in curious Japanese customers, who seldom had a chance to meet foreign women. And the girls liked the idea of the big money the clubs were willing to pay them to sit with an customer and pour his drinks—even if they found the work itself unbearably monotonous.

The attitude of a California girl known simply as Karina, a part time student, was typical. In a newspaper interview with an

American journalist some years ago, she said that being a hostess in Japan was the most boring job in the world. "They'd ask you the same pat questions," she complained, "and make the same pat remarks: Where are you from? What's the weather like in America? Did you know Japan has four seasons? A guy would get a few drinks in him, and he would turn red, like a traffic stoplight, and the sweet personality would disappear. He'd start singing songs off key and running his hands up and down my body, making crude jokes about the size of my breasts. The muscles in my mouth ached from having to smile so much, from having to pretend to laugh so much at the stupid jokes."

Karina, like so many other Western women, could not quite grasp the Japanese concept that, good or bad, that was the way it was supposed to be.

MAGGIE'S REVENGE

However, there were other ways for foreign women to make it in the mizu shobai besides hostessing, or going to work at a place like Danny's Inn, as an ebullient, auburn-haired Australian known as Maggie would ably demonstrate.

Maggie had come to Japan in the late seventies at a very young age after her boyfriend, a Melbourne underworld figure, was sent to prison. She initially tried her hand at being a Ginza hostess but, being boisterous by nature, she quickly discovered she lacked the subtlety of temperament required by the job. However she did display great networking skills long before the term became popular. She had a knack for making friends across a broad spectrum of society, from the underworld to the diplomatic community. She also knew how to have fun, holding loud rollicking parties that people talked about for weeks afterward. Those talents landed her a job as a greeting hostess and floor manager of Chaps, a country-and-western bar that opened up in Roppongi on the edge of its famous cemetery in 1982.

Chaps was the creation of a Tokyo couple named Miyoko and Art Naruse who also owned the nearby jazz clubs After 6 and

Casanova. Miyoko, an extraordinarily beautiful woman, known in some quarters as the Liz Taylor of Tokyo, and Art, a bass player by profession, were avid country-and-western music buffs who often traveled to Nashville to see the Grand Ol' Opry and other shows. They had long wanted to start a country-and-western bar of their own in Tokyo in the city, and Chaps—a basement-level affair with a bar, a few barstools, assorted wooden tables and a stage—was the realization of that dream. Art brought in a country-and-western singer from the States, hiring the gregarious Maggie as the finishing touch.

From the beginning, Chaps was packed, becoming the new in-place in the Roppongi–Akasaka area. Included in the nightly standing-room-only crowd were friends of Maggie, people from the movie industry, people from the media, assorted artists and models, sports figures like Roy White and Charlie Manuel—outfielders for the Yomiuri Giants and Yakult Swallows respectively—and an armada of after-hours nightclub hostesses and their clients, whose patronage Maggie had specifically cultivated. (Included in this group was a Japanese girl named Chako, one of the top girls at the famed Ginza nightclub the Hime—the Apalon's main rival. She would show up every night around midnight, straight from work, attired in a kimono, with her hair tied up in a bun, ready to do the country two-step and the line dance.)

Although Maggie did indeed bring in the business, Miyoko and Art were not entirely satisfied with her ways. They complained that she was giving out too many free drinks to her friends and regular customers. It wasn't the Japanese way, they said. Maggie responded that it might not be the Japanese way, but it was certainly her way: it was how you developed a loyal clientele. How else could you show your customers you appreciated their patronage and thank them for coming?

On the surface, the dispute seemed one of cultural differences. In most Japanese establishments the clients were already loyal to the proprietor and the staff. They came in part because of an existing attachment or connection of some kind. They felt a sense of obligation, if you will, to help their friends, and the friends of their friends, succeed. They *always* expected to pay and in some cases more than usual. In both systems, that of the Japanese and that of Maggie, the operative term was *ningen kankei*—personal relationships. However, in cost, as well as psychology, they were separated by 180 degrees.

The discord erupted into a long, loud argument one night, according to witnesses the words exchanged becoming more and more incendiary, until Maggie, in an uncontrollable burst of alcohol-propelled frustration, grabbed Art Naruse's favorite pair of sunglasses and threw them on the floor. Then she jumped up and down on them, smashing his beloved shades to pieces.

There are varying accounts of what happened next on that now famous evening. In one version, Maggie yelled, "I quit!" and stormed out of Chaps, taking all her clients with her. In another version, Maggie was physically thrown out of Chaps, which also prompted her friends to leave.

At any rate, the relationship between Maggie and the Naruses was indeed terminated. With Maggie's friends gone, business was never the same again. Soon Chaps was just another Roppongi bar in the process of dropping off the radar screen.

If Chaps was finished, however, Maggie was not. She still had something more to prove. She entered into a business deal with a consortium of Japanese and American businessmen who were opening up their own Roppongi nightspot and had asked Maggie to be their point man—or point woman, to put it more accurately.

The bar was to be Aussie-themed, serving up big thick juicy Australian steaks and live rock music. It was to be situated in Roppongi just around the corner from Chaps—a cruelly brief walk of about forty-five seconds—and it would be called Maggie's Revenge.

As had been the case with Chaps, Maggie's touch worked. From the opening day it was a hit. All Maggie's friends and acquaintances, the same crowd that had once graced the portals of Chaps, now gathering cobwebs nearby, descended on Maggie's Revenge. Moreover, it also attracted the attention of the burgeoning new hip crowd in Tokyo, the stockbroker set, who were capitalizing on the remarkable run up in the value of the Nikkei-Dow Japan Stock Market

Index—which was on its way to the all-time high of almost 40,000 that it would reach in December 1989—and of urban real estate.

In addition, since Maggie's Revenge was at street level and people walking by could hear the music and see the band playing through a big bay window, there was a lot of walk-in trade.

Maggie introduced a bizarre new ritual that alternately fascinated and horrified her clientele: necktie cutting. She said that she had envisioned Maggie's Revenge as a place where people cast aside their inhibitions, kicked back, relaxed and got drunk. Thus, customers wearing suits and neckties were, in Maggie's opinion, too uptight to enjoy themselves and therefore had to be loosened up. Maggie, in her typical balls-of-brass style, decided she would be the one to do it by taking a pair of scissors and snipping off any necktie attached to a human neck, then hanging the offending object on the "necktie trophy wall" on one side of the room.

"No necktie wearers," the irrepressible Aussie would cluck to her shocked customers, brandishing her scissors. "You're here to have a good time." And then she would give them a drink—on the house.

Maggie's partners included a longtime Roppongi restaurateur—a burly, red-bearded New Yorker named Al Stamp—and a onetime NHK Japan Broadcasting Corporation radio announcer and business executive named Toshiro Suzuki. Neither one of them had ever seen anybody like their shears-crazed partner. Suzuki was a graduate of Georgetown University and Georgetown was the home of some of the world's best pubs and restaurants. He had seen pubmasters have their quirks, but nothing like those that Maggie displayed. Stamp, for his part, had owned and managed several restaurants and studied Restaurant Management at Cornell University. He knew all about Japanese theories of management by consensus, as opposed to the American theories essentially based on dictatorship and he was familiar with the different ways of achieving all-important *ningen kankei* personal relationships, yet he had never run across anything in any of his business textbooks regarding scissors and neckties.

But the customers kept coming back. Maggie's Revenge, fully twice the size of Chaps, was always bulging at the seams. Regular customers included the ambassadors from Australia, New Zealand, Papua New Guinea, the UK and a host of other countries. Film-maker Itami Juzo was a patron. So were baseball stars Terry Whit-field and Osamu Higashio from the Seibu Lions, Randy Bass of the Hanshin Tigers and Warren Cromartie and Kiyoshi Nakahata of the Yomiuri Giants. High-ranking captains in the Sumiyoshi-kai—To-kyo's largest crime syndicate—also dropped by. All of them surren-dered their ties to Maggie's scissors.

But then her partners began to take uncomfortable notice of Maggie's deep streak of generosity. She was, it seemed to them, giv-ing away the store to her customers: magnums of champagne here, bottles of whiskey there, free pitchers of beer all around. Neigh-boring restaurateur Nicola Zappetti, who himself was not averse to giving away free pizza and beer to valued customers, was among those astonished at the largesse. "If you're not careful," he would say, on visits to chat with Stamp, surveying the nightly damage, "you're going to give away all your profits."

That wasn't all. Stamp also complained privately about the money Maggie was advancing herself from the till to cover pressing expenses. Two hundred thousand yen for a trip to Guam to treat her chronic asthma. A hundred thousand yen the next week for something else. The consortium was already paying her a substan-tial salary and a single digit percentage of profits in the venture. But still that didn't seem to be enough.

For a time, Stamp and the others said nothing to Maggie for fear she would leave. Instead, they let her do as she wished for several years because business was sailing along. But then in 1988, Maggie demanded a bigger share of ownership. Gratis. If they refused to give it to her, she reportedly said, then she would quit and take all her customers with her.

The consortium had calculated that if they gave Maggie what she was demanding, then there would be no profits left for the rest of them. This time, they refused to go along. In response, Maggie started taking more time off. On nights when she wasn't there, groups of mean-looking men, with bruised knuckles, ugly scars and missing fingertips would appear. Among them was a well-dressed local yakuza boss, a captain in the Sumiyoshi-kai, the city's largest gang, who kept an office nearby. As it turned out, he was doing business with Maggie's boyfriend, the Australian ex-jailbird who was sending up shipments of narcotics from down under.

The yakuza boss advised the floor manager on duty, a man named Inaba, to tell management to "cooperate" with Maggie, to give her what she wanted. He said he was a "big fan" of the lady from Australia and that he would hate to see her leave, because without Maggie, the restaurant would be nothing. He added that if for some reason she could not get what she wanted then there would be trouble.

Stamp and company demurred and continued to demur despite repeated threats. They did not know exactly why Maggie had such, shall we say, influential supporters. But Stamp was already familiar with the well-dressed Akasaka boss from a previous encounter. Maggie had shown him a letter from her boyfriend in Australia, addressed to the Sumiyoshi captain, and had asked Stamp, who was fluent in Japanese, to translate it for the man over the phone. Stamp did as requested. The letter was a notice to the effect that "there was a lot of fish available" for the boss in Akasaka if they could throw a crew together. When Stamp had finished translating, the boss said thank you and that was the end of that. It was only later that Stamp realized that the "fish" he had been talking about were drugs.

The final demand came late one night when the place had almost emptied out. The Akasaka boss had come in and told a terrified Inaba, holding down the fort by himself, that the negotiating phase was over. If they didn't agree to give Maggie what she wanted, the next time he came he would bring thirty or forty of his men with him. They would sit there and drink water and coke all night until closing time if need be, and stare at the other customers. And they would do it the next night and the next and the one after that.

Stamp called the police, who true to fashion, said they could do nothing until the threat actually materialized into action. Then the consortium lawyers organized a round of meetings and conferences and negotiations until finally an accord was reached. Maggie would sell her shares for a substantial sum of money.

This accomplished, in December 1988, Maggie left Japan.

Predictably, business did indeed eventually fall off, perhaps because there was no one brazen enough around to cut the customers neckties anymore.

Maggie's Revenge struggled on for about three more years until the stock and real estate bubble burst. In the ensuing recession, it was forced to shut down.

However, the legend of Maggie remained.

As one longtime observer of the scene put it, "Maggie was like a ten-year-long typhoon that blew through Roppongi. They ought to build a statue of her in front of the Roppongi cemetery."

By the end of the twentieth century, the Roppongi–Akasaka area had changed dramatically. Gone were the big band hostess clubs. The New Latin Quarter had fallen victim to a fire that gutted the Hotel New Japan and caused the deaths of many people, while the Mikado, with its 1,200 beeper-carrying girls, went bankrupt after the owner died and his daughter took over. (Local residents still remember the sight of the cabaret's hostesses, many in hair curlers and scarves, staging a huge daytime protest outside the Mikado over unpaid wages—which, unfortunately, would never be forthcoming.) In place of such clubs would come smaller, more intimate ones, as well as discos.

Although Akasaka still maintained a kind of quiet elegance, home as it was to the back street, high-walled geisha houses hidden behind towering new five-star hotels, the entertainment quarter of Roppongi once noted for its class and identified by the shiny limousines parked on its main drag, was now a neon-lit center of sleaze, more famous perhaps for its sidewalk pimps and touts, bearing placards appealing to all carnal appetites—cheap recession-induced karaoke bars and seedy clubs that featured strip shows and backroom lap dancing and the like.

On any given night one could find among the pedestrian swells, Japanese salarymen and habitués of the foreign business community; an eclectic mix of Southeast Asian drug dealers, petty crooks and drifters; Israeli and Iranian street vendors; Nigerian bouncers;

drunken GIs; and streetwalkers of all nationalities, mingling with the locals in déclassé watering holes with names like Gas Panic.

The economic crash of the nineties had caused many bankruptcies but Japan still remained the number two economy in the world, boasting one-third, if no longer one-half, of all the cash in the world's banks. The yen was one of the world's strongest currencies, reaching a high of 79 yen to the greenback in 1995 before retreating back to the 130 range by 2002. There were still people with money who were willing to spend it, despite the downturn, even on—or perhaps especially on—"entertainment."

Thus, in a massive wave of immigration that hit Japan in the in the last two decades of the twentieth century, both legal and illegal, there was a striking increase in female workers. According to the Japanese police, the number of illegal women workers quadrupled in the nineties from approximately five thousand in 1990 to twenty thousand in 2000 (while the number of illegal male workers stayed the same). By the end of the millennium, police estimated the number of Western women in Japan's *mizu shobai*, or "water trade," as it was called, was in the thousands and was far higher than at anytime in Japan's history. A great many of these women came on ninety-day tourist visas, simply because it was the easiest way to get into Japan for citizens from many Western countries. Under new simplified visa procedures, there was no paperwork at all required for entry. All you had to do was get off the plane and have your passport stamped.

LUCIE BLACKMAN

The world of the ninety-day hostess was not commonly known to most ordinary Japanese citizens. But that all changed when a young English hostess named Lucie Blackman, working in Tokyo, suddenly disappeared, and the subsequent investigation and media coverage exposed this aspect of Tokyo nightlife's dark underbelly.

Lucie was a bright, attractive twenty-year-old, a middle-class lass from England. A flight attendant with British Airways who had flown the London–Moscow route, she found such work low paying and dull and had quit the airline in the summer of 2000 to come to Tokyo, where she had heard there was a fortune to be made for English-speaking Caucasian blond women like herself in Tokyo's clubs. She planned to spend three months there, then return home to England to start thinking seriously about her future.

She entered Japan in June on a tourist visa, accompanied by another young English woman named Louise Phillips with whom she would share a small apartment in Yoyogi. The two women found hostess employment at the Roppongi club Casablanca, a small living-room-sized affair with deep, cushiony sofas. It was located in a modern, six-story building which also housed the notorious Seventh Heaven, the largest strip club in the city, known for its lap dances and other emoluments supplied by blond Russian girls and Las Vegas hookers.

Described by friends as "sweet, trusting, likable," she was quoted as saying after her first few days on the job, pouring drinks and "flirting a little" with Japanese businessmen two and three times her age, "I can't believe I'm being paid for doing this." She even found a boyfriend, an American sailor from the Yokosuka base near Tokyo.

Lucie had been on the job for about a month when one day she took off for an afternoon drive to the seashore with a client, telling her roommate that she would be back in time for an evening dinner date. She did not return. Calls to the police by her friends did no good.

Two days later her father came to Japan and launched a desperate search, sending out thirty thousand fliers and even enlisting the help of British prime minister Tony Blair, who was in Japan attending the G-8 summit in Okinawa. Blair, in turn, appealed to then prime minister of Japan, Yoshiro Mori.

Lucie's father became widely recognized around the nation after holding eight separate press conferences. But not everyone in Japan was sympathetic to Blackman's plight. Some observers said that taking a job at a place such as the Casablanca, which was hardly a bastion of moral probity, and working there without a work visa and other papers, was an invitation to trouble.

On February 9, 2001, authorities found the dismembered body

of a blond Caucasian woman buried in a cave in Zushi, a seaside town ninety minutes outside of Tokyo. The body had been cut into ten pieces and put inside separate bags. The head had been shaved and encased in cement. DNA tests revealed it was Lucie Blackman. Police believed that she had died of an overdose in the apartment of one Joji Obara, a Korean-Japanese millionaire real-estate investor who had became a money-laundering front for the Sumiyoshi-kai crime syndicate in the wake of the burst economic bubble. Seven years later, Obara was found guilty of multiple rape charges involving other foreign women, and manslaughter (although he was acquitted of Blackman's rape and murder for lack of direct evidence), and sentenced to life in prison. The case was recounted in an excellent book by the London *Times* newspaper reporter Richard Lloyd Parry, *People Who Eat Darkness* (Farrar, Straus & Giroux, 2011).

An American gang member in Roppongi known as Smoky, had this to say: "I think that her problem was that she started to get too involved with her customers. The smart girls come to work, serve their drinks, smile, act stupid and go home at midnight. They don't accept favors or gifts or after hours dinner dates from customers, especially from the yakuza type. That's the road to trouble . . . In fact, most of them out and out refuse to sleep with a Japanese man no matter how much they offer, which when you think about it is race discrimination, but that's the way it is. Look at all the nightclubs in this city that won't let Americans in."

In the end, the remarkable thing about the Lucy Blackman case aside from the grisliness of Obara's crimes (he would later be charged with three more rapes) and the absolute heartache it brought the Blackman family, was the media coverage and the impact it had on the public consciousness. Over the several months it took for the case to unfold, there were reams of stories about Lucie, making her face familiar to everyone in the country. Japanese TV, radio and print commentators analyzed the story from every conceivable angle—racial, sexist, legal, moral—trying to figure out what it revealed, if anything, about the Japanese psyche.

Did Japanese men have an unhealthy attraction to blond Western women?

Was Japan becoming an immoral country?

Did Japan really discriminate against foreigners?

The English-language press did its share of theorizing as well. In a breathless, grandiose cover story in *TIME* magazine Asia, for example, a writer equated the Lucie Blackman case to nothing less than a national wakeup call for Japan, terming Lucie "the poster child of a nation that was suddenly unaware of where it was going and of what was happening to it," and the case "synonymous with millennial Tokyo's anxieties, aspirations and insecurities . . ."

The fact that Obara lived in a multimillion-dollar suburban Tokyo mansion that had gone to seed in the wake of the deflated bubble and moribund economy—its iron gates rusting, facade crumbling and garden trash-filled—was to the *TIME* editors a clear metaphor for the sorry state of modern Japanese society as a whole.

HUMAN RIGHTS WATCH

What was missing from the frenzied coverage of Lucie Blackman (which at times appeared to match that surrounding the O.J. Simpson murder case in Los Angeles in 1995) was any sense of perspective. Seldom seen was any mention of the countless Southeast Asian women who had come to Japan to work in the mizu shobai "water trade" only to suffer similar misery—held in virtual slavery by their "sponsors," beaten, raped, drugged, robbed and forced to work in cramped sex sweatshops under heavy debt bondage. More than a few of them have disappeared and appeared to have died under mysterious circumstances.

Undeniably, Japan had, at the time, one of the most energetic sex industries in the world. It was estimated that it employed anywhere from 150,000 to 250,000 Japanese women in a wide array of traditional and "postmodern" sex entertainment establishments, which included "pink salons" where oral sex in a darkened booth was the norm, "image clubs" where nurse–patient or infant–nanny roleplaying was featured, "S&M clubs" featuring cross-dressing and anal sex, and "teleclubs" where romantic liaisons could be arranged by phone. It was an industry whose imagination knew no limits, from domestic child-pornography peddlers whose products were famous worldwide to the freelance fourteen-year-old junior high school girls who entertained middle-aged men with Lolita complexes in exchange for money to shop at Gucci. Whether all this activity represented sexual maturity, a sick culture or the result of cramped living conditions was open to debate. What was clear was how huge the demand was with the industry accounting for anywhere from one to three per cent of the GNP. (It is interesting to note, in light of all this activity, that, according to an international survey, Japanese married couples had the least sex of all the world's major countries, about thirty-five times a year.)

To fill Japan's throbbing need in this regard, there were tens of thousands of foreign women working in this industry. It was estimated that approximately 80 percent of the women came from other Asian countries like Thailand and the Philippines—a great many of them having been trafficked. According to a report issued by the Human Rights Watch (HRW) in September 2000, entitled "Owed Justice: Thai Women Trafficked Into Debt Bondage in Japan," literally thousands of such women have been lured into Japan every year. While admittedly, the majority of cases involved willing sex workers, many others were promised lucrative jobs as entertainers, beauticians, waitresses, factory workers and whatnot by "agents" in Thailand (who beat the bushes for talent much like professional baseball scouts) but upon arriving in Japan suddenly found themselves trapped by debt they couldn't possibly pay. Typically, they were picked up at Tokyo's Narita Airport by Japanese "agents," often members of organized crime groups, who ushered them into vans, confiscated their passports for "safekeeping" and drove them hours to a destination far outside Tokyo where they were forced to work in bars as prostitutes to pay back the exorbitant sums of money spent on them in "agent" and "transportation" fees. During the years it took to pay back this "debt," often amounting to thousands of dollars, they were forced to labor under highly coercive and abusive conditions. In their off-duty hours they often had to live in cramped, cockroach-infested apartments designed for one or two people, but sometimes crammed with as many as eight.

Upon release, many found their work visas were fake and that they were in the country illegally.

A Thai economist conservatively estimated the gross annual income generated by Thai sex workers as over US$3.3 billion. According to a June 2020 study published by the US State Department, Japan had not met even minimum requirements for the elimination of human trafficking.

One place HRW agents visited was Komoro, an agricultural town in Nagano and longtime trucking stop, with a population of forty thousand—two thousand of them prostitutes from Thailand, their presence evidenced by the myriad of bars and Thai restaurants and supermarkets there. One observer estimated that 40 percent of the prostitutes were there involuntarily, including a young woman who resisted the order to sexually service customers in the bar she was forced to work in and paid a heavy penalty for her disobedience—her head was dunked in a vat of hot water, until she begged for mercy and agreed to do what she was told. To set an example for the others, she was ordered to personally fulfill all the oral sex requests that came from the bar's customers.

According to the photojournalist Greg Davis who was familiar with the situation there, many girls who tried to escape from the town were usually stymied by roadblocks erected by both police and yakuza working together, the latter being the agents who had brought the Thai females to town in the first place. Occasionally a girl succeeded in making it all the way to Tokyo, but most escapees were hunted down and brought back.

The extreme isolation and daily intimidation many such women faced was described in a wrenching letter written by one Thai women (who has since disappeared) to her father.

> *I live without hope. What I do everyday is just have customers. I cannot go out. There are more than ten yakuza here. This letter must be hidden from them. If they find it, I will be beaten. If I try to run away from here, I will be killed and my body will be thrown to the sea . . . I do not know where I am now. All of us do not speak. There are lots of Thais and Filipinas. I am prohibited to talk to them . . .*

The yakuza are always watching me carefully. I am forced to stay at the place where yakuza live. The restaurant where I work is located on an island. The yakuza are threatening me . . . Living here is like living in hell. Yakuza sometimes take us somewhere in order for us to get customers. The pack us into a truck without windows. I cannot look outside.

The father who received this letter went to Japan to look for his daughter and could not find her.

Similar stories could be heard all over Japan, involving Colombian, Russian and Chinese women coerced into prostitution and prevented from trying to flee by threats of severe punishment and even death. Yet one saw only lukewarm coverage of their plight in the media, because they are not from the Western world. There are no widely attended press conferences, of the type Tim Blackman held, at the Thai or Philippine embassies and no police sweeps and searches for such kidnapped girls (only periodic crackdowns on illegal workers to send them back home). When Southeast Asian leaders came to Japan, they usually came with their hands out for economic aid, not to lobby for the well-being of migrant laborers.

Mizuho Fukushima, a female member of the Upper House of Japan's parliament who in 1989 helped establish a private center called HELP, which has assisted Asian women coerced into prostitution, has said, "I have taken foreign women who have been beaten up to the police of the Immigration Department who have said to my face, 'What are you doing here? These women are here illegally. What were these women expecting when they came here illegally?'"

Japanese officials have publicly expressed concern for the victims of trafficking, but can also remain bureaucratically obtuse, maintaining that incidents of coercion are rare. As the Director General of the Immigration Bureau, Yukio Machida, put it in the HRW report, "so-called trafficking victims are merely illegal migrants with crime syndicates behind them"—the attitude seeming to be "those that lie down with dogs should not complain if they catch fleas."

The reports pointed out cultural differences between Japan and other nations, in regard to treatment of minorities and those charged with criminal offenses, citing Japan's feudal, "pure-blooded" mentality as impediments to human rights. (The HRW cited immigration law revisions in 1990 that targeted illegal migrants from other Asian countries, causing mass raids and increased arrests for immigration offenses, but at the same time greatly expanded the availability of visas for second and third generation Japanese emigrants.)

The ultimate question asked by many: why did it take the disappearance of a white woman at the hands of the Japanese not only to make the cover of *TIME*, but to cause the authorities to move on behalf of an illegally working migrant? The answer seemed to have more to do with economic clout than anything else. Or was it indeed racism? Complaints by authorities from less-developed countries, it appeared, were just not worthy of the same attention as those from more developed, Occidental nations. Indeed, a similar phenomenon was seen with the March 2007 murder of UK English teacher Lucy Hawker at the hands of a Japanese martial artist who raped and strangled her to death. He was captured by police after two and a half years on the run and sentenced to life in prison. The case received national attention, but one involving the 2006 murder of a Japanese pimp by his Thai sex slave who had endured unspeakable abuse, received far less attention.

That does say something about priorities and Japan's relationship with the rest of the world.

As this book went to press in 2024, sadly, not much had changed. The 2023 Trafficking in Persons Report issued by the US State Department acknowledged that the Japanese government had made efforts to increase measures to combat trafficking, but went on to conclude: "The Government of Japan does not fully meet the minimum standards for the elimination of trafficking."

In its 2023 report, HRW noted Japan still does not have a human rights institution.

Gaijin Yakuza

UNDERWORLD GANGS have a long, rich history in Japan. As described in numerous books and academic theses, their origins can be traced all the way back to the illegal gamblers and the streetwise peddlers of the sixteenth century who professed to live by a strict samurai-inspired code of duty, honor and loyalty to the boss. A key feature of these criminal organizations—which gradually grew to include slum-dwelling dock workers and other laborers—was the *oyabun-kobun* relationship, a master-servant bond with strong Confucian patriarchal overtones. These gangs have been variously referred to over the years as yakuza, (a term for the worst score in a Japanese card game, thus meaning "loser"), as well as *gokudo* (villain), *boryokudan* (lit., "violence group") and *han-shakaiteki seiryoku* ("antisocial forces," a euphemistic term officially used in the present day by the Japanese government).

However, gangs have also prided themselves on having a certain romantic sense of obligation to society, often comparing themselves, with some exaggeration, to legendary characters like Jirocho Shimizu who fought to return the Japanese emperor to the throne during the Meiji Revolution in 1868, helping to end centuries of control by Japan's feudal lords. In the aftermath of the great 1923 earthquake, Tokyo mobsters displayed a social conscience by supplying food and medicine to the victims of the disaster, reacting more quickly and efficiently, in fact, than the government. Yakuza also came to the help of victims of the cataclysmic earthquakes that took place in 1995 in Kobe and in 2011 in Tohoku. A member of the Tokyo Inagawa-kai explained that such behavior was necessary if only to keep gangland's customer base active.

Thus, being of the underworld was not necessarily considered a terrible thing. In fact, authorities and the gang bosses shared a sort of tacit understanding in which certain gang activities were tolerated as long as they did not overly infringe on the rights of the man in the street or commit violence against the police. In addition to the big-money backroom card games, stimulant sales, brothels and other typical mob enterprises, these activities included debt collection, money lending and the arbitration of disputes—areas of endeavor which fell to the criminal underworld by default because of the relative paucity of civil courts (institutions which normally handled such matters in other countries, but in Japan were limited for reasons including the social dictates of *wa*, the ancient precept which demanded harmonious resolution of conflicts).

Of course, the indulgence of the powers that be had to be reciprocated by healthy election campaign donations and get-out-the-vote drives among other vital tasks of *wa* nurturing. In the prewar years, for instance, government authorities employed yakuza to break Socialist-inspired strikes on behalf of large corporations regarded as important to the Japanese economy. They formed the core of the paramilitary armies maintained by certain political parties before (and during) the Pacific War. During the postwar years, yakuza were mobilized by Japan's conservative government and its US supporters to join hands with police to put down pro-Communist demonstrations and intimidate suspected Communists.

Their presence in local communities was prominent, with branch offices bearing the gang crest on the front door. Citizens not infrequently turned to the crime groups rather than the authorities for help in dealing with problems in the neighborhood.

"We're not like Mafia," one would often hear the yakuza say. "Mafia guys are criminals who commit crimes for money, who sell their services to the highest bidder. But not the yakuza. We have a tradition of helping society."

Of course, to some observers, the concept of a benevolent gangster was a contradiction in terms, given the narcotics distribution, protection, usurious loan rates, apartment squatting, strong-arm real-estate takeovers and other such activities the underworld in Japan is known for.

As mob expert and crime author Yasuhara Honda declared famously, "When I stop and think about it, I don't believe I've ever seen or heard of such a thing as a good yakuza."

THE POSTWAR YEARS

It was in the years after the war that the biggest period of yakuza growth occurred. The prewar total of all gangsters in Japan ran less than twenty thousand, a typical gambling group being comprised of a few dozen men under one *oyabun* (boss). The aftermath of the Pacific War saw their ranks swell tenfold, as thousands of jobless and homeless young men, back from the front, filled the streets. They formed their own gangs in the rubble of shattered cities, moving into prostitution, narcotics, smuggling, loan sharking and protection, as well as the new fields of corporate extortion and casino gambling and any other areas where they could eke out a living.

Soon, there were ten large-scale underworld groups in the Tokyo area alone, foremost among them the Sumiyoshi-kai crime syndicate. Once a small prewar gambling organization of thirty-five people on the Ginza, one of fifty such groups in the metropolitan area, it gradually expanded its sphere of activity, moving into the amphetamine trade, then the nightclub and entertainment business and finally gaining control of the docks. A decade after the war ended, its membership stood at 11,000. Its main rival, the Inagawa-kai, began out of the port city of Yokosuka, eventually expanding into Tokyo and grew to 10,000. The Osaka-based Yamaguchi-gumi became the strongest of them all. It parlayed a series of hostile takeovers into widespread control of illegal gambling, extortion, prostitution, stevedore unions and show business. From humble dockside origins in Kobe, its membership reached a peak of 28,000 men in the pre–Tokyo Olympic year of 1963, a time when nationwide gangsterhood reached a total of 184,000, more than a dozen times its prewar high.

The large-scale organization of the yakuza was facilitated by the fortuitous advent of the Red Scare of the late forties caused by the Maoist takeover of China and the division of the Korean peninsula along ideological lines which in turn eventually led to the breakout of war there by 1950. There were massive Communist demonstrations in Japan, and the ruling Liberal Democratic Party (LDP) began to worry about a possible insurgent movement and the ability of the police and the weak, fledgling national defense forces of Japan known as JSDF, to deal with it. In desperation, they turned to the yakuza for help in maintaining social order (with the tacit blessing of American intelligence) and formed a security force the likes of which had no historical precedent in Japan.

Created for the LDP with the help of ultranationalist thug Yoshio Kodama, landlord of the Latin Quarter dinner club, it consisted of nearly thirty thousand mobsters and right-wingers. This unconventional army was designed to help police provide protection from leftists opposing the extension of the Security Treaty scheduled for 1960, whose galvanizing protests involving several hundred thousands of people disrupted a planned visit by US president Dwight Eisenhower to celebrate the treaty's extension. Although Ike's trip was ultimately canceled due to the escalating intensity of the riots, the government still found good use for the gangsters by having them guard the Diet Building the night of June 19 when the treaty extension was voted on, their presence in the main hall physically preventing leftists from carrying out a plan to storm the Diet and obstruct the vote.

Such patriotic contributions bestowed the gangsters with a certain kind of sociopolitical cachet with the Japanese authorities and with American intelligence agents, who quietly recognized the yakuza right to exist. In fact, many gang members went on to assume public poses as right-wingers to capitalize on their new status, which served, of course, as a convenient cover for their more nefarious activities.

By the 1964 Tokyo Olympics, however, the authorities had

enough firepower to deal with "antiestablishment" elements without help from their yakuza army wing. In fact, worried about the image of Japan that would be portrayed in the foreign media covering the Olympics and aided by a huge budget increase, the police undertook a massive crackdown on organized crime, resulting in the arrests of several oyabun, the dissolution of some of the smaller gangs and the halving of the "officially known" number of gangsters.

In response, some gangsters turned to the esoteric world of *sokaiya*—in which they would buy shares in a company and offer to "keep the peace" at general shareholders' meetings (known as *sokai*, in Japanese) for a price, or else dig up embarrassing information about company executives and demand money to keep it quiet. Many refurbished yakuza made fortunes through this particular brand of corporate extortion.

Others became *keizai yakuza* (financial gangsters), turning to real estate and securities transactions to make money, a phenomenon that grew during Japan's "bubble era" in the 1980s, when Japanese banks held more cash than the rest of the world combined. This state of affairs was brought about by the 1985 Plaza Accord when G-5 finance ministers engineered a revaluation of the Japanese yen to cope with a flood of exports of Japanese cameras, autos and TV sets that were destabilizing the world economy. The yen went from 240 to the dollar to 120, triggering a dramatic rise in Japan's stock and real-estate markets. The major Japanese banking institutions, hungry for loan customers in the soaring stock and property markets, practically threw money at affiliated housing loan companies, which used yakuza muscle to force tenants out of prime real estate needed for commercial development. The sometimes unwillingness of courts to enforce eminent domain laws in Japan necessitated such tactics. Thus, the keizai yakuza were able to participate in Japan's economic bubble and prosper. Physical threats and other forms of intimidation (dead cats or bags of feces on the doorstep) convinced reluctant real-estate owners to sell their properties to the housing-loan firms, who then turned around and sold their newly acquired real estate to the banks, repaying the original bank loan and pocketing a tidy profit. The banks then tore down the buildings on said properties and put up new office and residential structures which they sold or rented. Everyone made money.

The Nikkei Dow average rose sixfold to hit a peak of 38,957 on December 29, 1989, making many underworld criminals rich in the process.

The change in the nature of the gangs before and after the bubble began was striking. According to police reports, pre-bubble oyabun slept until noon, drank until all hours of the morning, wore kimono and lived on tribute from their underlings. As the bubble grew, however, and the underworld joined hands with high-finance, more top yakuza visibly moved up in the world. Many gang bosses assumed the habits and demeanor of corporate executives—arising at dawn, donning Italian suits and ties instead of kimono, then setting out for a long workday in a chauffeur-driven limousine.

The National Police Agency had estimated there were eighty thousand gangsters during this era, two-thirds of whom belonged to the brand-name gangs Yamaguchi-gumi, Sumiyoshi-kai and Inagawa-kai. Together, these three mega-groups controlled most of the organized criminal activity in Japan, including drug dealing, alien smuggling, prostitution, illegal gambling, gun trafficking, extortion and embezzlement. Their influence extended to almost every area of society—construction, entertainment, department stores, hotels, sports, politics, credit unions, newspapers, even health care. During the bubble era, their purchases of overseas businesses and property and significant investment in Wall Street for the purpose of money laundering and hiding assets, posed a threat to the global economy.

Overall mob influence was such that an FBI agent intimately familiar with international crime offered the following assessment at the time: "Outside of Russia, Japan offers the best example of what the mob can do to a society."

"If you're with a foreign firm and don't want to deal with the mob," offered a vice president at a major American investment company, "then you should probably leave Japan."

The Nikkei Dow began a long, precipitous slide after reaching that December 1989 high, which would take it all the way back down to the 7,054 level in March 2009, and cause many bankruptcies, including those of organized crime businesses. However, yakuza found new ways to operate further underground and in disguised form. Illegal drug transactions, for example, skyrocketed. Financial fraud cases and money-laundering crimes involving underworld groups also spiked.

Some American firms were impacted by organized crime in Japan, in particular brokerage houses and investment banks in the nonperforming loan business, who wound up selling distressed Japanese assets to yakuza groups in disguise. Conversely, executives from such firms also had problems with yakuza groups trying to block the disposal or sale of real estate assets that their loans were connected to, and, in other cases, yakuza underlings even occupied buildings purchased by unwitting American buyers. In an infamous incident, one of the managing directors of Cargill had his front porch firebombed, in a suspected underworld protest over a Cargill distressed asset purchase. The American company Lone Star made a huge investment in a Japanese golf course, and was then subjected to massive protest demonstrations by a right-wing-connected yakuza group. Such problems were one reason why companies like Goldman-Sachs and Morgan-Stanley saw fit to hire former FBI and CIA investigators fluent in Japanese to handle their security.

Said organized crime expert Grant Newsham, an American who was for a time in charge of security for a major American firm in Tokyo, "It seemed there wasn't an area of society or the economy in Japan where yakuza were not involved and we were not threatened, unless it was *sokaiya*, corporate extortion. And that was only because most American companies are not listed on the stock exchanges in Tokyo. I'd say half the time the mob was involved in prospective deals, be it just in the form of a company that makes minor tribute payments to operate in a particular area or be it in a company that is a mob subsidiary. Of this 50 percent, 10–20 percent are companies that we would simply not do business with."

In the early part of the twenty-first century, after the widely reported murder of two bank executives trying to collect unpaid loans from organized crime groups, a police crackdown caused badge-wearing membership in underworld gangs to drop from a hundred thousand at the turn of the century to ten thousand in 2021. Kudo-kai boss Satoru Nomura was given the death sentence that same year, after local authorities demolished the gang's headquarters in Fukuoka.

Accordingly, police noted, arrests fell at a rate corresponding to the drop in formal gang membership. But statistics could be deceiving. Among crimes whose numbers are recorded in the statistics, some 70 percent deal with common theft, such as bicycle theft, while 20 percent deal with reckless driving—neither of those exactly in the yakuza oeuvre.

At the same time, traditional sources of underworld income—gambling, prostitution and drugs—remained large and financial crimes were increasing. Yakuza were active in underground casinos, mobile gambling sites and mahjong parlors, as well as in online gambling, which, although illegal in Japan, experienced a dramatic spike. To cite one publicly known example, reported by the *Asahi Shimbun* newspaper, monthly online visits by Japanese to the Curacao-based casino site Vera and John increased 119-fold from 648,000 in December 2018 to 77.51 million in January 2020. Although the figure declined to 19.88 million in August 2020, it rose again to 49.38 million in 2022.

Yakuza also stepped up their activities in child prostitution and child pornography, with offenses in that category doubling in the second decade of the twenty-first century.

In the lucrative field of drugs, cannabis drug offenses nearly quadrupled since 2000, according to the 2019 White Paper on Crime issued by the police, while narcotic and psychotropic crimes have doubled in that same time frame.

Chinese triads and Mexican cartels replaced North Korean syndicates as prime suppliers of crystal methamphetamine and fentanyl in Japan and by the dawn of the third decade of the twenty-first century, according to police, there was more cocaine in Tokyo than ever before. In November 2019, for example, police had discovered an astonishing 400 kilograms (882 pounds) of cocaine in a shipping container in Kobe, until then an all-time record for Japan. It was said to be worth more than $75 million on the street.

In April 2020, customs authorities in Yokohama seized 700 kilograms (1,543 pounds) of cocaine with a street value of about $130 million. The cocaine was hidden in a shipping container on a vessel docked in the harbor, nestled amidst boxes of bananas.

A Finance Ministry official declared that Japan had now become "a major market" in the world of illegal drugs, noting that street prices for stimulants were higher than those overseas.

Money laundering also spiked in the wake of the rise of narcotics deals with yakuza gangs moving hundreds of billions of yen through Bitcoin and other cryptocurrencies. Another growing source of revenue could be seen in so-called specialized-fraud cases—impersonating family members, police officers or bank officials in order to raid the savings accounts of unsuspecting individuals, especially the elderly.

To sum up, while yakuza may have not been operating openly as before, they were just as active. They simply became more discreet.

GAIJIN YAKUZA: VLADIMIR

Foreigners themselves have played their own colorful role in the world of organized crime in Japan starting with the machinations of Occupation-era US intelligence officers who freed yakuza jailed for black-market activity and hired them to suppress Communist agitators, generously paving the way for their postwar growth and expansion.

Among the many gaijin reprobates who ran with the Japanese yakuza in the postwar era was Korean-American Jason Lee of the Mandarin and Tradewinds nightclub fame (see Chapter 2).

In addition to Lee, there was the sui generis Russian mobster Vladimir Granby Auscus, whose exploits earned him a spot in the yakuza history books. Known simply as Hitokiri Jimu ("Killer Jim" or "Jim the Slasher") to the other Tokyo yakuza who could not pronounce his real name, much less remember it, Jim was a stateless White Russian whose parents had come to Japan to flee the Russian Revolution of 1917. He had been born and raised in Tokyo, spoke fluent Japanese and, after spending the war in a POW camp, eked out a living running a small "catch bar" in the entertainment district of Shibuya during the 1950s. (The word "catch" referred to the behavior of the young females employed to stand in the street in front of his bar and snare passers-by.)

Vladimir's *hitokiri* moniker came about after several drunken brawls in which he had made chopped sashimi out of his foes with a samurai long sword he sometimes carried with him. Jim, it was said, was in a perpetual haze of vodka and bad temper. He was married to one of the very few Japanese female yakuza, who was covered in tattoos and said to be of a mean temperament.

His presence on the streets of Shibuya struck fear into all but the bravest of the ward's residents.

Jim spoke in a fluent, flowing Old Edo dialect, much to the astonishment of Shibuya residents, who had thought that he, being a white gaijin, was naturally an American. It was an assumption which most Japanese made of such Caucasians and one which greatly upset the Europeans, Canadians, Australians and New Zealanders living in Japan, as well as the White Russian community. Thus, Jim took a special disliking to Americans, and he had no compunction about bumping shoulders with passing GIs or flattening one of them with a sudden roundhouse right.

Jim's end came one day in the early sixties. He'd picked one too many fights with the local yakuza and it was they who dispatched him. As described in gang boss Noboru Ando's autobiography *Jiden* [Bunkasha, 2001], Jim had gotten into an argument with a notorious Ando-gang captain named Kei Hanagata one afternoon on a street in Shibuya. It was a chance shoulder-bumping encounter that had turned violent and Jim came out on the short end of the fisticuffs that ensued.

"*Kuso* [shit]," cried the Russian yakuza, picking himself off the ground. "Who do you think you're dealing with? I'm Hitokiri Jimu."

Jim dashed home, got his sword and accompanied by his gangster wife who had brought a revolver in her purse, set out to seek revenge. They found Hanagata later that evening sitting on a public park bench in the center of Shibuya.

"I've come to pay you back," he yelled. With that, he took a furious swing with his sword that sliced off the left shoulder pad of Hanagata's suit coat. Hanagata retaliated by knocking Jim to the ground and delivering several kicks to Jim's head. When he saw Jim's wife reaching inside her handbag, he kicked it out of her hand and punched her in the jaw, knocking her unconscious as well.

Vladimir Granby Auscus was carried to the hospital in a coma with a severe concussion and several days later Hitokiri Jimu died. Hanagata went to prison for manslaughter. Both men were immortalized in a pair of best-selling underworld books, *Yakuza to koso* [Gangsters in conflict] by Noboru Ando, and *Kizu* [Scar] by Yasuharu Honda, published years later.

GAIJIN YAKUZA: NICK

Nick Zappetti, a character featured in my book *Tokyo Underworld*, had Mafia relatives in New York and New Jersey and a bona fide criminal record in Tokyo. His "career statistics" included ten arrests—for black marketing, assault (twice on police officers), gun running, drug dealing and robbery—one deportation for illicit commerce in 1950 and the top spot on the Ministry of Justice blacklist of foreign residents in Japan, a ranking he held for several years until 1982 when a well-placed "political donation" restored his good standing and helped him gain Japanese citizenship. This sequence of events helped demonstrate yet again the power of money in Japan. Over the course of his career, the police raided Zappetti's residence numerous times on suspicion of black marketeering and gun smuggling and hauled him in numerous times for questioning. He was investigated by the FBI during the mid-sixties on suspicion of gun running and, on top of all that, he managed to get himself involved in some fourteen different lawsuits over the course of his career. He also ran a sizable illegal currency operation in the back of his popular Italian restaurant Nicola's in Roppongi, which helped many Japanese businessmen obtain tightly controlled US dollars to finance trips to the United States. A former US Marine boxer, he had prevailed in many brawls with local gangsters and was known for his famous parking-lot altercations with neighborhood gangsters who tried to test him by walking out on their bills. Tokyo police dubbed him "the Mafia boss" of the city.

Zappetti was famous for introducing pizza to Japan in his Roppongi Italian restaurant and subsequent chain stores, as delineated in the book *Tokyo Underworld*. However, he was also famous for his sexual appetite and tumultuous relationships. In 1968, to cite one memorable example, he married a teenage beauty queen, a girl barely out of high school and less than half his age, who appeared more interested in other young men, especially a long-haired Japanese pop singer, than she was in her own gaijin husband, who was pushing fifty. She spent much of her time outside their Roppongi home on afternoon "shopping expeditions."

News of her supposed infidelities had reached Zappetti's ears via his chauffeur who ferried the young Mrs. Zappetti around on her various adventures. Unfortunately, the chauffeur also told his company's telephone operator who in turn told everybody else in the Nicola's empire, to the proud Zappetti's chagrin and what happened next would become legend in the Roppongi–Akasaka area.

The young wife had returned to the palatial 10,000-square-foot (929-square-meter) residence that Zappetti called home to find her angry husband waiting for her. He told her he had had enough. And demanded that she commit suicide right then and there. If not, he would kill her himself, with his bare hands. Either way, he had said, there was no way that she was going to leave the house again alive. She had embarrassed him enough in front of his staff and employees. She had wounded his Italian male pride. Enough was enough.

And so, she had gone upstairs and pulled out a razor from the bathroom medicine cabinet. Then she sat down on the bedroom carpet and sliced her wrists. Ten minutes later, as chance would have it, Zappetti's young daughter from an earlier marriage came home from a night out on the Ginza to find her stepmother propped up against the bed, bleeding all over the carpet.

She screamed and ran to her father, who, as he told it, was sitting in a chair reading a copy of *Playboy* magazine.

"I hope she doesn't ruin the rug," he quoted himself as saying. "I paid a lot of money for that."

However, thanks to his daughter's insistence, a trip to the hospital ensued, as did a messy divorce proceeding, that ended in a court decision that required his young bride to pay him a settlement for wounding his male pride with her marital infidelity. It represented a first in Japanese jurisprudence.

UNITED NATIONS OF CRIME

The Japanese yakuza had metamorphosed in several stages, from the kimono-wearing, sword-carrying, tattooed characters of the prewar to the aping of the dress and manner of first Marlon Brando in *Guys and Dolls*, then Lee Marvin in *The Killers*, and from there to Michael Douglas in *Wall Street*.

By the late twentieth century, they were more conversant with the intricacies of casino gambling and designer drugs than they had ever been with the traditional *hanafuda* card games and crude Philopon methamphetamine stimulants of their ancestors. Instead of keeping their yen hidden in the futon, they put it in American junk bonds on the advice of their foreign underworld associates.

One could say that foreign gangland influence was far more successful in remolding the Japanese yakuza. (Also, of course, there was the CIA secretly funneling money to the LDP and their yakuza supporters, in a remarkable example of a dual US foreign policy.)

The impact individual foreign underworld actors had on Japanese society began to increase with the advent of Japan's great economic bubble-era boom, when the purchasing power of the yen doubled. The boom brought a surge in migration stimulated by Japanese investment and business activities overseas, as well as an increased domestic demand for unskilled and low-skilled labor. The wave of immigrants included laborers from Pakistan, merchants from Iran, pickpockets from Manila, drug dealers from China, prostitutes from Thailand and Caucasian hostesses, among others.

Up until then, foreign travel to and immigration into the country had been very limited. The number of foreigners, including both temporary visitors and migrant workers, did not even reach a million until 1980. By the end of the century, however, the figure would be nearly five times as much, including 1,400,000 long term residents and an estimated 300,000 illegal residents, the latter total triple that of a decade earlier. (And it would keep going. By 2021 the figure would reach three million.)

The situation grew so acute that in 1991 the Tokyo Metropolitan Police set up a special translation center on the seventh floor of the police headquarters building overlooking the Imperial Palace. It was staffed by over 150 people who could interview detainees in 50 different languages. It dealt with Colombian cocaine cartels, Taiwanese prostitution rings, Iranian opium dealers, "Nigerian Mafia" credit card scams, Korean pickpocket gangs working the Yamanote train line circling the city and members of triad gangs from China involved in everything from Golden Triangle drugs to white slavery.

It was a veritable United Nations of crime. During one memorable stretch in 1997, the Tokyo Detention House in the basement of the Tokyo Metropolitan Police Department building simultaneously held a British convenience store thief; a Chinese second-story man from Shanghai whose specialty was late night forays to alter the memory chips on pachinko machines; a professional kidnapper from Karachi who had attempted to abduct a Tokyo-based Pakistani businessman; and a Colombian arrested for trying to smuggle into Tokyo's Narita Airport seven kilos (fifteen pounds) of Peruvian cocaine hidden inside an American-made bowling ball.

A 2001 report by the National Police Agency in 2001 gave a breakdown of the grim statistics: 25,105 crimes. Of these, 75 percent were the work of Asians (nearly half of them Chinese) while the other 25 percent were committed by evildoers from the West.

Many of the immigrant criminals were able to establish close ties with Japanese organized crime, as the newcomers moved into major urban areas like Tokyo, Nagoya and Osaka where they paid dues to Japanese bosses to operate mahjong gambling clubs and on-the-street narcotics concessions, eventually forming their own new Japan-based gangs.

The Chinese comprised the largest single foreign criminal group in Japan, numbering in the thousands and hailing from all over Taiwan, Hong Kong and the mainland. Next were the Iranians, who like the Chinese, numbered in the thousands, and who were not afraid to challenge the Chinese on their own newly acquired turf in Japan, where they "integrated" into Japanese gangs.

Many of these individuals had military experience; some had fought in wars, and most had learned how to kill with efficiency. The police were simply not used to dealing with such people. In fact, until a policy change in 2002, Japanese police were hampered by regulations which required them to follow an insane four-step procedure or kata when apprehending an armed suspect. Step 1 was to point a warning finger. Step 2 was to unholster the police revolver. Step 3 was to fire a warning shot in the air. And Step 4 was to aim at the suspect's leg. As one retired police detective put it, "It was a senseless approach because you're unlikely to hit anything, and by Step 4 the knife is already in your belly, which is why most Japanese police were afraid to fight."

ROPPONGI

Ground zero for many other foreign criminals in Japan was, of course, the international area of Roppongi, where they paid tribute for the use of territory to conduct their business, which, more often than not, was the business of peddling drugs, the primary source of income for the underworld, with Ecstasy leading coke, ice and hashish in terms of consumer demands.

There were over a hundred Iranians in Roppongi, for example, on any given day. They controlled half a dozen bars and were heavily into drug dealing. There were even more Chinese who, among other things, controlled the pachinko parlors in the area and a variety of massage parlors where discount sexual services were offered—China's contribution to combating Japan's great recession of the nineties.

Another significant group was the Africans, coming from Nigeria and other countries, who specialized in drugs and stolen credit cards. They congregated in an area of Roppongi near the Creighton Coffee Shop known as "Wall Street." The Africans were aligned with a Japanese gang that burglarized restaurants and implanted memory chips in the credit card machines in use in those establishments. Then, some weeks later, they would re-burglarize the same places, retrieve the memory chips and download the magnetically embedded credit card serial numbers for use in making bogus purchases. Other groups included the Brazilians, the Colombians, the Israelis, the Australians and the New Zealanders, the latter a group of burly ex-rugby players who vied for a share of the on-the-street drug sales. A band of Filipinos ran an underground bank. Drunken GIs, in from the nearby military bases of Yokosuka and Yokota, dabbled in the "duty free" market, selling discount liquor from the base.

One of the more colorful of all the Roppongi gangland denizens was a Chinese nightclub owner named Kwan, who stood all of five feet two (1.5 m) and weighed 120 pounds (54 kg) soaking wet, yet had no compunction about picking a fight with someone twice his size. The only English phrase he understood was "fuck you," and when it was directed at him, it was like detonating a bomb.

People in Roppongi still talk about what happened the time a visiting US professional football player was foolish enough to utter that internationally famous epithet in Kwan's club. Denied admission by the doorman because he appeared to be intoxicated, the six-foot-six, 280-pound (2 m, 127 kg) linebacker yelled "Fuck you" at the top of his lungs. The next thing onlookers remember seeing was the diminutive mob boss hurtling across the room from a corner table, leaping atop the football player's shoulders and raining blow after crazed blow upon the stunned athlete until he collapsed on the floor unconscious. It remains one of the great Roppongi underworld stories.

GAIJIN YAKUZA: SMOKY

An indication of how things were changing in the Roppongi underworld was the fact that the Yamaguchi-gumi, in 2002, placed the important task of selling territory to the various foreign drug-dealing groups in the hands of a twenty-six-year-old American from Nebraska named "Smoky." It was surely some kind of first in Japanese organized crime. Such a job would naturally have fallen to a homegrown yakuza in earlier years, using interpreters to bridge the language gap. But now the large number of foreigners called for a different approach and Smoky had the right qualifications. He held black belts in karate and shorinji kempo. He was fluent in Japanese and English, and he had a measured IQ of 145 on the Stanford-Binet test. What's more, he attended university classes three times a week, where he studied Japanese politics, a subject any ambitious mobster in Japan would naturally want to master.

Born in Omaha, of part-Cherokee ancestry and the product of a broken home, Smoky had been in an out of reform schools most of his young life. But a teen romance with a Japanese girl and his special fascination with the martial arts, helped point his way to Japan in 1997, where he enrolled in a Tokyo-based international university and came to appreciate what he described as the "special pedestal on which many Japanese and other Asians often put white Americans."

One night in Roppongi, a local yakuza boss spotted Smoky breaking up a street fight. Impressed with what he saw, the boss hired Smoky to work as a bodyguard and escort for the troupe of foreign hostesses employed in a nightclub he owned. Smoky's job entailed keeping obnoxious drunks under control and walking the girls home at night to their apartments in a nearby building, famously known in Roppongi as "Pussy Palace" for its large resident population of imported barmaids. When business was slow, he and a couple of the girls were dispatched to stand on the street, passing out discount coupons to passersby.

Smoky also served as a bouncer at the nightclub where he found himself involved in at least one fight a night, mostly with unruly *chimpira* small time mobsters from rival gangs, but using his martial arts skills, he was usually able to end such altercations quickly. When the offender was a *katagi*, the word Japanese mobsters used for an ordinary citizen, Smoky employed a quick hammerlock to escort the antagonist to a taxi, tossing the driver extra cab fare to ensure a speedy departure. In the process, he earned a reputation as someone to be reckoned with.

His reward was a modest salary, all the food and drink he could consume at the club and a rent-free two-room apartment in the

"Palace." After a couple of years on the job, he became eligible to have his own *gumi* or subgroup. It was a first, he was told, for an American working for a Japanese yakuza group. Smoky was put in charge of a band of foreign youths whose task it was to sell designer drugs at nightspots in Roppongi. Included in his crew were a crack-addicted Brazilian, a Colombian exchange student and the son of an American diplomat stationed at the US embassy in Tokyo.

That venture was so successful that within a year he was given his very own nightclub to run, employing Western hostesses, and twelve months after that he was put in charge of the gang's foreign drug concessions division, doling out territorial rights to overseas dealers who were vying to participate in the tremendously lucrative narcotics business in Roppongi.

Smoky now had a desk in the gang's main office, located in a well-known twelve-story commercial building on the main Roppongi strip. As befitting a modern criminal organization, it was furnished with several computer work stations and a bank of fax machines, (which, unlike cell phones, were impossible to wiretap and thus represented an indispensable mode of communication). Adorning the walls were the only hints of the firm's dark underworld connections—photographs of previous yakuza bosses and a huge block of varnished oak bearing the inscription *Chisha Regi Ninkyo* (The Wise Man Takes the Path of Chivalry).

Smoky reported directly to the big boss, who put out orders to all jealous Japanese yakuza cohorts in the gang to keep their hands off his prized gaijin. He provided Smoky with a chauffeur-driven Benz and moved him into his own sprawling, multi-bedroom residence nearby, which was also occupied by several young females from Latvia, the Czech Republic and other Eastern European countries, should the need for companionship suddenly arise.

The only demand the *oyabun* made on Smoky, other than performing well, that is, was to stay away from Japanese women.

"Pick a Chinese girl, a Korean or a Taiwanese," the boss would say. "Or pick one of these Western girls to move in on. But young Japanese women these days are too whiny and too demanding. They will ruin you psychologically. So stay away from them."

Smoky's boss, a well-groomed, Armani-clad man in his fifties, was a new-wave underworld executive. He liked to refer to himself as "Mafia" as opposed to "yakuza," because he viewed the latter as outdated. He did not believe in many of the arcane customs, like the secret blood-letting initiation rituals or the engraving of tattoos that were so prevalent in other organizations. Wearing elaborate full- or half-body tattoos of fierce dragons and vengeful samurai, for example, was an old yakuza tradition dating back to the feudal era. Traditionally applied with a bamboo sliver, in an excruciatingly painful process that took weeks, tattoos were a sign of courage, a symbol of the ability of the wearer to endure torture and were thus worn by approximately 70 percent of pre- and postwar mobsters.

But times had changed. New laws, passed in 1992 and 1997, now penalized yakuza just for the very act of belonging to a gang, so why, wondered Smoky's boss, would you possibly want to advertise yourself with easily identifiable body markings? For the same reason, he also eschewed the gruesome custom of having to sever a finger tip to show remorse and atone for some real or imagined violation of the yakuza code of ethics. Moreover, he viewed such practices as anachronistic in a time mobsters everywhere carried cell phones and read the *Nihon Keizai Shimbun*, Japan's version of the *Wall Street Journal*.

"Forget the kimono," he would say. "Forget the sword. All that matters is making money."

By Smoky's fifth year in the gang, there was no underworld foreigner on the streets of Roppongi who ranked higher or who was more respected, as indicated by the deferential nods he received in the street. Dressed in khaki pants and a leather jacket, he would make his daily rounds—coffee with an Israeli at a local Starbucks, steak with an American cohort at the Roppongi Seryna, drinks with an Aussie client at one of the trendy brandy and cigar bars in the quarter and so forth—discussing rights and collecting concession fees. Although he preferred to use reason, calm and negotiating technique in his nightly sessions, it was often easier said than done.

"Most people in this business have at least one thing in common," Smoky told me over dinner one night. "A natural chemical imbalance which makes them chronically irritable and ready to fight at the first perceived insult. Most gangsters compensate by taking narcotics to mellow out. But sometimes the mix is not quite right and that is when trouble occurs."

There was always backup available, if Smoky found himself in trouble he could not handle. He could make a call and within seconds, some armed men in a black limousine would pull up, escort the offending party outside, and, in extreme cases, deposit him in the trunk, which might well be the very last anyone would see of him. It was nice to have the power of a ten-thousand-man gang behind you, Smoky said. If a situation got too dicey, Smoky liked to pull out his cell phone, hold it in the air, and make a short speech. "You have two choices," he would say. "You can calm down and behave yourself. Or I can push a button on my cell phone and some men will come and take you away. Believe me, you don't want option number two to happen."

Of course, things did not always go smoothly. One night, after a rather unsatisfactory meeting with a certain hot-tempered Iranian, a member of Smoky's circle was kidnapped. The abductee was a diminutive Brazilian crack addict named Nick. He was taken by a group of Iranians to an abandoned warehouse near Tokyo Bay and tortured for information on rival gang drug shipments. He was handcuffed to a chair and beaten. Then he was injected with Sodium Pentothal, but with some rather unexpected results. Nick, who had begun experiencing crack withdrawal when he was kidnapped, found that the Sodium Pentothal somehow counterbalanced the crack and miraculously restored his equilibrium. He removed a pin from his wristwatch, used it to unlock the handcuffs and escape. Shortly thereafter, the Iranian who had instigated the whole affair was intercepted by Smoky and his cohorts at a Roppongi nightspot called the Golden Gate (no relation to the infamous spot that was mentioned in Chapter 2) and taken to a back alley for retribution.

Smoky stayed in the Tokyo underworld because he thought Japan was one of the easiest places in the world to be a criminal. For one thing, he viewed the police as basically inept. With the exception of certain large-scale drug investigations, for example, undercover sting operations were prohibited by the authorities because within the National Police Agency, the practice was believed to be degrading ("stooping to the criminal's level," as one NPA official put it). Moreover, those sting operations that did take place were unlikely to include fluent English-speaking foreigners of the type that Smoky and friends associated with. Then too, there were convenient privacy laws that restricted the sharing of information by police with outside authorities—another practice that was frowned upon in any event by Japanese authorities who thought that cooperating with foreign law enforcement agents was tantamount to washing one's dirty laundry in public. On top of all this was the fact that Japan had yet to pass any RICO-type laws that were in effect in the United States giving extended criminal penalties for racketeering and corruption—icing on the cake.

But that was not all. In the event one *was* apprehended, the courts in Japan were ridiculously lenient. The Japanese system emphasized redemption over tough jail sentences, based on the Buddhist belief that "even the lowest cockroach has a spark of divinity." Prison sentences were notoriously light and, in fact, surveys over the last decade of the twentieth century showed that roughly 40 percent of all criminals were sentenced only to write a letter of apology, the judges deeming them capable of "self-correction." This is the state of affairs which gave Japan one of the lowest incarceration rates in the industrialized world.

In the unfortunate event one *was* sent away, however, Japanese prisons could be a problem since they were among the toughest in the world. For example, the regimen at Fuchu Prison in western Tokyo, the largest and oldest prison in Japan, with three thousand inmates, nearly half of whom were hardened criminals belonging to yakuza gangs, was downright draconian. There was no talking allowed or even looking aside while working, eating and marching. No telephone calls. No smoking in the cells. No exercise in the cells. Faces had to be visible while sleeping. Strip searches were conducted several times a day. Violators could be punished by being forced to sit in a fixed position for hours. The more disobedient prisoners could be bound hand and foot for days and forced to lap up their meals like dogs and urinate and defecate through holes ripped in their pants.

In the end, Smoky made up his mind to quit—to "wash his legs" in yakuza parlance—and move on to something else. One reason was the incredibly grinding lifestyle he was leading. His work day essentially lasted from dusk to dawn. He consumed magnums of champagne each evening in the course of entertaining business associates, while simultaneously taking speed to stay awake (and alert enough to fight at the drop of a hat if need be). Another reason was shame and embarrassment. Being a yakuza meant carrying a burden he did not want to carry anymore.

"I can't tell my father or any of my relatives what I do," he told me. "I can't take people to my office. It's only in Roppongi where I'm around people in the same business that I can hold my head high. There's only one reason to be a gangster," he said, summing up his experiences, "and that's to get girls. That's universal. That's why people go through the danger of dealing drugs, getting into fights, participating in shootouts. It's all to make money and to acquire power in order to attract members of the opposite sex. But now I find that all the girls I'm interested in are afraid of me.

"I appreciate the opportunity I was given and I could formally join the gang, do the whole bit, drink the blood in the sake cup, pin the badge underneath my lapel, if I wanted to. My Japanese is good enough. I know the rules. But there is another big problem. Once you're in you have to do what they say. That means hooking kids on drugs, killing someone if you're ordered to. You have to give up any sense of morality you might have and obey arbitrary rules—like the one about my not dating Japanese girls. It's not jail I'm scared of. The gangs can get you out if they really want to. And you can always get another passport to get back in the country. It's losing my sense of self that scares me. It's hard to keep whatever integrity you think you might have, as a real yakuza."

Smoky left the gang and (following a yakuza tradition of sorts) applied for a job with the Central Intelligence Agency.

CHAPTER 11

Gaijin CEOs

VERY FEW FOREIGNERS have succeeded in running a Japanese company. Most who tried discovered—considerable language barriers aside—that the cultural wall dividing Japan and other countries was simply too big an obstacle, and that at heart their fellow Japanese executives and underlings did not really want to accept the mostly Westernized changes the foreigners were brought in to make. A look at the history of such experiences is depressing.

The first major Japanese company to have a foreign president was the automaker Mazda. Mazda, in fact, would have three foreign presidents in the span of five years, all of them finishing in the red, financially. The first was Henry Wallace, Ford's group vice president for the Asia Pacific region, appointed in 1996. (Ford owned 30 percent of Mazda and had taken control of management in 1996). As the first gaijin to head a Japanese company, however, Wallace, a six-foot-two (1.9 meter) Scotsman, lasted only a year. Fears that the Ford executive would do away with Japan's hallowed seniority system or dismantle Mazda's interlocking keiretsu network of suppliers and other business relationships did not materialize. Mazda ads featuring Wallace speaking halting Japanese were popular and although Mazda was $80 million in the red for the fiscal year, it was also the only automaker whose sales did not shrink in the wake of post-bubble economic difficulties in the Japanese market which included a strengthening yen that made competing overseas more difficult. However, Wallace left Mazda because his wife was reportedly unhappy in Hiroshima where Mazda is based and also because he was, as he put it, tired of hearing the phrase, "You don't understand Japanese business practices."

Wallace was followed by James E. Miller, who resigned from the presidency and board of directors after two years for "personal and health reasons" at age fifty. He was replaced by thirty-eight-year old New Yorker Mark Fields, a Harvard graduate, who became the youngest CEO in the seniority-driven Japanese blue-chip corporations. (The average age of Mazda employees was 42.4.) Fields lasted two years as well, but managed to make inroads into the hallowed seniority system by promoting younger employees to high positions. By 2008 the joint venture was all but over, with the book *Collision Course* by Hans Gremiel and William Sposato (Harvard Business Review Press, 2021) later noting that Fields and Ford got "little credit for helping to put Mazda on a stronger footing," despite creating the hugely successful marketing tagline "Zoom, Zoom."

Away from the auto industry, Howard Stringer, onetime executive producer of the CBS Evening News, ran Sony from Tokyo from 1997 to 2012. He came in as an innovator intending to restore Sony to the glory of its Walkman days, in the process launching a massive restructuring that cut thousands of jobs. By the end of his last year, however, the price of Sony stock had fallen by 60 percent, thanks in part to the effects of exchange-rate fluctuations and the 2011 Tohoku earthquake, not to mention the Wall Street meltdown.

OLYMPUS

In the twenty-first century, one of the more noteworthy episodes illustrating the perils of being the imported head of a Japanese company was the Olympus affair, in which England's Michael Woodford was appointed as CEO of the famous optics manufacturer only to lose his job after he disclosed a major accounting fraud, which led to the resignation of the company's entire board and the arrest of several senior executives. He was later awarded £10 million in a court settlement.

In 1981 Woodford had joined KeyMed in the UK, a medical equipment unit of Olympus. He was twenty-one years old and fresh out of Millbank College of Commerce. Fastidious by nature, and known for his dedication and his precise, meticulous approach to his job, Woodford started out as a surgical salesman, advancing through the ranks to become executive managing director of the Olympus subsidiary Olympus Europa Holding GmbH, and a member of the board of directors in 2008.

That same year, Woodford learned that Olympus had paid $2.2 billion to purchase an obscure medical device company named Gyrus which generated an annual revenue of only $600,000. Moreover, he discovered that Olympus had also paid a broker's commission of some $687 million to two little-known firms, AXES and AXAM. The figure was several multiples of the fees brokers usually charged in such cases. Such a purchase would have normally been under Woodford's authority but had instead been arranged at the main office in Tokyo by the then chairman of the Olympus board, Tsuyoshi "Tom" Kikukawa. Kikukawa was a Keio University graduate who had spent considerable time in the United States looking after the interests of Olympus, Westernizing the company to a certain degree, and facilitating Olympus' entry into the market for high-resolution photographic products with its 810,000-pixel digital camera. Alarmed at the circumstances of the purchase, Woodford flew to Olympus headquarters in Tokyo to submit his resignation.

However, Kikukawa implored Woodford not to resign and instead offered him a promotion in the form of a position as chief of all of Olympus' European operations as well as a position on the Olympus board of directors. Woodford accepted, flew back to London and for a time, all was well.

In 2011, as a result of impressive sales growth in Europe, Woodford was promoted to company president, with Kikukawa staying on as chairman and CEO. Woodford thus became the first non-Japanese person to be so appointed, making Olympus one of the few Japanese firms headed by a foreigner. He was hailed as the new global face of Olympus.

However, Woodford's appointment to president, as soon became clear, was in name only, with Japanese executives back home in Tokyo retaining real power. The announcement of Woodford's promotion was made only on Olympus' English website, not the all-important Japanese-language one.

Many believed that Woodford, although hardworking and effective as a cost cutter in Europe, had only been promoted to president because board members thought he would be easy to control in dealing with the questionable financial issues the company faced. After all, he spoke no Japanese and was essentially out of the loop.

As an article in the July 2011 issue of the hard-hitting Japanese monthly economic magazine *Facta* put it: "The fact that the company picked a bottom-ranking foreign executive director with virtually no significant responsibilities from amongst a total pool of twenty-five potential candidates, including the vice president who was responsible for medical instruments [. . .] set tongues a-wagging." Some observers referred to Woodford as a mere figurehead to reassure Olympus' global partners that the company was "internationalizing," to use a popular term of the day, while behind the screen things went on as before.

Unfortunately for the Olympus brain trust, they made a wrong assumption. As Woodford soon discovered, thanks in part to the exposé in *Facta*, Olympus had been hiding massive losses for years by moving them from one set of books to another, a practice known as *tobashi* in Japanese. The ploy was designed to delay the repayment of bad loans and keep the company's stock price from collapsing. Olympus executives did this by purchasing obscure firms of dubious value, like Gyrus, paying far more than the market price to brokers based in the Cayman Islands tax haven, who hid the true nature of the transactions. They did this using several different front companies, many of which were based in the same building in the Cayman capital of Georgetown, with the same employees. This practice dated back to the stock market crash of the early nineties.

It also became apparent that organized crime was involved in the purchases. Publicly available information about the improper "money flows" included the name of a Japanese company that had earlier appeared on a leaked National Police Agency list of yakuza front companies. Investigators identified Tsubasa Net, a software maker acquired by Olympus, as a front for the Yamaguchi-gumi, Japan's largest yakuza gang. Several other such purchases were linked to Japan's underworld. But the authorities were slow to act.

A hastily arranged investigation led by a former Japanese Supreme Court justice, as well as later inquiries by Japanese financial regulators, determined this was simply a run-of-the-mill accounting fraud to cover up financial losses and that, in the investigators' version of reality, yakuza were nowhere to be found.

Grant Newsham, a senior research fellow at the Japan Forum for Strategic Studies who wrote about the case, had this to say: "At the time, it was deemed too embarrassing to Japanese authorities and regulators to admit that a flagship Japanese company was up to its eyeballs in yakuza. Moreover, an official admission to this effect would have required delisting Olympus from the Tokyo Stock Exchange and potentially risked its overseas listings as well [. . .] Thus did the authorities fail to act [. . .] Ironically, that same year, the Obama administration declared that the main yakuza group behind the scandal, the Yamaguchi-gumi, was a transnational criminal organization and a threat to US national security while issuing an order freezing its assets—even if the US authorities didn't know where those assets precisely were.

"The perpetrators were not tattooed guys," said Newsham. "They were Nomura Securities guys who knew how to create front companies and shift funds internationally."

In late September 2011, Kikukawa resigned as CEO, and engineered Woodford's appointment to that post, thinking the move would divert attention from the growing scandal. However, Woodford persisted in seeking answers to the organized crime issue, appointing an outside auditing firm to investigate. As a result, he was abruptly dismissed, less than a fortnight after his appointment to the top Olympus post. Kikukawa returned to his old position and immediately accused Woodford of attempting to "seize power." This prompted Woodford to take his concerns outside the company even as he retained his seat on the board of directors.

Thus it was that on November 17, 2011, the *New York Times* ran a report that the Yamaguchi-gumi had been blackmailing a senior Olympus executive to establish a foothold in the company and then systemically fleece it on the threat of exposing the compromising information. (It was later revealed that a top Japanese executive at Olympus had gambled at a club in Yokohama with Tadamasa Goto, head of the powerful Goto wing of the Yamaguchi-gumi and had fallen into considerable debt. This, along with the gang's knowledge of creative accounting, according to one confidential report, led to the Yamaguchi-gumi taking over $200 million a year out of Olympus.)

A week later, Woodford held a widely attended press conference at the Foreign Correspondents' Club in Tokyo, in which he revealed all that he knew about the Olympus financial shenanigans, and left Japan immediately thereafter, his life reportedly in danger from underworld death threats. Back in London, he operated behind bulletproof glass with police protection he had requested, but given that no attacks on his life materialized, observers wondered how real the threats on his life had actually been.

On November 30, Woodford and Kikukawa simultaneously resigned from the board.

The Olympus scandal rocked corporate Japan despite protestations from Olympus's top executives, and many in the Japanese media, that the foreigner didn't understand Japan or was simply paranoid. Kikukawa and other executives argued that they had only been trying to protect their predecessors from losing face over their entirely understandable actions which came about as a result of the devastating stock market crash that burst Japan's economic bubble and did grievous damage to the nation.

They pointed to a third-party investigation report commissioned by Olympus inferring that there had been no need to tell Woodford about what had happened because the fraud had finally been cleaned up by the time Woodford took the job. They attacked Woodford for leaking secret company information which had further affected the deteriorating stock price of Olympus shares.

Woodford subsequently returned to Japan from the UK, under police protection, to speak with investigators and also stage a proxy fight for control of Olympus. However, he was ultimately rejected by Olympus' institutional investors because they were said to be uncomfortable with the "Englishman's combative style" and his plans to recapitalize the firm through private equity.

The scandal led to the resignation of the entire Olympus board and the arrests of seven Olympus executives, including Kikukawa. Two Nomura Securities brokers who had engineered the accounting maneuvers, were eventually sentenced to prison for three to four years. Others, including Kikukawa, received suspended sentences. Kikukawa and two fellow executives were fined nearly US$600 million in a shareholder derivative suit. It was the largest fine of any shareholder derivative suit in Japanese history. The Supreme Court of Japan upheld the ruling on October 22, 2020.

Back in London once more, Woodford sued for defamation and wrongful dismissal, ultimately winning his massive £10 million in an out-of-court settlement with Olympus. He was also showered with awards, including the Foreign Correspondents' Club of Japan's first Freedom of the Press Award and the *Financial Times* Person of the Year Award. He was given similar honors by the *Sunday Times*, the *Independent* and the *Sun*, and wrote a best-selling book about his experiences entitled *Exposure: Inside the Olympus Scandal: How I Went from CEO to Whistleblower* (Portfolio, 2012).

The folks back at Olympus were not so lucky however. In the wake of the scandal, the price of Olympus stock had dropped by more than 75 percent and the company was forced to downsize its workforce by 2,700 jobs and its manufacturing plants by 40 percent to reduce costs. It also faced a $7 million fine and several civil lawsuits amounting to billions of yen.

Many observers in the Japanese media openly wondered how Olympus would have fared if Woodford, who went on to forge a second career as a consultant on corporate governance, human rights and whistleblower laws, had never been plucked from the ranks to occupy the firm's (ostensible) top spot—a slot, many insiders agreed, he was not entirely qualified for. After all, as Tokyo-based financial analyst Peter Tasker pointed out, Olympus had just about paid off its losses and the company's endoscope business was going great guns worldwide, promising to take the rest of the enterprise with it.

"All Woodford had to do was keep his silence," said Tasker. "It would have technically been a violation of the law, but everyone, including the authorities, would have been happier in the end."

Writing a memorable piece in the *Financial Times*, Tasker opined that had Woodford done that, "the reputation of a hundred-year-old company would not have been besmirched. Its forty thousand employees would not be worrying about the future. Billions of dollars of market capitalization would not have been destroyed. Everyone would have been better off."

He noted the irony that whereas Western observers viewed Woodford as a kind of Gary Cooper in *High Noon*, Japanese were more likely to see him as the disloyal retainer in a samurai movie who sold out his benefactors to the enemy. The heroes of the film would be the men who engineered the brilliantly complex mergers and acquisitions scheme, taking a huge personal risk for the sake of the company.

"It was a classic Japanese scandal," said Tasker, "being about hiding losses. Nobody got rich. Woodford was way out of his depth. And nobody believed any nonsense about yakuza hit men."

During a subsequent Woodford appearance at the Foreign Correspondents' Club, reporter Andrew Horvat asked the whistleblower if he felt any responsibility to Olympus employees and investors who had suffered financially from his actions. Woodford bristled at the suggestion his actions were anything less than cloaked in nobility, but Horvat later remarked:

Although I sympathized with Woodford because he was being lied to, I did not consider him to be a hero in the same way that some others did. Just think of the interests of a huge number of employees not only of Olympus but all of its suppliers and subcontractors whose lives would have been upended had the company collapsed. In Japan the labor market is far less liquid than in the US or even the UK so if your company collapses it is fair to say you will never get a job as good as the one you had before. To me, the Woodford Olympus case was not quite as black and white as it was for the far too well-paid members of the financial industry. In a very narrow definition of fiduciary duty, Woodford did the right thing. From a larger, societal perspective, he risked the livelihoods of thousands in order to clean up the company's books. And in the end, what was achieved? What was the punishment meted out against the Olympus executives? Not a single one of them went to jail.

I also think that the Olympus board of directors had a completely unrealistic view of "foreign talent," seeing Woodford as essentially someone who could generate sales and profits, sort of like a new kind of robot, someone who performs miracles but doesn't ask questions. They did not understand that going global is a two-way street and that you need to take into account the different ways of thinking of the foreigners you hire. But the same criticism can be applied to Woodford, who spoke no Japanese. How can one work for a foreign firm and think that somehow the values of that firm are identical to one's own? He too had a strictly mechanical—acultural—view of his own role. I suppose it is sort of like waking up after a night of great sex with a lover whose language you do not know and discover that you don't want the same things for breakfast, or lunch, or dinner, or in fact anything at all.

In the end, however, one lesson from the Olympus scandal was completely clear. The culture of saving face over shareholder interests, so long dominant in Japan with its big corporate networks of banks and insurance companies, did not suit a globalized economy. The Japanese system of corporate governance, which essentially resembled a private club, did not know how to deal with the pesky foreigners thrust into their midst.

Of course, there never would have been an issue in the first place if Olympus had not been cooking the books, so criticizing Woodford for damaging the corporate image is akin to killing the messenger, especially given the fact that *Facta* magazine had already published the basic facts of the wrongdoing. Hiding corporate malfeasance can hardly be considered a good thing. Indeed, one might also argue that the more the misdeeds of companies like Olympus were outed, the better it would be in the end for the health of enterprises as a whole, unless of course the corporate stock nosedives, the company goes bankrupt and everybody winds up on the street.

NISSAN

By far the most successful foreign executive in Japanese history was Carlos Ghosn, the Brazilian-born auto executive who held dual French and Lebanese nationalities, as well as a Brazilian passport. Before his 2018 arrest in Tokyo on charges of false accounting, he had dramatically reversed the sagging fortunes of Nissan Motors, the giant Japanese car manufacturer. He had also taken over Renault, making him the only person in history to head two of the world's leading automakers at the same time.

Ghosn had gotten his start in the auto business at Michelin, joining the huge tire maker in 1978 after graduating in France, first from the prestigious Ecole Polytechnique and then the Ecole des Mines de Paris, one of the world's top engineering schools, initially training and working in several plants in France and Germany. In 1985, Ghosn rose to the post of chief operating officer (COO) of Michelin's South American operations, after having turned around the company's Brazilian operation by forming what media reports called "unique multicultural management teams." After a stint in Greenville, South Carolina, where he was promoted to COO of Michelin North America, Ghosn moved to Renault and the company's French headquarters near Paris where he headed up its South American division. Three years later, he joined the Yokohama-based auto firm Nissan, where he was named CEO in 2001, becoming only the fourth foreign CEO of an auto company in Japan after the aforementioned Mazda gaijin triad.

When Ghosn first arrived, the company was buried in debt—$20 billion worth, due to mediocre, bureaucratic management. Ghosn engineered a life-saving infusion of cash from Renault, which made it Nissan's largest shareholder, Renault owning 43 percent of Nissan stock, and instituted a "Nissan Revival Plan," which called for the elimination of 14 percent of the work force—a total of 21,000 job losses with the majority in Japan (some through retirement)—and the closure of five Japanese plants. These were actions that no Japanese executive, raised in an environment that promoted lifetime employment, would have *ever* had the vision or nerve to take, especially in the domestic market. Ghosn further defied long-standing convention in Japan by decreasing seniority-based promotions and dismantling the long established keiretsu system. He also changed the firm's official language from Japanese to English. Ghosn, who could speak four languages, although not Japanese, was noted for his results-and-execution–oriented style in business meetings as well as for forming cross-cultural and cross-functional team groupings. He enthusiastically solicited workers' opinions.

Ghosn also managed to transform an unattractive lineup of vehicles with underpowered engines into a very attractive high-powered engine lineup, improved business performance in key markets such as the US, and entered new markets such as China.

Under Ghosn, Nissan climbed out of the red and into profitability in a few short years. In 2001 he topped *TIME* magazine's list of global influential people, ahead of Bill Gates. By 2005 Ghosn was named president and CEO of Renault, the first person in history to run two different companies on the Fortune Global 500 at the same time. He led the Renault–Nissan alliance into the electric car market, manufacturing the Nissan Leaf, which became the world's best-selling electric car. He envisioned adding Mitsubishi Motors to the alliance as well as Fiat Chrysler Automobiles.

Ghosn's nickname in the Japanese media was 7-Eleven, for his morning to late night work habits. He logged 150,000 frequent flier miles per year. *Forbes* termed Ghosn "the hardest working man in the car business."

During the aftermath of the March 11, 2011 earthquake and tsunami in the Tohoku region, Ghosn further burnished his already sterling reputation by heading to the afflicted area and personally taking charge of Nissan operations there.

The Tohoku quake, at a magnitude of 9.1, was the most powerful earthquake ever to hit Japan and the fourth most powerful earthquake recorded on earth since measurements began in 1900.

It was later discovered that Honshu, the main island of Japan, had been moved 8 feet (2.5 meters) to the east and that the axis of the earth had been shifted several inches by the impact of the quake. The quake also triggered tsunamis, arriving an hour after the initial tremor, of over 130 feet (40 meters) in height. The waves traveled upriver as far as six miles (10 km), carrying with them vehicles, buildings, fishing boats and debris. In the process, they destroyed highways and other infrastructure, wiping entire towns off the face of the earth.

The disaster left nearly 16,000 dead—more than 90 percent by drowning—including several hundred school children. The scope of the tragedy overwhelmed morgues and crematoria, forcing mass graves to be dug. A total of 2,562 went missing, never to be found, and thousands more were injured.

More than 200,000 would be left homeless, including 80,000 forcibly evacuated from their homes due to concerns over radiation leaks from damaged nuclear reactors in Fukushima Prefecture. Many evacuees were forced to live for months in cramped, crowded evacuation centers, often with no running water or other basic amenities. The threat from radiation, along with hundreds of very substantial aftershocks, exacerbated their fears.

The enormous scale of destruction—in all, about one-third of Japan economy was impacted by the disaster—dwarfed anything that anyone had ever seen. Some residential houses and condo buildings built on reclaimed land in Chiba Prefecture, hundreds of miles from the epicenter, sank or tilted due to ground liquefaction and had to be abandoned. Roads, railways and dams suffered structural damage.

In the midst of all this tremendous destruction, Ghosn was a visible presence in the area, appearing often in the media offering encouragement to the populace, while helping to restore full operations at the Nissan Iwaki plant in the afflicted region.

Over the course of his Nissan career, Ghosn won several Businessman of the Year Awards, as well as a Lifetime Achievement Award from the Strategic Management Society, the first person in the auto industry to win that particular honor. Observers called

Renault–Nissan the most successful auto alliance in history. In October 2016, Ghosn became chairman of Mitsubishi as well, after Nissan acquired a controlling stake in that firm. The Renault-Nissan Alliance became the Renault-Nissan-Mitsubishi Alliance, with the three companies partnered in a cross-sharing agreement. Notably, that year, some seventeen years after he joined Nissan, the company sold 5.7 million vehicles as compared to 2.5 million vehicles in 1999 when Ghosn first arrived, earned $6.7 billion in net profits compared to staggering losses in the 1990s, and had $15 billion in the bank as compared to $20 billion of debt in 1999. He also had in place a highly talented top management team which oversaw the thousands of employees he had hired. All in all, it was a remarkable track record.

Ghosn stepped down as CEO in April 2017, to be succeeded by Nissan vice president Hirota Saikawa, while remaining as chairman, and he began planning for his retirement.

Then the wheels came off.

ARREST

On November 19, 2018, as Ghosn arrived at Tokyo's Haneda Airport, he was met by Tokyo district prosecutors who boarded his plane and arrested him over allegations of false accounting. Ghosn aide, Greg Kelly, sixty-two, a Nissan director and head of Human Resources, was also arrested upon his arrival from the US later that day for "conspiring to underreport Carlos Ghosn compensation."

Both men had been lured back to Japan on the false pretext of an emergency meeting at Nissan. They were detained based on information provided by two Nissan executives—Toshiaki Ohnuma, the head of the Secretariat Office and Hari Nada, the head of the CEO Office and vice president in Nissan's legal department.

Ohnuma and Nada had struck a deal with prosecutors in Japan's newly established plea-bargaining system, relating to questionable work they had done regarding Carlos Ghosn's compensation. The deal would give them immunity from prosecution in exchange for cooperation in fingering Ghosn and Kelly. In fact, as part of the deal, Nada had even tricked a reluctant Kelly into coming back to Japan by enticing him to travel on a private jet Hari had arranged, all the while knowing Kelly needed urgent neck surgery.

The issue at hand was whether Nissan, in its annual securities reports, should have included unfinalized nonbinding documents stating Ghosn's financial compensation for continuing a working relationship with Nissan post-retirement. These documents were being considered by Kelly, by the then CEO Hirota Saikawa, and by other executives; they had been drawn up by Nissan's attorneys and were subject to review by the board. The prosecutors alleged that the documents were a pretext for paying for Ghosn's past services. The case had its roots in fiscal 2010 when Ghosn's $20 million salary was cut to $10 million, prompted by French business practices and new executive pay disclosure rules in Japan. A salary of $20 million was in line with the Ford CEO's $25 million, but much more than that of the Toyota CEO, who didn't even make $1 million.

On the same day as the Ghosn and Kelly arrests, Nissan chief executive Saikawa called a press conference to announce that Ghosn had also been fired from the board and stripped of all rights as a Nissan employee. He told assembled reporters the surprise move was the result of an "internal inquiry" by Nissan into the "underreporting" of Ghosn's future retirement compensation from Nissan, which had "violated Japan's 2010 Security law" requiring full disclosure of all future employee compensation to investors in advance.

Saikawa further claimed that over the years Ghosn had misused Nissan's corporate assets in buying luxury residences for himself around the globe at Nissan's expense. Saikawa told assembled reporters of his profound "disappointment, indignation and despair" at Ghosn's conduct, which also included using company funds for personal investments and otherwise misusing corporate assets.

"These are acts that cannot be tolerated," he said, "and are sufficient grounds for dismissal."

In published reports, it was later alleged that Ghosn had used Nissan funds via shell companies to purchase luxury homes in Rio de Janeiro, Paris, Amsterdam and Beirut, as well as a yacht.

Both Ghosn and Kelly were detained at the Tokyo Detention

House. Japanese law allowed prosecutors to hold suspects in jail for up to twenty-three days without filing charges and to extend their confinement for an additional ten to twenty days once charges had been determined and announced. This process could be repeated indefinitely, with a string of rearrests. Thus prosecutors artificially split the (suspicion of) underreporting offenses into two different charges, one that covered the fiscal years 2010 to 2014 and a second that covered the years 2015 to 2017. Then, on December 21, 2018, Ghosn was arrested again, this time on charges of shifting personal losses of over $16 million to Nissan's books. This allowed for an additional three weeks of incarceration prior to a bail hearing.

Kelly was released on bail on Christmas Day, however, Ghosn was arrested for a third time on January 11, 2019, on new charges of aggravated breach of trust and crimes of financial misconduct and, three weeks after that, subjected to still another arrest, this time authorities charging him with "enriching himself through $5 million in payments to a Middle East car dealership and for breach of trust for temporarily transferring personal financial losses to his employer's books." And on it went.

Bloomberg reporter Reed Stevenson reported that Hari Nada was mastermind of the campaign to unseat then chairman Ghosn on criminal financial allegations, operating in league with a small group of other senior executives with ulterior motives. Nada, a smooth-talking, Malaysian-born lawyer of Indian descent who "wore strong cologne and French cuffs, and smoked Marlboro cigarettes," as described by Stevenson, had opposed a proposed merger between Nissan and Renault that was being discussed in early 2018. The French government, under new president Emmanuel Macron, was more invested in its controlling interest in Renault and not satisfied with the status of the Nissan-Renault alliance. Macron wanted a fifty-fifty merger of the two automakers and more auto production in France, to bring more jobs. Nada and other veteran Nissan executives strongly opposed this, believing it would destroy Nissan's independence and identity. Nada had regular meetings with fellow executives Hitoshi Kawaguchi, head of government affairs, and Toshiaki Imazu, chief statutory auditor, to discuss actions that could be taken to block a merger. As a result of those meetings in April and May 2018, detailed written scenario plans were developed under Nada's direction to ensure Ghosn continued as chairman of Nissan if Ghosn opposed the merger (and if the French government tried to oust him, which Macron had threatened to do). They had also created a detailed second set of plans for ousting Ghosn if he agreed with the French government to merge the companies. Ghosn—and Kelly, as it turned out—would agree to support the merger and the die was cast for a corporate overthrow.

"Nada arranged for a hack into Nissan's computer systems and Ghosn's corporate email account without informing key information-technology staff or the chief executive officer," Stevenson wrote in a lengthy article published on August 27, 2020. "That was months before he began working with prosecutors who later arrested the former chairman, according to current and former IT employees at the company."

TV Tokyo reporters later uncovered a confidential document Nada had written to Saikawa a few days before Ghosn's arrest, which clearly revealed the extent of Nada's involvement. It was solely focused on how to use Ghosn's arrest as leverage to oust him from the company and to achieve separation from Renault:

> Prosecutors want to make the arrest for underreporting compensation. I think we should push for breach-of-trust reasons for arrest supported by media campaign for insurance of destroying CG reputation hard enough. Particular attention should be given to France.

This was significant because corporate breach of trust was generally considered to be a more serious crime than underreporting, or false disclosure of income.

The TV Tokyo crew accosted Nada one January morning in 2021 as he was strolling down the street of his Azabu neighborhood in ragged velour pajamas with coffee and Marlboro cigarette in hand and showed him the document.

"That's a confidential email," Nada can be heard to say, clearly stunned. "How did you get it?"

In another email Nada had sent to Saikawa on November 18, 2018 (the day before Ghosn's arrest), with a draft of briefing points attached, he stated that Nissan executives should inform Renault that it was "Nissan's position that Ghosn's removal was a fundamental change to the Alliance and that a new governance for the Alliance must be found." The draft briefing points set forth the demands that should be made by Nissan executives in order to prevent a merger and make Nissan more independent from Renault.

Nada would later testify in court that Ghosn had concealed the scale of his compensation at Nissan primarily because he feared the French government would force him out of Renault it if was discovered how much he really earned.

Through it all, Ghosn heatedly denied any wrongdoing and claimed that in reality he was simply the victim of a boardroom plot by his former Nissan colleagues who feared, more than anything else, that Ghosn would push through the planned merger between Nissan and Renault that would cause Nissan to lose whatever autonomy it had.

Kelly, for his part, insisted that he had acted in a legal manner in the compensation matter and argued he had followed the advice of outside law firms as well as the Financial Services Agency, a Japanese government-run financial regulator responsible for overseeing banking, securities and exchanges.

In all, Ghosn would spend three and a half miserable months in the austere Tokyo Detention House (where the Soviet spy Richard Sorge had been executed), sleeping in a small, solitary unheated cell with a toilet and washbasin, no hot water, and the ceiling light on twenty-four hours a day. When not being interrogated, he was forced to sit upright with his back against the wall in silence. He was allowed thirty minutes of fresh air on weekdays, but none on the weekends. He was not allowed to wear a watch or to receive family visits. Ghosn later compared his experience to torture and characterized the Japanese legal system as one of "hostage justice."

"We thought Japan was part of the G-7, that it's the third-largest economy and looks so civilized," Ghosn's wife Carole said in an interview with *Forbes*. "But then you find out you can get interviewed with no lawyer present and get detained for as long as they want even though they have no proof.

"It's a fake democracy," she added.

Ghosn was eventually granted bail, to the tune of ¥1 billion ($8.93 million), and released on March 6, after 108 days in jail. However, he was subject to stringent conditions. He was not allowed to travel abroad and had to remain at one address with twenty-four-hour camera surveillance. He had no access to the Internet.

Upon his release, Ghosn announced he would hold a press conference at the Foreign Correspondents' Club of Japan to tell his side of the story, scheduling it for April 11, 2019. But much to his shock was rearrested yet again, a week later, on entirely new charges—these stemming from suspicions of financial misconduct concerning alleged dealings via Oman. Four days later, Nissan shareholders voted to remove him, and Kelly, from the board. During this time Ghosn was also compelled to step down as head of Renault.

Ghosn was released again on bail—¥1.5 billion ($14 million) this time around—in late April but was forbidden even to have contact with his wife whom prosecutors had also considered charging with complicity in the crimes, given that she was a shareholder in a Virgin Islands company that received payments from a Nissan distributor in the Middle East. At one point, she said, Japanese authorities seized her phone, her laptop, her diary and the private letters she'd been sending to Ghosn each day.

In June, French prosecutors in Nanterre opened their own investigation of Ghosn.

COUNTERCHARGE

Both Ghosn and Kelly argued that they had been set up, that the accusations about hidden pay were simply red herrings to disguise the corporate coup. The discussions about post-retirement compensation were just that. Nothing was executed and there had been no board approval. As for the properties that Ghosn had supposedly purchased, they were in reality bought under Nissan's Delegation of Authority and were provided for Ghosn to use for business purposes and approved by outside legal counsel. Even the prosecutor eventually recognized that.

Contrary to popular belief, and the odd shareholder angry over the firings, the sensitivities of the Japanese people had nothing do with the 50 percent salary cut Ghosn had taken in 2010. In 2014, Nikesh Arora, CEO of Softbank made $100 million. Nobody in Japan was up in arms when Arora's compensation was disclosed. Several other directors in publicly traded Japanese companies also earned much more than Ghosn. Even Toyota CEO, Akio Toyoda, who owned a great deal of Toyota stock, made about $10 million per year from Toyota dividend payments. In fact, Akio Toyoda's net worth grew from $310 million in 2009 to over $1 billion, in contrast to Ghosn's total worth which was estimated to be around $150 million. It just wasn't talked about.

In fact, every year Nissan requested shareholders to submit written questions for the annual shareholders' meeting, but less than a tenth of a percent of the shareholders asked about Carlos Ghosn's compensation. Everyone appreciated Ghosn's accomplishments, given the increased profits and the fact that Nissan's workforce was considerably larger in 2018 than it was in 2000, with several thousand jobs having been added during his tenure.

Ghosn had halved his annual salary only because he knew the left-leaning French were uncomfortable with greed, capitalism and sky-high executive compensation. French shareholders (who included the French government) would not have approved of the $20 million in pay for Ghosn when his salary became public due to the new disclosure rule in Japan, and had the power to oust Ghosn as Renault CEO if they so desired.

In September 2019, the United States Securities and Exchange Commission (SEC) filed "settled fraud charges" against Ghosn and Kelly related to false financial disclosures that omitted more than $140 million to be paid to Ghosn in retirement. The charges were described in the following manner in the SEC filing dated September 23, 2019 (based on information provided by the Japanese government):

From 2009 until his arrest in Tokyo in November 2018, Ghosn, with substantial assistance from Kelly and subordinates at Nissan, engaged in a scheme to conceal more than $90 million of compensation from public disclosure, while also taking steps to increase Ghosn's retirement allowance by more than $50 million. Each year, Ghosn fixed a total amount of compensation for himself, with a certain amount paid and disclosed and an additional amount that was unpaid and undisclosed. Ghosn and his subordinates, including Kelly, crafted various ways to structure payment of the undisclosed compensation after Ghosn's retirement, such as entering into secret contracts, backdating letters to grant Ghosn interests in Nissan's Long Term Incentive Plan, and changing the calculation of Ghosn's pension allowance to provide more than $50 million in additional benefits. Kelly and Ghosn's Nissan subordinates misled Nissan's CFO, and Nissan issued a misleading disclosure in connection with the increased pension allowance. The $140 million in undisclosed compensation and retirement benefits was never paid out to Ghosn.

Similar charges were filed against Nissan. For his part, Kelly agreed to pay $100,000 and submit to a five-year ban on serving as a senior executive of any public company to settle the charges. Ghosn agreed to pay a $1 million fine and submit to a ten-year ban, while Nissan agreed to pay $15 million to settle charges of civil fraud.

However, like the Ghosn and Kelly arrests, the SEC filing was not what it seemed either. No admission or denial of guilt was required by the SEC from any of the three parties. Moreover, the SEC filing noted in its final sentence that the so-called undisclosed compensation agreement had never been executed. It was simply far, far cheaper, and m less exhausting to pay up, everyone agreed, than to fight two cases simultaneously in court, one in Japan, one in the US.

It was noteworthy that the SEC had based its charges solely on information from the Japanese government, which had originally been provided by the aforementioned Nissan executives, and had not been subjected to cross-examination. It was also noteworthy that as part of its announcement the SEC thanked the Japanese prosecutor for the information the prosecutor provided the SEC.

Had the SEC delayed their civil action until the facts came out in court, as should have been the case, there may not have been any charges filed at all because there were no secret contracts and there was no evidence of secret payments or of any approval for such by the Nissan board. The compensation memos were simply suggestions and points for discussion. Period.

The documentary evidence would show at trial that if a post-retirement agreement had been entered into by Nissan with Carlos Ghosn, the terms of the agreement and the amount of compensation to be paid under the agreement would have had to be publicly disclosed.

Indeed, one of those documents was a September 24, 2018 memo prepared by Arun Bajaj (senior vice president of HR for Nissan, Renault, and Mitsubishi) and Peter Gundy (senior compensation consultant for Willis Towers Watson, a global insurance services firm). It expressly stated that the terms of a post-retirement agreement that Nissan might enter with Carlos Ghosn and the amount of compensation that would be paid under the agreement would have to be fully disclosed. Kelly reviewed the document with Ghosn and Ghosn relayed to Kelly that he understood the terms.

Another of those documents was a statement made by Nada to the Latham & Watkins law firm, with his attorney present, on July 3, 2019, more than a year before Greg Kelly's Tokyo trial began. In it, Nada admitted that Ghosn had not concealed his compensation. Nada confirmed that the draft nonbinding post-retirement documents prepared by Nada were for future services Ghosn would perform as a consultant for Nissan after his retirement and a covenant not to compete, and not for past services. (Unfortunately, this statement, which exonerated Kelly, was never provided by Nissan or the prosecutor to Kelly's attorneys until after the trial was over.)

THE GREAT ESCAPE

In December 2019, with his trial delayed until the end of 2020 and still forbidden to see his wife, Ghosn decided to flee Japan. He left his house on the twenty-ninth of that month and headed for the

Grand Hyatt hotel in Roppongi, losing the plainclothesmen who had been following him as he entered the building. Sometime later he boarded a bullet train to Osaka with two other men. They were part of a team Ghosn's wife Carole had hired to help him escape, at a cost of nearly $1.5 million. The team was led by a former US Army Green Beret turned private security contractor named Michael Taylor, who had figured out a way for Ghosn to leave the country without being detected. At a hotel near Osaka's Kansai International Airport, Ghosn was secreted inside a large audio speaker equipment box—the type of equipment that was too large to fit inside an X-ray machine and that customs officials at Kansai routinely allowed to pass through without opening up for inspection. The box was then loaded aboard a private jet for Istanbul, where Ghosn was transferred to a private jet for Beirut.

Ghosn then took up residence in Lebanon, a country that does not have an extradition treaty with Japan. Shortly after his arrival, Ghosn held a well-attended press conference, which was beamed around the world, to once again declare his innocence. He hired Hollywood heavyweight agent Michael Ovitz to handle a book on his life—which the now international fugitive would write—and which would subsequently be turned into a film. In the meantime, Interpol had issued a "wanted" notice at the request of the French government which was investigating Ghosn over possible tax evasion, questioning whether or not he should have been legally considered a French resident. Ghosn declared in 2012 that he had moved to the Netherlands as a "symbol of neutrality" since he headed the multinational Renault–Nissan auto manufacturer alliance and that he should be treated as a nonresident, but the Ministre de la Justice wasn't buying that claim.

The Lebanese government, for their part, slapped a travel ban on Ghosn and confiscated his passport, while they conducted their own investigation.

Taylor and his son, Ghosn's escape coconspirators, who had argued, incomprehensibly, that they were immune from prosecution in Japan because there was no criminal statute prohibiting jumping bail—ignoring the fact they had broken laws getting Ghosn out of the country by sneaking him past immigration—were later arrested in the US at the request of the Japanese government and extradited to Japan, where, in July 2021, they were sentenced to prison terms of two years and one year and eight months respectively. Also, four individuals who had participated in the escape plan at Istanbul Airport wound up in a Turkish jail, extending the wide swath of collateral damage caused by Ghosn's escape. This also included Greg Kelly, who had been arrested, many believed, primarily so that prosecutors could force him to testify against Ghosn and who was now left to face the music in Japan by himself.

Kelly's trial would begin in September 2020 and last for more than a year.

"INSIDE MAN"

Outside of Nissan, few people had ever heard of Kelly, a bespectacled, mild-mannered trial lawyer from Chicago, a graduate of Loyola University School of Law (and diehard Chicago Cubs fan). He had joined Nissan in 1988, after having been recruited from his law firm, Barnes & Thornburg, in South Bend, Indiana, and was assigned to work at the Nissan Smyrna Assembly Plant in Tennessee—now North America's largest assembly plant—as senior manager and associate legal counsel.

During a training stint in Yokohama in 1992, Kelly spent time familiarizing himself with all aspects of the Nissan operation, which included stints in Nissan's smoke-filled legal offices in Tokyo, in the HR Department, in product engineering as well as a spell on the assembly line in the town of Oppama outside Tokyo.

"I spent my first day on the line putting the wrong screw in each car as it passed which required the guy next to me to repair my work as well as do his," Kelly recalled.

Kelly advanced quickly and by 2005 he was running the Nissan HR Department for all of North America. He personally recruited dozens of replacements for executives who had balked at moving when the company shifted its US headquarters from Gardenia, California, to Nashville, Tennessee.

He and his energetic wife, Dee, raised two sons while living in a Nashville suburb and regularly attended a local Episcopalian church, before being transferred to Japan in 2008.

In 2012, he was elevated to the Nissan board of directors, becoming the first American board member for the Japanese automaker. At the time, Nissan had a total of five non-Japanese executives on its nine-member board. Two years later, Kelly was also appointed head of Alliance Talent Management.

Kelly absolutely loved Nissan. He believed it was a great auto manufacturer destined for ever bigger and better things, thanks to its tie-ups with Renault and Mitsubishi. Friends and coworkers described him as intelligent, a man of the highest integrity, and extremely hardworking.

As the man in charge of HR, and CEO of Ghosn's office, Kelly deeply resented the labels "Ghosn's Right Hand Man," "Inside Man" or "CEO Whisperer" which the press had bestowed on him after the arrests hit the media. He maintained that his relationship with his boss was "not that close," pointing out that he although he was on the board, he was not on Nissan's top operating committee, the executive committee. He met Ghosn but twice a month on average.

However, Kelly did view Ghosn as the most brilliant business executive he had ever met.

"The man ran two globally ranked auto companies at the same time, Nissan and Renault," he marveled. "How many people are capable of doing that?"

Over the years at Nissan, Kelly periodically took up the subject of Ghosn's retirement. If Ghosn left Nissan they were certain a rival auto firm would snap him up and pay him at global standards. Kelly believed, as did Saikawa, that that would be disastrous for Nissan. They had to keep him in the fold as a consultant in some capacity.

By 2015, Kelly had retired from day-to-day management, though he remained a Nissan director. He was spending more and more time at his homes in Nashville and on Sanibel Island, Florida. In November 2018, when he was initially urged by Nissan executive Hari Nada to return to Japan for an emergency board meeting, Kelly had demurred. He explained that he had been scheduled for neck fusion surgery at Vanderbilt University Medical Center and that he was unable even to walk properly due to the numbness he was experiencing in his extremities. Nada insisted it was necessary that Kelly come in person, saying that the company would send a plane to pick him up and have him back home in three days, in time for Thanksgiving and his surgery. After landing in Tokyo, however, his van into the city center was suddenly stopped by police vehicles and he was arrested. He spent the next thirty-seven days in solitary confinement in a cell at the Tokyo Detention House, sleeping on a futon on the floor.

Three and a half years later Kelly was still in Japan, out on bail, mired in legal work and having been forced to have his surgery in Tokyo, which, unfortunately, did not relieve all of his symptoms.

THE JUDGMENT

The evolution of Carlos Ghosn's image during his years at Nissan was often remarked upon. In the beginning, many Japanese observers commented that Ghosn resembled Mr. Bean, the comedic character developed by Rowan Atkinson, joking that the two must have been separated at birth. Over time, however, as Ghosn achieved success after success, he developed a rock-star-like aura in Japan. His life story was featured in a superhero comic-book series, as well as in several other books. His was an almost worshipful following.

Said Tokyo-based lawyer Steven Givens: "You could see him evolve as the years passed and he became more and more successful and the object of more and more media coverage. He was transformed from a geeky, funny-looking guy into a sex symbol."

In 2012, Ghosn had divorced his wife of twenty-six years and mother of his four children, Lebanese Rita Kordahl and, in 2016, married a shapely, blond-haired Lebanese-American New Yorker Carole Nahas. He threw a lavish Marie-Antoinette–themed party at the Palace of Versailles in France to celebrate the wedding and his new wife's fiftieth birthday. The couple was also photographed on the red carpet at the 2017 Cannes film festival. This sparked false reports Ghosn had used Nissan money to purchase five different private homes—in Tokyo, Paris, Rio de Janeiro, Amsterdam and Beirut. The excess prompted many observers to opine that Ghosn had gone too far. General Motors' crusty former vice-chairman Robert Lutz told the CNBC news network that Ghosn "showed all the signs of believing himself to be omnipotent."

Such criticisms were perhaps overblown. The annual operating costs of those properties Ghosn used was probably about $500,000. Combined with Ghosn's compensation package at Nissan of $10 million per year, that made for $10.5 million—far below Ford CEO Alan Mulally's compensation of $25 million annually from 2010 to 2014 and Fiat-Chrysler CEO Sergio Marchionne's compensation of $35 million annually from 2010 to 2016. Indeed, the prosecutor and Nissan's law firm Latham & Watkins both would later acknowledge there was no problem with the properties.

But, as noted earlier, there was more to this story than just plain greed and Ghosn's ever growing ego, illustrated by his increasing conviction that Nissan did indeed need a full-blown merger with Renault and Mitsubishi, moving beyond the existing alliance in which the three firms shared certain specific functions like purchasing and research.

Ghosn's support of a fifty-fifty merger angered certain top Nissan executives in Yokohama, in part because Nissan was generating most of the profit in the alliance and partly because Nissan's Japanese brain trust did not want their company to lose its identity as a *Japanese* firm. (Hari Nada, though not a Japanese national, opposed the merger because, it was said, he feared he would lose his position of power within the firm if it went through.)

Ghosn's wife, Carole, in a January 3, 2020 interview with *Forbes*, complained that Japan had "never shed its nationalist and anti-foreign heritage." She claimed that some Nissan executives conspired directly with the Japanese government's Ministry of Economy, Trade and Industry in order to take down Ghosn and sabotage the planned merger.

"They did not want the merger with Renault," she said. "They don't want anything to do with the French."

There was blame on both sides, as once again the old dynamic of Japanese-versus-foreigner, so common in cross-cultural ventures, made its presence felt, sowing seeds of distrust.

As Peter Daniel Miller, the noted Japan-based sociologist, put it:

These stories share a common theme: the desire of Japanese business circles to stay up-to-date in the world by importing foreign talent. The process involves 1) awareness through various listening posts that something new in the world is afoot, 2) the perception that "we Japanese" have no idea how to do this new thing or use it to our advantage, and 3) a decision to import some practitioner of this foreign magic under tightly controlled conditions so that "we Japanese" can learn how to do it. You could liken it to a Japanese baseball team importing MLB players for home-run production. And when these grandiose expectations prove unrealistic, confidence in native Japanese ability is restored. Alternatively if the imported talent succeeds, the gaijin gets an exaggerated notion of his own importance [see Valentine in the next chapter] and feels free to put aside the Japanese inhibitions he should have learned about not taking too much personal credit, minimizing his own role, instead of setting up a personal cult or wangling blockbuster deals.

Prime Minister Shinzo Abe, (one of the saner voices during all the brouhaha), argued that the case should have been handled internally by the Nissan board. And never should have gone to criminal court.

After his release on bail, Kelly and his wife Dee moved to a small apartment in Hanzomon, near the Imperial Palace in central Tokyo, with a microwave, but no stove. Dee was allowed to stay in Japan on a student visa as long as she faithfully attended Japanese classes and scored high enough on her exams to satisfy the authorities. In preparation for his trial, Kelly made a daily trek to his lawyer's office, where he spent hour upon hour reviewing items from an enormous document dump of close to one billion pages delivered by the prosecutor's office. (One billion pages is the equivalent of eleven terabytes. The Library of Congress has ten terabytes.) As if that were not enough of a roadblock, the prosecution had forbidden the defense to use Internet-based tools to search the electronic records. In cases involving a great deal of electronic data, law firms routinely use such tools because that allows attorneys to collaborate and work together. But not in this case. The Kelly team was hamstrung.

Said Dee, "It would take a hundred lawyers a hundred years to view all the info on a search engine."

Moreover, access to some pages required a password which was not forthcoming either. Yet another obstacle.

It was not a particularly document-heavy case, according to Kelly's attorneys. There were around a hundred to two hundred documents that were relevant. The reason one billion pages were provided to the defense, they surmised, was to hide the documents that exonerated Kelly. Only through extraordinary hard work and resourcefulness were Kelly's attorneys able to find documents that demonstrated the case was not a criminal matter.

Kelly's trial lasted just over a year, from September 2020 to October 2021, encompassing over sixty-seven separate court sessions. Prosecutors specifically alleged that Kelly had been involved in trying to help Ghosn hide compensation starting in 2010, the year Japan changed its corporate reporting rules to require companies to disclose individual executive pay packages of more than ¥100 million ($942,500) a year. Ghosn, they argued, wanted to avoid scrutiny in Japan and France, where public mores frown on large compensation packages.

The trial featured testimony by Saikawa, among other witnesses, who surprisingly praised Ghosn as "a brilliant business leader" and said he agreed with the assessment by Ghosn and Kelly that Ghosn was indeed underpaid compared to the compensation received by other global CEOs of Ghosn's rank (although compared to the pay of other company heads in Japan it was excessive). The post-retirement package had only been an attempt to alleviate that problem as well as to keep Ghosn from going to work for a competitor.

Saikawa said he and Kelly had both feared Ghosn might jump ship. "We simply could not expect Mr. Ghosn to keep working for Nissan," he said. "He was indeed an extremely talented manager."

Saikawa described the retirement agreements as drafts pertaining to "future services" and not as payback for compensation cuts incurred after the disclosure of high executive pay became required in Japan in 2010. He noted that the compact could not take effect in any event without a full set of signatures and board approval. Copies of the drafts presented in court showed the signatures of Saikawa and Kelly, but the documents lacked Ghosn's signature and were left undated.

When prosecutors presented as evidence tables on Ghosn's "unpaid salary" kept meticulously by another Nissan official, Kelly's Japanese lawyer Yoichi Kitamura introduced documents (retrieved from that massive data dump) showing that Kelly had not known about the tables. The documents also demonstrated that Kelly had clearly advised Ghosn that any of Ghosn's compensation as director could not be deferred without disclosure. They demonstrated that Nissan CEO Saikawa, Kelly and others were only trying to ensure that Ghosn stayed connected to Nissan after his eventual retirement as chairman, that Ghosn would provide a variety of post-retirement services and that Ghosn would not work for rival companies. Documents further showed that the retirement compensation plans, estimated to be in the neighborhood of $100 million over a period of around ten years, were thoroughly vetted by internal and external lawyers, and, what's more, had not even been finalized.

Defense attorneys emphasized again and again that Ghosn had not taken any of the money in question. He had been arrested for future bonuses that he had not even signed off on and neither had the board. Nissan lawyers and accountants oversaw every move. So where was the harm, one might rightly ask. Did it really warrant all those arrests and a criminal trial?

Roger Schreffler, a veteran reporter for *Ward's AutoWorld* magazine, further noted in an article for the *Asia Times* that was highly critical of Japan's prosecutors, that Kelly could simply not have committed the crime he was accused of—falsifying financial reports in regard to Ghosn's compensation package because "Kelly, like Ghosn, doesn't read, write or speak Japanese. Financial reports are submitted in Japanese after being reviewed and approved by

Nissan's board, accountants, internal auditors and lawyers—all people who read, write and speak Japanese.

"It didn't happen the way Tokyo prosecutors have alleged," said Schreffler. "They have misled the public about the case from the beginning. Kelly's trial is a kangaroo court. And Ghosn's trial, had he stayed in Japan, would have been a kangaroo court. The way accusations were made in secret, it already qualifies as a Star Chamber."

Indeed, there was evidence that as early as spring 2018, a Nissan official had gone to Japan's Ministry of Economy, Trade and Industry about blocking the merger and was advised to find a crime and go to the prosecutor's office, which, among other things, resulted in Nada luring Kelly back to Japan.

The case captured the attention of America. One of many voices arguing Kelly was "set up" was that of US Senator Bill Hagerty, former US Ambassador to Japan, who echoed the claim that Kelly was a victim of Japan's "hostage justice" system.

Senator Roger Wicker took to the Senate floor to say "This needless ordeal sends a message: if you do business in Japan, watch your back. When it suits the Japanese, they could set a trap for you."

The verdict was finally handed down March 3, 2022, with the American defendant being acquitted of seven of eight charges involving unreported compensation for Ghosn in the fiscal years 2010 to 2016. The court said Kelly was not responsible for most of the planned compensation for Ghosn.

The court said instead that the concealed unpaid income was the fault of Ghosn and Ohnuma, the Nissan executive who had kept track of the reduction in Ghosn's compensation. The court found he had supported a document prepared by a pair of high-ranking Nissan executives named Toshiyuki Shiga and Itaru Koeda, who had undertaken a plan to commit to paying Ghosn for lost salary after he retired. Even though subject to eventual board approval, it was nevertheless a technical violation of Japan's security disclosure laws, simply because it was a "suggestion" that the shareholders had a right to know. This was unbeknownst to Saikawa and Kelly. Ohnuma had, of course, been granted immunity in exchange for his testimony, as had Hari Nada.

However, the court did rule that Kelly was aware of cash compensation for Ghosn in 2017 to the tune of $8 million that was concealed from regulators, again, a legal violation. The court made this ruling on the basis of testimony from Ohnuma, who said he had told Kelly of the 2017 arrangement, thereby making Kelly an accessory. It seemed to many as a face-saving gift to the prosecution.

The chief judge in the case, Kenji Shimotsu, gave Kelly a six-month sentence, suspended for three years, and declared the American free to go back to the United States. Prosecutors had sought two years of jail time.

Kelly was stunned by the court's decision. He argued the 2017 matter centered around a ten-minute meeting he had attended and a resulting document which did not have his name on it and which he had never seen. He further said it was surprising that Shimotsu's decision relied upon the testimony of the same prosecution witness Ohnuma, whom the court had earlier indicated was largely untruthful and unreliable, as borne out by the acquittals.

However, the ruling amounted to a rejection of much of the Japanese prosecutors' case against Kelly, even though Nissan, also a defendant in the case, pleaded guilty and was ordered to pay a ¥200 million fine.

Tokyo attorney Stephen Givens was scathing in his review of the proceedings: "In finding Kelly seven-eighths innocent, the court acknowledged the flimsiness of the underlying case. The guilty verdict on a single count is unpersuasive and reads like a sop to spare the prosecution complete humiliation. The de facto verdict of 'mostly innocent' is wholly consistent with Japan's instinct to avoid stark either-or choices and seek compromises and soft landings where possible. In Kelly's case, justice was more or less disserved, in a murky and unsatisfying way unique to Japanistan."

The verdict concluded the first and possibly only trial regarding the charges on which Mr. Ghosn was arrested in late 2018.

From Beirut, Ghosn, insisted he and Kelly were innocent and that Japanese prosecutors worked to help Nissan push them out in a "palace coup." Said Ghosn: "If Kelly's guilty, many Japanese should also be in prison."

The fallout from the incident did great damage to the auto alliance. There was a precipitous fall in the shares of both Nissan and Renault after Ghosn's arrest, with the post-Ghosn profit margin not much different than when Ghosn first arrived. Nissan announced a $6.3 billion loss. Twenty-eight months after Ghosn's ouster, in March of 2021, Nissan's market capitalization was only halfway back and the automaker was projecting a ¥200 billion ($1.8 billion) operating loss and a nearly ¥530 billion (nearly $5 billion) net loss when it closed its books at the end of the financial year.

Both Nada and Ohnuma remained with Nissan. Nada, who had worried that he would lose power in a Renault merger, was demoted to Senior Advisor, unreported compensation issues of his own having come to light, a demotion in name only as it was reported by several journalists that Nada was still a senior vice president, that he regularly attended executive committee meetings and he was the architect of Nissan's 2023 realignment from Renault, which reduced the French automaker's stake in the Renault–Nissan–Mitsubishi Alliance to just 15 percent. Nissan CEO Saikawa, implicated in a separate payout scandal, was compelled to resign—although not indicted.

Two other foreign executives were also caught up in the damage. José Muñoz, former head of Nissan North America under Ghosn left shortly after his boss's arrest to become global COO for Hyundai Motor. Ravinder Passi, general counsel for Nissan under Ghosn, was, according to Bloomberg reports, demoted, after flagging conflicts of interest within Nissan's investigation into Ghosn.

In Lebanon, Ghosn was treated as a hero by the public and feted on billboards. But in Japan, public sentiment was just the opposite. He was seen as someone who could use his wealth to flee legal penalties in a way nobody else could. According to Tokyo securities analyst Koji Endo "Ghosn's flight means there will never be a judicial decision the Japanese public will accept."

For Carole Ghosn, what happened to her husband was part of the worldwide populist backlash against globalization itself. "I think Japan is going back to Japan Inc.," she said. "They're a country which has always been known as very nationalistic. Look at the history. Nothing has changed."

Kelly, for his part, was phlegmatic despite his ordeal, which caused him sleepless nights and bouts of depression long after he had returned to Nashville. "I am very proud to have worked for this amazing company, Nissan, for over thirty years," he said. "It has been an honor. It's too bad this had to happen. They ruined a great company because of their fear of foreign ownership."

The trial in Japan was unusual to Western observers because of a stunning speech made by the presiding judge after announcing the final verdict that Ghosn had indeed plotted illegal compensation with Ohnuma. He declared Carlos Ghosn was a "dictator" and an "evil person" who showed "greed and malice"—surprising vitriol given Ghosn's track record with Nissan.

A company like Nissan is incredibly complex. You have to deal with problems on the assembly line, say, like a robot part not fitting. At the same time you have to make plans on how to market cars in China. It takes a special kind of person who has both a broad and deep understanding of the automotive business. Ghosn was that special type of person.

Was he greedy? Perhaps. But no more than other highly paid CEOs. And he was incredibly hardworking. He logged more frequent flier miles than the US Secretary of State. Some might argue that he was underpaid.

Japan's longest serving prime minister, Shinzo Abe, had come to power in 2012 promising to make Japan a place that would welcome the global capitalist elite and, at the same time, push corporate Japan to pay more attention to shareholders and outside directors and disclose the cozy, often inefficient cross-shareholdings that characterized Japanese business—the latter a major target for Ghosn when he first arrived in Tokyo. When Abe resigned in September 2019, that possibility was sorely diminished. Foreign executives of Ghosn's rank would think twice before coming to Japan.

All said and done, an unpleasant truth to consider is that the law in Japan may be just another tool for the powers that be to selectively use to control society. Ghosn was deemed undesirable because he promoted a merger that would have cost a Japanese carmaker its special "identity," so the authorities manipulated the law in the interests of societal goals. Woodford followed the law as it was written but was also regarded as an undesirable by many Japanese because he too broke societal harmony. In both cases, it was convenient for the foreigner to suffer (although Woodford got his money). The press served as the public relations tool throughout it all and there was little real journalism, except for the occasional magazine article.

The cases in this chapter don't just point to Japanese insularity. Said business journalist Mary Iida, in a discussion at the Foreign Correspondents' Club of Japan: "There has never been much of a demand for Japanese CEOs outside of their country, even at the height of Japan Inc. Simply not many at any rank could excel in the global market, only in the Japan market context."

That, too, may be an unpleasant truth for the Japanese business world to consider.

CHAPTER 12

Valentine's Way

FOREIGN MANAGERS in Japanese baseball have been, by definition, outsiders, like other characters in this book. Indeed, there have only been a handful of American managers in Japanese professional baseball since it began in 1935 and most of them have been unsuccessful. In general they have been regarded as suspect due to their fundamentally different philosophies, including comparatively relaxed ideas on training which conflict with Japan's intense martial-arts based approach. As one Central League president was famously quoted as saying, "American managers are not suitable for Japan. They're simply too easy."

Hawaiian nisei Wally Yonamine was a Hall of Fame player for Tokyo's Yomiuri Giants. A seven-time All-Star, he graduated to managing and led the Chunichi Dragons to a Central League pennant in 1974, breaking the Giants' run of nine consecutive titles. Liberal thinkers applauded his American-style progressive methods but old-guard managers like the Giants' Tetsuharu Kawakami considered him beneath their respect. Kawakami and Yonamine had been teammates during the fifties but Kawakami, the team's cleanup hitter, and others, were slow to warm to Yonamine because, as they constantly reminded him, he came from a group of people—Japanese-American US citizens—that had fought against Japan during World War Two and were thus regarded as traitors by Japanese nationals to Emperor Hirohito. Indeed, for the first few seasons, his name on the roster was not Wally Yonamine but Kaname Yonamine (Kaname was his middle name, as in Wallace Kaname Yonamine) because it was embarrassing to be seen to have a gaijin on the team. The frigid treatment became worse when Yonamine started breaking Kawakami's records. When Kawakami retired as a player and became manager he sent Yonamine packing to the Nagoya-based Dragons. But Yonamine did eventually exact his revenge through his success with the Dragons.

The Hiroshima Carp hired Joe Lutz as a manager in 1975, with Lutz becoming the first "white pilot" in Japanese baseball history, one who, unlike Yonamine could not speak a word of Japanese. The Carp general manager was quoted as saying, "Appointing Mr. Lutz was one of the greatest gambles I ever made in my life and I considered seppuku if it didn't work."

Lutz lasted less than a month into the regular season. The American's constant battles with the umpires had been a source of embarrassment to the team. The situation came to a head one day when Lutz protested to an umpire and, after some bumping and shoving, was ordered out of the game. Lutz refused to go, arguing for ten minutes until the Carp general manager felt compelled to come down from the grandstand onto the field to ask him to leave. For Lutz, this was an unforgivable embarrassment and after the game he submitted his resignation.

"I didn't feel I was in control, anyway," he said later. "The front office would make decisions about fining players for curfew violations and other things and I would learn about it from reporters. I really felt I didn't know what was going on."

Some people said that the idea of a noisy gaijin manager was just too much for the fans in a city like Hiroshima, a provincial capital that had once been destroyed by an American atomic bomb. Carp player Gail Hopkins later revealed that Lutz had, in fact, been fired. Indeed, Hopkins claimed the Carp organization had been so uncomfortable with foreigners in their midst that in the beginning they darkened the white faces of gaijin in the team photo so they wouldn't look so different from the rest.

Next up was American Don Blasingame, a former St. Louis Cardinals infielder, who signed to manage the popular Hanshin Tigers in 1979, but was gone by mid-season the following year, mired in a controversy over his choice of players in the starting lineup, having gone with a veteran American instead of a prized rookie who had been a nationally famous star in college. Blazer, as Blasingame was known, received death threats and hate mail and the car he was riding in after one game was nearly overturned by angry fans.

It was the American Bobby Valentine, however, who had the stormiest career of all, filled with astonishing highs and mortifying lows. His dynamic leadership electrified Lotte Marines fans in the port city of Chiba, east of Tokyo, and changed the face of Japanese baseball. It also got him fired—twice—and caused a team executive to term Valentine's hiring a "huge mistake," one that had so upset the equilibrium of the organization that it "damaged team harmony beyond repair." There has been no better display of the difficulties involved in being a foreign executive in Japan.

Bobby Valentine was born in 1950 and raised in Connecticut, where he was chosen one of the most outstanding high school athletes in the history of the state in a survey by the popular American magazine *Sports Illustrated.*

He was recruited by the University of Southern California, whose football coach expected him to fill the shoes of departing All-American running back, O.J. Simpson, but he dropped out after meeting Tommy Lasorda, then a manager in the Los Angeles Dodgers' minor league system, who persuaded him that he should switch to professional baseball.

Valentine worked his way up the minor-league ladder to the big leagues, but did not fulfill his early promise and was traded by the Dodgers to the California Angels in 1973. In his first year in Anaheim, he ran into a chain-link fence and suffered a multiple compound fracture from which he never fully recovered. He spent a total of nine years as a part-time player in the major leagues with several different teams before retiring in 1979.

Valentine managed in the minor leagues for a time, then in

1985 took over a chronically weak Texas Rangers team. He won the United Press International's Manager of the Year award two years later when he led the club to a second-place finish.

He had a knack for molding young players into winners and was generally regarded as one of the most intelligent, visionary and charismatic managers in Major League Baseball. At the same time, however, he had an abrasive, condescending, sarcastic side that resulted in a history of conflict with certain players, front office executives, umpires and sportswriters.

It was a testament to his high-octane personality that in one twelve-month span, the New York Press Photographers Association would give him its annual "Good Guy Award" and *The Sporting News* would run a cover story on him which asked the question, "Why Does Everyone Hate Bobby Valentine?"

Fired by the Rangers in 1992, Valentine took a job managing the Triple-A Norfolk Tides, the New York Mets' top farm club. While there he was approached by Tatsuro Hirooka, the famed former manager of Japan's Yakult Swallows and the Seibu Lions, who had just taken over as general manager of the Chiba Lotte Marines, a baseball team owned by the multinational corporation Lotte. Hirooka persuaded him to come to Japan and join the club as field manager in 1995.

The Marines had just moved from Kawasaki in the heart of Japan's industrial belt. There, they had been known as the Lotte Orions, and had played in a rusting, polluted, headache-inducing stadium, habitually occupying the nether regions of the Pacific League. Now they found themselves in Chiba's Makuhari, a newly built high-tech industrial center of antiseptic office towers and residences, exhibition venues and concert halls.

Hirooka had brought Valentine in primarily as a novelty item, a way to stimulate fan interest, while he, Hirooka, rebuilt the organization. Unbeknownst to Valentine, Hirooka had only intended to keep his American manager for two years, whereupon he would replace him with farm team manager Akira Eijiri, whom Hirooka was grooming for the job.

The Marines did well despite playing in a modern concrete bowl that was as windy as the San Francisco Giants notorious former seaside baseball stadium, Candlestick Park and, in the early spring, just as dank and frigid. However, there were frequent clashes between Valentine and the coaches Hirooka had hired to assist him. The coaches preferred the established way, meaning the martial-arts approach to the game, which dated back to the nineteenth century, when baseball was first introduced to Japan.

It was a system that manifested itself in dawn-to-dusk days in spring training camps that were weeks longer than in the US. There was a focus on so-called guts drills where players were made to field balls to the point of exhaustion and the approach sometimes entailed corporal punishment, where coaches would kick and slap recalcitrant players.

Valentine instituted his own hybrid method of practice—three hours a day in camp, not nine as with many other Japanese teams—and during the season he held softer pregame workouts, to conserve energy for the games. He reduced the number and length of pregame meetings that required the attendance of the entire team and also shunned the use of the sacrifice bunt, a favorite tactic of nearly all Japanese managers, believing the meetings a waste of time and the sacrifice bunt a waste of an out.

However, throughout most of the season, it became clear that Valentine was never completely in charge. The Japanese coaches, uncomfortable with Valentine's Western-style ways, sometimes countermanded his instructions after consulting with Hirooka and held secret practices without Valentine's knowledge.

A memorable incident occurred in the September of Valentine's first year with the Marines, after the team returned from a long, arduous road trip in the midst of a wilting heat wave, and Valentine elected to give everyone a full day off before the next regularly scheduled game. When Valentine visited the stadium on that supposed off-day, however, he found, much to his surprise, the entire team in full practice mode, with General Manager Hirooka himself directing the proceedings.

The Marines finished the season in second place. It was the team's best showing in years and some of the top Marines players praised Valentine for trying to make baseball fun—some of them even averred, off the record, that the martial-arts approach of Hirooka and the Japanese coaches was unsuitable for the modern Japanese game.

Valentine, believing he was operating from a position of strength, wrote a letter to acting owner Akio Shigemitsu suggesting that the coaching staff be changed. The coaches, however, told Hirooka that they would resign unless Valentine was fired. One of them, Shozo Eto, a respected veteran of the baseball wars in Japan, said that Valentine did not make enough of an effort to understand the psychological value of the traditional Japanese approach, or show enough respect to the people trying to help him. Eto called his season with Valentine "the worst year of my life."

General Manager Hirooka took Eto's side. In Hirooka's end-of-season report to Akio Shigemitsu, he lamented that the philosophical differences were simply too great between the two sides. He said that tactical errors by Valentine, which, not surprisingly, included a failure to employ the sacrifice bunt, had cost the team fifteen victories (although he somehow neglected to notice in his mathematical calculations those decisions Valentine had made which had helped the team win twenty-seven more games than the previous season). In the end, Shigemitsu agreed with Hirooka to fire Valentine.

The next season, with Valentine gone, the Marines suffered a return to the lower depths. Now it was Hirooka and his coaches who were replaced at year's end.

The franchise stayed near the bottom of the league under a succession of Japanese managers. Meanwhile, over in the US, Valentine had taken over the New York Mets in 1996 and had guided them to several impressive seasons, winning the National League pennant in 2000, before losing to the Yankees in the World Series in five games.

After Valentine was fired by New York in 2002 amid a conflict with Mets executives, Shigemitsu, now convinced he had made a mistake in letting Valentine go, decided to invite him to return to Japan and manage the Marines once more—and at a salary of $4 million a year, a record for a manager in Japan.

THE ZEN OF BOBBY V

The "air," as the Japanese say, had changed in the interim. The influx of Japanese baseball stars into American Major League Baseball that began in the mid-1990s with Hideo Nomo and continued with Ichiro Suzuki and Hideki Matsui, served to soften anti-outsider thinking in the Japanese game. The flood of daily gamecasts and TV programs about the freer, looser American style of play, seemed to inspire a new willingness on the part of Nippon Professional Baseball (NPB) to accept American ideas.

As Koichi Tabuchi, a former Hanshin Tigers star, would famously put it in 2005, "Now, people are watching a lot of American ball and have gained a real appreciation for it. There's no prejudice anymore."

As a result, the NPB began to rethink its practices against hiring foreign managers. In 2003, the Nippon Ham Fighters selected as their new manager Trey Hillman, the former farm director for the Texas Rangers. This preceded Valentine's return to reassume the helm of the Chiba Lotte Marines in 2004. In 2005 Valentine became the first American manager ever to win a Japan Series title, doing it in a most convincing fashion, leading many observers to conclude the corner had been turned in Japan as far as gaijin managers went.

Valentine had, as before, eschewed the endless workouts and authoritarian discipline typical of Japanese sport in favor of proper rest and shorter, snappier practices, while giving all his players ample opportunities to play regardless of age or experience. This time, no one was unhappy with the result, given the fact that Lotte had not had a winning season in nearly a decade and was one of the least popular teams in Japan. After finishing second in regular season play, the well-rested Marines blew through the playoffs, defeating defending Japan champions the Seibu Lions and the heavily favored Fukuoka Softbank Hawks in five games, and then obliterated their Central League opponent the Hanshin Tigers in four straight games, outscoring them 33–4. It was the most lopsided Japan Series in history.

Moreover, Valentine gave Marines supporters a special boost when he challenged the 2005 MLB champions, the Chicago White

Sox, to a "Real World Series"—a long-held dream of many Japanese baseball fans—claiming that his team could hold its own with any club on the globe. White Sox manager Ozzie Guillen scoffed at the idea, as no doubt would have any other big league manager, but the point had been made.

Valentine was widely applauded for his accomplishments. He was voted Manager of the Year in many media polls, and chosen as "ideal boss" by readers of *Weekly Spa*, a popular magazine that caters to young businessmen. A newspaper editorial called on Japanese firms to begin treating employees "the same way Bobby does," and curb their tradition of harsh management and overwork—a sixty-to-seventy-hour week was not unusual.

It was estimated by advertising agency Hakuhodo that the national media exposure enjoyed by team owner Lotte—a vast worldwide conglomerate of hotels, candy, chewing gum, fast-food restaurants and financial services—immediately following the Marines' Japan Series victory was worth the equivalent of more than $30 million in free advertising.

Lotte acting owner Akio Shigemitsu was beside himself with pride. "This is the greatest day of my life," he was heard to say during the Marines' victory parade through downtown Chiba.

He rewarded Valentine with a new four-year contract worth $20 million, making him the second-highest-paid baseball manager in the world behind then New York Yankees skipper, Joe Torre.

Shigemitsu also signed onto a number of MLB-style additions to windblown Chiba Marine Stadium in Makuhari suggested by Valentine, including a new sports bar, luxury boxes, deluxe suites, picnic tables and an HD screen. He welcomed a myriad of promotional events inviting fans onto the field to interact with Valentine and his players, all of which added to the new appeal and helped cause a marked jump in attendance and revenue.

The revitalization efforts featured the contributions of one Shigeo Araki, a youthful, brainy director of business operations who had joined Lotte upon Valentine's return. As Araki explained in an interview, "Makuhari, where Chiba Marine Stadium is located, is out of the way and it is difficult to get to. We had to give people special motivation to make the trip. So in addition to the game it-self, we created all sorts of amusements.

"We set up a concert stage for entertainment and an area for street performers in front of the main gate. We set up food and souvenir stalls and other concessions outside, which was also helpful because, in the beginning, we did not get a cut from concessions inside, as the rights to them were owned by the stadium.

"Then, after the game, we allowed kids to come on the field to run the bases and then have their pictures taken with their favorite stars. We allowed their parents to come down on the field and pose with them, too.

"So at times in the 2005 season, we had hundreds, up to a thousand kids in line waiting their turn to run the bases."

It is perhaps accurate to say that no manager has ever worked harder than Valentine to promote his team. It was estimated he signed a hundred thousand autographs in a year. He also sent out thousands of signed New Year's cards to Lotte faithful, as well as hundreds of congratulatory telegrams to schools in the Chiba area during the April school-entrance period.

Furthermore, he participated in a plethora of events he helped design to get the fans involved, such as "Handshake Day" and "Blood Pressure Awareness Day." On top of that, he also granted an unending stream of interview requests to anyone and everyone who asked, be it to representatives from the major media, or graduate students writing papers about his management style.

Time and again, he stressed the need to get involved with the citizens of Chiba. "I see very little effort made from coaches of other teams and the managers of other teams to do anything other than winning the game they are playing," he said. "Players really have more responsibility to the community and to the fans—it's not just going out and playing."

The result of his efforts was that the Chiba Lotte Marines drew over 1,300,000 in attendance in 2005, doubling their 2004 total, and were ranked number one in all "fan service" surveys.

Declan O'Connell, a longtime foreign resident of Chiba and a hard-core Marines fan who hails from Ireland, said, "It is difficult to exaggerate the effect Bobby had on the locals, in particular in 2005. I was working in a small city in rural Chiba at that time, and there was literally an extra spring in people's steps that fall. It was wonderful to see kids in Chiba Lotte Marines hats and talking excitedly about their local team—young players at that time were wonderful role models.

"Sport matters to the community, it really does," O'Connell added. "It has to do with people's self-image and it has to do with pride of place, pride in where you come from."

Valentine's exploits drew the attention of major media from North America as well as Japan. He was profiled by the *Washington Post*, the *New York Times* and by HBO in a TV feature, giving the name Lotte a healthy dose of exposure in the US. He was also the subject of a documentary produced by a trio of New York filmmakers entitled *The Zen of Bobby V*, which premiered in the spring of 2008 at the Tribeca Film Festival and then aired on ESPN.

In an interview with CBS News, Valentine said "It's my destiny to be in Japan."

As it turned out, however, it was not his destiny to remain there.

THE DECLINE AND FALL OF BOBBY V

Valentine failed to win a second pennant . His team finished in 2006 and missed by a game in 2007, as Trey Hillman's Nippon Fighters won two consecutive Pacific League flags and one Japan Series ('06). However, attendance at and revenue from Chiba Lotte Marines games had quadrupled under Valentine's watch. The former Texas Rangers and New York Mets pilot was riding a wave of success that many commentators on Japanese baseball had thought impossible for a gaijin manager to attain. In fact, Chiba Lotte Marines acting owner Akio Shigemitsu even began talking about a lifetime extension of Valentine's contract. Valentine's supporters boasted that he was headed for the Japanese Hall of Fame.

But such talk did not last.

The 2008 Marines finished in the second division—albeit barely—in a four-team race for the flag. It was not the kind of record people expected from one of the world's most expensive managers. Moreover, attendance had grown by only 2.7 percent during that '08 campaign, not nearly enough to cover costs.

Thus it was that in December, Valentine was called back to Japan from the US and unceremoniously informed that when his contract expired in 2009 he would not be invited back.

The Marines had a newly elevated president Ryuzo Setoyama, imported by Shigemitsu from Fukuoka—where he had been managing director of the Daiei Hawks—to handle an internal auditing issue. He was kept on to run the front office. Setoyama explained to the media that the baseball team had been losing money to the tune of $30 to $40 million a year, despite the unprecedented buzz the Marines had created in the Chiba community. Although revenue from ticket sales had *indeed* risen, so had expenses, including player salaries and stadium improvements. New video boards and HDTV broadcasting equipment alone had cost more than $8 million a year.

At the same time, TV revenue had remained virtually nonexistent. Local television stations continued to pay a paltry $1,500 to televise a single Marines home contest, a tiny fraction of what the more popular Yomiuri Giants commanded.

The Marines baseball team, you must keep in mind, was a subsidiary of Lotte Corporation, whose Japan and Korea operations were bleeding money in the wake of the '08 global financial meltdown, and was unable to help the ball club.

Shigemitsu had stated earlier that he would decide on Valentine's future at the conclusion of the 2009 season, when Valentine's contract expired, after examining the team's performance and gauging the wishes of the fans. However, the fact of the matter was that his father, Takeo Shigemitsu, the Seoul-born eighty-five-year-old chairman and patriarch of the Lotte empire, who had single-handedly built the business up from a small chewing gum stand (at a time when most Koreans in Japan were relegated to menial jobs like shining shoes, or to roles in the nighttime entertainment business or the *yakuza* underworld) had never been happy with the $20 million deal his son had given to Valentine in the first place and had decreed that the contract could not be extended at that exorbitant price.

Moreover, in an offseason tripartite summit of the father, the son and the team president, the father ordered the ballclub's deficit to be reduced to a manageable ¥2 billion ($20 million), and the president, Setoyama, was assigned the task of making the budget cuts. Setoyama reckoned that under these circumstances Valentine was simply too expensive, especially for someone, in his opinion, who seemed to be going backward. Furthermore, Setoyama said, if you counted all the dozen or so people who had been enlisted in the Valentine effort to modernize the team, then, by the team president's calculation, he was costing Lotte a total of $8 million a year.

The "Valentine Family," as the media dubbed the group of American and Japanese advisers Valentine had hired, included the aforementioned Araki, a former IBM executive and IT whiz who had been brought in to update business operations; Shun Kakazu, a young Harvard graduate who had constructed a sophisticated player database; and Larry Rocca, a former New York sports writer who had initiated American-style promotions (ladies' night, salaryman's night, disco night) and successfully solicited several million dollars' worth of corporate sponsorships for the Marines.

Setoyama asked them all, and several others, to submit their resignations and accept a buyout—the polite way of getting rid of unwanted personnel in Japan. Noteworthy in this blitzkrieg of change was that none of those getting the ax, including, notably, Valentine, was given a chance to discuss and renegotiate his contract downward. The decision to dismiss them was as final as it was swift.

Valentine, stunned at suddenly going from "lifetime" manager to lame duck, attempted to appeal directly to Akio Shigemitsu for an explanation of this disastrous turn of events. But the acting owner refused to return Valentine's phone calls or answer emails.

More than any other team in the NPB, the Marines during the Valentine era had been identified by their American manager. At the entrance to the park, a flat-screen TV showed continuous loops of Bobby greeting fans. The concourse walkways inside the park were lined with ten-feet (three-meter) high Bobby murals, inscribed with his aphorisms like "The team is a family. A happy family makes the team stronger."

Even the food there had his image on it: the Bobby box-lunch; a brand of sake with his picture on the label; a beer named after him; and Bobby bubble gum; while near the main entrance to the stadium there was a small shrine in his honor, featuring his papier-mâché image, and not far away, a street named after him, Valentine Way. To some, it had overtones of a personality cult. But now, Setoyama began dismantling every reminder of Valentine's influence. Down came the shrine, the main gate video presentation, the murals and posters on the walls. The beer, the hamburgers and other Bobby V. products also gradually disappeared.

Valentine's many supporters wondered what the hell had happened. How could he sink so low, so fast?

The members of the Marines *oendan* (cheering section) and various fan groups were furious at this turn of events. They had formed a special bond with Valentine during his years with the Marines. Not only had he given them a team worth cheering about, but he also made them an integral part of the organization, unlike Japanese managers, who tended to keep their distance from the outfield hoi polloi.

He had always made himself available to sign autographs inside and outside the stadium. He had participated in pep rallies and after home games had made it a point to see that his players walked out to the right-field stand area, where the oendan stationed themselves, to shake hands with the fans and express their thanks.

He had taken to calling the Lotte oendan "No. 26" because with their raucous enthusiastic cheering, they were the equivalent of an extra player on the 25-man team roster. He declared many times over that they were the best fans in the world.

As oendan member Kazuhiro Yasuzumi put it, "I went to Lotte games for years. It was always easy to get a ticket to sit in the outfield stands, because it was usually half empty. But that all changed after Bobby came. You had to stand in line. He made Lotte special. He made Lotte a big part of the community, whereas before it wasn't.

"Bobby has been a phenomenally successful manager, both on and off the field. He's also been a great ambassador for baseball generally, especially American baseball. It was clear it would take a while for the changes he was making to reap benefits. But it didn't make sense to get rid of him. There are other ways to deal with the economic problems."

Daigo Asada, a young sports marketing executive who could be found in the outfield cheering section for nearly every home game, was incredulous. "How can they do this?" he cried. "Valentine is a man who said we were good enough to play in a real World Series. Who else has ever been able to say that? Considering the Marines cannot afford a payroll with a lineup of stars and free agents like the Yomiuri Giants or the Softbank Hawks can, Bobby has been doing a superb job. You can't get anybody better than Bobby V. This is treason against Japanese baseball. This is about Japanese society. This shows that you try to change things and you get hammered down."

Anger at the sudden changes in the Lotte baseball organization thus set the stage for one of the more confrontational seasons in the history of the NPB. From Opening Day 2009, hometown fans in the outfield seats declared war on Setoyama. They hoisted banners pillorying Marines executives for their decision to let Valentine go.

"Clap Your Hands If You Want Setoyama To Resign," read one sign. "What An Unforgivable Disgrace," went another. "Death to Lotte Management," said one more.

Stadium security would eject fans raising particularly offensive banners, but other banners quickly took their place. Mitch Murata, a corporate adviser and ardent Marines fan, observed wryly, "These guys are more organized than al-Qaeda."

At the same time, oendan members launched a drive to collect signatures demanding Valentine's return.

The response from Setoyama and his supporters within the organization was to begin a smear campaign to sully Valentine's reputation. They floated rumors that he was taking kickbacks from foreign players, that he had even recruited one gaijin player from a local bar, and that he had hired his own son to design new Lotte uniforms, while collecting a hefty royalty on their sale.

They also claimed that he had sexually harassed Lotte female employees, that he was anti-Japanese and even racist, noting he had been heard using terms like "the fucking Japanese way." Truth be told, they would say, Valentine was a very bad individual, more suited for the uniform of a Fuchu Prison inmate than that of a Chiba Lotte Marine.

A new assistant general manager named Akira Ishikawa, hired by Setoyama in the middle of the 2008 season, seemed intent on making Valentine's life as miserable as possible. He reportedly countermanded Valentine's instructions to players before and during games. Also, on two different occasions when Valentine had become involved in on-field disputes with the umpires, Ishikawa had come down to take the side of the men in blue.

As previously indicated, Valentine had his abrasive side. In Japan, as in the US, he had had his share of run-ins, not only with umpires, but also with opposing players and league officials. At one point he had called Central League officials "idiots" for their refusal to embrace reform. He had had an awkward shouting match with the manager of the Orix Blue Wave over the latter's delaying tactics and his habit of directing his charges while standing in the coach's box on the third base side of the infield, as opposed to staying in the dugout as other managers did. Valentine had hurled a string of insults in English at the Orix pilot, who yelled back angrily, "Speak Japanese." Such behavior was used against him by his enemies.

Valentine's considerable ego was another issue. Noted author Toru Takagi, who wrote the book *Valentine-ryu manejimento no gyakushu* [A Counterattack to Valentine-style management, published by Kodansha, 2006] about Valentine and directed two television documentaries him, praised his skill in developing young players but was quoted as saying that Valentine's "need to constantly be the center of attention, to self-flatter, is a cause for concern. It makes it difficult for him to demonstrate his good side."

A key, if unusual, combatant in the effort to discredit Valentine was a moon-faced, middle-aged woman named Yoko Yoneda, who, at the start of the 2009 season, had been elevated to the No. 3 spot in the front office by Akio Shigemitsu, in charge of media relations and VIP suites. With a fondness for garish fashion—zebra-striped polyester shirts and loud pink dresses—while carrying a mauve business card that described her as a "fortune teller" who did "character and color analysis," she was surely one of the strangest NPB executives in the annals of the game.

Yoneda made news at the beginning of the season, when she ordered reporters to stop wearing jeans and to use formal language when speaking to the players. This was the cause of great mirth to some observers, since most reporters had nothing else in their wardrobe and most players, for their part, were so uneducated they could not easily understand honorific Japanese.

A former cheerleader at high school baseball powerhouse PL Gakuen and an employee at Otsuka Pharmaceutical Co. Ltd., Yoneda had been introduced to Akio Shigemitsu by the president of Otsuka, and had been given a job in the Marines' front office in 2006. No one could figure out what the nature of her relationship was with the diffident billionaire's son, who denied there was anything romantic going on. He simply explained in a news conference that Yoneda was an "eccentric character" who told his fortune.

Setoyama was just as surprised at Yoneda's elevation to the top ranks of Lotte as everyone else. Nevertheless, she dove head first into her duties. From spring training on, Yoneda pressured scribes to criticize Valentine more often in print and, in one case, demanded that a reporter write that Valentine had chosen the wrong pitcher. She complained that Valentine's lifelong friend, coach Frank Ramppen, could not even hit fungoes properly.

As head of the VIP suites, she cut off access to Valentine's wealthy supporters—one of whom was an American corporate executive who spent $15,000 a year on tickets to Marines games. Yoneda claimed that he had damaged the carpet of a VIP room. She then turned around and granted special access to VIP areas to the families of select Marines players, including star infielder Tsuyoshi Nishioka, in an effort to curry favor with them, and she was even spotted playing Nintendo Wii video games in one of the two-thousand-dollar suites.

Setoyama and his staff were employing the ancient Japanese tactic of village ostracism, to make Valentine's final season as miserable as possible, and perhaps force him to quit early and save the front office part of his salary—or at least affect Valentine's ability to run the team successfully.

The last thing Setoyama seemed to want was for Lotte to win another Japan Series and cause such a groundswell of support for Valentine that the organization would have no choice but to offer him a new contract.

A month into the 2009 season, the battle of the Chiba Lotte Marines entered a new phase, when a Valentine sympathizer in the front office leaked the minutes of an executive meeting in which Setoyama, shedding his mask of congeniality, dismissed complaints from the oendan and the petition they were circulating, as worthless.

"The fans are like carp, they will eat anything you feed them," Setoyama was quoted as saying, adding, "Regarding those people in the right-field stands that are pro-Valentine, we should think about changing locations if they're going to damage our image. If we have unworthy fans like this, let's just move our home stadium. It's just a bunch of stupid Chiba fans anyway."

Setoyama claimed the minutes were a forgery, but they were later proven real. And the public revelation of his remarks prompted the appearance of even more protest banners, including one sign that alluded to front office graft as a motivation for his actions and another that alluded to Setoyama's own misadventures in sexual harassment, along with others offering helpful suggestions as to what Setoyama could do with himself.

The most memorable, however, was a banner, reading "Bobby Forever," that was so huge it stretched across half the outfield and was thirty rows high. After one game, angry fans supporting Valentine congregated outside the stadium demanding an audience with Setoyama, forcing the team president and his assistants to hide inside until they dispersed.

Valentine himself kept silent, aware that a clause in his contract forbade him from criticizing the team under penalty of being fired and losing his salary. But by mid-season, the oendan petition had reached 112,000 signatures. It was presented to the elder Shigemitsu, who rotated between Tokyo and the Seoul office of Lotte

Korea, on one of his regular visits to Japan. The wizened patriarch was so upset at the bad publicity the Marines were getting, and the way his son Akio was handling things in general, that he ordered a special investigation of his own into the goings-on at Lotte.

Valentine and his supporters held out hope that the investigation would result in the firings of Setoyama, Ishikawa and Yoneda, once the elder Shigemitsu discovered just how badly they had behaved. Indeed, many staff members expected that to happen. But it was not to be. The final report of the investigation, which was not released to the public, did indeed conclude that the rumors being spread about Valentine were untrue. In fact, most of the interviewees, if not all, had supported Valentine.

However, in the end, the old man decided that the American manager would still have to go. Perhaps it was simply to save his son from further embarrassment, or perhaps he did not know what else to do, since he knew next to nothing about the baseball team he had owned for several decades.

Either way, he wasn't saying.

"MR. VALENTINE'S 'USE-BY' DATE HAS EXPIRED"

In retrospect, there were many reasons why Bobby Valentine lost favor with the Chiba Lotte Marines organization. It wasn't just his prohibitive salary of $4 million per year.

For example, some observers thought it all came down to a case of "gaijin fatigue." After all, they said, six years is a long time for one man to be manager of a team, especially when said manager is by far the highest paid, a foreigner and surrounded by so many foreign faces or *gaijin kusai* Japanese (Japanese who "stink of foreigner" as the pejorative expression goes).

Valentine began to suffer by comparison with fellow American and Nippon Ham Fighters manager Trey Hillman who had achieved further success and done it by eventually incorporating certain Japanese ways into his management style.

As Hillman explained in an interview with the *Yukan Fuji* newspaper: "In the beginning, I held spring training sessions the

American way, three to four hours then go home. But it was clear that what I was doing wasn't working. The team wasn't winning. So I asked my players and coaches for suggestions. First, they told me they wanted longer practices—no more of this half-day routine—in camp. So, against everything I believed, I kept them there until 5 p.m., working on defense, among other things.

"They also wanted more bunting, which is typical for Japan, but went against my big-inning offensive philosophy. But again I said OK, because this time we had a lot of good pitching."

In that 2006 season, Hillman's Fighters set a new club record for sacrifice bunts, triple the number of the year before, and the entire outfield won Golden Gloves.

With the help of a solid mound corps, led by a twenty-year-old sensation named Yu Darvish, and a spacious home park, the Sapporo Dome, Nippon Ham had its best win–loss record in forty-six years and won the Japan Series. At the end of the season, a news announcer for Japan's NHK broadcasting corporation lauded Hillman for understanding the Japanese way, saying "Hillman-san is the first American manager ever to make the switch from an American approach to the game to a Japanese one."

Hillman, who left Japan at the end of the 2007 season to manage the Kansas City Royals, and Valentine, were not the only foreign managers at the time. There was the gregarious Marty Brown who managed the Hiroshima Carp for three also-ran seasons and followed that with a lone unsuccessful season at the helm of the Rakuten Golden Eagles before being invited to turn in his visa. There was also Terry Collins, hyper and combative, who quit after little more than a year managing the Orix Buffaloes in 2007, in protest at front office interference. "They brought me over to change things," he said upon exiting Japan, "but they refused to change." Former Chiba Lotte Marines and Yakult Swallows star Leon Lee managed Orix for a year in 2003 before being fired. Puerto Rican Alex Ramirez managed the Yokohama Bay Stars for five years, winning a pennant in 2017 but losing the Japan Series. He was canned in 2020. But among them all only Valentine's tenure featured such Shakespearean drama.

For Valentine, however, the deciding factor may have simply been his inability, or unwillingness, from the beginning, to coexist with the team president Ryuzo Setoyama. Setoyama had initially found himself marginalized while Valentine and his crew basked in the glow of the Marines' 2005 success. It was a delicate situation that called for tact and understanding, both of which proved to be in short supply given the cultural differences and personalities of the individuals involved on both sides, and the inability of the foreign contingent to appreciate Setoyama's backstory.

Setoyama was a "salaryman," a baseball executive who had never played professional baseball. After graduating from Osaka Shiritsu University in 1977, he had joined the Daiei Corporation, a gigantic supermarket chain and retail conglomerate that had expanded rapidly in bubble-era Japan with the help, it was reported, of shady real-estate sharks and other underworld connections. Setoyama had started out in the meat department of a Daiei supermarket branch in Osaka and worked his way up the ladder, catching the eye of Daiei owner and founder Isao Nakauchi in the process. In 1988, when Daiei purchased the Nankai Hawks of Osaka, Setoyama was tapped to organize the relocation of the team to Fukuoka.

Setoyama was invariably described as a likable, friendly, easygoing sort—a "nice *ojisan*" (uncle) is the way one NHK broadcasting corporation producer put it. He was respected throughout the NPB for his workmanlike business abilities and was singled out by then NPB commissioner Ichiro Yoshikuni as an executive to be emulated for his skill in organizing the Hawks' move to Fukuoka, which entailed the construction of the Fukuoka Dome and the adjacent "Hawks Town" shopping mall and hotel, as well as the purchase of the land on which it all stood.

Although the Hawks produced only losing seasons during their first eight years in Fukuoka, the team regularly drew over two million fans a season, an impressive figure for a small-market team. The Hawks also enjoyed the third-highest TV revenue after the Yomiuri Giants and the Hanshin Tigers.

During Setoyama's tenure, the Hawks gradually managed to turn things around, under former slugger Sadaharu Oh (see Chapter 8) who took over as manager, replacing Rikuo Nemoto, who moved up to assume the post of team president.

Setoyama's assistant, scout Akira Ishikawa, a former Hawks ballplayer of little note, successfully recruited a number of notable young amateur players who became stars and turned the franchise into a baseball powerhouse. The Hawks accomplished the signings of these highly sought-after players by reportedly paying under-the-table subsidies that exceeded the ¥100 million signing bonus limit set by the NPB. Although such payments were certainly questionable, it was a practice that was customary at the time until revised draft rules reduced the power of eligible draftees to choose their teams. Many high school and college managers demanded money for their schools before they would agree to steer their charges to one professional franchise over another.

In 1997, when the tax office charged several individuals with tax evasion linked to the under-the-table payments, Setoyama took responsibility by resigning. He was called back and remained long enough to take some of the credit for the two Japan championships and three pennants the Hawks won.

Setoyama resigned again in 2003, this time for good, after losing an internal power struggle, but was called to the Marines in 2004, on the recommendation of Daiei owner, Nakauchi, who had long-standing ties to the elder Shigemitsu. Nakauchi and Shigemitsu had also established joint business ventures in South Korea in the 1970s and 1980s.

The two men were, in fact, planning a merger of the Lotte and Daiei baseball teams as part of an overall NPB plan to contract from twelve to eight teams and in March 2004, they had picked Setoyama to oversee it. The planned contraction fell through, however, thanks in part to a player strike, but Setoyama stayed on in the Lotte front office with the blessing of newly arrived manager Valentine. From the fall of 2004, Setoyama occupied the post of general manager, which, unfortunately, did not leave him with a lot to do, since Valentine, for all intents and purposes, was already functioning as his own general manager. Setoyama, who, in any event, did not know very much about the team, was thus relegated to rubber-stamping

Valentine's to-do list—a general manager in name only, on his way to being appointed team president a year later.

Setoyama was further handicapped by his inability to speak English and also by the fact that he did not know how to use the Internet and email, tools that Valentine and Shigeo Araki, the business operations manager, employed nearly all their waking hours. Moreover, Setoyama was old-school, accustomed to long discussions with subordinates, taking his time, mulling decisions, while Valentine and Araki simply figured out the right thing to do and with a minimum of talk and cursory notification upstairs, took the ball and ran with it. Indeed, it was Valentine who had taken the lead in getting the operating rights to Chiba Marine Stadium from the Chiba governor, a job that normally the president of the team should have undertaken.

It was an awkward situation. The president of the team was supposed to have been the field manager's boss, but at Lotte, the tail was wagging the dog.

There had been a brief dustup in 2006, when Valentine had publicly charged that NPB team representatives were still making under-the-table payments to hot amateur prospects, despite their vow to cease doing so. The remark created such an uproar among executives on other NPB teams that Valentine was ordered by Akio Shigemitsu to apologize in front of reporters. Appearing before the media pregame at Miyagi Stadium in Sendai with Setoyama standing by his side, Valentine said, "My remarks were not based on accurate information. I apologize if I offended anyone."

Sports dailies ran a comical photo of the Chiba Lotte Marines team president bowing deeply, sincerely, beside Valentine who, instead of bowing himself, stood head up, his arms folded, a defiant expression on his face.

(In March 2007, Valentine was vindicated when an executive from the Pacific League Seibu Lions organization admitted that the team had still been making secret payments to a high school star to prevent him from signing with another pro team.)

Valentine had been particularly unhappy that Setoyama had volunteered the services of seven of Lotte's top players to join Team

Japan for the 2006 World Baseball Classic, including four of the team's best pitchers. Valentine claimed that the absence of so many of his key players had prevented the team from preparing properly in spring training for the '06 season and was the primary reason the club finished in the second division that year, 16.5 games out of first place.

Setoyama's hole card was his power over the budget. From the time Setoyama took over as president, Lotte headquarters complained constantly that the $30 to $40 million annual deficit was too much and kept asking for Setoyama to make budget cuts. One of the budget items Setoyama consequently eliminated was so-called fight money (cash prizes paid to the best players in each game), reportedly explaining to Valentine and his subordinates that the money was needed to build a new indoor practice facility for the team, a project that showed no signs of ever getting under way.

Valentine, who had a long personal history of loaning money to friends and acquaintances in need, and of contributing to charities, reacted to the cuts by continuing to make the fight money payments out of his own pocket. He also gave financial assistance to other staff members whose benefits had been similarly cropped.

Valentine had assumed it was just a matter of time before the various improvements he had overseen in the organization would begin reaping benefits and the Marines would turn a profit—even if it meant a few more years in the red. But that assumption had also presupposed an eventual increase in media revenue, which was nearly nonexistent.

Valentine and Araki had helped to set up a podcast series involving Pacific League teams, but Valentine's hope was that some sort of MLB-style integrated TV rights and revenue-sharing system would be established involving all NPB teams, as with the MLB. But the Japanese pro game had only two really big money-making organizations: the Central League's Yomiuri Giants and the Hanshin Tigers, and they were loathe to share their wealth, as were the other four Central League clubs who benefited from playing them.

Valentine was not averse to taking a substantial pay cut in order to stay with Lotte. That was how attached he had become to the fans and players. But, as previously noted, he was never given an opportunity to renegotiate a new contract extension downward, which, at that stage, was in Setoyama's power to offer.

And for that, perhaps, Valentine had himself to blame.

Consider, for example, the article which appeared in *Sports Illustrated* in November 2007, written by Chris Ballard, entitled "Bobby V's Super Terrific Happy Hour." In it, Ballard described Valentine offering Setoyama's job to farm team manager Hide Koga earlier that year, which was interpreted by some as a sign of disrespect on Valentine's part toward the higher-ranked Lotte executive.

Valentine complained he had been misunderstood, that he had only been offering Koga the general manager post which Setoyama had recently vacated when he assumed the team presidency. He sought to repair the damage by apologizing on his blog, *Bobby's Way*, and praising Setoyama for his "fine contributions to the team."

However, the incident begged the question of why Valentine assumed that he, and not the team president, had the power to offer the general manager's position to anyone in the first place.

Then, in April 2008, the documentary *The Zen of Bobby V* was released. Instead of being a film about the Chiba Lotte Marines over the course of the 2007 season, as the project was initially described to acting owner Akio Shigemitsu and Setoyama, it turned out to be a paean to Bobby Valentine depicting how much he was loved by Lotte fans. In the final cut of the eighty-six-minute film, Setoyama, the team president, who had specifically asked to be included, was nowhere to be seen. It was yet another painful embarrassment.

With the Marines struggling to play .500 ball during the first half of the 2008 season, the situation came to a head in a July 20 meeting over dinner and drinks, involving Valentine, Setoyama, the Harvard grad Shun Kakazu and Araki. Setoyama suddenly announced he was going to quit. Lotte was a terrible organization, he said, and he was going to the Orix Buffaloes, who had made him an attractive offer. He said Valentine should consider resigning as well.

"If you think Lotte is bad, then you should leave," Valentine responded. "But I'm not like you. I can do without someone who has no desire to make us better. We can get by without you."

More words were exchanged and a drunken shouting match ensued. Setoyama did not show up in the front office for a month.

THE LIFETIME OF A CAT

Acting owner Akio Shigemitsu, not usually described as a strong-willed person, was reluctant to lose Setoyama. He had respect for Setoyama's resume, which was, after all, the reason for bringing him to Chiba in the first place. And there was also the history involved with Daiei founder and owner Isao Nakauchi (who had passed away in September 2005). It was an important consideration. Deep business ties with South Korean and ethnic minority groups permeated both organizations. Someone might have pointed out this fact to Valentine, as well, at the outset.

At the same time, Shigemitsu had also begun to revise his opinion of Valentine. Although he had indeed said Valentine could have the job of manager for life, a close associate said that the remark had been a light-hearted one—a spur-of-the-moment declaration that was not necessarily engraved in stone.

Shigemitsu had reportedly not appreciated Valentine's subsequent boasts of his "lifetime status" to the American media. He was said to be annoyed over what he viewed as Valentine's "condescending" and "conceited" attitude.

After hearing of Setoyama's account of the explosive July dinner, Shigemitsu was quoted as saying, "I never heard of a field manager of a ballclub telling the president of the team he wasn't needed. It's highly unusual."

The upshot of it all was that Setoyama returned to the team in September, his relations with Valentine steadily worsening, especially after Valentine revealed the extent of the internal feud, heretofore kept secret from the press, when he remarked to reporters, "Someone is trying to get rid of me."

The remark forced Setoyama to publicly deny he was trying to dump Valentine and angered Shigemitsu, who was upset that Valentine had aired the team's dirty laundry in public. According to the *Sankei Shimbun* newspaper it was this remark, combined with Lotte's failure to make the playoffs, that sealed Valentine's fate. "Had Valentine not disclosed the family feud," wrote Sayaka Kanda, a reporter who covered Lotte baseball for that daily newspaper, "I tend to think the team would not have announced that his contract would not be extended."

Valentine went home at season's end, but in December, Ishikawa called on him to return to Japan from the US for an urgent meeting and then coldly informed him upon his arrival that 2009 would be his last year. Valentine tried to appeal to Shigemitsu. But "Junior" (as Shigemitsu was sometimes called, condescendingly, behind his back in Valentine's circle), was through listening. He refused to return Valentine's calls. Instead of replying to Valentine's emails, he passed them on to Setoyama's office

"I guess when Shigemitsu was talking about a lifetime contract," sighed Valentine to the *Sankei*, "he meant the lifetime of a cat."

It was later revealed that after the final investigation report had been completed that it was the elder Shigemitsu who had made the decision that Valentine would have to go.

Of course, part of the blame for the way things turned out lay with Akio Shigemitsu, who set the stage for trouble when he agreed to give Valentine such a huge contract without considering the ramifications, and put Setoyama at the helm of an operation he was clearly not capable of understanding. However, Valentine bore some responsibility, as well. There is a tradition in Japan that employees carry a weak or unqualified boss and let him share in the glory—like a team of festival participants carrying a portable shrine to the local temple. Valentine should have been aware of that.

As one former employee put it, "Akio might not be too bright, but Bobby is too bright—and he knows it. He always has to prove he is the smartest guy in the room and that was not a good recipe for group harmony at Lotte. It was a problem."

If there is a lesson to this tale, as with others in this book, it is that change does not come easy in Japan. It is not easy to replace the old way with the new way. It is still necessary in this day and age to keep proper order.

At the end of the 2009 season, with Lotte having finished 18.5

games out of first place, Valentine said a tearful, touching goodbye, reading a speech to the fans in halting Japanese, following a rain-soaked final home game. He was memorably gracious in praising and thanking the fans and the players for their support.

"My dream," he'd said in an earlier interview, "is for the business of Japanese baseball to rise to the level where it can compete both on the field and off the field with other great leagues of the world and prevent what they call Major League Baseball from expanding into Asia and beyond. But I don't think that's going to happen as quickly as it should because of the lack of leadership here in Japan."

In that same interview, he also pointed to what he saw as "secrecy" in the Japanese culture, a tendency to "keep what they know to themselves," and added, "I think they would rather have outsiders remain outside."

Norifumi Nishimura, Valentine's bench coach, was appointed the new Lotte manager. He promptly vowed to have one-on-one conversations with the players to "understand their hearts," a remark that seemed to be a swipe at his former boss's inability to speak the language well, and promised to "restore the harmony of the team," seemingly another swipe at his old boss.

He made *wa* (harmony) the team slogan for 2010. He also ordered a full-blown autumn training camp for the off-season. It was the first autumn camp Lotte held in seven years and was a pointed rebuke of Valentine's policy of postseason rest, a policy that was, of course, totally at odds with that of other NPB teams.

Said former member of the Valentine Family Larry Rocca, summing up the general feeling of the Valentine regime, "We thought it would be different for us compared to other gaijin who had come over and tried to change things and failed. But in the end, we were just like everybody else."

The Zen of Bobby V, incidentally, was never shown in Japan.

POSTSCRIPT

The Bobby Valentine shrine, once displayed inside the stadium in the corner of the lobby during day games, disappeared. There are suspicions that it was destroyed. Moreover, shortly after Valentine left Japan, representatives from Setoyama's office visited city officials who had been in charge of naming "Valentine Way" nearby and requested the name be changed back. However, angry residents, who had been neighbors and fans of Valentine, quickly countered with a proposal to keep the name as it was and further commemorate Valentine with a memorial showcase. The officials agreed, thereby guaranteeing permanent residency for the Valentine name. Valentine donated an old uniform and other memorabilia for the display.

In 2011, the team slipped back into mediocrity and attendance fell, partially due to the aftereffects of the Tohoku earthquake and tsunami. As a result Setoyama submitted his resignation. Ishikawa and Yoneda followed.

Akio Shigemitsu, for his part, wound up going to prison. Shin Dong-bin, as he was known in South Korea, was sentenced in 2018 to thirty months in jail for bribing an associate of former president Park Geun-hye, both of whom were sent to the penitentiary. An appellate court later suspended Shigemitsu's sentence for four years pending good behavior, essentially granting him parole. Park and her associate were released in 2021 and pardoned.

CHAPTER 13

The Bitcoin Crimes

THE FOREIGN POPULATION of Japan reached 2.93 million in 2020 with 567,000 in Tokyo, both all-time highs, before the Coronavirus pandemic of 2020–2021 caused a temporary decline. By that time, one out of every eight residents in Shinjuku was a foreign national. Mass emigration from rising economic superpower China had served to triple the number of foreigners in the capital. As of January 1, 2020, there were 367,000 Chinese immigrants living in the city, doubling the combined total of South and North Koreans, who had previously been the largest minority. The percentage of Americans in the foreign population living in Tokyo had consequently halved since 1985. There were 20,000 Americans in the city, although the US embassy would tell you there were actually 100,000 Americans there at any one time if you counted tourists and others without resident cards (or at least there were before the pandemic hit). There were approximately 6,000 French nationals and 6,000 citizens of the UK.

Twenty-first century Tokyo had fallen behind other major capitals in some respects, starting with a severe labor shortage. The government was struggling to cope with a severely declining birth rate—one that was attributed to cramped housing, long commutes and lack of nearby family support—and an aging population. Thanks in part to a superior, if increasingly costly, national health care system, life expectancy was now eighty-seven years, among the highest in the world. In Tokyo, the decrease in the number of young people had resulted in twice as many job vacancies as applicants.

To deal with this problem, the government had further loosened requirements for those foreigners with specific, in-demand, professional skills. Among other things this brought in forty thousand Southeast Asians to work at 7-Eleven, Lawson and other convenience stores. This influx was accompanied by a government program to attract more tourists, raising the number of foreign visitors from a little more than 8 million in 2012 to more than 30 million in 2018, with well over a third of these sightseers coming from mainland China. The stated goal of this plan was to reach 40 million by the start of the 2020 Olympics. However, both the program and the games themselves were interrupted by the appearance of the Novel Coronavirus pandemic as it was called in Japan, also known as Covid-19 elsewhere.

There was a good side to the increased immigration. Japanese in the twenty-first century were more receptive to the gaijin in their midst than their predecessors as evidenced by government survey results. In 1988, the government-run survey, the "Study on the Japanese National Character," began asking the question in its periodic polls "Suppose your child said: 'I want to marry a foreigner.' Would you approve or disapprove?" In that initial survey, only 29 percent said "approve." By the 2013 survey, however, 56 percent would say they would approve of such a union.

That being said, most Japanese opposed the idea of mass immigration, pointing inevitably to the inability of the interlopers to adjust to Japanese ways, starting, one might surmise, with the country's finely detailed system of garbage collection, which was divided into eight distinct categories and required user identification marked on each bag of trash, and other important social etiquette, and ending with the unfortunate fact that the more foreigners the country admitted, the more illegal narcotics use increased.

As discussed in Chapter 10, Japan had become a major market in the world of illegal drugs. Police in Roppongi adopted a policy of stop-and-frisk for narcotics. A lawyer friend of mine, a man from Vancouver, stopped to watch one such early-morning frisking by a group of four policeman and was himself searched because the lead cop thought he was "acting suspiciously."

Said former special ops agent Hiroki Allen, a native of Japan, "Cocaine has long become the drug of choice for young rich people in Tokyo. It is glamorous, while *shabu* (meth) is seen as a working man's thing. The young and the rich refers to those under forty who can afford expensive sports cars. The cops won't fuck with these guys because the entire legal system is designed to allow the side with the most money to win. They might arrest an entertainer from time to time but those people aren't really that rich."

Yakuza gangs were, not surprisingly, active participants in the illicit international drug trade. Although, new anti–organized-crime laws restricting underworld access to bank accounts, office space and respectable business channels had served to deplete the formal ranks of the yakuza by more than 75 percent, financial fraud cases and money-laundering crimes involving underworld figures had spiked. It went without saying that the traditional underworld sources of income—gambling and prostitution—did not suffer declines either, with quasi-gangsters from motorcycle gangs with names like Kanto Rengo now doing most of the grunt work.

The hand of the CIA was not as pervasive as it once was. The organization that had once donated $1 million a month to the Liberal Democratic Party had phased out its support as the Communist threat in Japan receded, the Vietnam War expanded and US–Japan trade disputes grew, (although it should be noted that the US embassy in Japan and the FBI had facilitated the visa of a prominent crime lord to receive a queue-jumping liver transplant at the UCLA Medical Center in 2001).

Now it was American Drug Enforcement Administration agents based at the US embassy in Japan who were more active, trying to stem the tide of narcotics from gangs in China and Mexico.

Poster boy for the new wave of criminals was one Edward James Montague Reid, as the official police reports referred to him, a British national in his early forties, who, lived in Tokyo's tony Minami-Azabu district and had worked, for a time, for Nomura Securities on the currency desk and for the Sony Corporation in the

Investor Relations Department. He was a flashy presence around town, the one-time owner of a Lamborghini.

The Tokyo Metropolitan Police suspected he was dealing cocaine and other drugs in the nightlife quarter of Roppongi so one morning in September 2017, detectives burst into his apartment and arrested him after seizing 239 grams of cocaine and 92 grams of other stimulant drugs, with a combined street value of about ¥20 million. The amount of drugs in his possession obviously intended for sale, he was given a ten-year prison sentence.

Police believed Reid sold illegal drugs from April to July to between forty and fifty customers who frequented clubs in the Roppongi area, making his transactions in Bitcoin.

According to his friends, Reid had been battling depression and had become addicted to drugs as a result, a state of affairs that made him prey to organized crime figures who blackmailed him into becoming a dealer to drug dealers. Foreign male criminals were normally sent to Fuchu prison outside Tokyo, but the court became aware of possible yakuza attacks on Reid if he were sent there, so, for his safety, he was incarcerated in the city of Fukuoka instead.

Japanese drug laws were, and are, scarily strict. Drug use alone is a serious criminal matter. In some states in the USA it's legal to smoke pot openly. In others it's a mere misdemeanor which the police will not bother themselves with. In Japan, however, mere possession of marijuana can result in a prison sentence, deportation or both. The idea is to eradicate narcotic stimulants through intolerance and punishment.

Japanese detention centers continued to be deeply unpleasant places, with occupants allowed but two showers per week and lights kept on all night. During the winter, inmates constantly complain of not enough blankets or warm clothes, enduring the cold being part of their punishment. UN rapporteurs have called such treatment a basic violation of fundamental human rights and even likened it to torture. But their complaints have done little to improve conditions.

Conviction rates in Japan are over 95 percent and sentencing is harsh and consistent. A first time offender will most likely receive a sentence of one to two years, suspended, if said offender is duly penitent. A second offense results in prison for a couple of years or more. A twenty-five-year-old Canadian man who brought in a suitcase full of cocaine in 2016 on consignment—on his first visit to Japan—was given fourteen years in a Yokohama prison.

Public opinion surveys show widespread and overwhelming condemnation of drug use by the public. They view drug use as a question of individual morality, not the result of disadvantaged circumstances as many might see it in the West.

Fortunately for Reid and others in his situation, Japanese government policy toward foreign prisoners underwent some changes in the early part of the twenty-first century.

In 2003, Japan became a signatory to the Convention on the Transfer of Sentenced Persons along with members of the Council of Europe and the United States. The Convention was an international treaty designed to help rehabilitate and reintegrate convicted criminals by allowing them to serve their sentences in their home countries. A related domestic law was put into force in June 2003.

Over a subsequent sixteen-year period, Japan repatriated 423 foreign prisoners. The UK topped the list with 61 prisoners, followed by the United States at 54, the Netherlands at 51, Canada with 44 and South Korea at 43, according to the Justice Ministry.

Japan, for its part, has had ten of its nationals repatriated, with five returning from the United States, three from Thailand and two from South Korea, in case you are interested. The abovementioned Ed Reid was transferred to Wandsworth Prison in the UK in December 2021.

For those who could not be sent home (or did not wish to go) some Japanese prisons began to offer meals, specific beds and language services catered to their needs.

Tokyo's Fuchu Prison held the country's largest foreign prisoner contingent, as of 2021, with 332 prisoners from other countries, about 20 percent of the total prison population. They were housed in a three-story building for foreign prisoners with each room equipped with a bed, rather than a futon. Rules and regulations were available in multiple languages, so were vegetarian meals, while the prison moved meal times to the evening for Muslims during Ramadan when their faith prohibited them eating in day-light hours. However, the Japanese authorities had their limits and strict military-like discipline, as has previously been described, was still the order of the day.

THE BITCOIN KING

Frenchman Mark Karpelès was another individual who would make his mark on the Tokyo criminal justice system. Karpelès ran a To-kyo-based Bitcoin exchange named Mt. Gox, which at one point, he claimed, was handling 80 percent of the world's Bitcoin trans-actions. However, Karpelès' company was shut down due to bank-ruptcy in 2014 after 850,000 Bitcoins—worth an estimated ¥48 billion at the time—disappeared from its digital vaults, prompting angry investors to question the security of cryptocurrencies. People came from as far away as Scotland to protest against the evapora-tion of their crypto wealth.

Karpelès was arrested in 2015 at the age of thirty, after an in-vestigation by the Cybercrimes Unit of the Metropolitan Police Department which accused him of embezzling a total of ¥341 mil-lion belonging to customers that was kept in Mt. Gox accounts and falsifying electronic data which harmed his clients. He was alleged to have transferred the money to his own account and to have used the money to live a lavish lifestyle.

Karpelès, who claimed he was a victim of a massive hacking attack, spent eleven months in detention while awaiting trial, un-dergoing interrogation for several hours a day. His case drew global attention, as cryptocurrencies were a relatively new phenomenon to the public. During the court proceedings, police officers on the stand admitted that they had begun the investigation believing that Karpelès had stolen the coins himself and hoped to obtain a confes-sion. They also stated they had stopped looking for a hacker.

On March 14, 2019, Karpelès was found guilty by the Tokyo District Court of one count, which charged that he had actually transferred roughly $33.5 million to a bank account operated by a Bitcoin exchange based in Dallas across twenty-one transactions made between February and September 2013, that he had done it using his personal computer and that he had covered his tracks by falsifying company records.

In reading the verdict, the judge opined that Karpelès had inflicted "massive harm to the trust of his users."

It was noteworthy, however, that Karpelès was also found not guilty on two other counts and that the judge saw fit to suspend the four-year sentence he had handed down (prosecutors had demanded ten years) meaning Karpelès would not go to prison if he behaved himself. As with the Greg Kelly trial, it was a rare victory in a country in which the post-indictment conviction rate is above 95 percent.

Karpelès appealed his conviction. His defense attorneys argued that prosecutors had not understood how cryptocurrency exchanges—an entirely unregulated business in Japan at the time—really worked and were trying to pin the blame for a massive cybercrime on Karpelès, who was just a victim trying to protect his clients. Karpelès was adamant that he had not pocketed client funds that went missing when Mt. Gox collapsed in 2014. However, his appeal was unsuccessful and the verdict was upheld by a Japanese high court in 2019.

Mark Karpelès, also known as MagicalTux, his online alias, was not your typical gaijin criminal, if indeed there is such a type. He was raised in Dijon, France and completed his education at Lycée Louis Armand in Paris, according to a profile in on the Phys.org news aggregator website. He was a computer prodigy, and according to his mother, speaking in a 2017 documentary, had few friends at school as he was "unable to find a buddy who could talk like he could about IT and quantum physics." The "only thing that interested" her "talented" son, said the mother, was computer science.

Karpelès, whose real first name is Robert, admitted on French television that he would spend entire days in front of the computer screen without any physical activity, a "geek who stuffed himself with snacks in front of his computer," ballooning his weight.

Entering the professional world, he quickly found himself at odds with his French company, Linux Cyberjoueurs, which found irregularities in its data and brought a case against Karpelès to the authorities in 2010, for "fraudulent access of an automated data processing system" and "fraudulent altering of data." Karpelès received a year's suspended sentence in absentia in France.

Karpelès also had a keen interest in Japanese anime and video games and in 2009 after several visits to Japan, moved there, where he developed his interest in Bitcoin.

By 2011, he had bought his own cryptocurrency exchange, Mt. Gox, which stood for "Magic: The Gathering Online eXchange."

Jake Adelstein, the coauthor of a book about Karpelès, *Pay the Devil in Bitcoin* (Kindle Single, 2017), said, "The platform had originally been meant to trade cards in a popular game known as Magic: The Gathering, which bears some similarity to Pokemon. The system had never been meant to handle cryptocurrency and there were flaws galore. When Mark took over the company, it already had a substantial number of missing Bitcoins."

Nevertheless, as the popularity of Bitcoin surged after it was found to be the perfect currency to buy drugs and illegal items on the Silk Road black-market website, so did their customer base. Mt. Gox grew so rapidly that at one point, it claimed to control 80 percent of all global Bitcoin transactions.

Karpelès enjoyed the trappings of success, living in an $11,000-per-month luxury apartment with a king-sized bed worth tens of thousands of dollars. He married a Japanese woman and became a father. But, everything came crashing down in 2014, when Mt. Gox lost the estimated 850,000 Bitcoins, worth just under half a billion dollars at that time, in what Karpelès claimed was a "massive" hack attack. Mt. Gox collapsed and filed for bankruptcy protection, as prosecutors pursued Karpelès for allegedly falsifying data and pilfering around $3 million from customers' accounts.

After being arrested and rearrested several times and spending a total of a year in Japanese detention, as is possible under the legal system in Japan, and interrogated for several hours each day, the corpulent Karpelès lost a huge amount of weight. Released on bail, he presented a svelte clean-cut image at his first hearing.

In the succeeding bankruptcy hearings, the Mt. Gox firm was ordered to reimburse its creditors to the tune of US$483 per Bitcoin, (making for a total of ¥45.6 billion or US$400 million).

Fortunately for Karpelès, he had turned over to trustees the remaining 200,000 Bitcoins in the company and during his detention period their value had increased exponentially, meaning creditors' were to actually receive more value than they had lost from the bankruptcy. While an estimated 50,000 Bitcoins were sold circa 2017 by the trustee for some US$600 million, an estimated US$6 billion worth remained at the time of this writing.

In the end, it appeared that there was ample reason to believe that Karpelès had been targeted unfairly. A Swedish engineer named Kim Nilsson, who had lost a considerable amount of Bitcoins in the collapse of Mt. Gox, began sharing information with federal authorities in the United States while Karpelès was in the Tokyo Detention House. A task force led by the Internal Revenue Service concluded that Mt. Gox had indeed been hacked by an outsider who had siphoned off more than 600,000 Bitcoins in a period between 2011 and late 2013.

Tigran "Blockchain Wizard" Gambaryan, a special agent in the Internal Revenue Service approached the National Police Agency and the Tokyo Metropolitan Police Department asking for their cooperation in capturing the hacker, by sharing Mt. Gox data. They refused. Karpelès' supporters believed that the Tokyo police feared that if the real criminal was caught it would make their efforts to force Karpelès to confess to the theft appear cruel and misguided.

However, Jake Adelstein took a copy of the Mt. Gox database to the FBI in San Francisco which aided the investigation. Eventually US authorities were able to trace the bulk of stolen Bitcoins to one individual, a Russian Bitcoin exchange operator named Alexander Vinnik. On July 25, 2017, US authorities had Vinnik detained in Greece. He was indicted on twenty-one counts of money laundering and several other charges, some relating to Mt. Gox. The United States requested Vinnik's extradition, citing fraud and hacking offenses, but so did France and Russia.

Over a year later, in November 2018, Vinnik went on a three-month hunger strike in protest at his prolonged detention in Greece. In January he was finally extradited to France where he was tried and convicted on charges of money laundering and sentenced to five years in prison.

In June 2020, New Zealand police announced the seizure of US$90 million from WME Capital Management, a company in New Zealand registered to Vinnik.

Karpelès, for his part, went on to establish a new company, UNGOX, in then spring of 2022, which provided ratings for cryptocurrency exchanges and related entities by conducting checks in key areas such as technology, transparency, people and legal context.

NORTH KOREA: THE LEADING FOREIGN CRIME SYNDICATE

One of the leading foreign crime syndicates in Japan, as of this writing is the government of North Korea, also known as the Democratic People's Republic of Korea (DPRK). Through operatives and agents, it is, and has long been, engaged in a wide variety of illegal activities in Japan designed to raise money for the development of nuclear missiles in North Korea for their own use as well as for sale to clients in the Middle East and Africa.

These activities include the illegal manufacture and sale of narcotics including cocaine, heroin, high-grade methamphetamine and fentanyl, along with synthetic pharmaceuticals like Viagra. Counterfeit currency is another hot-selling product. North Korea has traditionally used yakuza gangs like the Yamaguchi-gumi with high *zainichi* (ethnic Korean in Japan) membership to peddle its wares. Money laundering is off the charts.

North Korea is unique in that it controls such criminal activities completely, from top down, starting with Kim Jong-un. It is power that a Mafia boss would envy.

According to Mark Gollom of the Canadian Broadcast Corporation (CBC), who has reported extensively on the subject, "Many of the schemes are run out of 'Central Committee Bureau 39' of the Workers' Party of Korea, which enlists military officials, bureaucrats and members of the diplomatic corps to organize and participate in the manufacture and distribution of criminal goods."

The North Korean government has used its diplomatic corps posted to Japan (informally, since the two countries do not have formal diplomatic relations) to collect proceeds from these activities and deposit them in various local banks, he said. Many North Korean diplomats, in fact, are sent to countries overseas for that specific reason—to launder money and send proceeds from their criminal enterprises back to the regime, he said. In Japan, where relations have never been formally established, officials have operated through Chongryon (or Chosen Soren in Japanese), a Japan-based organization with ties to Pyongyang and the Japan Korean Economic and Cultural Exchange Association (JKCE) a nonprofit affiliate that focuses on trade.

Many Chinese citizens of Korean ethnicity living in Japan are also involved with the North Korean trade. One base of operations is Nishi Kawaguchi in Saitama which has become another Chinatown, largely populated with mainland Chinese and controlled by gangsters from the former Manchuria region now known as Dongbei. In addition, much of the trade between Japan and North Korea is assisted by Mindan, the zainichi group with ties to South Korea. They move transshipments through their networks in China or South Korea and launder the money via pachinko (Japanese pinball), underground casinos or other businesses.

Relations between North Korea and Japan have been seriously strained over the years because of the kidnapping of Japanese citizens by North Korean agents and also by the North Korean government's nuclear program, in which many missiles have been fired in the vicinity of Japanese waters. These issues have turned more than 90 percent of the people of Japan against North Korea, according to public opinion polls. However trade goes on beneath the surface.

Over the years, the top three North Korean cash cows in Japan have been meth, fake US dollars and counterfeit US or European cigarettes. Of the three, meth smuggling has had the least risk, and has also offered more profit than the other two businesses, so that is what the North Koreans have focused on in Japan.

Since 1989 the United States Secret Service estimates North Korea has printed over $40 million in counterfeit US currency at the Pyongsong Trademark Printing Factory near Pyongyang. In the early 2000s, the US government dubbed North Korea's counterfeit US$100 bills "supernotes" and the US Treasury was forced to change its currency and come up with specialized paper and holographic images. The extent of counterfeiting is currently unclear because production techniques have become increasingly sophisticated. In addition, said special ops agent Hiroki Allen, "There are violent crimes, pachinko, and electronic fraud, in great abundance. There is lots of smuggling as well, with transshipment of people and goods. Human trafficking by North Korea involves transporting foreigners into Japan via South Korea."

The human trafficking referenced here is accomplished by using the large numbers of SPR—special permanent residents—Koreans of both north and south heritage that live in Japan, most noticeably in the Kansai or greater Osaka area. SPR is a category of resident in Japan that dates back to the conclusion of the American Occupation in 1952, when the Japanese government gave the half-million ethnic Koreans in Japan the option of choosing one of three status categories if they wanted to stay in the country: as a citizen of Japan; as a citizen of the new Republic of Korea formed in South Korea in 1948; or stateless as a Special Permanent Resident. This latter category was created for those who did not want to be solely identified with the new reclusive Democratic People's Republic of Korea in the north, but instead chose to wait it out until the two Korean states would eventually reunify one day. These SPRs have the same privileges of overseas travel as Japanese citizens, and they go through the same immigration line as Japanese when they return to Tokyo Narita or other Japanese airports. Their ability to move back and forth freely between Japan and the two Koreas is a decided trafficking advantage.

"During the 2020–2021 Covid-19 crisis," said Allen, "loads of foreigners infected with the Coronavirus were coming into Japan. SPRs working in the sex industry had a particularly high rate of virus transmission."

"Want to know why so many mutant Coronavirus cases started popping up all over Osaka?" Allen asked. "Kansai is heavily *kim-chee*. The business of transshipments of foreigners through South Korea to send them into Japan—it's quite lucrative."

Foreign firms in Japan also used the Korea route to bring in Europeans and even English-speaking IT talent from India, Singapore, Pakistan and other countries. (Sex workers were only part of the mix.) These so-called *gaishi-kei* firms would pay more to use the Korea route to smuggle in people from nations that were banned officially. For example, a French firm might want to bring in a Frenchman from Paris but travelers from France might be banned by policies in place at the time. So, the Frenchman would fly to South Korea, spend a few days in Seoul and then travel to Japan. At the airport, he would claim only Korea as his last place of residence, since Korea would be on the "preferred" list for entry into Japan due to pressure from North and South Korea. This system rendered meaningless the Japan "travel ban" on certain countries.

"SPRs consist of both North and South Korean zainichi, and many are involved in some sort of illegal activity from hard crime to tax evasion," said Allen. "These particular zainichi are the enablers for government or criminal gangs in both the North and the South."

Finally, North Korea and its allies have been heavily involved in financial fraud in Japan: stock price manipulation, fake real estate deals, counterfeit products and hacking attacks. Smuggling operations have also flourished, particularly with animal and plant products prohibited from trade by CITES, the Convention on International Trade in Endangered Species.

All in all, this represents a lot of crime, deeply ingrained in Japanese society and seemingly impossible to stop.

CHAPTER 14

The Korean Taxi Barons

KOREA WAS A COLONY of Japan from 1910 to 1945 and, as previously noted, it has historically been the Koreans who comprised the largest and most influential non-Japanese ethnic group in Japan. The quintessence of outsiderdom, they have suffered more than a century of bigotry and injustice at the hands of the Japanese. To cite but one example of this abuse, more than 670,000 Koreans were estimated to have been conscripted into forced labor by the Japanese government during World War II, with some 20 percent of all the Korean laborers sent to work in mines and on construction projects in Hokkaido and other northern islands that belonged to Japan at the time. When Japan surrendered, more than 100,000 of these individuals were simply left behind on the island of Sakhalin when it was taken over by the Soviet Union.

After the end of the war, life was not easy for ethnic Koreans living in Japan (referred to in Japanese as *zainichi*). Many found their career paths limited due to discrimination by Japan's top universities and corporations and wound up working in bottom-rung jobs, such as the so-called 3-D (dirty, dangerous and demeaning) industries—such as pachinko, construction or *yakiniku* restaurants—or turned to the criminal underworld. The fact that many Japanese landlords refused to rent to zainichi Koreans added to their difficulties. As a result, the majority of zainichi opted to hide their identities by adopting Japanese names.

The indignities were many and varied. A Japanese government sponsored repatriation program that began in 1959 and continued through 1984 encouraged a total of 93,340 people to migrate to North Korea, persuading them they would be moving to a Socialist paradise. Instead, the migrants to North Korea endured brutal conditions—starvation, imprisonment, torture. Many believed the repatriation program was established by the Japanese government to get rid of Koreans in Japan who were believed by some in the upper echelons of the Japanese government to be Communist sympathizers and troublemakers.

In the immediate postwar era, intermarriage between Japanese and Koreans was rare due to an anti-Korean stigma in Japan. But prejudices slowly eased and in succeeding years many zainichi did marry Japanese. In 1985 the Japanese government changed its laws so as to grant Japanese citizenship to a child with either parent being Japanese, the said child having to choose Korean or Japanese nationality after reaching the age of twenty-one.

Some ethnic Koreans forged impressive careers in sports and entertainment. Masaichi Kaneda, born to Korean parents, became the most successful pitcher of all time in Japanese baseball, winning four hundred career games. Rikidozan was a pro-wrestling icon who jump-started the postwar TV industry. Masayoshi Son created the Softbank Corporation in 1981.

But perhaps the most famous of them all in Japan was Sadao Aoki, a prewar Korean immigrant who rose from abject poverty to revolutionize the taxi industry, starting in Kyoto and expanding into Tokyo in the mid-nineties. His MK Taxi company came to symbolize the highest quality service possible and led all competitors in revenue. Aoki was the first person in history to sue the Japanese government and win. He also had a son, Masaaki, who became as famous as his father for his award-winning high-tech business acumen, which prompted Harvard Business School to teach a course about him, as well as for a wild personal lifestyle that often landed him in jail. Ma-chan, as the son was called, was like something out of Shakespeare—or the *National Enquirer*.

THE FATHER

Sadao Aoki was born in 1928, as Bon Sig Yoo, in a small village out-side the city of Busan in the southern part of the Korean Peninsula. He was one of six children whose parents ran a roadside hotel. He was sent to Kyoto, Japan by his parents in 1943 at the age of fifteen to live with his older brother. It was there in August 1945 that he listened to Emperor Hirohito's speech over the radio in which Hiro-hito did not use the word surrender but nevertheless implored the citizens of Japan to bear the unbearable as the Americans prepared to arrive on Japanese soil.

As detailed in Katsumi Kato's book *MK Aoki Sadao no takushi kakumei* [MK Aoki Sadao's taxi revolution, published by Toyo Keizai, 1994], Sadao entered the law department of Kyoto's Ritsu-meikan University in 1946 and moved into the boarding house of a German woman named Rosie. She proved to be a pivotal character in his life. Rosie, whose husband was a professor at Kyoto Univer-sity, was a linguist who spoke German, English and Spanish and worked as a tutor, but it was the way she ran her lodging that pro-vided Aoki with his first lessons about business.

She fixed the amount of gas to be consumed per month and forced her tenants to conserve energy. If Aoki went to sleep upstairs without turning the lights off downstairs, Rosie made sure to call him back down and have him flip the switch himself. In time, he developed the habit of double-checking. Even after ascending the stairs and climbing into bed, he would get up and go back down-stairs to re-check.

There was more. If Aoki or any of the other tenants grabbed a breakfast roll from the kitchen for a midnight snack, that tenant would get no roll for his breakfast from Rosie the next morning. She kept a careful count. In fact Rosie would not even allow that tenant to go out to the store to buy a replacement. It's important to learn to plan properly, she would say. If you know you're going to get hungry when studying all night, make sure to prepare your own food in advance. It was from Rosie that Aoki learned the important lesson in business to always go the extra mile.

Rosie would also clean the lint from Sadao's trouser cuffs and pockets and provide him with a clean handkerchief everyday. Rosie taught him not to buy new clothes but repair the old ones instead, and reuse wrapping paper from purchased items.

Postwar life in Kyoto was somewhat better than in other cities because the historic town had been spared from Allied bombings due to its cultural heritage. Thus hostility toward Americans during the Occupation years from 1945 to 1952, was muted and incidence of postwar illness and disease was less than in Tokyo, Osaka or A-bombed Hiroshima where effects of radiation sickness had affected the populace and generated strong anti-American sentiment. That said, there were open sewers everywhere, few flush toilets, 25 percent of well water was unfit to drink and tap water risky. Smallpox, cholera, dysentery, typhus, diphtheria and scarlet fever were all common. Most of the Kyoto population suffered from tapeworms. Moreover, VD was rampant and streetwalkers were everywhere. Kyoto was run by an Allied military government and for a time military police arrested any "likely" women out on the street. However the Americans did provide food and medical supplies, and conditions gradually improved. Average life expectancy rose from fifty years in 1945 to sixty-two years in 1953 for men, and from fifty-four to sixty-six years for women.

In 1952, Sadao took a job at Nagai Sekiyu, a gasoline and oil company, and a Korean neighbor arranged a marriage for him with the daughter of a Korean man who ran a weaving factory in Osaka. Her name was Fumiko Kanemoto (her Korean name Kim Jon Sun) and she was twenty-three years old when she had her *omiai*—meeting with a view toward marriage—with Sadao Aoki. She had led such a sheltered life that she had never even been inside a teahouse or coffee shop. *Hako iri musume*, the Japanese said of such young women, "daughter kept in a box."

Sadao Aoki liked to tell people that he had never been discriminated against in his life, that he grew up thinking he was Japanese because, after all, Korea was part of Japan. In fact, the only time he ever spoke Korean, he said, was to his father who could not speak any other language. His new wife Fumiko, however, was just the opposite. She remembered as a child living in a dilapidated tool shed on a farm in Hyogo Prefecture and hearing taunts of "*Chosen-jin!*"—a derogatory term for Koreans—and other insulting words from neighbors. She also remembered being falsely accused of misdeeds in school, of stealing and other crimes, just because she was Korean.

Fumiko's new husband was completely obsessed with work. He spent much of his wedding day delivering fuel and he showed up at the wedding hall dressed in his work clothes, apologizing deeply to all. Later that evening, when Fumiko's father escorted her, as per Korean custom, to the room above his company where he lived, nobody was there. Sadao was out working. Although Sadao, by this time, was well enough off financially, his room looked to Fumiko like a haunted house. In the middle of the room was bed made of iron pipes. In one corner was a trunk. A pile of sales slips occupied another corner. That was it. Fumiko and her father were shocked. Sadao's younger brother Hideo and three employees occupied other rooms on the second floor.

Sadao's philosophy was that women should not work and that his new wife should not ask questions about his work. She was given enough money to run the house and told to stay in her lane and that he would stay in his.

In 1957 the couple had their first child, a daughter born in the eighth month of pregnancy. The baby was brain damaged, believed to be due to a fall down the stairs that Fumiko experienced.

Sadao arose at five o'clock every morning and drove his "tank lorry" to Kobe to fill it with fuel. He stayed on the job until midnight. Indeed, Sadao was so consumed with his job that once his head hit the futon at night he could not be roused. On one occasion where his wife developed a severe fever, she was unable to wake him up. She wound up asking his younger brother for help. Hideo called a doctor to the house to treat her. Sadao never noticed. It was odd, Fumiko thought, that Sadao could be roused in the middle of the night by a customer banging at the door or calling him on the phone but not by his wife requiring a doctor's visit.

Sadao's reputation grew. If a car broke down at three o'clock in the morning and the driver telephoned the police, the police would advise him to call Aoki at Nagai Sekiyu and provide him with the number. There were so few gasoline stands at the time in Kyoto that drivers would even take a taxi to Nagai Sekiyu, gasoline container in hand, to get help. They knew that all they had to do was pound on the door and Aoki would get up to help.

In 1959 Nagai Sekiyu went bankrupt, but Sadao took over and revived the business by providing free greasing and other services to win back customers. That same year he applied for a license to start a taxi company and was approved. Originally named Minami Taxi, it was the beginning of what would later come to be known as MK Taxi and gain national renown.

Cabs in Japan at the time were notorious for taking poor care of customers. Cabs were often unclean and drivers unknowledgeable. Kyoto taxi firms had no incentive to do better because the industry was tightly regulated by the government which set fares, decided when more cabs should be added to the fleets of the major taxi firms in the area and determined who would get the licenses to operate the new cabs.

When he got his first set of cab licenses, ten in all, Sadao Aoki set out to change all that. He insisted his cars be kept spotlessly clean, and demanded his drivers be courteous at all times, which was unusual in an industry known for its rudeness. Drivers usually said nothing, or just grunted. Aoki also trained his people on geography and best routes from any spot on the Kyoto map to another, which, again, was unusual in an industry where drivers were famous for taking the long way around.

Drivers were told to say one of four greetings to their customers:

"Thank you. I'm your driver, X, and I will be taking you to your destination safely."

"Is Y the place you are going to?"

"Please check if you have all your belongings."

"Thank you for using our taxi."

When a female passenger got out of one of Aoki's cabs late at night, the driver had to keep the lights on to show her the way in the dark. Drivers were also required to have umbrellas at the ready to hand over to passengers if rain suddenly started to fall. Aoki insisted that a cab ride should offer passengers an old-fashioned yet refreshing and sentimental experience.

At the time it was common for taxis to ignore passengers, especially around midnight after the trains had stopped running. Drivers demanded several times the meter fare to accept a passenger and would take only those traveling long distances. Aoki's taxis, however, accepted anyone and at meter price, so people took an immense liking to the company.

Aoki hired college graduates to be his drivers, another unusual practice at the time, and encouraged them to study English. The English language abilities of MK drivers made them favorites of foreign tourists visiting Kyoto, naturally, with MK offering personal tours as well as regular metered taxi services.

As revenue increased, he built a waiting lounge for customers at the city's main train station and gave his drivers uniforms designed by Hanae Mori, known at the time as the doyenne of the Japanese fashion industry. He paid above-average salaries, provided his employees with apartments to live in and encouraged them to continue their education in night classes, instilling a sense of self-respect and self-confidence.

By 1965, Aoki had two sons, as well as a second daughter, and had put up his first building, his home office from where he ran MK Taxi as well as Nagai Sekiyu which was doing well under his ownership. He began recruiting employees from among the ranks of students from top schools around the country. Issuing stock in his companies was part of his sales package. Freshman employees at Nagai Sekiyu went through a rigorous training process. They were required to live in the company dormitory. They awoke at six in the morning to clean the premises, study for one hour, eat breakfast and report for work at the gasoline stand at eight thirty. Then they went on sales rounds in search of new customers. They carried rags in their back pockets which they used to clean and shine cars they encountered parked in front of houses.

"This is a service provided by Nagai Sekiyu," they would say to startled owners who would emerge from their houses and ask them what the hell they were doing. Owners would quite often invite them in for tea, and the employees would pass out free service tickets to their gasoline stands They repeated this process, again, and again, day after day, growing the business. Trainees returned home at 6 p.m. for dinner, then hit the books. "Study, reflect and exercise" was a sign on one of the dormitory walls.

Aoki would always stress how competitive business was and how he had to compete in tiny units of one or two yen to gain an edge. He preached that what, when and where the customer decided to buy was often based on the people that the customer liked, which made the importance of human relations in the business paramount.

By 1969 Aoki had put up a company housing complex consisting of forty-six housing units, and provided housing loans to his employees so they could buy them. His employees could afford them because he paid the highest salaries in the industry.

Aoki believed in involving his employees in his business, so that they could see where all the money required to run them went. He believed that his employees were all part of one big family.

"You have to communicate through the uniform," he would say. "Eat dinner together, drink at a bar or nightclub together, thereby forming important bonds."

At times, he got so carried away with the evening sessions with his employees that he wound up staying at the employees dormitory. Other times he would bring them home to eat, unexpectedly, which made life difficult for Fumiko, who had to prepare extra food at short notice. On New Year's Eve he would go to the company dormitory to help the kitchen staff prepare New Year's dinner for everyone there.

He believed being an employee of his firm was a twenty-four hour a day, seven days a week proposition.

In February 1970, Aoki established a Housewives Association for the wives of drivers, with the goal of creating stability in the drivers' lives. The company also established an in-house education program, bringing in outside experts, professors and lecturers every month to address all employees about all aspects of life. The idea was to increase a sense of self-worth among drivers to combat the common perception that taxi drivers were low class and not worthy of respect. At the time the social position of taxi drivers was still so low that their wives were embarrassed to admit their husbands drove cabs.

In December, Aoki began publishing an in-house newspaper for his employees. He adopted a policy to take orphans to the Osaka Exposition.

By the end of 1970, Aoki had become the taxi operator with the highest revenue in Kyoto. Its success set the stage for engagements with the taxi regulators the following year when he first applied for permission for his drivers to park their taxis at home so as to dispense with the time-wasting commute to the office. Regulatory distinctions between commercial and noncommercial vehicles at the time were such that even a minor issue like this took a year to resolve. But, once approved, it eventually served to make those efficiency gains and reduce the accident rate.

In April 1972, Aoki began a movement called "Let's Return Taxis To the People," adopting a policy of never refusing a passenger, even wheelchair users, those taken ill or those about to give birth. This was something unheard of in the taxi business. He also established late-night taxi stations, becoming the first taxi company to operate between midnight and six o'clock in the morning, and adopted the heart symbol as the taxi firm's insignia.

It was also around this time that Sadao began to enjoy his new wealth. He bought a brand new American car, a Lincoln Continental and took his family on a week long vacation. He drove the family to Hakone, almost two hundred miles (three hundred kilometers) distant, then to Tokyo, a further hundred kilometers, where they stayed at the Imperial Hotel. In 1973, Aoki took his second son Masaaki to his first movie, *The Godfather*, then showing at the Kyoto Scalaza.

Masaaki, who was then in primary school, was unhappy with discriminatory attitudes toward Koreans in Japanese schools. He often got into fistfights with classmates who called him names insulting his Korean background. He had three cousins who attended a pro-North Korean school in Kyoto. They liked to beat up Japanese. This defiant attitude impressed young Masaaki and he decided to assert his identity. He convinced the rest of the family to change their names to Korean ones on the family registry and become South Korean citizens, although it in the end it was really only a symbolic gesture. As with all ethnic Koreans in Japan, everyone continued to use their Japanese names in daily life for practical reasons and pretended to be one of the crowd whenever possible. It was just easier to get along.

Aoki's company formally changed its name to MK Corporation in 1977, after merging with Katsura Taxi, and began expanding into other businesses. However, his relationship with government regulators entered a new and toxic phase in 1981, when he proposed lowering the taxi fares on the theory that cheaper fares would yield more passengers. It was a time when the other forty-two cab companies in Kyoto had banded together to call for yet another fare increase. Aoki felt that higher fares were pricing taxis out of the urban transportation market, given the growth of the bus, train and subway system in the Kansai area and the proliferation of private car ownership.

Transport Ministry officials in Osaka were not amused and, after consultation with the Minister of Transport Masajuro Shiokawa in Tokyo, rejected his application.

"The taxi industry is based on the principle of one region, one fare," said Shiokawa, a powerful politician who would later become finance minister. "They should fall in line with others and apply for an increase."

A lengthy battle with the authorities began. Sadao Aoki engaged a young lawyer named Kaneko in Osaka to sue the government to prevent the aforementioned taxi companies from unilaterally raising their prices, which would affect the taxi business in Kyoto and five or six other cities across Japan. He wanted prices in Kyoto to stay the same for the time being and eventually go down. Kaneko did not know anything about the taxi business. What's more, no one had ever sued the Japanese government before. It was assumed by all that the odds of winning were almost zero. But Kaneko was impressed with Aoki's energy and passion and took the case on, making preparations for a lawsuit.

This incurred the wrath of Shiokawa.

At a meeting between himself and Aoki at the Transport Ministry, Shiokawa grew livid and shouted, "We are going to break you down and destroy you."

Said second son Masaaki, who accompanied his father to that meeting as a teenager "I wanted to punch him in the mouth."

Aoki was challenging an entrenched system kept in place by under-the-table bribes. He faced threats to his physical well-being from right-wing thugs who despised Koreans. Ultranationalist sound trucks with loudspeakers blocked the streets to the Aoki home and blared messages of hate—*Go Home You Lousy Korean! Get the hell out of Japan!*—night and day.

"It was a terrible time," Masaaki later recalled.

It took three years, until January 31, 1985, before the Osaka District Court ruled that the government's rejection of MK's fare-reduction application was unfair and had no basis in law. The victory was huge news. It hit the front page in all the newspapers and was the lead story on the evening NHK news telecast, whose announcer said, "One region, one price, everyone paying the same taxi fare is a system we have all thought normal. But today's verdict in Osaka changes all that."

It was the first time anyone had taken on the all-powerful bureaucracy in Japan in a court, and won, and it had huge impact on society across the board. Aoki himself was so surprised that he could not think of anything to say when the evening daily reporters contacted him for comment. He hadn't thought it possible he could win.

Said his attorney Kaneko, "What was strange about the trial was that the taxi company executives, the taxi union officials and government bureaucrats all testified as witnesses for the government. It was really strange to see that Mr. Aoki was the only one fighting for the consumer. Even the judge in court thought it was unusual. The judge said he thought the whole idea of one region, one price was *okashi* (strange)."

The government prepared to appeal to a higher court. At the same time, however, the government's lawyers asked Aoki to consider a *wakai*, a kind of compromise by which the imposition of price decreases would be implemented at a later date. The reason the government asked for the wakai is because officials were afraid of losing in the appeals court and that would be a terrible loss of face. Kaneko did not want Aoki to accept this compromise. He wanted to go for a complete victory. Aoki was afraid of pushing his victory too far. He did not want to rub it in so he went against his lawyer's wishes, leaving Kaneko an unhappy man who was so upset that he would refuse to represent Aoki ever again as a result.

The agreement in place, the appeals court authorized the wakai, but it was one nevertheless in which the appeals court judges ordered the government to give in and publicly "acknowledge the role MK Taxi had played in energizing the taxi industry and improving customer convenience." That statement alone was worth its weight in gold.

It took several years, until 1994, when MK Taxi was finally given the all clear to fix its own prices. Even then, harassment by rival taxi companies remained a problem. It included trucks ramming MK cabs, pachinko balls being hurled through open windows at MK drivers and Kyoto yakuza intimidating prospective passengers at MK Taxi stations. Some people threw feces at the front doors of MK buildings. Cab drivers from other companies would go out on their day off, get drunk and then climb in the back of an MK taxi solely to cause trouble.

The fact that MK Taxi was a firm run by ethnic Koreans only added to the anger of rival companies.

Two trips to North Korea by Aoki during this period, to donate used cabs and develop tourism, further infuriated the ultranationalists. The MK headquarters was besieged by intimidating phone calls and letters with messages like: "You die! You son of a bitch!" "I'll kill your kids." "Commit suicide!"

Despite this, MK occupancy increased 10 percent while that of the competitors fell. MK Taxi expanded operations to include Osaka, Japan's second largest city, and Kobe. When Nagoya officials, in solidarity with the traditional taxi firms, rejected Aoki's application for MK to operate with its cut-rate fees in that city of 2.2 million people, Aoki turned to the courts and won an OK to operate a free taxi service instead, which he continued until the city relented and allowed him to compete using his own prices. Sadao Aoki went on to win all sorts of awards for his business achievements.

Masaaki compared his father to Ho Chin Minh, the Vietnamese revolutionary, whom Masaaki considered the greatest Asian figure in modern history, a man who set the stage for Mao Tse Tung and brought about the defeat of two great powers—France and the United States of America.

"My father was a self-made billionaire who single handedly changed the face of the taxi industry in Japan," said the younger Aoki in a 2021 interview, "and did it in the face of great discrimination against Koreans. He was a trailblazer, a white knight. Sam Walton. He had struck a blow for the little guy. He was a hero to the Japanese public."

Sadao Aoki had given control of the Osaka franchise of MK Taxi to the oldest son, Nobuaki, and of the Nagoya franchise to the youngest son, Yoshiaki. However, second son Masaaki did not want to be part of the family business. He was the most like his father of the three sons. He was tall, good-looking and had a string of girlfriends. He was not a good student but he was adventurous and outspoken. Instead of staying with MK Taxi, he decided to go abroad. He backpacked around Europe, had ménage à trois with two Italian girls and then moved to the US. It was where everything was happening, the country of Madonna, Michael Jackson and Prince. It was where everyone wanted to be. Besides, his older brother would be going into the business as per Korean custom. Masaaki wanted independence from the family and to find his own identity.

Ultimately, however, it would be this second son Masaaki taking over, who would return to save the company when the Japanese economic bubble of the 1980s burst and brought MK Taxi to near ruin. He would become known as the man who had conquered the cab market in the world's largest city and the man who invented an Uber-like System in Japan, winning all sorts of awards, including businessman of the year.

He would also go on to be known as the enfant terrible of the Tokyo taxi world.

THE SON

Masaaki Aoki had initially enrolled at the University of Southern California in 1987 at age twenty-one, where, much to his chagrin, he encountered a different type of discrimination than the anti-Korean prejudice he had experienced in Japan—the disdain the all-white USC student body displayed toward Asians en masse.

"It was worse than being a Korean in Japan," the blunt-spoken Masaaki said during an interview in 2021. "White chicks would blow you off it you tried to talk to them, especially if you couldn't speak English well. It's changed now that Asians are rich. But back then it was awful. The white chicks wouldn't touch me. So I had to date the nisei girls."

He went on to become a successful businessman in California, exporting American-made golf clubs to Japan and selling them for several times cost. He also became a scratch golfer who often played at Pebble Beach.

"I was living in Newport Beach," he recalled, "making money and having a great time. But I picked up the *Wall Street Journal* one day and saw my dad's face on the front page! The paper had done a story on the new breed of Japanese entrepreneurs. And my dad was the lead figure. That was really cool. They did one of those ink sketches. I started to think that it might actually be fun to help with the family business."

"My dad had made a fortune and gotten into the golf course business in the mid- to late-eighties, buying a golf club near Lake Biwako. He asked me to come back to Japan and run his golf business. I love golf. I mean I fucking love golf. I thought it was a wonderful idea. I was twenty-seven. Moreover, in the late eighties and early nineties the US was in bad shape. Inflation was a big problem. 10 percent at one point. Interest rates were so high: 15 to 16 percent at Federal Reserve under Paul Volcker. That meant your housing mortgage was 20 percent. There was the Savings and Loan Crisis in which so many people lost their money. Charles Keating would go to prison. So I sold my business in the United States and went back to Japan in 1991."

His timing could not have been worse.

Japan had just experienced an economic bubble without parallel in world history. It had been precipitated by the Plaza Accord of 1985 when G-5 finance ministers sought to put a break on the flood of exports emanating from Japan in the form of automobiles, TV sets and cameras by intentionally revaluing the yen. Within eighteen months the yen had doubled against the world's major currencies. The top ten banks in the world in terms of asset size were all Japanese and there was money everywhere. The stock exchange tripled as the Japanese government sought to stimulate domestic demand. Japanese firms started buying up iconic American properties like the Pebble Beach Company, Rockefeller Center and Columbia Pictures. Tokyoites flew to Sapporo for lunch, spent weekends in Hawaii and ate sushi with gold flakes sprinkled on top. Expensive Louis Vuitton and Gucci bags flew off the shelves. It was a crazy time. Rapacious. Degenerate. One could see girls at the discos regularly stripping down to their underwear and dancing on the stage.

By the time Aoki had returned to Japan, this bubble had already burst, but it took a couple of years for everyone to notice.

The Nikkei 225 stock index had reached its all-time high of ¥38,916 on December 29, 1989. Then, as the Bank of Japan began raising interest rates—to a peak of 6 percent in 1990—to tamp down an overheated economy and the Ministry of Finance put restrictions on the total loan volume of real estate lending and large-scale land transactions, prices started to fall. From there, the Nikkei 225 embarked on a white-knuckle ride that would see it lose nearly 60 percent of its value by December 1992. A decade later it would reach a low of ¥8,579. Accordingly, land prices (residential, commercial and industrial) in Tokyo also fell sharply. The yen, for its part, would continue to appreciate, hitting ¥83 to the US dollar in May 1995 and peaking at ¥76 in August 2011.

Neither Japanese stocks nor Tokyo property prices—nor the Japanese people, for that matter—ever fully recovered those previous giddy heights. Instead, years of torpor and stagnant growth ensued, in what came to be known as Japan's "Lost Decade," then "Lost Decades." News reports during that time were filled with accounts of long-established businesses going bankrupt and leaving their employees out in the cold.

People who had taken out million-dollar loans to buy Tokyo apartments now found themselves out of work and unable to pay off the debt. Selling the apartment they were living in and moving to a cheaper place was not an option because values had plummeted 80 percent from their peak. Banks continued their policy of easy mortgages, far beyond what the family incomes should have allowed, to the bitter end. The fallout extended to family, friends and business associates who signed as "guarantors."

Vacation homes, pleasure boats and new ski condos in high demand during the bubble, and purchased at peak prices by investors or vacationers, were now being sold at bargain-basement prices, some ski condos going for the rock bottom price of ¥50,000. Nobody wanted them because the taxes and maintenance fees were too high.

"It was skydiving without a parachute," said Masaaki of being in business at that time. "My father's business suffered a lot in the wake of the economic collapse of the 1990s. We were really rich. We had $2 billion at one point. But the crash in the stock and real-estate markets really hurt."

To cite one example, Masaaki's father owned land in front of Kyoto Station that had been worth $160 million at the peak of the bubble. A premium location. After the bubble burst the value of that land sank to $10 million within five to six years. His father's business was devastated by the losses. He was forced to borrow $700 million from the bank to keep his taxi companies in Kyoto, Osaka and Kobe afloat.

Back in Japan, Masaaki worked in the MK company at different jobs, including a stint as a taxi driver. His father trained him in the MK philosophy. Everything went well enough, considering the economic environment, until he met the Nissan girl, a receptionist at the Kyoto branch showroom of the famed automaker.

Then it didn't go so well at all.

Outsiderdom took on an entirely new meaning.

THE NISSAN GIRL

MK Taxi bought its cars from Nissan and as a result Masaaki visited the automaker's offices in Kyoto quite often. It was there that he struck up an acquaintance with the receptionist. Several dates followed and romance blossomed.

"She was perfect," he recalled. "She was beautiful. Drop-dead knockout. She had a great way about her. Easygoing. Never got upset. Lovely. Everybody liked her. I had four different girlfriends at the time, so many girls. You know I was driving a nice car. I still had a lot of money. I was the son of the president of MK Taxi. Girls liked that sort of thing. So I asked her out. Took her to a steakhouse. I fell madly in love with her. She loved me back. We dated for six months. She always walked behind me, which I liked."

He wanted to marry her and she him. So he took her home to meet his mother and father for a formal meeting about marriage. Tea was served. Everything went smoothly until the girl made a remark in passing to the fact that she was Japanese—pure-blooded.

Masaaki knew that his second sister Kyomi, born in 1961, had been forbidden to even date a Japanese man. But he thought his father was just being overprotective and that he had also mellowed over time.

"The Japanese are our customers," his father would always say. "We have to nurture them."

Instead, his father exploded in anger at the mention of "Japanese" and threw a lamp across the room.

"Jesus Christ!" screamed the elder Aoki. "You want to marry a Japanese?! What the hell is wrong with you?"

His mother started crying.

It was a terrible scene. His parents would not even tolerate her presence in the house.

"Get out!" they both screamed.

The Nissan girl was mortified. She broke into tears. But she was also very scared.

"I never saw my father so angry," Masaaki recalled. "It shocked me. Until that day I never knew my father harbored so much hatred for the Japanese. He had always told us to respect the Japanese, that they were our business customers and we had to treat them right. That's what he always said. So I was stunned at his reaction."

"It was the first time I had ever seen him get really mad. That was when I really understood how badly my mom and dad had been treated by the Japanese. He was often quoted as saying he had never suffered discrimination at the hands of the Japanese. My uncle said the same thing. But I think it was just PR. BS. That day the truth came out."

And so sadly that was the end of Masaaki's relationship with the Nissan girl. He had been forced to choose between his parents and the girl he loved, and as painful as it was, there was no other choice but to break it off.

"If I had gone against their wishes," he said, "I would have been shut out of the family business. So that was that. I never ever talked to the girl again. And she refused to speak to me whenever I went over to the Nissan Showroom."

1997: MK TAXI TOKYO

In 1997 Masaaki was assigned by his father to manage the newly established MK Taxi of Tokyo. MK had long been kept out of Japan's biggest taxi market but the family kept up pressure on the Japanese government and eventually won the right to operate eighty-four cabs in the capital. At age thirty-two, Masaaki moved to Tokyo to set up shop.

It was the so-called Lost Decade. Real estate and housing price deflation was horrible. The stock market was a disaster and 1997 was the year the long established Yamaichi Securities, one of the four major Japanese brokerages, went under, their president making a tearful public apology after the former chairman had acknowledged illegal dealings. It was also the year the Hokkaido Takushoku Bank went under as well, destroyed by a mountain of bad debt. It was the absolute worst time for the Aoki family finances. MK Kyoto was $700 million in debt. Tokyo had become doubly important.

Aoki started the Tokyo business with only $200,000. He rented a location, leased vehicles from Nissan and because the Japanese government was subsidizing the hiring of older workers, employed drivers in their forties and fifties. With unemployment at 10 percent, it wasn't hard to get drivers.

The Japanese media followed Aoki around for a solid year.

At the time MK Taxi Tokyo got started, Tokyo cabs were among the world's cleanest and most modern, with white-gloved drivers and passenger doors that opened and closed automatically. To make MK different, Aoki painted his cars black so they resembled limousines more than taxis and eliminated the automatic passenger doors. He trained his drivers to exit the car and open the door for each fare. As a result of such initiatives, MK appeared to customers more like a chauffeur service than a taxi company.

"That's what we wanted," said Masaaki. "The average fare when one of our taxis was flagged down on the street was one-sixth the average fare when one was dispatched to a customer. The dispatch service was used by our corporate clients to take people across town to a meeting or home to the suburbs at the end of the day. It was a great business for us and we got entire companies to sign up with us because we feel more like a limo ride than a cab ride. We got 90 percent of our fares via dispatch while most of our competitors got 20 percent this way.

Nippon TV reporter Masahi Kikuchi, who covered the Tokyo MK venture from the very beginning, summed up their success in a lengthy interview: "MK started a revolution in the taxi business. What was impressive about MK was that they had very polite drivers who always said 'Welcome' and 'Thank you.' They gave change with both hands. MK trained them very thoroughly. The cars were nice. Crown. Cedric. The fares were low and the service was great. It was the polar opposite of the Tokyo taxi system until then, which was high prices and relatively bad service. The old system was 60 percent for the driver and 40 percent for the taxi company. MK introduced the franchise or lease system to Tokyo. The driver leases the car, pays expenses and keeps all the profit. It was a zero salary system. Since MK came on the scene, the Tokyo taxi business has never been the same . . . "

Masaaki also established PCS or Private Chauffeur Service, using a web-enabled mobile-phone program, a system he had created with the help of Japanese telecommunications company NTT, that allowed users to automatically find the MK cab closest to them and then speak directly with the driver or bypass the customer driver phone conversation altogether using the PCS system. It reduced the need for a dispatch system, which had been a problem because during busy times there were not enough staff members to answer calls, thus increasing wait times for the customers. Once a customer did get a dispatcher on the line it then took several minutes to find and coordinate a cab nearby. On an average day, the call center received 2,000 phone calls and dispatched 1,200 cabs to customers.

The PCS system brought great savings to MK.

"It was Uber app before Uber was ever invented," said Masaaki, bursting with uncontained pride.

PCS

The PCS system venture was so successful, Aoki was able to afford to construct his own building from the resultant profits. He won several businessman-of-the-year awards. His competitors were calling him "an absolute genius." He was regularly invited to speak at bankers groups and other business associations and was frequently interviewed by newspapers, magazines and TV stations. He was the toast of the town.

A professor at Harvard named Andrew McAfee took notice and wrote a paper on the Tokyo MK operation, entitled "MK Taxi:

Private Chauffeur Service" and then fashioned a course on Masaaki
Aoki's approach to business. In 2004 he even invited Masaaki to
address a Harvard Business School class on the MK Taxi business
philosophy. "Yu-chan," as Masaaki was affectionately called by his
friends, was roundly applauded for his calm, relaxed, confident
performance. He was so well received he was invited back again to
participate in a panel discussion. No one realized he was stoned.

"A friend from Newport Beach had given me some pot," he recalled. "I smoked it in the bathroom, like Eddie Murphy in *Trading
Places*. So I was super relaxed when I spoke."

Masaaki's success with PCS in Tokyo saved the family businesses in Kyoto and Osaka—which were now part of a conglomerate known as MK Group—from bankruptcy. Profits from Tokyo
allowed the respective companies there to overcome the negative
effects of MK-owned property in Kyoto having dropped in value
from $2 billion to half that amount.

His father had also made some drastic and—in the eyes of the
Japanese authorities—highly questionable moves to save the MK
enterprises. The seventy-three year-old Sadao had bought a 40 per-
cent interest in an institution known as the Kinki Sangyo Credit
Union, aka Kinki Industrial Credit Union, and appointed himself
Representative Director and Chairman. The Kinki Sangyo Credit
Union then took over the business of three bankrupt credit associa-
tions with (public) funds totaling hundreds of billions of yen.

Subsequently, from March to August 2004, Sadao Aoki and the
Kinki Sangyo Bank loaned large sums of money to four MK companies in financial trouble: Kyoto MK Taxi (¥5.2 billion), Kobe MK
Taxi (¥500 million), Osaka MK Taxi (¥1 billion) and MK Petroleum
(¥1.9 billion). Also receiving a loan was the shipping company MK
Taiyo of Kyoto owned by Masaaki's older brother Hideo. All in all,
the total amount lent out to family companies totaled ¥11 billion.

The loans were granted at below market interest rates and drew
the attention of the regional finance bureau which deemed them
illegal and ordered them to be withdrawn.

The family was in a serious bind and it fell to Masaaki to have to
bail the family out, which he did by selling the new building he had

just put up in the Kachidoki district of Tokyo and using the profits to rescue the MK Kyoto, MK Osaka and MK Nagoya companies.

Said Masaaki: "The Kachidoki building was constructed in 2006 and I sold it in 2008 for a profit of several billion yen. We also had to grease some palms to make the issue go away, because the Upper House Committee on Financial Affairs in the National Diet had started looking into the matter.

"'You saved my ass,' is what my father said to me," recalled Masaaki. "That's what I remembered most."

David Shin, the former Fox Networks executive who had followed the younger Aoki's career, thought Masaaki a perfect symbol of modern Japan.

"The postwar generation was led by visionary entrepreneurs, people like Soichiro Honda and Konosuke Matsushita, who created the great Japanese economy," he said. "But their sons were content to ride on the established structure. It took a renegade like Masaaki to shake things up."

NTV reporter Masashi Kikuchi called him "a cross between Sonny and Michael in The Godfather."

Renowned lawyer Tasuku Matsuo, who represented Paul McCartney when he was arrested at Tokyo's Narita Airport for marijuana possession and successfully got him released, singled Masaaki out for praise in an interview, saying: "There were four taxi companies in Tokyo that controlled everything: Nihon Kotsu, Teito, Daiwa and Kokusai. We call them Dai-Nippon Teikoku or the Great Empire of Japan. That MK was able to challenge this system in Tokyo is a great thing. It's a tribute to the ability of Masaaki Aoki. That he comes from a minority background makes it all the more impressive."

ANGER MANAGEMENT

Whomever he resembled, the glow from Masaaki's success did not last long, thanks to a turbulent, self-destructive personal life that almost did him in.

He had gone through over two hundred *omiai* matchmaking meetings arranged by his parents, who wanted him to get married and produce some offspring, but he used the process as his own Adult Friend Finder.

"It was a good way to meet girls and to get laid," he said. "Each one would run its course until it became clear I wasn't interested in getting married. I had a girlfriend I liked. A Korean Air flight attendant. What a doll. But she couldn't speak Japanese. My family didn't care for her because of it. So that was the end of that."

Finally, in 2004, to please his parents, he settled on a woman he liked more than the others he'd been matched with, and they tied the knot.

But he hardly ever went home. He worked at the MK dispatch center from six in the morning until the early hours of the following morning. Sometimes he would leave around ten in the evening to hit the Ginza nightclubs before they closed. He wound up spending more and more of his nights in hotels with Ginza hostesses.

His wife gave birth to a son in 2006, but by 2008 she filed for divorce citing infidelity. The daughter of a Korean yakuza loan shark, she moved back home to her father's palatial estate and never talked to him again.

More alarming than the infidelities were a series of unpleasant "incidents," which caused some observers to suggest he was more like Sonny Corleone than Michael. For example, on March 13, 2005, Masaaki woke up to find himself lying on the ground in the parking lot of Saginuma Station outside Tokyo. It was eleven in the morning. He had been drinking all night and had passed out. Hungover, in a foul mood and realizing he had missed an important appointment, he grabbed a station employee and punched the hapless man in the face.

"Why the hell didn't you wake me up?" he screamed.

Someone called the police. Patrolmen quickly arrived on the scene to arrest Masaaki, while the station employee was rushed to the hospital where he spent several days recovering. Masaaki avoided jail time but was forced to pay compensation, as well as apologize, in a very public way, at a press conference and resign his position as well. His absence from the company lasted a year, but then he was back at the Tokyo MK president's desk.

In 2008 he found himself in jail again, this time arrested at eight thirty on the morning of April 9 at Tokyo Station for causing yet another fight with a station attendant.

"I needed a wheelchair for my sister," explained Masaaki. "Japan Railways is supposed to provide them. But the guy behind the counter said they didn't have one. So I got mad and I pulled him over the counter. The police came and arrested me and they hauled me off to a detention house in Marunouchi."

Another fine, another suspended sentence and resignation followed, requiring another year away from the company before he could be reinstated.

Masaaki's arrests were accompanied by other problems that seriously jeopardized the company's viability. Such as a Diet investigation in which a member of the Lower House declared that Tokyo MK tactics were illegal. The MK system was based on leasing cars to drivers who were paid under a formula "sales and benefits minus expense equals salary." An MP named Ueda claimed this system was illegal and a violation of the Road Transport Act.

"Only workers are losing and the company is not losing money," said Ueda. "Under this system MK just lends the car and the driver is liable for all expenses for maintenance and repair of the car. The company makes a profit and the workers lose money." According to Ueda this resulted in "irresponsible management decisions."

It was right at this juncture that Masaaki Aoki had a stroke.

"I spent the night with this gorgeous nightclub hostess but I couldn't get it up," he explained. "So I took a lot of Viagra. Three or four. Still no good. I woke up at seven thirty feeling funny. The girl said that one side of my face was paralyzed. I could not inhale any smoke when I lit up a cigarette. I couldn't stand up. She took me to the hospital and I was there for two weeks."

As if ordained by the Shinto gods, Tokyo MK was hit by a wave of civil lawsuits during this period from former and current drivers.

The first one arrived in November 2011 when a Tokyo MK driver filed a multimillion-dollar lawsuit for damages against Masaaki, who, at the time, had just returned to his post as president of Tokyo MK. Aoki was captured for all to see on the MK taxi video system riding in the back seat of an MK Taxi as part of the company's internal checks system, training a driver. When the driver nearly ran into a pedestrian, Aoki exploded in anger. He kicked the back of the seat and screamed *bakayaro* (you idiot), several times. He jumped out of the car, forced the driver out from behind the wheel and fired him on the spot. Aoki then got in the driver's seat and drove away. It was an ugly, nauseating scene, one which quickly found its way onto the Internet, to the great embarrassment of the MK family.

The driver filed a suit complaining of whiplash, lumbar contusions, emotional distress and other troubles, demanding compensation to the amount of ¥23 million. Four other MK drivers joined in the suit complaining of being similarly assaulted by their boss. Aoki was forced to resign yet again, setting some kind of record.

"I'm a strict boss," protested Aoki. "I control my drivers' hairstyle. The way they smell. If something can offend the customer I make them change it. The way they handle the steering wheel. I'm better than my dad in that way. I'm looking for perfection. I tell them don't use GPS. Looking at it while driving can cause an accident. Use the voice guide. Keep your eyes on the road at all times.

"But part of the problem was that 90 percent of the drivers did not follow my rules. They were driving recklessly, like kamikaze. I tried to train them. I did it nicely the first two or three times, but it didn't work. They just ignored me and kept doing the same thing. So I changed my tactics and became harsher. I would yell at them. Kick the back of the seat. You have to be like that. That's the Japanese system of education. You see it in sports. In the schools. Corporal punishment. It's common. What made it worse is that drivers were always busy, because our fares were cheaper and our service was better. There was excessive overtime. They were overworked, putting in eighteen- to twenty-one-hour shifts. They were falling asleep driving down the street. The accident rate was sky-high. That added pressure. *I* wanted to change the system to ten-hour shifts twelve days a month but the drivers refused. The existing system was convenient for them because they got the next two days off after a shift. I wanted to put them on a fixed salary system. They didn't like that. I wanted to put some of them in BMWs. They didn't want that either. They didn't want to be put above other drivers. They didn't want to be different from other drivers."

Inspired by the whiplash suit, ten other drivers banded together and sued Aoki for power harassment, complaining as well about overtime work. More people joined the lawsuit. Twenty. Then it increased to sixty.

The drivers were spreading stories that Aoki was forcing them to wash their cars for two hours everyday. Some drivers called him up just to shout "You Fucking Korean!" into the phone. They actually challenged him to a fight in the square at Shimbashi Station in front of the old nineteenth-century locomotive on permanent display there. Aoki went down to accommodate them. He faced off against twenty men, to the bewilderment of commuters on their way home. He was going to take them all on.

"I would have punched the motherfuckers," he said, with characteristic bravado. "But it was rush hour and then the cops came and broke it up."

It took a suicide to bail him out of all the trouble he was in.

SUICIDE

In 2015, there was another issue at Tokyo MK, this one over misuse of union funds, and this time it had nothing to do with Masaaki Aoki. Instead, it involved the number two man in the Tokyo MK Union, the union secretary general—an individual named Kenji Nishiyama—who was discovered to have embezzled money from union dues accounts. Half a million dollars' worth, in fact. He had spent it all on nightclub hostesses and generally having a good time.

Aoki challenged the union members to cease their attacks on him and go after their own union over the misspent money.

"If you don't sue," said Aoki, "then you are part of a criminal conspiracy."

When they demurred, Aoki accused them of conspiring with the union embezzler and started firing workers. He fired almost 300 of them (out of a total of 550 drivers) over a period of a year and a half, replacing them with new hires.

The problem dissipated on May 15, 2015, when Kenji Nishiyama jumped from the fourth floor of his apartment building, committing suicide, leaving a wife and two children behind. After that, few MK employees had the stomach to continue fighting.

CHAOS

The final blow in the Masaaki Aoki drama was a breach with his parents. The *Asahi Shimbun* newspaper had published an article about Masaaki on January 3, 2011, detailing the fights with the driver, his three arrests and the lawsuits that the Aoki family's second son had triggered. It was followed with another article in the popular weekly magazine *Friday*, with a link to a YouTube video of Masaaki's assault on the trainee driver. It drew over a million views. This came at a time when MK Taxi ranked third of most efficient businesses in the nation according to a survey conducted by *President* magazine. Second was All Nippon Airways and first was Tokyo Disneyland.

His mother was beyond enraged. "The entire MK Taxi Company is going to collapse because of you!" she railed at him.

For Masaaki, this was the last straw. For sure, he had acted like a dope. That he well knew. But on the other hand he had bailed the company out of more than one jam, hadn't he, and he thought his mother should be more appreciative. But she wasn't. And as a result he never spoke to her again. Not even after she suffered a stroke in 2017 and became incapacitated.

He also stopped speaking to his father after his younger brother was given permission to marry a Japanese woman. He was shocked beyond belief to learn the news. His father had destroyed his dream of marrying the Nissan girl, the love of his life, solely because she was Japanese, yet he allowed his third son to marry one. It was colossally unfair, he thought. It angered him so much that he could not even bring himself to attend his father's funeral after his father passed away from bronchial pneumonia in 2017 at the age of eighty-eight.

More lawsuits followed. In May 2017 the court ordered MK

Taxi to pay unpaid wages of ¥20 million. That same month, twenty of Aoki's drivers banded together to file suit against him for power harassment. Approximately forty more workers joined the suit.

On December 21, 2017, Masaaki was arrested yet again, this time in Shimbashi for assaulting a driver who had refused to pick him up. Witnesses say he threw a shoe in the face of the man, which caused some bruising. A police officer on patrol made the arrest. Aoki claimed he was drunk and could not remember what he had done. Tokyo MK was obliged to make, yet again, another public apology and arrangements for his dismissal from the company. Masaaki was beginning to lose count of the times he had had to resign to take responsibility for some misdeed or other.

The *Shukan Shincho* news magazine wrote a bruising article about his behavior. "A violent life without reflection," said the magazine. "A drunken moron."

MEETING MASAAKI

I first met Masaaki Aoki in the summer of 2019, invited by a mutual acquaintance David Shin, then president of Fox Networks in Japan. Aoki had read my book on crime and corruption *Tokyo Underworld*, said David, and wanted to meet.

It was lunchtime at the Conrad Hilton, the deluxe five-star hotel overlooking Hamarikyu Gardens and the distant Tokyo Bay where Aoki kept a suite. He was sitting in the French dining room Collage on the thirty-seventh floor, working on a large draft beer. He had been up all night, he said, with a group of nightclub hostesses polishing off several cases of expensive Dom Perignon champagne.

"I liked your book," he said, standing up to shake my hand vigorously. "But I'm surprised you are still alive. The right wing must be really pissed at you. But fuck the motherfuckers."

Thus began several hours of a nonstop monologue, by Aoki-san, or Yu-chan, as he likes to be called. He was a compulsive talker—the most compulsive talker I had ever met—in addition to his other gifts which, it became apparent, included limitless energy. He was bubbly, endearing, crude and exhausting, and incapable of listening.

The topics he expounded on ranged from the story of Black baseball player Jackie Robinson and racism in the United States, to the Central Park reunion scene in the film *Kramer vs. Kramer*.

"I cry every time I see that," he said.

The afternoon with Aoki stretched into the evening and he invited us to a hostess bar, where he followed up the dozen or so glasses of beer he managed to consume with numerous shots of whiskey, talking all the while.

He wanted to discuss a project David Shin had proposed, a movie and a book about his father who had founded the original MK taxi company in Kyoto, which Masaaki Aoki had expanded into Tokyo in a most dramatic way, and so a weekend in that ancient capital followed where he introduced my wife and me to the city's main temples and dining spots, providing a nonstop commentary all the way through.

At Eikando Temple, he had disappeared to take a phone call. Twenty minutes later, he came back beaming.

"I just made $300,000 in a twenty-minute cell-phone call standing in the middle of a temple in Kyoto," he said, ebullient. "How many people can do that?"

The evenings featured visits to several haunts in Gion, the famous geisha district. One of the attending *geiko* (as geisha are called in Gion), was a stunningly beautiful twenty-six-year-old named Satsuki. Aoki had discovered her when she was sixteen years old and paid for all her training as a *maiko*, or apprentice. Now she was one of the most famous geiko of all, her image adorning the cover of glossy Kyoto travel magazines and train station posters. Aoki was crazy about her, he said, and wanted them to live together but she was too focused on her career and kept putting him off.

On our last night in Kyoto we watched Japan defeat Korea in the finals of the Premier 12 baseball tournament. Aoki, who had consumed twelve beers and a fifth of Jim Beam whiskey, was devastated. He launched into a monologue about what it was like to be a *zainichi* ethnic Korean, someone who had endured discrimination growing up in Kyoto, suffering insults daily, like *chon-ko* or *shipseki*, both derogatory Korean terms which often led to schoolyard fights.

He said he could not understand Japanese people who could shrug off the wartime atrocities their forefathers had committed as if they had never happened.

He let it be known that he had $200 million in the bank and that he wanted to use it all to demolish Japan's right wing and anyone who supported them.

Later, back in Tokyo, he had stood up in a crowded hostess bar and yelled at the hostesses, "How in hell can you screw Japanese men? You fuck Japanese businessmen? Shame on you."

The mama-san had to calm him down.

I'd met a lot of foreigners living in Japan who, paradoxically, harbored resentments about their adopted home. Some of them had lived in the country for decades. It struck me that Masaaki Aoki, who had lived his whole life in Japan as a member of an ethnic minority, claimed the heavyweight title in that regard.

I wondered what a clinical psychiatrist would make of him.

The last time I saw Aoki was in the fall of 2020, over dinner at the Foreign Correspondents Club of Japan in Tokyo. The film and the book project had fallen through, the remnants of which you are reading here, but he was in good spirits. He had stopped drinking, started exercising, and was talking about emigrating to the States.

Some foreign reporter friends from the club joined us and I spent the next hour or so telling them about Aoki's exploits, and the considerable accomplishments of Masaaki and his father Sadao. There was a lot to relate. It struck me that of all the people in this book who have made an impact on Japanese society, including the city of Tokyo, few had done more to change the established way of doing things than Masaaki's father, the only individual in the history of the nation who had sued the Japanese government and won—and perhaps Masaaki himself with his inventive PCS system.

It was a story that deserved to be told and I am glad that I was finally able to do it.

CHAPTER 15

The Moonies

THE SHOOTING to death of Shinzo Abe, the former prime minister of Japan on July 8, 2022, shocked the nation. Abe had been making a campaign speech for a Liberal Democratic Party (LDP) candidate for the Upper House of the Diet on a Friday morning in the city of Nara, when he was attacked by a man who emerged from the crowd wielding a homemade device that resembled a double-barreled shotgun.

The man somehow managed to get within several feet of Abe, despite the presence of a Security Police team, and shot him in the shoulder and neck. Abe collapsed to the ground as the police immediately subdued the assailant. Medical attendants found Abe's heart had stopped and their resuscitation efforts failed. He was pronounced dead at a nearby hospital several hours later. Media coverage of the event dominated the news for months afterward.

Gun violence is rare in Japan thanks to strict Firearm and Sword Possession Control Law. However, Japanese political history is filled with assassinations and assassination attempts. Abe's own grandfather, Nobusuke Kishi, one time prime minister of Japan was the victim of an assassination attempt in 1960. An assailant believed to have been hired by a rival political group stabbed him in the thigh six times before being subdued. Kishi lost considerable blood but survived, after receiving thirty stitches to close his wounds.

That same year, Japan Socialist Party head Inejiro Asanuma was stabbed to death in the middle of a speech by a crazed right-wing assailant. In subsequent years Prime Minister Takeo Miki, Deputy Prime Minister Shin Kanemaru and Prime Minister Morihiro Hokosawa all survived assassination attempts. Nagasaki mayor Hitoshi Nakanishi was shot by an ultranationalist in 1990 but survived. Another Nagasaki mayor, Itcho Ito, was shot and killed while campaigning in 2007 by a gangster. Shinzo Abe is just the latest.

Abe's assassin was a forty-one-year-old male named Tetsuya Yamagami, a former member of Japan's Maritime Self-Defense Force, who told police that he was motivated by his hatred for the religious group the Korean Unification Church (UC), an organization long supported by the Abe family. Yamagami was quoted as saying the Unification Church had brainwashed his mother, a member, bankrupted the family and ruined his life. It was later revealed that Yamagami's father had committed suicide and that his mother had subsequently donated the entire family wealth to the UC. This prevented Yamagami from being able to go to university. He stated that he had originally planned to assassinate the current UC leader, Hak Ja Han, who is the widow of the Church's founder the Reverend Sun Yung Moon, a Korean preacher, entrepreneur and political activist who declared himself to be a Messiah.

"After my mother joined the Church (in the 1990s), my entire teenage years are gone with some ¥100 million ($735,0000) wasted," Yamagami wrote in a typed letter sent to a blogger the day before the assassination. "It's not an exaggeration to say that my experience during that time had kept distorting my entire life."

Unable to get close enough to the Moon widow to carry out his plan, however, Yamagami set his sights on Abe, after learning that Abe had sent a congratulatory video message to a UC-related group event in September 2021 and had otherwise supported the group.

Originally known as the Holy Spirit Association for the Unification of World Christianity, founded in 1954, the Church championed family values, capitalism and the unification of the Korean Peninsula, which had been split between the totalitarian pro-Communist north and democratic south in 1948. The Church grew dramatically, spreading out to establish bases in 194 countries including the United States. The Japan branch was established in

1959 and, ironically, was greatly helped by Shinzo Abe's maternal grandfather, Nobusuke Kishi and the nation's prime minister at the time. Kishi, who held strong right-wing views, had thrown his support behind the UC because of the Church's strong anti-Communist stance and advocacy for world peace.

The UC was certified as a Christian religious organization in 1964 and later changed its name to its current one—Family Federation for World Peace and Unification—but was more commonly known as the Unification Church. It became famous for holding mass wedding ceremonies between followers, dubbed "Moonies." The couples to be married were matched by Church founder Moon who dictated an outlandish series of purification rituals couples had to complete, including beating each other with a bat and performing a three-day sex ceremony involving prescribed positions in front of Moon's portrait. Among those followers was a famous singer named Junko Sakurada who got married in one of these mass ceremonies, effectively ending her career as an entertainer.

The Church also became known for aggressive—and often fraudulent—sales tactics in persuading people to buy Church-manufactured pottery, books and seals and other products at exorbitant prices, as well as for intrusive conversion methods and mind control of young people in search of some meaning to their lives. Critics pointed to an abnormal number of bankruptcies, divorces and suicides among Japanese believers, which had caused some high-ranking officials to resign.

After the Abe assassination, a number of former UC adherents came forward to disclose that they had been subjected to mind control and other forms of abuse by the Church, until they came to their senses and left the organization.

The Abe assassination focused new attention on the murky relationship between the long-ruling conservative Liberal Democratic Party, to which Kishi had also belonged, and the Korean Unification Church. Also involved in this relationship were the CIA and the Korean Central Intelligence Agency (KCIA). They had all found common ground in their opposition to Communism. Despite being foreign institutions, the Church and the intelligence agencies wielded extraordinary influence in Japan during the postwar era and beyond, impacting the course of history. The new attention that was brought to bear on the UC served as a reminder of its dark past.

Reverend Moon was born in 1920 in Korea at a time when it had been annexed by Japan. He was raised Christian and taught Sunday School at a Presbyterian Church. After World War II ended and Korea's subsequent partition along the 38th parallel, Moon began preaching the word of God, reporting later that Jesus had appeared to him and said God had chosen him to establish the Kingdom of Heaven on earth. He traveled to Pyongyang in North Korea where he was arrested and accused of spreading falsehoods and deceiving innocent people for their money. Charged with enticing wives away from their husbands, destroying family institutions and bringing disorder to society, he spent three years in prison before returning to Seoul to establish the Korean Unification Church, which expanded rapidly with centers around the country, then moved into Japan, as well as the Philippines and the USA. He was arrested twice in Seoul on suspicion of having religious sex orgies and ducking the military draft, but both charges were ultimately dropped.

Moon was not a particularly gifted orator or an especially charismatic individual. But he was ambitious and he stood out for his anti-Communist activism. This helped earn him the attention of Japan's Liberal Democratic Party which viewed the rise of Mao Tse Tung in China and Kim Il Sung in the Democratic People's Republic of Korea as a threat to Japan's national interests, and solidified the support of the LDP's Kishi, who had assumed the post of prime minister in 1957. Kishi was backed, politically and financially, by the CIA, which, in turn had helped create the KCIA, an organization that became deeply intertwined with the UC.

The LDP stayed in power for years to come, thanks in great part to CIA payments which amounted to a million dollars a month during the fifties and sixties, delivered by American businessmen, with unwitting politicians told the money was a gift from corporate America. Kishi adviser Okinori Kaya, a former finance minister in Japan's wartime cabinet and convicted war criminal who was elected to the Diet in 1958, was a key conduit, described in Timo-thy Weiner's book *Legacy of Ashes* (Anchor, 2008). That relationship continued through the regime of prime minister Eisaku Sato (1964–1972), Kishi's brother, when the big issue was Okinawa, where US military bases operated as a staging area for the Vietnam War.

All of this dovetailed nicely with the Unification Church's an-ti-Communist stance and its burgeoning relationship with the Ko-rean Central Intelligence Agency, established in 1961 with funding provided by the CIA, and modeled after that organization. The KCIA had been designed to keep Communist North Korea in check and protect the pro-capitalist Republic of Korea, where the United States also maintained a substantial military force. The KCIA had been founded by Brigadier General Kim Chong Pil who shortly thereafter participated in the 1961 South Korean coup which de-posed anti-American Syngman Rhee and installed President Park Chung-Hee, who became pro-American (and who would sign the long-delayed 1965 peace treaty formally establishing diplomatic re-lations between Japan and its former colony).

Kim Chong Pil, a Korean War vet who had trained at Fort Ben-ning, Georgia, and who had also taken an early interest in the UC and its virulent anti-Communism, imbedded several KCIA agents in the Church. According to Middlebury professor Jeffrey M. Bale, a specialist in religious extremism, one was Moon's right hand man in the Church, high-ranking KCIA agent Bo-Hi Pak, an assistant military attaché at the South Korean embassy in Washington, D.C. from 1961 to 1964, where he functioned as liaison between the KCIA and the US intelligence agencies. There were several other UC members from the KCIA who achieved prominence, including Bud Han, a translator for President Park Chung Hee; Steve Kim, a liaison between the KCIA and the CIA who would later run the global Moon media group; and Sang-Kil Han, a military attaché at the South Korean embassy in Washington in the late 1960s, a posi-tion involving intelligence work. Sang-Kil Han later became Moon's personal secretary and the tutor for his children. It was quite a team. Whether they were all there to serve the Church first and their governments second, or vice-versa, was open to interpretation.

However, it was evident that had it not been for Kishi's support (facilitated by Tokyo-based CIA agent Clyde McAvoy), the UC, which had struggled in acquiring members in the beginning, would not have grown to the size it eventually did. In 1958, its first year in Japan, the UC had but 158 followers. However, it would later grow to its membership of approximately 600,000 at the time of writing.

Kishi's close relationship with the Church was publicly known in Japan (unlike his relationship with the CIA). The Church headquarters at one point was even housed next to Kishi's Tokyo residence, on land previously owned by the prime minister. Kishi was seen with Moon in photos taken at the Church and published in UC group publications. In fact, the relationship was so openly cozy that according to media reports Abe's assassin Yamagami believed that it was Kishi who had originally brought the Church to Japan.

Kishi and President Park became close friends, while ties between the LDP and UC-affiliated organizations developed further over the years. As the Church expanded, with CIA backing, it provided solid political support in the form of funds and votes for governing party candidates who, in turn, continued to provide them with a sense of legitimacy and political cover in return. Once Kishi had embraced the Moonies in the 1950s he allowed the rank and file LDP to do the same and receive free money and labor from the Moonie cult members.

"Japanese leaders at the time saw the Church as a tool to promote anti-Communist views in Japan," said Masaki Kito, a lawyer and expert on religious businesses, in a report published by the American National Broadcasting Corporation (NBC) in 2022 in the wake of the Abe assassination. "For their part, the UC group viewed showcasing close ties with prominent politicians as a surefire way to get endorsement for its activities."

The movement's anti-Communist activities also received continued financial support from powerful ultranationalist Yoshio Kodama and his right-wing cohort, the motorboat-racing millionaire Ryoichi Sasakawa.

By the 1980s, Japan reportedly provided roughly 80 percent of Unification Church revenues worldwide, an astonishing figure.

Money-raising techniques included members of the Unification Church randomly approaching people on the street and offering free fortune-telling without identifying themselves as Church representatives. They then urged their targets to purchase expensive items, often amulets, to "shake off bad karma" created by their ancestors, especially those who had maltreated Koreans during Japanese rule of the peninsula. Complaints about this led to an association called the National Network of Lawyers Against Spiritual Sales to be eventually set up to help such victims.

South Korean president Park Chung Hee was assassinated in 1979 while Kishi died of natural causes in 1987. But the influence of the UC lived on. Kishi's LDP faction passed into the hands of his son-in-law, Shintaro Abe, father of Shinzo Abe, and later to Shinzo Abe, who became prime minister—twice. LDP power broker Shin Kanemaru was a supporter of the UC and in 1992 it was reported in the *Shukan Asahi* news magazine that he had pressured the Ministry of Justice to ease restrictions it had placed on Sun Myung Moon and allow him to enter the country.

In 1999, a survey of 128 LDP lawmakers obtained from the National Police Agency and published in *Shukan Gendai* magazine revealed that most of them had attended events organized by the UC's anti-Communism affiliate, the International Federation for Victory Over Communism, and more than 20 of these lawmakers had at least one Church member in their offices as a volunteer.

In 2005, then up-and-coming LDP politician Shinzo Abe, chief secretary of the LDP, was introduced at a mass wedding of UC members as the most promising candidate for the next party leader. He was met with thunderous applause. An article in *Friday Magazine* October 27, 2006, led with the headline "Prime Minister Abe May Be Just A Bit Too Chummy With Rev. Moon Song Myong's Unification Church."

In the wake of the 2011 earthquake and tsunami in Tohoku, the Unification Church was among the most successful religious groups raising funds for victims in the devastated areas. Weekly magazine *Flash* ran an article about the heretofore unreported nexus between the 2011 Tohoku earthquake and religion. Several religious groups were among the largest donors, with Buddhist group Soka Gakkai and the Unification Church donating huge amounts.

Shinzo Abe first became prime minister in 2006 before resigning due to ill health a year later. He ascended to the post again in 2012, remaining there until 2020, when he again resigned claiming ill health. He had a good relationship with Park Chung Hee's daughter, Park Gyeun-hye, who became South Korean president in 2012. Later relations between South Korea and Japan soured over a revival of prewar issues, particularly including that of the Korean comfort women—referring to those reportedly forced into sexual slavery during Japan's colonization of Korea (1910–1945) by the Imperial Japanese Army. (Madam Park's presidency ended in her impeachment in 2016 and removal from office in 2017. She was sentenced to twenty-four years in prison on April 6, 2018 on charges of abuse of power and coercion, and released in 2021.)

In 2019, the anti-LDP evening tabloid *Nikkan Gendai* termed the new Abe Cabinet a "cult," reporting that six of thirteen new ministers appointed in Abe's latest cabinet reshuffle belonged to the anti-leftist Unification Church and that twelve high-ranking government members also had UC connections.

In July 2022, the Kyodo News agency reported that at least twenty Japanese lawmakers appointed as deputies for cabinet members in the government of Prime Minister Fumio Kishida had links to the controversial religious group. It further emerged that Minister of Education, Culture, Sports, Science and Technology, Shinsuke Suematsu had members of the religious group purchase tickets for a political funding party, while Defense Minister Nobuo Kishi, Shinzo Abe's younger brother, also confessed that he had received help in past elections from members of the Unification Church. Upper House member Yoshiyuki Inoue, meanwhile, acknowledged that he was an "endorsing member" of the religious organization.

In the wake of these revelations about his party's involvement with the UC, Prime Minister Fumio Kishida replaced seven cabinet members who had acknowledged links to the Church, including defense minister, Nobuo Kishi.

Kishida stressed that the new cabinet would have all members closely examined for their relationship with the UC. However, it was subsequently reported that at least 30 members of the reshuffled cabinet were still related to the UC to various degrees and that more than 100 parliamentarians out of the 712 total number of Japanese lawmakers had ties to the UC and nearly 80 percent of them belonged to the ruling Liberal Democratic Party. A later report revised that figure upward to 146 LDP lawmakers.

Mitsuhiro Suganuma, aged eighty-six, a former high-ranking officer of the Public Security Intelligence Agency in Japan, admitted in an interview with the *Diplomat* magazine in July 2022, that the relationship between the ruling Liberal Democratic Party and the Unification Church was "a serious problem," in that the Church had embedded itself in Japanese society in various ways.

He also said that the authorities had unfortunately been unable to stop the Church's influence because of the freedom of religion guaranteed in the constitution.

MOON'S MONEY

Reverend Moon had moved to the United States in 1971, although he remained a citizen of the Republic of Korea and returned there for mass gatherings, like the one held by the Holy Spirit Association for the Unification of World Christianity (HSA–UWC) in 1975 in Seoul, to rally the nation against the Communist threat from North Korea in the north after the fall of Saigon. Attended by 1,200,000 people it was one of the largest such gatherings in history. He also gave a series of well-attended public speeches in the States including one in front of the Washington Monument where he spoke on "God's Hope for America" to 300,000 people.

The UC aligned itself with Christian fundamentalists in America, condemning premarital sex, divorce and homosexuality—with Moon comparing gay people to "dirty dung-eating dogs"—while encouraging gun ownership. Moon was also able to attract well-educated, disaffected youths opposed to America's involvement in the Vietnam War. However, along with some other new religious movements like Scientology, it became a target of anti-cult activists who accused the movement of having brainwashed its members.

One such brainwashing victim was Steven Hassan who joined the Unification Church in the early 1970s, after becoming friends with UC recruiters. He was put through an intensive forty-day initiation period where he could not communicate with family or friends, and remained a member for over two years before his father rescued him. He told his story to the *Guardian* newspaper in 2012:

> [When I first joined] little did I know within a few weeks I would be told to drop out of school, donate my bank account, look at Moon as my true parent, and believe my parents were Satan. I didn't even believe in Satan until I met the group.
>
> "I was with the Moonies for two and a half years. I worked twenty-one hours a day, seven days a week—in prayer for between one and three hours. Then I would spend the rest of the day doing PR or lectures for the group, recruiting and fundraising. Everyone on my team was told they had to raise a minimum of $100 a day, otherwise they wouldn't be allowed to sleep, and as a good leader, if they couldn't sleep, then I couldn't either. When I crashed a van into the back of a tractor trailer, I had gone three days without sleep.

Hassan left the group after his father intervened and had him deprogrammed. He went on to be a counselor and write books about cults and their techniques.

Moonie volunteers in the United States worked in Washington congressional offices, and the Church campaigned in support of conservative politicians including US president Richard Nixon. The UC also funded the Korean Cultural Freedom Foundation, a non-profit organization that conducted a public diplomacy campaign for the Republic of Korea.

In 1977, the Church became the subject of a US Congressional investigation, led by Democratic congressman Donald Fraser of Minnesota. Fraser's subcommittee issued a 444-page congressional report that alleged Moonie involvement with bribery, bank fraud, illegal kickbacks and arms sales. The report concluded that Moon's

20,000-member Unification Church was the creation of the Korean Central Intelligence Agency (KCIA).

It was a charge UC leadership vigorously denied, citing the indisputable fact that the UC had actually been established before the KCIA. However, it was quite clear that the Church never would have grown as it did without the support of the KCIA—and one might add, the CIA, given that the American CIA was the agency primarily responsible for founding the KCIA. (It was also believed in some circles that the CIA had provided contacts and seed money for Moon's US businesses.)

The Congressional committee also investigated possible KCIA influence on the Unification Church's campaign in support of Nixon and charged that Moonies had been working with KCIA Director Kim Chong Phil as a political instrument to influence US foreign policy. UC leaders denied these accusations as well. The Fraser report described the Church as being "paramilitary" and "tightly controlled," and documented that Moon was "paid by the KCIA to stage demonstrations at the United Nations and run pro-South Korean propaganda campaigns."

An investigator for the Fraser committee summed up its findings by saying, "We determine that their [the Moonies'] primary interest, at least in the US at that time, was not religion at all but was political, it was an attempt to gain power, influence and authority."

Moon earned further notoriety in the so-called Koreagate scandal of 1976, which involved the KCIA allegedly funneling bribes and favors through a Korean businessman named Tongsun Park to influence policy. (The reversal of Nixon's decision to withdraw US troops stationed in South Korea is thought to have been one of their primary objectives.) Female followers of the Unification Church were accused of "entertaining" US congressmen at a Washington Hilton Hotel suite rented by the Moonies and keeping confidential files on those they "lobbied." The US Senate held hearings concerning Moon's "programmatic bribery of US officials, journalists and others as part of an operation by the KCIA to influence the course of US foreign policy."

Ignoring the devastating indictment, Moon went on to create

a multinational business empire of hotels, fishing fleets, weapons and a vast range of other products. He opened his checkbook to leading Republican politicians. In 1982, the Unification Church founded the daily newspaper the *Washington Times*, intended as a conservative counterweight to the liberal *Washington Post*. Moon's credentials soared in conservative circles. The Church had to subsidize the *Times*, which had one-seventh the circulation of the *Post*, to the tune of $40 million a year. The *Times* became President Ronald Reagan's paper of choice, while Reagan's vice president and successor in the White House, George H.W. Bush, gave it a ringing public endorsement as "an independent voice." Bush immediately saw the value of forging an alliance with the politically powerful Moon organization, an alliance that Moon would later claim made Bush president. (One former Moonie website claims that during the 1988 Bush–Dukakis battle for president, Reverend Moon told his followers that if the evil Dukakis won, they would be kicked out of the US.) It is well to keep in mind that Bush was Director of the Central Intelligence Agency from 1976 to 1980 and was more than familiar with the UC-KCIA-CIA-LDP alliance in Japan.

It was something to behold. The man accused of being a brainwasher and covert operative, had moved into the mainstream of Republican America, much as he had in Japan. Not even indictment and conviction in the United States for filing false federal income tax returns as well as for conspiracy—for which Moon served thirteen months in Danbury federal prison—seemed to affect him. After his prison sentence ended Moon officially conferred the title of "Messiah" on himself in 1992. In 1995, he gained further credibility when ex-president George Bush spent a week in Japan on behalf of a Moonie front organization, the Women's Federation for World Peace, founded and led by Moon's wife. He addressed a capacity crowd of fifty thousand in the Tokyo Dome stadium. Bush's payday was estimated to be in the millions of dollars.

The improbable political alliance between the Bushes and Reverend Moon paid off in early 2000 when George W. Bush faltered in early campaigning in the New Hampshire presidential primary. Moon's shadowy, cultish right-wing network came to his rescue reinforcing Bush's campaign with phone banks, radio ads and mailings enabling the younger Bush's victory. They repeated the favor in the South Carolina primary, helping to turn what looked like certain defeat into a double-digit victory.

According to the Free Press, "It was one of "the dirty little secrets of CIA involvement in US domestic politics."

Ultimately, it was Japan that was, and has always been, the biggest source of funds for the Unification Church. As mentioned earlier, the Church has long been known for coercing donations from Japanese individuals by making them feel guilty about Japan's treatment of Koreans during the years 1910–1945 when Korea was part of the Japanese empire and the citizenry was forbidden to speak their native language and reportedly subjected to other abuses.

According to Mitsuhiro Suganuma, the former high-ranking Japanese intelligence officer, quoted in the *Diplomat* magazine, "The Church gives Japanese believers a sermon that 'your descendants are suffering because your ancestors have committed so many sins. That's why you have to cancel the sin.'"

In 2022, the *Mainichi Shimbun* interviewed a former senior official of the Church who claimed that the religious organization had an annual "donations target" in Japan of around ¥30 billion (US$210 million) during the time he worked there, from 1998 to 2017. The collected funds not distributed to LDP politicians and other supporters in Japan were then transferred to South Korea where the Church's business interests, according to the *Financial Times*,"include ski, ocean and golf resorts, a construction group, a defense company, a chemicals group, an auto parts business and a newspaper."

All in all it was a remarkable confluence of interests—a political system based on CIA-LDP cooperation with the UC and KCIA, one that helped to inspire a term in Japan called *kozo oshoku* or structural corruption.

When Moon died in 2012, the Unification Church had millions of members around the globe, including several hundred thousand in Japan, mourn his passing.

YOSHIO KODAMA AND RYOCHI SASAKAWA

Two of the more remarkable figures in the unholy alliance described above were Yoshio Kodama, the larger than life right-winger, CIA bagman and landlord of the Latin Quarter dinner club, also known as godfather to Japan's yakuza bosses; and Ryoichi Sasakawa, an eccentric right-winger who was one of the wealthiest men in the world thanks to his motorboat racing monopoly.

Kodama's story has already been told in Chapter 2. Suffice it to add that he was tightly allied with Tokyo's ethnic Korean yakuza boss Hisayuki Machii and KCIA director Kim Chong Pil, the man who had brought about the downfall of the anti-Japanese South Korean leader Syngman Rhee and installed pro-Japanese Park Chung Hee into power, aligning himself with Moon.

Sasakawa had made his first fortune in the prewar era by speculating in rice markets and then established his own paramilitary force of fifteen thousand soldiers—with their own airport and twenty-two fighter planes—garbed in dark uniforms modeled on those of Italian dictator Benito Mussolini's blackshirts. Some of his soldiers served with Kodama in China, pillaging the countryside on behalf of the Tojo war cabinet. He once led his squadron of planes and pilots on a bizarre mission to Italy to meet Il Duce. Sasakawa later donated to the Japanese war effort and served in the Japanese parliament during the war and with the help of his men, made a small fortune in Shanghai. At war's end, he was ordered incarcerated by GHQ authorities at Sugamo Prison, where he was reunited with his longtime friend Kodama. Sasakawa had turned himself in by driving through the streets of Tokyo to Sugamo Prison accompanied by a brass band and shouting "Banzai!" while claiming he was offering himself in place of Emperor Hirohito.

Like Kodama, Sasakawa was released without going to trial after agreeing to help the GHQ fight the growing threat of Communism (although some American intelligence officers had warned against him, as they had with Kodama, regarding him as a security risk).

Upon his release in 1948, Sasakawa persuaded Japanese parliamentarians—with the help of some under-the-table donations—to pass a law allowing state operated motorboat racing and associated betting. The management and distribution of monies from this would be assigned to Sasakawa's Japan Shipbuilding Industry Foundation, an organization he had established to help rebuild the nation's shipbuilding industry. It was a body that eventually came to be known as the Nippon Foundation, with Sasakawa the chairman.

Sasakawa built twenty-four venues around Japan, designed as small moats with grandstands overlooking them, where drivers would race powerboats. Motorboat racing would make billions of dollars annually, with a tidy 3.3 percent commission going to various charities around the world, totaling more than $13 billion over the next thirty years.

"I am the world's richest fascist," Sasakawa liked to say.

Sasakawa, like Kodama, was a force in Japanese politics. He assisted Kodama in securing the election of Kishi's brother Eisaku Sato as prime minister in 1964, and helped Kakuei Tanaka defeat his Kodama-backed LDP rival Takeo Fukuda in the 1972 party and prime-ministerial elections.

Along with his friends authoritarian South Korean president Syngman Rhee and Chinese nationalist leader Chiang Kai-shek, Sasakawa helped found the Asian People's Anti-Communist League in 1954 and then helped create the World Anti-Communist League in 1966. He jogged with US president Jimmy Carter, dined with Elizabeth Taylor and established his own private army.

From the very beginning, both Sasakawa and Kodama were strong supporters of the Korea Unification Church. So why had two of the most powerful and influential figures in postwar Japan taken such an interest in an obscure, struggling Korea-based religious sect like the UC, back in its beginnings?

Middlebury professor Jeffrey M. Bale, in a lengthy 1991 article in the intelligence-oriented UK magazine *Lobster*, gave an answer:

In my opinion, the key lies [. . .] with the KCIA founder Jong-Pil Kim [. . .] Kim had established links with Moon even <u>before</u> the 1961 Park coup, and that following this [Park] coup—if not earlier—he had decided to covertly support the expansion of the UC in return for its provision of "cover" for various KCIA operations, both in South

Korea and the US. It is therefore entirely reasonable to suppose that he hoped to make similar use of the UC branch in Japan, which was at that time unable to make any real headway in recruiting followers.

One of the most problematic issues in postwar Asian reconstruction was the so-called normalization of South Korean–Japanese relations. The harsh and exploitative nature of Japanese colonial rule in Korea from 1910–1945 had led to bitter hostility between the two countries, which inhibited their ability to reestablish mutually beneficial political and economic relations after the war was over. These attitudes were exacerbated by both the unwillingness of Japanese leaders to acknowledge the destructive effects of their nation's occupation of Korea and [former president] Syngman Rhee's unshakable hatred and distrust of Japan, and were manifested in a series of squabbles over specific issues of interest to both countries, including the question of Japanese reparations for damages inflicted on Korea, the return of stolen Korean property, the controversy over the fishing boundary between the two nations, and the problem posed by the Koreans residing in Japan. Despite sporadic efforts to resolve these issues, no bilateral agreement could be reached as long as Rhee remained in power. Moreover, his intransigence undermined US efforts to create a regional anti-Communist alliance structure in Northeast Asia, whether formally, in the manner of NATO, or informally through "private" organizations like the Asian People's Anti-Communist League.

In 1963, newly installed South Korean president Park Chung Hee selected Jong-Pil Kim to initiate informal normalization talks in Japan with concerned figures, and Kim turned to Kodama who set up meetings with LDP bigwigs. Kim explained to Kodama that he was planning to use Moon's Church in Korea as cover for the KCIA and to help finance various anti-Communist political activities initiated by the agency. He suggested that the wirepullers Kodama and Sasakawa provide similar backing for the struggling UC branch in Japan.

Kodama and Kim, along with yakuza boss Hisayuki Machii, thus formed part of a secret cabal that met at the Akasaka penthouse of

wrestling icon (and ethnic Korean) Rikidozan with LDP and South
Korean officials to hammer out the 1965 peace treaty which nor-
malized relations between Japan and South Korea, and under which
Korea received $300 million from Japan, money which the cabal
helped spend. Machii subsequently took ownership of the Kampu
Ferry that ran between South Korea and Japan, and was a major
conduit for drugs.

When the KCIA decided to get rid of left-wing political activist
Kim Dae-Jung, on his way back from asylum in the USA to South
Korea to run for office, the agency outsourced the job to ethnic
Korean yakuza, who kidnapped him from a Tokyo hotel in 1973.
Only the last-minute intervention of the Americans saved Kim
from being tossed overboard from a ship in the Japan Sea. A Japa-
nese military helicopter was dispatched to hover over the vessel as it
made its way to the Korean Peninsula and ensure Kim's release. Kim
Dae-Jung later became the South Korean president.

The formation of the Asian People's Anti-Communist League,
a Korean-style anti-Communist movement operating under the
umbrella of the World Anti-Communist League (WACL), followed.
As well as furthering Moon's crusade, it lent the Japanese underworld—which both Kodama and Sasakawa were intimately familiar with—a respectable new facade. In 1970, Sasakawa helped fund
the Japanese branch of the WACL, Shokyo Rengo, which hosted
the Fourth WACL Conference in Tokyo, addressed by prominent
Japanese politicians, including Kishi and Sato. The Shokyo Rengo
remained active in the affairs of APACL and WACL for years.

"WACL and its lower level personnel have from the outset been
drawn primarily from the ranks of UC affiliated organizations," said
Bale. "They have provided the door-to-door political campaigning
and fund raising grunt work that the organization needed.

"Like the UC-KCIA-CIA-LDP connection, Moon's links to
WACL provide further evidence of his associations with an international nexus consisting of hardline intelligence personnel, gangsters, leading conservative politicians and far right extremists, many
of whom are in turn members of a bewildering variety of other 'private' anti-Communist organizations."

An investigative report in the Indian political magazine *Front-line* named Ryoichi Sasakawa as the key money source behind Moon's far-flung world religious and business empire.

POSTWAR RELIGIONS

The Unification Church was one of a number of new religious sects that sprang up in Japan after the Second World War, many of them Christian groups inspired by Douglas MacArthur's call for thousands of missionaries. This was something the GHQ head felt necessary to counter the moral decay that characterized Japan during the US Occupation, when the streets were flooded with *pan-pan* girls soliciting young American soldiers. Among the flood of ministers invading Japan were those proselytizing for Jehovah's Witnesses and the Mormons, to mention just two of the many groups.

Despite the influx of Christian missionaries, less than 1 percent of Japanese converted to Christianity. The vast majority of new religions that started after the war were Buddhist-related or Shinto-related sects, including the Reiyukai, the Rissho Kosei-kai and the Shinnyo-en, which focused on spiritual healing and social harmony.

The largest of the Japanese new religions was the Nichiren Buddhist Soka Gakkai which was actually founded in 1930 in Japan, but disbanded by the wartime government of Hideki Tojo, because of its anti-emperor and anti-Shinto platform. It expanded greatly during the postwar era reaching 750,000 members by 1958. Today, it claims the largest membership among all Nichiren Buddhist groups, with over 12 million followers, attracted by the religion's focus on inner peace achieved by rigorous chanting. It is estimated that up to 20 percent of the Japanese population belongs to a new religion.

Like the UC, the Soka Gakkai gradually became a major influence in politics, in the latter's case thanks to the religion's affiliation with the Komeito party, which it founded in 1964. The Komeito became aligned with the LDP and served as a junior partner in the coalition running the Japanese government.

Soka Gakkai founder and president Daisaku Ikeda was a charismatic leader who rose from a modest seaweed farming family to international fame as a religious educator, nuclear-disarmament advocate and political activist who openly cultivated political leaders like former LDP bigwig Ichiro Ozawa with huge donations. Ikeda was criticized for violating the separation of church and state and in 1991 was excommunicated by the Nichiren Shoshu Buddhist sect.

The Soka Gakkai and the UC shared certain similarities in that they have both solicited money from followers and increasingly sought political power. Moreover, both organizations have been heavily influenced by followers of Korean heritage but neither one could have survived without Japan and the money of its citizens—an ironic fact of life for those Koreans and Japanese who disliked each other—and there were many. It was a bittersweet irony.

The Soka Gakkai and Komeito have long pushed for voting rights for *zainichi* ethnic Koreans living in Japan, and this is part of the Komeito Party manifesto. Ikeda himself, reportedly a former UC member, is rumored to be zainichi.

Both groups have claimed they have no relation to each other, although there have been reports that Ikeda was sent by the UC to the Soka Gakkai to solidify political power through a Komeito-LDP alliance along with reports of UC members and "volunteers" supporting Komeito political campaigns via funding, donations and honey-trap operations.

"The UC claims to be Christian and has more of the globalist, cognoscenti appeal while the masses get more appeal from Buddhism," said former special ops agent Hiroki Allen. "Since both are Korean in nature, one could say the UC is the Genesis, the luxury brand of Hyundai and the SG is the Sonata of the same corporation. Same origin, different branding. The UC targets the wealthy like those who own homes or businesses, while the SG targets the lower-income classes to harvest their votes. You might say the UC is a business-class cult while SG is more like an economy-class cult.

Like the UC, the Soka Gakkai has its dark side. There have been charges of overaggressive recruiting, brainwashing and even reports that the Church invested its funds in the cocaine business in Manuel Noriega's Panama during the 1980s, donating much of the profits to the influential LDP politician and ally Ichiro Ozawa. The

Church had even constructed a Noriega Garden in Fujinomiya, near Mount Fuji, but it was destroyed shortly after news of Noriega's capture by US forces and imprisonment in Florida.

As a side note, former CIA director George H.W. Bush had actually worked with Noriega to disrupt Cuban Castro and Central American rebel groups such as those in Nicaragua, pretending not to notice Noriega's smuggling of cocaine into the United States. When Bush became president, however, that all changed. The US invaded Panama in December 1989. By January 1990 Noriega was in US custody and facing trial. Bush reportedly obtained evidence of drug connection between the Soka Gakkai and Noriega and used it to control Ozawa and fellow LDP power broker Shin Kanemaru, through US Ambassador to Japan Michael H. Armacost.

Over the years, the Soka Gakkai developed deep ties with giant Japanese advertising agency Dentsu; their logos, in fact, are similar. The SG has also had many adherents in Japan's entertainment industry, including actor Sonny Chiba, songstress Namie Amuro and singer Aska, who was arrested twice for drug use—drugs that were said to be supplied by the Soka Gakkai organization.

There were accusations that the Soka Gakkai was involved in the death of film director Juzo Itami in December 1996, when he fell from the roof of an apartment building, because Itami had been making an anti-Soka movie. On his desk was found a suicide note stating he had been falsely accused of an extramarital affair and was taking his life to clear his name. Two days later, a tabloid magazine published a report of such an affair. But no one in Itami's family believed the suicide note was written by him or that the story was true. In 2008, reporter Jake Adelstein stated that a member of the yakuza group the Goto-gumi had told him the group had murdered Itami by forcing him to jump as retribution for an anti-yakuza film he had made. Another explanation is that the Soka Gakkai had hired Goto soldiers to do the deed, as detailed on the Japanese news website Cherish, because of the intended anti-Soka film.

The same article mentioned the unsolved death of Yutaka Ozaki, a popular young singer who died in 1992 under mysterious circumstances. Ozaki's parents had both been Soka cultists and there were rumors that Ozaki was going to attack the group publicly. Ozaki, who was a drug addict, was found naked, drunk and unconscious in a Tokyo alleyway, dying hours later in a hospital.

However, the Soka Gakkai filed a lawsuit against the Cherish website, claiming that the allegations were groundless. In February 2009, Tokyo District Court accepted the claim of the plaintiff Soka Gakkai and ordered the defendant to pay damages of ¥800,000.

The Soka Gakkai was attacked in the book *I Denounce Soka Gakkai* (Nisshin Hodo, 1970) by Hirotatsu Fujiwara, in which the author accused it of dealing with Japanese yakuza.

Adherents of the Soka Gakkai outside Japan have included Chow Yun Fat, Orlando Bloom, Tina Turner, Patrick Swayze, Herbie Hancock. And Los Angeles Dodgers star outfielder Willie Davis.

Davis' religion became a point of contention when he spent a memorable year in Japan with the Chunichi Dragons in 1977. Davis was a serious longtime believer in Nichiren Buddhism and he chanted regularly, in the clubhouse, on the bench, riding on the team bus, in the team bath, on the road, at the hotel. No matter where the team was, he would pull out his beads and off he would go: *"Namu myoho renge-kyo, namu myho renge-kyo . . ."*

When not chanting himself, he would play tapes of it on his portable cassette tape recorder. His teammates couldn't stand it and begged the team captain to make him stop. "I thought everyone who heard this chant would feel peace and goodwill," said Davis. "Isn't Japan the birthplace of the Soka Gakkai? "

What Davis did not know was that such chanting was only heard at Buddhist funerals in Japan and that his teammates found it depressing to hear it nonstop. The following season Davis was sent to the Crown Lighter Lions of Fukuoka, a Pacific League backwater.

The UC and the Soka Gakkai have not been the only religious groups used by the CIA—it has also had quite a few Mormons in its ranks. In fact many observers have commented on the similarity between the Mormons and the Moonies. The CIA is said to prefer to recruit from the Latter Day Saints (LDS) Church possibly because Mormons, like the Moonies and the Soka followers, are conditioned to follow authoritative organizations. But there are also other reasons that LDS members would be attractive to the CIA. As the Mormon website MORMONR explained: "The LDS global missionary program regularly produces men and women who are fluent in another language and familiar with other cultures. Many members also have stable family relationships and a clear sense of personal and professional purpose. This makes them attractive recruits for government agencies."

The Moonies purchased a chapel in Washington, D.C. from the Mormons, so certain business ties between the two groups clearly did exist.

Some observers object to the UC classification as a religion and argue it is better described as a criminal syndicate disguised as an anti-Communist political tool run by extortionists and tax dodgers, in conjunction with corrupt politicians and bureaucrats. The so-called spiritual sales by the Unification Church and other groups, for example, have cost followers nearly a billion dollars and resulted in some 35,000 compensation claims since 1987, according to the National Network of Lawyers Against Spiritual Sales.

However you want to describe it, Reverend Moon's Unification Church certainly belongs in the pantheon of outsiders that have profoundly impacted the nation of Japan and the city of Tokyo. It has helped shape the political landscape of the country and has had its uses in combating Communism, given the often violent history of the Japanese Communist Party and its supporters in postwar Japan. Members of the Japanese Red Army, the East Asia Anti-Japan Armed Front and related radical far-left groups were all dedicated Communists and were responsible for a number of airline hijackings, bombings of Tokyo corporate headquarters and incidents like the Lod Airport massacre in Israel during the 1970s. Although such acts of violence were condemned and denied by the Japanese Communist Party, it is widely acknowledged that the perpetrators did in fact come from its ranks.

With help from the UC, the LDP has maintained power in Japan for nearly all of its existence. Shinzo Abe, Japan's longest serving prime minister at eight years and eight months, was, like his predecessors, living proof of the efficacy of the LDP alliance with the outsiders the CIA, the KCIA and the UC. Abe's government pushed an unabashedly pro-nationalist agenda, with new anti-terrorism laws limiting public protests, the muting of criticism of Japan's wartime excesses, and a sustained effort to revise Japan's constitution, which bans the maintenance of a standing army (Japan's Self-Defense Forces are already the eighth-largest military in the world). Abe pushed for legislation that permitted Japanese troops to fight overseas for the first time. As Japan legal expert Lawrence Repeta put it, the Abe administration achieved great success in expanding police power, passing legislation LDP leaders had sought for decades. They expanded wiretapping authority, formally recognized plea bargaining, expanded state secrecy powers and passed legislation creating the crime of "conspiracy."

"The Abe team did all this," Repeta said, "despite opposition from the bar associations, much of the news media and public intelligentsia and tens of thousands of protesters that repeatedly gathered before the Diet. This a tremendous record of achievement."

Such changes were just the kind of thing that Kishi, Kodama, Sasakawa, Kim Chong-Pil and the CIA would have applauded, although those on the left, like Repeta, did not approve of them at all.

In the end, irony of ironies, the former prime minister's relationship with the Church that helped keep him in power came back to haunt him—not to mention his party—as outrage over the cozy LDP–UC relationship mounted. The drip, drip, drip of revelations of the UC's deep political ties in the wake of Abe's death and the angry public testimony of hundreds of former UC members who lost their life savings through exorbitant donations demanded by the Church, eventually reached critical mass. In October 2023, the government of Japan, under Prime Minister Fumio Kishida, filed a request for a court order to revoke the religious corporation status of the Unification Church and essentially dissolve it. But the case faced years in the Japanese court system and what it would mean for the future of the UC in Japan, still a very wealthy entity, was by no means clear.

Afterword

A COMMON THREAD appearing and reappearing throughout this book is that of a Japan which remains suspicious of foreigners (with good reason in some cases) and rather biased about its own "uniqueness," albeit at the same time generally curious about the outside world and eager to be seen in a favorable light internationally. Japanese leaders, both government and corporate, have found a strange comfort in the rigidity of their ways, which renders them incapable of seeing the damage of what their treatment of foreign CEOs, for example, has wrought to their reputation, as well as the damage Japanese court cases involving gaijin criminals has done to the reputation of Japan's judicial system and global relations.

This feudal insularity remains in plain sight and makes the Japanese look rather as though they still live in the hermit kingdom they occupied when the Black Ships first forced open their gates at the end of the nineteenth century. Today, as of this writing, seventy years after the Occupation ended, the average Japanese, highly educated and literate though they may be, cannot access news unfolding in real time online because their English is not good enough. Worse yet is the abysmal foreign language ability of most of the country's leaders in government, business and other fields.

One wonders whatever happened to the seeds of entrepreneurship that produced world-renowned titans like Sony and Honda in the 1950s and 1960s and put Japan on technology's cutting edge?

The country's blue-chip manufacturers, which had a brief foray into pioneering technology, have now been replaced by purveyors of the government's "Cool Japan" strategy. The nation is now the world's favorite tourist destination, and its biggest growth sectors are anime, game software and related products such as movies, and game music—a phenomenon described in detail by Matt Alt in his classic book *Pure Invention* (Crown, 2021). It is worthy of mention that the public has played the biggest role in making these into some of the world's leading industries, without too much government or corporate leadership.

Japan still bears the virtues which helped the world fall in love with it at the 1964 Olympics—low crime, orderliness, cleanliness and politeness—as well as low incidence of Coronavirus in the Covid era. The nation's leaders, on the other hand, are ironically, increasingly out of touch with the world, and, unfortunately, too often corrupt, as we have seen in these pages.

Japan may be number one in the world in efficient train and subway systems, safety, Michelin-starred restaurants, fashion and global Fortune 500 headquarters. It is regarded in many surveys as the most livable place on earth. But it is sinking in other, equally important, rankings.

The comfort zone for wirepuller Shinzo Abe, during his decade-long reign as prime minister, and his LDP cronies, was a nation that was NOT well informed, and NOT English speaking . . . just like the last days of the shogunate! The inability to assess the character and motivations of visitors from abroad has always provided fertile territory for shady operators.

The results, as this book has shown, have not often been pretty.

Sources and Further Reading

My sources for this book are a combination of direct interviews I conducted with protagonists; friends and acquaintances of protagonists; and journalists; and information taken from books, newspapers, magazines and websites. The key sources are listed below, for anyone who wishes to do any further reading. The details of many of the publications I referred to during the writing of this book are given in the relevant chapter text. Further questions regarding sources can be addressed to the author at whiting.robert@gmail.com.

CHAPTER 1: The Canon Agency

Interviewees: Alonzo Shattuck, Victor Matsui

English-language articles

Esselstrom, Erik. "From Wartime Friend to ColdWar Fiend." *Journal of Cold War Studies*, Vol. 17. No.3 (Summer 2015.)

Whiting, Robert. "Inside story of US black ops in post-war Japan." *Asia Times*, August 19, 2020. asiatimes.com/2020/08/inside-story-of-us-black-ops-in-post-war-japan/

Japanese-language books

Inomata, Kozo. *Dokusen gun no hanzai* [Occupation army crimes], Tosho Shuppan, 1979.

Kimura, Katsumi. *Shishaku fujin Torio Tsuruyo* [Viscountess Torio Tsuruyo], Tachikaze, 1991.

Tachibana, Kagari. *Kodo no koi. "GHQ no onna" to yobarete koshaku fujin* [Scorched-earth love: the viscountess known as "the GHQ woman."]. Shodensha, 2011.

CHAPTER 2: Soldiers of Fortune

Interviewees and sources: Doctor Eugene Aksenoff; artist Frances Baker; lawyer Thomas Blakemore; club manager Jim Blessin; attorney Raymond Bushell; *Stars & Stripes* librarian Toshi Cooper; journalists Donald Richie and Rekichi Sumiya; and black marketeer Nick Zappetti. The Johnny Wetzstein story came from longtime Japan-based newspaperman Corky Alexander and Nick Zappetti.

Descriptions of Wally Gayda and the Golden Gate came from friends and acquaintances Corky Alexander, Jack Howard, Vince Acurso, attorney-at-law Tsuyoshi Fukuda, promoter Steve Parker, show agent Dan Sawyer, Al Shattuck and journalist Donald Richie. Also interviewed was Rosa Roal, who was briefly married to Wally.

Descriptions of Club Mandarin and Club Cherry from Jack Dinken and Jim Blessin. Donald Richie recounted his tale of an evening out with Ava Gardner in Yoshiwara and Asakusa in an interview with the author.

Ted Lewin's wartime experiences were related to me by Al Shattuck and Jack Howard who heard them from Lewin and from contemporaries of Lewin. Lester Tenney, fellow POW with Lewin at Omuta provided the author with his account in an interview.

Tokyo lawyer Raymond Bushell, an acquaintance of Lewin, also gave information, as did Dr. Eugene Aksenoff, aircraft consultant Jim Phillips, film producer Steve Parker, and Dan Sawyer.

Manila-based businesswomen Bobby Greenwood and Nina Avancena also added perspective on Lewin, whom they both met in the Philippines. The military scrip counterfeiting tale appeared in Joseph Burkholder Smith's *Portrait of a Cold Warrior*, p.285. I also interviewed the grandson of Filipino Vice President Lopez, the boy Lewin kidnapped and brought back to Manila in 1952, fifty years later. He still remembers "Uncle Ted" fondly.

Lewin was discussed in Hidehiko Ushijima's book *Mo hitotsu no Showa-shi* [Another Showa history], unknown binding, 1978, pp. 224–228 and Shinsuke Itagaki's book *Kono jiyuto* [This Liberal Party], Genronsha, 1952, Volume 2, pp. 214–215. Lewin's association with the FBI in Tokyo is related in Itagaki's book, pps. 214–15.

The private casino in the Latin Quarter and the origins of Al Shattuck's relationship with Lewin are discussed in music promoter Jiro Uchino's book *Yume no warutsu* [Waltz of dreams], Kodansha, 1997, pp. 74-80.

The bugging of Lewin's penthouse apartment in the Shellburne hotel was described in Joseph Burkholder Smith's *Portrait of a Cold Warrior*, p. 295. Lewin's activities as a courier for the CIA were described in Kozo Inomata's book *Dokusen gun no hanzai* [Occupation army crimes], page 287.

The activities of the infamous Yoshio Kodama have been described in a wealth of magazine articles and books. Foremost among them is *Kodama Yoshio to wa nani ka?* [What is Yoshio Kodama?] in monthly magazine *Bungei Shunju*, May 1976, pps. 94-130. Also informative is a 4-part weekly series beginning in the April 15, 1976 issue of the weekly *Shukan Bunshun* and entitled *CIA to Yoshio Kodama* [Yoshio Kodama and the CIA].

Dan Sawyer provided information on the Tradewinds. Dr. Eugene Aksenoff provided information about Jason Lee, whom he treated for a gunshot wound. Jason Arcaro has written a screenplay about Jason Lee's life, having extensively researched it.

English-language articles

Fujita, Shig. "Recollection of Tokyo Night Life in the Days of Few but Elite Clubs." Asahi Evening News, November 30, 1976.

"The Plug Ugly American" [about Ted Lewin]. *TIME* magazine, December 21, 1959.

Tominomori, Eiji. "The Endemic Roots of Corruption." Asahi Evening News, March 17, 1976.

Japanese-language articles

Gaikokujin makaritoru [The foreigners have their own way]. *Shukan Yomiuri* magazine, October 10, 1954, pp. 4-11.

Kurabu mandarin [Club Mandarin]. *Asahi Shimbun*, July 18, 1953

English-language books

Brines, Russell. *MacArthur's Japan*. Lippincott, 1948.

Burkholder Smith, Joseph. *Portrait of a Cold Warrior*. G. P. Putnam's Sons, 1976

Dawes, Gavan. *Prisoners of the Japanese*. William Morrow Paperbacks, 1996.

Gayn, Mark. *Japan Diary*. Tuttle, 1989.

Tenney, Lester I. *My Hitch in Hell: The Bataan Death Marches*. Potomac Books, Inc., 2000.

CHAPTER 3: The Girard and Quackenbush Killings
English-language articles

Mann, David. "Eisenhower Weighed Asia Pullout in '50s, Files Show." *Los Angeles Times*, September 23, 1991. latimes.com/archives/la-xpm-1991-09-23-mn-2050-story.html

Japanese-language articles

Girado hanketsu to futari no josei [Two women and the Girard verdict]. *Shukan Josei* magazine, December 8, 1957, pp. 22–23.

Ichiman yonsen ken: Akahata, hyoron tokushu-ban, beigunjin no hanzai tokei [14,000 infractions: Statistics on crime by American soldiers]. October 30, 1995 (based on material provided by the Japan Self Defense Force Headquarters and the National Police Agency)

Nihon josei wo koroshita beihei girado ni totsuide 10 nen, ima . . ." [The woman who was married for ten years to the American soldier Girard, killer of a Japanese woman, is now . . .]. *Yangu reidi* [Young lady] magazine November 27, 1967, pps. 38–40.

CHAPTER 4: Elint Agents
English-language articles
"Heroin Dens." *Nippon Times*, November 5, 1953.
Mitchell, Jon. "Okinawa's first nuclear missile men break silence." *The Japan Times*, July 8, 2012. japantimes.co.jp/life/2012/07/08/general/okinawas-first-nuclear-missile-men-break-silence/
Whiting, Robert. "The U-2 spy plane: white knuckles from the get-go." *Asia Times*, January 22, 2022. asiatimes.com/2022/01/the-u-2-spy-plane-white-knuckles-from-the-get-go/

English-language books
Pocock, Chris. *The Black Bats: CIA Spy Flights over China from Taiwan.* Schiffer Military History, 2010.

CHAPTER 5: Saints
Interviewees: Eugene Aksenoff, Ray Bushell, Frances and Thomas Blakemore, Rosser Brockman and Yin-Wah-Ma Brockman.

Online sources
www.blakemorefoundation.org/
en.wikipedia.org/wiki/Frances_Blakemore
en.wikipedia.org/wiki/Thomas_Blakemore
wolfhoundpack.org/wolfhounds-and-the-holy-family-home/

CHAPTER 6: Con Artists
Interviews and sources: Mr. T is a pseudonym for an individual described by Richard Roa.

The Donald Zubriskie story was reported in several dispatches in the *Asahi Shimbun*, see below.

The Howard Baron episode was related by business acquaintances Steve Parker, Vince Acurso and Dick Bush, the latter of whom was Tokyo American Club president at the time of Baron's schemes.

Descriptions of Yokota Air Base, IOS and sales environment of the late '60s and early '70s from

my Tokyo contemporaries Martin P. Steinberg, Richard Roa, Dick Bush.

Eric Drew associate Eugene Aksenoff provided extra material in addition to newspaper sources below as well as did an unnamed participant held for police questioning in the affair, who wishes to remain anonymous.

Eric Money is a pseudonym.

The Persian restaurant episode about Mages was taken from interviews with reluctant business associate and eyewitness Richard Roa.

In addition to the articles about Craig Spence listed below, information came from interviews with Spence acquaintances Murray Sayle, Dwight Spenser and an interview with Spence by author. Sayle, a noted Japan-based Australian journalist who first met Spence in Saigon during the Vietnam War wrote Spence's obituary in the February issue of the Foreign Correspondents Press Club of Japan newsletter, *The No. 1 Shimbun*.

English-language articles
Muscatine, Alison and Caryle Murphy. "KGB Defector Wages War Against Soviet System." *The Washington Post*, May 29, 1983. washingtonpost.com/archive/politics/1983/05/29/kgb-defector-wages-war-against-soviet-system/731ef1ca-62d5-4ed4-a44f-a42d1b94c8a5/

English-language books
Tarpley, Webster G., and Anton Chaitkin. *George Bush: The Unauthorized Biography."* Progressive Press, 2004.

Sources for the stories of Stanislav Levchenko and Viktor Belenko:
Barron, John. *KGB Today: The Hidden Hand.* Berkley, 1985.
Brook-Shepherd, Gordon. *The Storm Birds: Soviet Post-War Defectors.* Henry Holt, 1989.
Laffin, John. *Brassey's Book of Espionage.* Potomac Books Inc., 1997.

Sources for the Donald Zubriskie story
Ginza de kogite sagi [Check scam on the Ginza]. *Asahi Shimbun*, May 23, 1967.
Zubriskie taiho [Zubriskie arrested]. *Asahi Shimbun*, May 24, 1967.
Arate no sa waza [New riddles arise]. *Asahi Shimbun*, May 25, 1967.

Kogite wa gizo to dantei [Fake checks confirmed]. *Asahi Shimbun*, May 26, 1967.

Yakekuso 25 ken [25 desperate incidents]. *Asahi Shimbun*, July 6, 1967.

Sagi mitome, gizo wo kyohi [Admits scam, denies forgery]. *Asahi Shimbun*, July 6, 1967.

Sources for the Eric Drew story

Roshiya jin ni nagasu [Flushing out the Russian]. *Asahi Shimbun*, October 24, 1976.

Hawaii beigun kara mo? [From an American soldier in Hawaii too?]. *Asahi Shimbun*, October 26, 1976.

Kokuritsu dai kyoju mo kankei [National university professor involved as well]. *Asahi Shimbun*, November 5, 1976.

Source for the Donald Mages story

Yon sen go hyaku man yen sagi [450 million yen scam]. *Asahi Shimbun*, March 4, 1986.

Source for the Genevieve de Vilmorin story

Sherman, Anne and E.H. Lunn. "Tale of Three Hucksters." *Tokyo Journal*, Feb 2, 1992.

Sources for the Craig Spence story

Hedges, Michael and Jerry Seper. "Power Broker Served Drugs, Sex at Parties Primed For Blackmail." *Washington Times*, June 29, 1989.

Dedman, Bill. "White House Guard Says He Accepted Watch; Lobbyist Asked Him To Intervene In Drunken-Driving Arrest." *Washington Post*, July 12, 1989.

Mintz, John, Martha Sherrill and Elsa Walsh. "The Shadow World of Craig Spence." *Washington Post*, July 18, 1989.

Carlson, Margaret. "Washington's Man From Nowhere." *TIME* magazine, July 24, 1989.

Randolph, Eleanor. "The Bombshell That Didn't Explode. Behind The Times's 'Scoop' And Press Coverage Of The Call Boy Ring." *Washington Post*, August 1, 1989.

Hedges, Michael and Jerry Seper. "Spence Arrested in New York; Bizarre Interview is No Night on Town." *Washington Times*, August 8, 1989.

Dedman, Bill. "Spence Faces Drug, Weapon Charges After Being Found in New York Hotel." *Washington Post*, August 9, 1989.

Hedges, Michael and Jerry Seper. "Spence Arrested in New York; Once Host to Powerful reduced to Sleeping in Park." *Washington Times*, August 9, 1989.

Weil, Martin. "Craig Spence, Figure In D.C. Sex Case, Found Dead in Boston." *Washington Post*, November 12, 1989.

Hedges, Michael and Jerry Seper. "In Death Spence Stayed True To Form." *Washington Times*, November 13, 1989.

Sherman, Anne and E.H. Lunn. "Tale of Three Hucksters." *Tokyo Journal*, Feb 2, 1992.

CHAPTER 7: Danny's Inn

Interviews and sources: Rick Roa, who bartended at Danny's. Working next door, I often went there myself and saw firsthand the goings on and heard all the stories, as did my coworker Dwight Spenser.

Japanese-language article

San men kyo [Three-sided mirror]. *Asashi Shimbun*, November 11, 1978.

CHAPTER 8: The Sadaharu Oh Story

Interviewees: Sadaharu Oh, Warren Cromartie, Shigeo Nagashima, Hiroshi Gondo, Yutaka Enatsu, Masayuki Tamaki, Gene Bacque, Daryl Spencer, Clete Boyer, Davey Johnson, Tuffy Rhodes, Kozo Abe, Randy Bass, Keith Comstock, Peter Daniel Miller, Itaru Kobayashi, Clyde Wright.

English-language articles

Whiting, Robert. "The Emperor of Swat." *New York Times*, Aug. 9, 2007.

Whiting, Robert. "Devoted to the game: Looking back at Oh's career." *The Japan Times*, October 29, 2008. japantimes.co.jp/sports/2008/10/29/baseball/japanese-baseball/devoted-to-the-game-looking-back-at-ohs-career/

Whiting, Robert. "Hank Aaron, US baseball legend, and great friend of Japanese rival Sadaharu Oh." *Nikkei Asia*, January 25, 2021. asia.nikkei.com/Life-Arts/Obituaries/Hank-Aaron-US-baseball-legend-and-great-friend-of-Japanese-rival-Sadaharu-Oh

Japanese-language article

Kyojin retsuden [Yomiuri Giants biographies]. *Takarajima* magazine, October 1, 1991.

Japanese-language book

Saito, Takashi. *Oh Sadaharu ni manabu nihon jin no ikikata* [What the Japanese can learn about how to live from Sadaharu Oh]. NHK Shuppan, 2009.

CHAPTER 9: Hostesses

Interviewees: Richard Roa, Maggie, Al Stamp, Joe Suzuki, Nick Zappetti, Greg Davis, Mark Schreiber, Jack Stamm, Tom Scully, Fraser Steele, Charlie Manuel.

English-language articles and reports

French, Howard. "Vanishing Havens of the High and Mighty." *New York Times*, May 5, 2001.

Human Rights Watch. "OWED JUSTICE. Thai Women Trafficked into Debt Bondage in Japan," © September 2000. hrw.org/reports/2000/japan/

Human Rights Watch. "World Report, 2023, Japan." hrw.org/world-report/2023/country-chapters/Japan

"Japan Lax on Human Trafficking, Says U.S." *Kyodo News Service*, July 13, 2001.

Wright, Evan Alan. "Death in Japan." *TIME* magazine, May 14, 2001.

U.S. Department of State. "2023 Trafficking in Persons Report: Japan"

Japanese-language articles

Thai josei kyuzo, ura no soshiki [The organization behind the sudden increase in Thai women]. *Asahi Shimbun*, July 5, 1988.

Rushi no Obara to saigo no hibi [Lucie's last days with Obara]. *Shukan Post*, March 2, 2001.

CHAPTER 10: Gaijin Yakuza

Interviewees: Smoky, Nick Zappetti, Patricia Zappetti, Joji Abe, Eugene Aksenoff, Clark Frogley (FBI), Jiro Numata (Sumiyoshi rengo-kai), Garron Elder, Benjamin Fulford, Velisarious Kattoulas, Raiusuke Miwyaki, Manabu Miyazaki, Richard Nagao, Grant Newsham, Misao Takahashi (Nat. Police Agency)

English-language articles and reports

Japanese National Police Agency. "The White Paper on Police 2021." npa.go.jp/english/publication/hakusyo2021.html

Milhaupt, Curtis J. and Mark D. West. "The Dark Side of Private Ordering: an Institutional and Empirical Crime." *University of Chicago Law Review*, Winter 2000.

"More Foreigners Join Japanese Yakuza." *Asahi Evening News*, August 17, 1991.

"More Japanese gambling online, many unaware that it's illegal." *Asahi Shimbun*, February 20, 2021. asahi.com/ajw/articles/14172844

Japanese-language book

Ando, Noboru. *Jiden* [Autobiography]. Bunkasha, 2001.

Ino, Kenji. *Yakuza to nihonjin* [Yakuza and the Japanese]. Chikuma Bunko, 1999.

Ninkyo dai hyakka [Great encyclopedia of chivalry]. Ninkyo Kenkyukai, 1986.

CHAPTER 11: Gaijin CEOs

Interviewees: Andrew Horvat, Peter Tasker, Greg Kelly, Roger Schreffler, Peter Daniel Miller, Mari Iida, Grant Newsham, Steven Givens, Tatsuo Ninoseki, Daisuke Fujiwara, Joe Schmelzeis, Mitch Murata.

English-language articles and reports

Givens, Stephen. "Greg Kelly is found seven-eighths innocent." *Nikkei Asia*, March 4, 2022. asia.nikkei.com/Opinion/Greg-Kelly-is-found-seven-eighths-innocent

Greimel, Hans. "Nissan's Saikawa praises ex-boss Ghosn during trial." *Automotive News*, March 1, 2021. archive.is/uVfuj

Lippert, John. "Prior To Carlos Ghosn's Daring Escape, His Wife Talked Of Japan's 'Fake Democracy.'" Forbes, January 3, 2020. forbes.com/sites/johnlippert/2020/01/03/prior-to-carlos-ghosns-daring-escape-his-wife-talked-of-japans-fake-democracy/?sh=740b6f991e65

Muller, Joann. "The Impatient Mr. Ghosn." *Forbes*, May 12, 2006.

Newsham, Grant. "Yakuza: A Tough Mess To Clean Up." *The Asia Times*, December 5, 2020. asiatimes.com/2020/12/yakuza-a-tough-mess-to-clean-up/

Schreffler, Roger. "Ghosn case puts Japan's 'hostage justice' on trial." *Asia Times*, March 30, 2021. asiatimes.com/2021/03/ghosn-case-puts-japans-hostage-justice-on-trial/

Schreffler, Roger. "Documents blow Nissan's Kelly case to smithereens." *Asia Times*, January 3, 2022. asiatimes.com/2022/01/making-the-case-that-nissans-kelly-is-innocent/

Schreffler, Roger. "Nissan coup: Pulling back more curtain on Kelly's trial." *Asia Times*, May 23, 2022. asiatimes.com/2022/05/hold-brad-pulling-back-more-curtain-shiga-confesses/

Schreffler, Roger. "Former Nissan executive Greg Kelly sums up ordeal." *Asia Times*, June 20, 2022. asiatimes.com/2022/06/former-nissan-execu-tive-greg-kelly-sums-up-ordeal/

"SEC Charges Nissan, Former CEO, and Former Director with Fraudulently Concealing from Investors More Than $140 Million of Compensation and Retirement Benefits." Litigation Release No. 24606 / September 23, 2019. Accounting and Auditing Release No. 4088 / September 23, 2019. *Securities and Exchange Commission v. Carlos Ghosn and Gregory L. Kelly*, No. 1:19-civ-08798 (S.D.N.Y. filed September 23, 2019). sec.gov/lit-igation/litreleases/lr-24606. Stevenson, Reed. "How a Powerful Nissan Insider Tore Apart Carlos Ghosn's Legacy." *Bloomberg*, August 28, 2020.

Sugiyama, Satoshi. "Takedown: The monu-mental fall of auto titan Carlos Ghosn." *The Japan Times*, November 18, 2019. japantimes. co.jp/news/2019/11/18/business/nissan-car-los-ghosn-scandal-anniversary/

Tasker, Peter. "Olympus epic is less Hollywood and more samurai." *The Financial Times*, November 25, 2011. ft.com/content/54dff8b0-15f2-11e1-a691-00144feabdc0

Japanese-language articles

Nissan 'Ghosn kainin keikaku' gokuhi bunsho o nyushu [Nissan obtains confidential docu-ments regarding Ghosn's dismissal plan]. *TV Tokyo*, January 14, 2021. txbiz.tv-tokyo.co.jp/wbs/feature/218804

Yamaguchi, Yoshimasa. "*Orinpasu: Mubo M&A kyo-gaku sonshitsu no kai.*" [Olympus: reckless M&A causes huge losses], *FACTA*, July 26, 2011 facta. co.jp/article/201108021.html

English-language books

Ghosn, Carlos and Philippe Riès. *Broken Alliances: Inside the Rise and Fall of a Global Automotive Empire*. Tanooki Press, 2021.

Kostov, Nick and Sean McLain. *Boundless: The Rise, Fall, and Escape of Carlos Ghosn*. Harper Business, 2022.

CHAPTER 12: Valentine's Way
Parts of this chapter are sourced from my inter-view with Ryuji Suzuki in August 1980 for my book *You Gotta Have Wa*. Other interviewees include Bobby Valentine, Mitch Murata, Larry Rocca, Don Blasingame, Wally Yonamine, Akio Shigemitsu, Trey Hillman, Declan O'Connell, Toru Takagi, Jim Allen, Jack Gallagher. Also Joe Lutz, Marty Kueh-nert, Jim Lyttle, Shigeo Araki, Itaru Kobayashi, Peter Miller, Rob Smaal, Ira Stevens, Michael Westbay.

English-language articles

Ballard, Chris. "Bobby V's Super Terrific Happy Hour." *Sports Illustrated*, November 8, 2007.

"Does Everybody Hate Bobby Valentine?" *The Sporting News*, September 27, 1999.

French, Howard. "BASEBALL; Japanese Are Playing Favorites." *New York Times*, September 15, 2001.

Kepner, Tyler. "Bobby Valentine, the American Tsu-nami." *New York Times*, March 4, 2007.

"The 50 Greatest Sports Figures From Connecticut." *Sports Illustrated*, December 27, 1999.

Wallace, Bruce. "A Made Man in Japan." *The Los Angeles Times*, November 1, 2005. latimes.com/archives/la-xpm-2005-nov-01-sp-valentine1-story.html

Whiting, Robert. "Open Mind Key to Hillman's Suc-cess." *The Japan Times*, May 31, 2009. (First of two parts)

Whiting, Robert. "Clandestine campaign led to Valentine's demise." *The Japan Times*, January 17, 2010. japantimes.co.jp/sports/2010/01/17/baseball/japanese-baseball/clandestine-cam-paign-led-to-valentines-demise/

Whiting, Robert. "Valentine's philosophy brought Marines glory, money." *The Japan Times*, January 24, 2010. japantimes.co.jp/sports/2010/01/24/baseball/valentines-philosophy-brought-ma-rines-glory-money/

Whiting, Robert. "Resentment of Valentine's power factored in downfall." *The Japan Times*, January 31, 2010. japantimes.co.jp/sports/2010/01/31/baseball/resentment-of-valentines-power-fac-tored-in-downfall/

Whiting, Robert. "History, tradition, helped to undermine Valentine." *The Japan Times*, February 7, 2010. japantimes.co.jp/sports/2010/02/07/baseball/history-tradition-helped-to-undermine-valentine/

Japanese-language source
Internal Memo [*jijiroku*] from Chiba Lotte Marines executive meeting chaired by team president Ryozo Setoyama, April 7, 2009. Referenced here: s03.megalodon.jp/2009-0929-1048-14/ameblo.jp/mvp-ishida/entry-10353033863.html

English-language book
Valentine, Bobby and Peter Golenbock. *Valentine's Way: My Adventurous Life and Times*. Permuted Press, 2021.

CHAPTER 13: The Bitcoin Crimes
Interviewees: Jake Adelstein, Leo Lewis, Hiroki Allen, Grant Newsham, Andrew Lawson.

English-language articles and reports
Bechtol Bruce, E., Jr., "North Korean Illicit Activities and Sanctions: A National Security Dilemna," Cornell International Law Journal, Vol 51, No. 1. (2018) scholarship.law.cornell.edu/cilj/vol51/iss1/2/
Butler, Gavin. "Candyland: The Secret Life of a Tokyo Coke Baron." *Vice.com*, May 19, 2022. vice.com/en/article/qjb7nd/the-secret-life-of-a-tokyo-coke-dealer?utm_source=reddit.com
"Cocaine spread in Roppongi," *Sankei News*, October 3, 2017.
Gollom, Mark. "Drugs, counterfeiting: How North Korea survives on proceeds of Crime," *CBC News*, December 8, 2017. cbc.ca/news/world/north-korea-criminal-empire-drugs-trafficking-1.4435265
Japan National Character Institute Survey, 1988. ism.ac.jp/kokuminsei/en/table/data/html/ss9/9_14/9_14_19882.htm
Japan National Character Institute Survey, 2013 ism.ac.jp/kokuminsei/en/table/data/html/ss9/9_14/9_14_20132.htm
"Karpeles: Bitcoin baron brought down with a bump," *phys.org*, March 13, 2019. phys.org/news/2019-03-karpeles-bitcoin-baron-brought.html
Karpelès Court Transcript: docketbird.com/court-documents/Greene-v-Karpeles-et-al/

REPLY-by-Defendant-Mark-Karpeles-in-Support-of-His-Rule-37-Motion-to-Strike-and-Exclude-Exhibits-D-and-G-to-Plaintiff-s-Motion-for-Class-Certification/ilnd-1:2014-cv-01437-00533
"Sony's CEO Hosts Corporate Strategy Meeting Conference Call for Overseas Investors (Transcript)," *The Street*, April 12, 2012. thestreet.com/story/11493575/1/sonys-ceo-hosts-corporate-strategy-meeting-conference-call-for-overseas-investors-transcript.html
"Tokyo cops nab British national in bitcoin sales of cocaine in Roppongi," *Tokyo Reporter*, September 26, 2017.

CHAPTER 14: The Korean Taxi Barons
Interviewees: Masaaki Aoki, David Shin, Masashi Kikuchi, Tasuku Matsuo, Hisanori Kimura, Kyomi Matsubara, Masaharu Aoki, Takashi Naito, Masahiro Matsuya, multiple MK Taxi and sister company employees.

English-language articles
McAfee, Andrew, "MK Taxi: Private Chauffeur Service." Harvard Business Publishing, August 25, 2004.
"Trashing Tradition: Some Maverick Firms in Japan Are Changing Its Business Climate." *Wall Street Journal*, April 29, 1994.

Japanese-language articles and reports
Kigyo Rankingu [Business rankings]. *President* magazine, September 14, 2015.
"Minutes of the 171st National Diet, Land, Infrastructure, Transport and Tourism Committee No. 23." June 9, 2021. shugiin.go.jp/internet/itdb_kaigirokua.nsf/html/kaigirokua/009917120090609023.htm
MK takushi Tokyo Emukei shacho (cho) pawahara & keri renpatsu de mata haiso shogeki shashin [MK Taxi Tokyo MK president (super) loses case again due to power harassment and repeated kicks, shocking photos]. *Friday* magazine, March 23, 2015 friday.gold/article/47790
Tokyo MK shacho Yu Chan Wan/Aoki Masaaki yogisha no hansei naki "boryoku jinsei" [Tokyo MK President Yu Chang Wan/Masaaki Aoki: Suspect's "Violent Life" Without Reflection]. Shukan Shincho magazine, December 23, 2017. dailyshincho.jp/article/2017/12231600/

Japanese-language books

Kato, Katsumi. *MK no kiseki* [The MK miracle]. JATEC, Tokyo,1985

Kato, Katsumi. *MK Taxi no takushi kakumei* [The MK taxi revolution]. Toyo Keizai, 1994.

Nakamura, Kenji and Koichi Noguchi. *Hai, MK Taxi no Aoki Sadao desu* [Yes, I'm Sadao Aoki of MK Taxi]. Diamond-sha, 2004.

CHAPTER15: The Moonies
English-language articles and reports

Bale, Dr. Jeffery M. "The Unification Church and the KCIA –'Privatizing' covert action: the case of the UC." howwelldoyouknowyourmoon.tumblr. com/post/147695217233/the-unification-church-and-the-kcia

Davies, Christian and Song Jung-a. "Church or cult? Inside the Moonies' 'world of delusion.'" *Financial Times*, July 16, 2022.

Fitrakis, Bob. "Reverend Moon: Cult leader, CIA asset and Bush family friend." *Scoop*, September 5, 2012. scoop.co.nz/stories/HL1209/S00029/reverend-moon-cult-leader-cia-asset-and-bush-family-friend.htm

Isikoff, Michael. "Church Spends Millions On Its Image." *The Washington Post*, September 17, 1984. washingtonpost.com/wp-srv/national/longterm/cult/unification/image.htm

Kingston, Jeff. "Shinzo Abe is gone, but his controversial vision for Japan lives on." *The Guardian*, July 12, 2022. theguardian.com/commentisfree/2022/jul/12/shinzo-abe-controversial-vision-japan-constitution?CMP=Share_iOSApp_Other

"Koreagate," *Wikipedia*. wikipedia.org/wiki/Koreagate

"Korean yakuza Daisaku Ikeda's SGI/Komeito amassed wealth & power via organized crime, political corruption, illegal drugs, money-laundering, N. Korea, & Bush's CIA. (part 3)" *reddit*. reddit.com/r/sgiwhistleblowers/comments/4925jo/korean_yakuza_daisaku_ikedas_sgikomeito_amassed/

Kyodo. "At least 20 deputies of Japan Cabinet ministers found to have ties to Unification Church." *The Japan Times*, August 13, 2022. japantimes.co.jp/news/2022/08/13/national/politics-diplomacy/kishida-unification-church-vice-ministers/

Kyodo. "At least 146 LDP lawmakers have had dealings with Unification Church." *Japan Today*, September 4, 2022. japantoday.com/category/politics/at-least-146-ldp-lawmakers-had-deal-ings-with-unification-church

"Let's talk about that persistent rumor that Ikeda is of Korean ancestry." *reddit*. reddit.com/r/sgi-whistleblowers/comments/fh3jhn/lets_talk_about_that_persistent_rumor_that_ikeda/

"Maybe joining the SGI was a mistake." *reddit*. reddit.com/r/sgiwhistleblowers/comments/x4otse/maybe_joining_the_sgi_was_a_mistake/

McGill, Peter. "The Dark Shadow Cast by Moon Sun Myung's Unification Church and Abe Shinzo." *The Asia-Pacific Journal*, October 15, 2022. apjjf.org/2022/17/McGill.html

Penn, Michael. "Unification Church and Freedom of Religion." *Shingetsu News Agency*, September 15, 2022.

Samuels, Richard. "Kishi and Corruption: An Anatomy of the 1955 System." Japan Policy Research Institute working paper, 2001.

Saner, Emine. "I Was A Moonie Cult Leader." *The Guardian*, September 3, 2012. theguardian.com/world/2012/sep/03/moonie-cult-leader.

Schreiber, Mark. "Weeklies take a look at faiths, (misplaced) hopes and charities." *The Japan Times*, May 6, 2012.

Takahashi, Kosuke. "The LDP's Tangled Ties to the Unification Church." *The Diplomat*, July 28, 2022. thediplomat.com/2022/07/the-ldps-tangled-ties-to-the-unification-church/

"The Resurrection of Reverend Moon." *PBS Frontline*, January 21, 1992. pbs.org/wgbh/frontline/documentary/the-resurrection-of-reverend-moon/

"Unification Church had $210 mil. annual donation target in Japan: ex-top official." *The Mainichi*, September 13, 2022. mainichi.jp/english/articles/20220913/p2a/00m/0na/018000c

"United States Congressional investigation of the Unification Church" (aka "The Fraser Report"). October 31, 1978. en.wikisource.org/wiki/United_States_Congressional_investigation_of_the_Unification_Church

Weiner, Tim. "C.I.A. Spent Millions to Support Japanese Right in '50s and '60s." *New York Times*, October 9, 1994. nytimes.com/1994/10/09/world/cia-spent-millions-to-support-japanese-right-in-50-s-and-60-s.html

Yamaguchi, Mari. "What Is the Unification Church and How Is It Related to Shinzo Abe's Assassination?" *NBC Miami*, July 15, 2022. nbc-miami.com/news/national-international/unification-church-at-center-of-abe-assassination-under-increased-scrutiny/2805935/

Yamaguchi, Mari. "The Unification Church's ties to Japan's politics." *AP*, July 17, 2022.

Yamaguchi, Mari. "Abe murder suspect says life destroyed by mother's religion." *AP*, 27 August, 2022.

Japanese-language articles and reports

(Dentsu no shuen) tonai no kanren shisetsu o tsugitsugi to baikyaku [(The end of Dentsu) sold related facilities in Tokyo one after another]. *RAPT+aTHEORY*, April 2, 2021. rapt-plusalpha.com/5382/

Ikeda Daisaku-san wa motomoto wa toitsu kyokai datta. Toitsu kyokai = sokagakkai [Daisaku Ikeda was originally a member of the Unification Church. Unification Church = Soka Gakkai]. *Daiwaryu*, July 30, 2022. daiwaryu1121.com/post-61672/

Itami Juzo no shin wa jisatsu de wa nai? Shi no shinso to Sokagakkai to no kankei to wa [Was Juzu Itami's cause of death not suicide? What is the truth behind his death and its relationship with Soka Gakkai?]. *Cherish*, May 20, 2021. cherish-media.jp/posts/10305)

Kyu Toitsukyokai to "kankei ari" kokkai giin risuto nyushu! Rekidai seiken no juyo posuto keiken-sha ga 34-ri mo [Obtain a list of Diet members "related to" the former Unification Church! 34 people have experience in important positions in successive governments]. *Nikkan Gendai*, July 17, 2022. nikkan-gendai.com/articles/view/life/308409

Sokkagakkai wa Nihon saidai no mayaku baibai soshiki de aru [Soka Gakkai is Japan's largest drug trafficking organization]. *Rapt*, May 23, 2014, rapt-neo.com/?p=10158

Sokagakkai-kei soshiki ni shitagai tsudzukete, korosa rezu ni ikinobite iru geinojin no uragawa ya jittai o kosatsu suru [Following the Soka Gakkai organization, we examine the behind-the-scenes facts and realities of celebrities who have survived without being killed]. *real-world*, October 31, 2020. real-world.tokyo/inbo/cult-14/

English-language book

Samuels, Richard. *Machiavelli's Children: Leaders and their Legacies in Italy and Japan*. Cornell University Press, 2005.

Japanese-language book

Tsurumi, Yoshihiro. "*Amerika Goro no Chohachisei*." Tokuma Shoten, 1994.

Acknowledgments

Writing this book was a long, involved process dating back to 2001 with the publication of *Tokyo Outsiders* in Japanese, a sequel to *Tokyo Underworld* which hit #1 on many charts in Japan. It consisted of seven chapters and 70,000 words which I had intended on expanding and publishing in English when a planned film version of Tokyo Underworld debuted in North America. However, said film project kept being delayed. It went through Dreamworks, Warner Brothers, HBO, Amazon Prime and Legendary Global over a period of twenty years and during this time I kept revising and adding to the book through additional research and interviews until it eventually reached critical mass—around the time of my eightieth birthday. You are looking at the result: fifteen chapters and 150,000 words under the title of *Gamblers, Fraudsters, Dreamers and Spies.*

A number of people helped me along the way getting the manuscript into its present shape and I owe them all a huge debt of gratitude. David Shapiro edited a shorter earlier draft many years ago. Murray Sayle, Greg Davis, Al Stamp, Joe Suzuki, Rick Roa, Tom Blakemore, Frances Blakemore, Raymond Bushell, Frances Bushell, Jim Adachi, Jack Howard, Hal Drake, Corky Alexander, Beate Sirota Gordon and Dan Sawyer all read parts of this version and offered helpful advice.

Mary Corbett went through the longer draft when it was finished in in 2022 and offered many valuable suggestions. Among those who looked at this version of the book in its various stages and made useful comments were Gwen Robinson, Mitch Murata, Hiroki Allen, Peter Daniel Miller, Jeff Kingston, Peter Tasker, Andrew Horvat, Jake Adelstein, Greg Kelly, Joe Schmelzeis, Mark Schreiber, Douglas Victoria, Jason Arcaro, Al Shattuck, Niki Gayda, Kevin Novak and David Shin.

Brad Martin at the *Asia Times* ran excerpts of The Canon Agency and the Elint Agents chapters, applying his editorial expertise to the material. Jack Gallagher did the same for the Sadaharu Oh and Bobby Valentine chapters which originally ran in the *Japan Times* in series form. So did Peter O'Connor who ran excerpts of the Kades/Torio romance in the Foreign Correspondents Club of Japan (FCCJ) monthly magazine *Number 1 Shimbun*.

I would like to give special thanks to the estimable Trevor Hill, who painstakingly went over the penultimate draft in great detail with his blue pen before I turned it in. Tuttle editor Cathy Layne deserves a prize for the outstanding work she has done. I've dealt with many editors over the years in New York and Tokyo. None have been better.

On the research side, thanks to Lester Harvey, Robin Moyer and the staff at the Fernando Lopez Library in Manila; Hal Drake and the staff at Pacific Stars and Stripes Archives in Tokyo; the staff at the International House Library in Roppongi; Hiroko Moriwaki and the FCCJ Library: the staff at the Oya Soichi Bunko in Setagaya, the National Diet Library of Japan, the New York Public Library, the Library of Congress and the National Archives. Also I would like to express my undying gratitude to Midori Matsui, Tetsuharu Sugahara and Satoshi Gunji of Kadokawa Publishing.

For help with photos, thanks to the Bungei Shunju,Niki Gayda, Jason Arcaro, the Mainichi Shimbun, the Sankei Shimbun, Lee Shattuck, Alamy, Jake Adelstein, Tetsuharu Sugahara of Kadokawa publishing, Kyodo, Shutterstock and AP.

Finally thanks to Miko Yamanouchi and Amanda Urban of the Japan Uni and ICM literary agencies.

Robert Whiting

Copyrights and Permissions

Some portions of this book were published previously in newspapers and magazines (print and digital), but have been revised, edited and rewritten for *Gamblers, Fraudsters, Dreamers & Spies*. The chapters below were published previously as indicated:

The Canon Agency (*Asia Times*, 2021; Substack *Robert Whiting's Japan*, 2021)
The Sadaharu Oh Story (*Japan Times*, 2008)
Valentine's Way (*Japan Times*, 2010)
Elint Agents (*Asia Times*, 2022; Substack *Robert Whiting's Japan*, 2022)
Hostesses (Substack *Robert Whiting's Japan, 2022*)
Saints (Substack *Robert Whiting's Japan, 2022*)

Photo credits (all numbers refer to the pages of the photographic insert)

Page 1; page 2 (bottom); page 4 (bottom); page 7 (bottom); page 12: public domain.
Page 2 (top); page 5; page 8 (top): Wikimedia Commons;
Page 3 (top): Bungei Shunju
Page 4 (top and middle); page 6 (top and bottom); page 7 (top); page 9 top and bottom; page 10 all: courtesy of the author
Page 6 (middle): courtesy Niki Gayda.
Page 8 (bottom); page 13 (bottom); page 14 (bottom); page 14–15 (top), Alamy.
Page 9 (bottom); page 12: Wikipedia.
Page 10: Andrei Kholmov, Shutterstock.
Page 13 (top): Jake Adelstein.
page 16: AP